THE DYNAMIC INFORMATION SOCIETY
MASTERING THE CHALLENGES

REVISED PRINTING

EDITED BY
JEAN M. HAMILTON

Cover image courtesy of Stock Illustration Source.

Taken from:

Introduction to Engineering Technology, Fourth Edition,
by Robert J. Pond
Copyright © 1999, 1996 by Prentice-Hall, Inc.
A Pearson Education Company
Upper Saddle River, New Jersey 07458

Social Problems: An Ecological Perspective, by Samuel E. Wallace
Copyright © 1999 by Pearson Custom Publishing
Boston, Massachusetts 02116

Engineering Success, by Peter Schiavone
Copyright © 1999 by Prentice-Hall, Inc.

Internet Investigations in Electronics, by Cynthia B. Leshin
Copyright © 1997 by Prentice-Hall, Inc.

Dictionary of the World Wide Web, by Cynthia B. Leshin
Copyright © 1998 by Prentice-Hall, Inc.

The Critical Edge: Thinking and Researching in a Virtual Society,
by Emily Thiroux
Copyright © 1999 by Prentice-Hall, Inc.

A Guide to the World Wide Web, by Lory Hawkes, Ph.D.
Copyright © 1999 by Prentice-Hall, Inc.

Social Problems: Globalization in the Twenty-First Century, by
R. Dean Peterson, Delores F. Wunder, and Harlan L. Mueller
Copyright © 1999 by Prentice-Hall, Inc.

Keys to Thinking and Learning: Creating Options and Opportunities,
by Carol Carter, Joyce Bishop, and Sarah Lyman Kravits
Copyright © 2000 by Prentice-Hall, Inc.

Pathways to Success, Volume 1, by Carol Carter, Carol Ozee,
and Sarah Lyman Kravits,
Copyright © 1999 by Pearson Custom Publishing

Pathways to Success, Volume 1, Second Edition, by Carol
Carter, Carol Ozee, and Sarah Lyman Kravits
Copyright © 1999 by Pearson Custom Publishing

Cornerstone: Building on Your Best, Second Edition, by Rhonda
J. Montgomery, Patricia G. Moody, and Robert M. Sherfield
Copyright © 1997 by Allyn and Bacon
Copyright © 2000 by Prentice-Hall, Inc.

*Strategies for Successful Writing: Written Communication in the
Modern World,* Compiled by Pamela J. Gurman
Copyright © 1999 by Pearson Custom Publishing

Mastering Public Speaking, Third Edition, by George L. Grice
and John F. Skinner
Copyright © 1998, 1995, 1993 by Allyn & Bacon
Needham Heights, Massachusetts 02494

Literacy, Technology, and Society: Confronting the Issues,
Edited by Gail E. Hawisher and Cynthia L. Selfe
Copyright © 1997 by Prentice-Hall, Inc.

Reading with Confidence, by Joan Monahan
Copyright © 2000 by Allyn and Bacon

The Reading Context: Developing College Reading Skills,
Second Edition, by Dorothy U. Seyler
Copyright © 2000, 1997 by Allyn and Bacon

PEARSON CUSTOM PUBLISHING
75 Arlington Street, Suite 300, Boston, MA 02116
A Pearson Education Company

Copyright Acknowledgments

Contents

PART I
Overview of the Technical and Information Society

1

What Is the World of Technology?

All of us wish to understand the world we live in and to know our place in it. As children we depended on our parents to protect and feed us and establish a secure family environment on which we could depend. In those early years, stability was necessary for normal development. As we became adolescents we experienced changes at school and with our friends. That unpredictable world was frightening and intimidating at first, but we learned to adapt. Most of us even learned to look forward to and expect change.

Change creates opportunities for those who prepare themselves with the skills, knowledge, and attitudes to solve problems. This book is about technology, and about the skills, knowledge and attitudes possessed by the technologists who live and work in a world where "the only constant is change."

You may become a part of the exciting world of technology. To do so you will need to acquire a practical knowledge of mathematics and science. You must also learn how to communicate well with others. But, above all, you must be prepared to constantly adapt to the everchanging world of technology.

Technologists are responsible for providing the material things necessary for human subsistence and comfort. Automobiles, transportation systems, buildings we work in, efficiently automated industrial and business processes, improved power systems, new materials, more powerful computers, and highly integrated communication systems (Figure 1.1) are but a few of the commodities we expect from technologists.

Figure 1.1 Technicians installed the elaborate communications sysems of the 1996 Atlanta Olympics. (Courtesy of International Business Machines Corporation. Unauthorized use not permitted.)

Technology has improved our lives. At the turn of the century, half of the population of the United States lived on farms, working from sunup to sundown merely to feed everyone. Now, with advanced farming techniques made possible by our modern technology, only 3 percent of the population feeds the entire United States plus a significant proportion of the rest of the world. And, while today's farmer may still work from sunrise to sunset, the work is much less labor-intensive.

Only since 1950 was the first commercially available computer born—HAL's great-great-grandfather. People first visited space. The first efforts at providing communications for the masses—e.g., direct long-distance dialing—were introduced. The first fax machine standards allowed different brands of machines to communicate.

People live much better than they did just 25 years ago. Consider the following: The number of autos per person has increased from 61 percent in 1970 to 73 percent in 1991. Gas mileage has more than doubled, while newly developed safety accessories like air bags and antilock brakes have been added. The average new home grew by 300 square feet between 1970 and 1992. An increasing number of the newer homes have central air and labor-saving devices like dishwashers, washing machines, and dryers. The price of a television set was $530 in 1970, compared with today's average price of less than $250. Home videocassette recorders didn't even exist in 1970, and now two-thirds of all households have a VCR. Other innovations in the last 25 years include compact disc players, microwave ovens, cellular phones, fax and answering machines, and personal computers. The personal computer had 4000 bytes of memory in the 1970s, while today's memory usually exceeds 8,000,000 bytes. The Internet (developed in the 1960s) and the World Wide Web (a new interface introduced in 1981) allow each of us to access information that only a privileged few had access to before their introduction.

Technology offers the world unparalleled opportunities. This textbook will help you better understand the world of technology while discovering how you might best enter that world and enjoy an exciting and profitable career as a technologist.

HISTORY OF ENGINEERING AND TECHNOLOGY

Ancestral Engineering—Humankind's Search for Identity

To fully appreciate the world of technology we begin with some early history. The technologists and craftspeople of early civilizations built huge objects. The Great Wall of China was built by those who learned through trial and error. But its construction also required precise surveying and an amazing talent to use the lever and the inclined plane. Algebra and trigonometry were well understood and applied during those early years. Construction of the pyramids of Egypt and of Central and South America required experience (trial and error) and the labor of many people. In addition, however, many of the pyramids are oriented with great accuracy to the movement of the sun (Figure 1.2) or to the cardinal points of the compass. Such accurate positioning required the use of a well-developed system of mathematics and science. Sophisticated long-range planning was necessary in all of the great, early projects.

These huge constructions, so precisely located, helped humankind establish an identity and satisfied the basic need to build and create. Engineering and technology activities satisfy this same basic need. The early builders were the forerunners of today's civil, mechanical, and mining engineers.

Sociological Changes

As civilization progressed, so did the evolution of technology and its lasting effect on society. Infrastructures were designed and built; tools, machinery, and their products were pro-

Figure 1.2 This Mayan pyramid (Yucatan Peninsula, Mexico) was precisely oriented to form the shadow of the seven triangles of the serpent's back only on the vernal and autumnal equinoxes, which occur in spring and fall, respectively.

duced; methods have been devised to safely and efficiently extract minerals from the earth, which are used to heat homes and provide fuel for transportation; chemistry applications are used in such industries as manufacturing, pharmaceuticals, healthcare, food processing, and biotechnology; and electrical technology is used in such areas as multimedia computing, robotics, and global communications. Clearly, technology continues to profoundly impact social and economic changes throughout the world.

The Cybernetic Age

The "dawning of a new age" has been announced for three or four decades, some would say first in 1956 with Daniel Bell's Post-Industrial Society. The dates given for its birth, its dominant characteristics, and the names given it have varied widely: Electronic, Information, Computer, Global, and Service. What name best captures the vast changes now transforming society? In our assessment, the new age most closely centers around "computers that control various processes, including assembly, guidance, data, and communication." Such use of computers is called **cybernation**. To cybernate is to control by cybernation. Related terms are cyberspace, cyberphobia, cyberphobe, cyberphobic, cybernectic, cyberneticist, and cybernetician.

Given the centrality of cybernation in the revolutionary changes now sweeping our planet, we thought the term *cybernetic* best described the new age we have now entered. This term is used however, merely as a summary of the many changes now going on and anticipated in the future. Our usage is parallel to the way in which the term *industrial* is used to describe the Industrial Revolution. Thus the structural change to the nuclear family is held to be part of the changes induced by industrialization, although strictly speaking family form changed only indirectly as a result of industrialization.

In many ways it is easier to understand the Industrial Age than it is to understand the emerging **Cybernetic Age**. By now, industrialization is at least 200 years old. Therefore, we have had sufficient time to experience, study, and analyze it, and to observe many if not most of its consequences. Industrialization is also a thing of the past, at least as far as the developed nations are concerned. As something that has already happened, it does not trigger the emotional response that current and anticipated changes do.

Here in the developed nations of the world, cybernation is creating another transformation, another series of social and economic changes that are so profound as to be revolutionary. As with the Industrial Revolution, the changes now taking place through cybernation are eliminating old lines of work, old ways of communicating, learning, relating, and even living. Leaving the old and familiar as the new age pushes and pulls us is not easy even when we know where we are going. But to leave the old and familiar for destinations unknown is simply too much. It is no wonder that we experience "future shock" as Alvin Toffler (1970) observed years ago.

Overloaded with change, fearing to leave the familiar, and even more fearful of the future, we fight and resist change, we deny that anything is different, and we search for scapegoats on whom to blame this change. We do so many things except identify the changes now transforming us. We insist on looking backward rather than trying to see where these changes are taking us. In an effort to understand the changes now under way, let us discuss the evolving Cybernetic Age by comparing its changes with the transformation from the Agricultural to the Industrial Age. We will do so in terms of nine dimensions: employment, residence, family, economy, government, moral ecology, environmental consciousness, composition, and scale.

Employment

Just as industrialization eliminated farming as a source of financial support for millions, so cybernation is eliminating the manufacturing base of industrial society. Before industrialization, 75 percent of the workforce was engaged in agriculture; afterwards, that number dropped to about 5 percent. In 1950, 45 percent of the workforce was employed in manufacturing; today that figure is less than half of what it was in 1950. The proportion in manufacturing is predicted to drop further to less than 10 percent by 2010.

Although a number of the manufacturing jobs are performed outside the U.S., a far greater number are simply disappearing. Just as the industrialization of agriculture eliminated the need for millions of farm workers, so technology today is eliminating millions of jobs in manufacturing. Millions of the formerly employed are simply no longer needed. This is the reality behind the decline in real wages of the last several decades.

In a valiant effort to make up for this decline in real wages, a second wage earner in the household has now become a necessity; necessary not to provide luxuries like vacations, but simply to put food on the table. The American dream of owning a home and late model car are increasingly beyond the means of ordinary middle class families.

The strategies formerly used by workers to secure higher wages and benefits are no longer effective. What good are strikes or unions when jobs are being eliminated and regular workers are being replaced by temporary employees? New jobs are being created but there are far fewer of them and the level of skills they require is far beyond what was needed in the jobs that were lost.

Residence

Virtually the entire population of the U.S. moved from the country to the city with industrialization. In the Northeast, where industrialization began and spread most quickly, the region's population went from being 75 percent rural to 75 percent urban in 1990.

	Age		
	Agricultural	Industrial	Cybernetic
Employment	Farm	Factory	Corporation
Residence	Rural	Urban	Anywhere
Family	Extended	Nuclear	Household
Government	Village/City	Nation	World
Moral Ecology	Localism/	Urbanism/	Environmentalism/
	Religion	Secularism	Spiritualism
Environmental	TEP	HEP	NEP
Consciousness	Local	National	Global

Suburbs began with rail transit, became popular with horse-drawn street cars, and mushroomed in growth when automobiles appeared (Warner, 1964). Today, cybernation has unchained urbanization, permitting people to relocate anywhere. Where do the "symbolic analysts" (Reich; 1990) of the cybernetic age live? They can and do live anywhere; anywhere they can take and operate their computers; anywhere served by cell phones; anywhere, including geographically remote locations.

Family

The structural change from the extended to the nuclear family has already been noted. In the Cybernetic Age, the shift is to the household as family; i.e., those who live together. Such families include those blended from previous marriages; those with and without children; those of the same and opposite sex; and many other combinations, including students and senior citizens.

The passions aroused by change are especially evident when changes in the family are noted. As industrialization got under way and the old extended and multigenerational family began to diminish in importance, preachers and other professional moralists thundered from their pulpits that surely the work of the devil was evident in the death of the "Farm Family." Today, as gay and lesbian couples seek, and at times are granted, some of the rights traditionally given only to heterosexual unions, there is a similar outcry. Some, like William Bennett, even became quite wealthy denouncing such changes.

Economy

The economy of the Agricultural Age was based primarily on exchange and barter. To the limited extent that there was a cash economy, it was based on crafts. In the Industrial Era, the economy shifted to the mining and manufacturing of a cash economy. In the Cybernetic Age, the labor force shifts to the service sector, with electronic transfers and credit cards predominating.

Government

Social order in the Agricultural Age was maintained by local folkways and mores in its villages and cities. Law as wielded by the nation was the governing body in the Industrial Age. What will emerge to govern lives in the Cybernetic Age? A New World Order? A United Nations? A Consortium of developed nations? Perhaps transnational corporations.

Moral Ecology

The blueprint for living in the Agricultural Age was found in religion and local customs. When the population was massed in the great metropolises of the Industrial Age, the moral ecology was urbanism and secularism. Today it is the related themes of environmentalism and spiritualism.

Environmental Consciousness

Working farms, forests, and fields, people of the Agricultural Age had to be aware of their environments if they were to prosper or even to survive. Without knowledge of the cycles of reproduction, guided growth, decay, and regeneration, the agricultural worker could not practice the necessary husbandry. Their set of environmental practices was guided by what we call the **Traditional Ecological Paradigm** (TEP).

Urban populations are less religious than their rural counterparts. They were (and are) more urbane and secular. In terms of their environmental awareness, they are typically unaware, believing that humans are the center of all things. As Dunlap and Catton (1976) put it, they hold to the **Human Exceptionalism Paradigm** (HEP), the belief that humans are not subject to the ecological principles that govern all other life forms.

Populations in the Cybernetic Age have demonstrated a remarkable resurgence of concern for the environment. Since the 1960s, support for the broad program called environmentalism has grown in spite of governmental and corporate opposition. Whether that public support will lead to biocentrism or biotechnology is too early to tell. It seems clear, however, that the HEP is being abandoned. **The New Ecological Paradigm** (NEP) is slowly emerging.

Composition

The social world of the ruralite was homogeneous and that of the urbanite, heterogeneous. The composition of the social world of the cybernetic is diverse. Today, to be literate it is necessary to be fluent in English, in a second major foreign language, and in computers; these skills are essential for communication in the diverse world in which we now live.

Scale

The scale of one's relationships can be mapped by locating in space those with whom one communicates. Whatever the nature of the interaction, be it work, friendship, or perhaps recreational, the scale is generally from the local to the national and thence to the global in each of the three ages reviewed.

When compared together, the three ages make evident the revolutionary changes that continue to sweep Planet Earth. But at a more microscopic level, such change is intimately connected to change in individuals. As mentioned at the beginning of this chapter, change creates opportunities for those who are well prepared and ready to constantly adapt to an everchanging world. Let's examine the opportunities available to technicians and technologists, and the skills, knowledge, and attitudes needed to participate successfully in an industrial team.

THE INDUSTRIAL TEAM

Today's industries are divided into two fundamentally different types: manufacturing and service industries. Manufacturing industries make products. The need for the technician was first recognized in manufacturing.

Service industries provide services. A great number of technicians are needed in the high-growth service sector. Technologists in the service industries are needed to properly connect and repair the increasingly complex equipment used in our homes and offices. Most of this equipment utilizes computers, and computer-service technologists are in strong demand. Other technologists are needed to make service industries more efficient. Those technologists will play an increasing role in the areas of quality control, supervision, and sales.

In both manufacturing and service sectors, teamwork will be required if companies wish to survive. Teamwork in manufacturing means that the scientist, engineer, accountant, technician, technologist, and the skilled worker all cooperate in bringing improvements to manufacturing processes that produce goods. Teamwork in service means that the owner or manager of the organization trains and supports technologists to achieve customer satisfaction. The computer-service technologist sent to a customer's computer facility to solve a problem that has resulted in downtime will be under extreme pressure to fix the problem in a very short time. With the proper resources available from his or her company, the knowledgeable and well-trained technologist will not only satisfy, but delight the customer. The result will be increased business for the service company.

The Role of the Technician and Technologist

The technician and technologist work in key positions on the industrial team. Persons holding two-year (technician-level) and four-year (technologist-level) degrees act as

1. communicators, providing clear communication between engineer and skilled worker;
2. implementors, interpreting the ideas of the engineer and implementing them;
3. calibrators and testers, performing complicated tests in engineering laboratories; and
4. manufacturing engineers, supervising skilled and semiskilled personnel solving problems in manufacturing processes.

The technician acts as *communicator*, illustrating complex technical ideas so they may be understood by others in the workforce. This task is often accomplished by the preparation of engineering drawings or charts and graphs, and by direct communication with the skilled employee. The technologist is responsible for planning and supervising. The supervisor requires excellent interpersonal communication skills, which include *listening* as well as speaking and writing skills.

For example, the civil engineering technician takes the plans of the civil engineer and prepares detailed drawings of a certain part of the project. The technologist then takes the drawings to the bridge or highway being constructed and directly supervises the construction personnel in the field.

Technicians and technologists must be able to speak clearly and accurately to enjoy credibility with coworkers and managers. They must not use confusing language when discussing detailed factual material.

Technicians and technologists take on active roles in *implementation*. This frees engineers to continue the flow of creative design ideas (Figure 1.3A) and to deal with broad concerns such as the personnel, managerial, and economic consequences of a project. Technicians implement the engineer's ideas, making the ideas reality (Figure 1.3B). They measure the quality of production, install new equipment, interpret the chart recordings and gauges monitoring a manufacturing process, or supervise the construction of the superstructure (steel skeleton) of a large office building.

In research and development (R&D), technicians work with engineers to introduce new materials and processes and to test new materials for such qualities as strength and durability.

Calibration of test equipment is vital in today's industry. Heat sensors, flow meters, fluid-pressure sensors, and electrical measuring equipment such as oscilloscopes and voltmeters are a few of the many types of instruments used to measure industrial processes. The technician, trained to read schematic drawings of industrial measuring instruments and possessing the knowledge of how the instruments operate, must often repair, maintain, and calibrate them. The technician in Figure 1.4 repairs and calibrates communication equipment, ensuring reliable, accurate operation.

Technologists are today's *manufacturing engineers*. The typical four-year technology curriculum provides a background equivalent to that of the baccalaureate engineer's curriculum of the 1950s. The technologist is often more willing and better suited to be involved with the day-to-day problems of manufacturing than is today's more scientifically educated engineer.

Figure 1.3A The design equations of the engineer and scientist (A) becomes reality with the work of the technician and technologist.

Figure 1.3B Aeronautical engineers work on a computer aided design (CAD) for jet aircraft while at work under a jet engine with exposed parts. Copyright © 1998 by Brownie Harris.

For example, a fiberglass insulation line slows because of the material sticking to the rollers. The supervisor of manufacturing engineering assigns the problem to a technologist. The technologist first analyzes the problem in light of the physical characteristics of the material, a task involving an applied knowledge of chemistry and physics. The technologist measures the temperature and humidity with a sling psychrometer and determines that humidity is higher than normal. Skilled workers are then assigned to inspect the duct system and find that a large ventilating fan is inoperative. The technologist then reports the problem and recommends the fan be replaced.

The preceeding discussion illustrates the four essential services expected of technicians and technologists: communicator, implementor, calibrator and tester, and manufacturing engineer. By studying to become a technician in two years and perhaps continuing for a four-year bachelor of science in engineering technology (B.S.E.T.) degree,

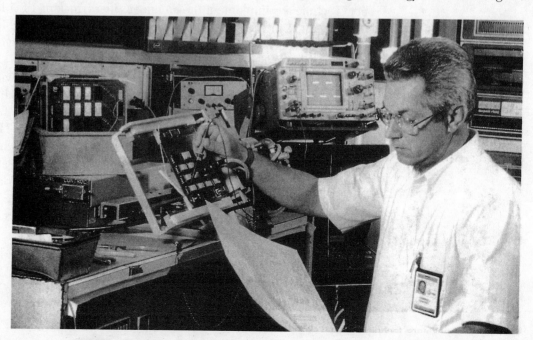

Figure 1.4 Technicians and technologists repair, maintain, and calibrate sensitive measurement equipment. (Courtesy AT&T Network Systems)

you will be well prepared to find a position in industry that will be both challenging and rewarding for years to come.

Teamwork in Manufacturing

Manufacturing industries require the teamwork of the scientist, engineer, technician and technologist, and skilled worker (Figure 1.5). The *scientist* is engaged principally in research and the development of new material—in advancing the state of the art.

The *engineer* provides system design and technical management. The *technician* and *technologist* provide the practical, hands-on, manufacturing expertise. The *skilled worker* operates and repairs specialized machinery. Table 1.1 depicts the amount of theory and applied knowledge needed for these five industrial classifications.

The skilled worker performs tasks requiring some mathematics and other theoretical knowledge, but relies mostly on hands-on experience. Examples of skilled workers are machinists and electronic assembly workers. Indispensable to production and used often in maintenance, the skilled workers must be included in the industrial team.

In industry, the roles of the engineering technician or technologist and of the engineer may be clarified by comparing and contrasting their occupational tasks. To illustrate, the electronic engineer (EE, or "double E") is responsible for *designing* new computer systems, *directing fabrication* of mainframe computer systems, and *developing applications* for new technologies such as laser diodes. Occupational tasks of an electronic engineering technician (EET) are similar to those of the EEs in some areas, but differ markedly in others. Some occupational tasks the EET is responsible for are *designing the interfacing circuit* for a computer circuit board, *supervising the assembly* of specific electronic equipment, and *breadboarding circuits* designed by the engineer.

The italicized words in the preceding paragraph are key words that aid in comparing and contrasting the duties of the engineer and engineering technician. The engineer *designs systems,* but the technician *designs individual circuits;* the engineer *directs fabrication of systems,* but the technician *supervises the assembly of specific electronic subsystems,* the engineer *develops new systems,* but the technician *breadboards* such systems, *troubleshoots and improves circuitry,* and *brings the system into the real world.*

Another difference between engineers and technicians is how quickly they must

Figure 1.5 Engineers, technicians, and skilled workers team up to solve a manufacturing problem. (Courtesy AT&T Network Systems)

Table 1.1 **The Industrial Team—Duties and Education**

Duties	% Theory	% Applied	Education Required/Degree
Scientist—hypothesizes, verifies laws of nature	90	10	Five to seven years of college M.S. or Ph.D
Engineer—designs and creates hardware and software from scientific ideas and laws of nature	70	30	Four or five years of college B.S. or M.S.
Technologist—makes design prototype, suggests redesign or modification, acts as manufacturing engineer	60	40	Four years of college B.S.E.T.
Technician—makes model of prototype, tests and troubleshoots prototypes and hardware/ software in actual production use, acts as manufacturing supervisor	50	50	Two years of college A.S.E.T.
Skilled worker (craftsperson)—produces parts (e.g., holding fixtures) from completed designs, installs and runs hardware	20	80	Four years of on-the-job training (OJT) and/or vocational high school High school diploma and training/experience

M.S. = Master of Science, Ph.D = Doctor of Philosophy, B.S.E.T. = Bachelor of Science in Engineering Technology, A.S.E.T. = Associate of Science in Engineering Technology

learn their jobs. Because technicians are prepared in college for hands-on (practical) applications as well as theoretical applications (Figure 1.6), employers expect a technician to learn a new process or to perform a new laboratory test in a very short time. Employers have admitted that they expect a technician to be fully productive within 30 to 60 days after beginning employment. On the other hand, an engineer might take up to a year on the job to become familiar with the manufacturing process and become fully productive.

How may the members of the manufacturing team work together? Consider, for example, a hydraulic pump that continues to overheat because of inadequate system design or defective parts (Figure 1.7). An engineering technician, prepared to deal with the real-world problems of industry, is called in. An electromechanical, mechanical, or fluid-power technician is trained to test pumps and know what conditions must be present for pumps to operate effectively. The technician quickly isolates the problem by determining that (1) a specific type of relief valve incorporated into the inadequate system will solve the problem, (2) the oil reservoir is too small, or (3) the pump is defective.

If new parts are required (e.g., oil reservoir, pump) the technician will order the substitutes by establishing the correct replacement specifications, researching suppliers' catalogs, and making telephone calls to determine availability. The skilled worker will complete the necessary maintenance by installing the new parts. Alternatively, repair of a part may be necessary. If the pump is determined to be defective, for instance, the skilled mechanic would be better qualified to tear down and rebuild the hydraulic pump than would the technician who has been trained only to test pumps, not to deal with the placement of seals and other internal components.

Figure 1.6 Technical students couple hands-on experience with theory in the process control laboratory. (Courtesy of Trident Technical College)

Example 1.1

If the faulty hydraulic circuit in Figure 1.7 is diagnosed to require a different type of relief valve, which ports hydraulic fluid to the reservoir if system pressure becomes too great, who would specify the new relief valve? Who would determine the problem if complex piping or hose runs are at fault?

Solution If the relief valve is at fault, the technician is quite capable of determining the specifications of the new valve and will specify a suitable replacement. If, on the other hand, the piping or hose (conductor) runs are long and complex, then the engineer is often needed to redesign the system and solve complicated fluid-mechanics problems. These problems may require sophisticated mathematics not possessed by the technician.

Communication and the Industrial Team

One of the critical roles technicians or technologists play is that of communicator. They "glue the industrial team together" and make it function as a whole (Figure 1.8). Technicians and technologists are best prepared to communicate with the skilled worker

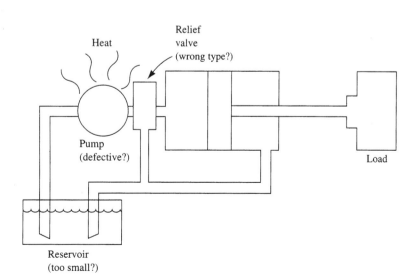

Figure 1.7 Training prepares a technician to troubleshoot a faulty hydraulic system.

because of a technical education that includes a great deal of laboratory experience, including work with the actual tools and machinery used in industry.

During college, technicians and technologists are exposed to the language of the engineer, who uses information from mathematics, physics, chemistry, and other sciences to solve theoretical problems and to design new systems. The technician's college education requires a sound base of algebra and trigonometry (sometimes calculus) and at least two courses in physics or chemistry. The technologist's curriculum includes mathematics through calculus and advanced applied science courses.

Knowledge of the symbols and words used by both the skilled worker and the engineer enables the technician or technologist to become a critical link between them. Forging this link between the quite different worlds of the skilled worker and engineer is challenging. How do technologists build bridges and assure communication occurs between people who are expected to perform markedly different work (see Figure 1.9)? Technologists can accomplish these tasks only if they

1. have confidence in the real skills and knowledge they possess,
2. can logically and reasonably transmit their messages to others, and
3. know and can use the appropriate conventions of the language, for instance, good spelling, good grammar, and good sentence and paragraph structure.

Of course, *good human relations skills must be added to all of the above criteria.* One critical factor in human relations is listening to others. The technologist who can listen to the skilled worker will be much more effective and will learn a great deal more than those who can only direct others.

Organizational Structures and the Industrial Team

Medium to large companies must have an organizational plan for the industrial team to function correctly. The organizational plan fixes decision-making responsibilities, showing specifically how the members of the team interact and who makes decisions at a particular level. The plan may be shown as an *organizational diagram* or *organizational chart.*

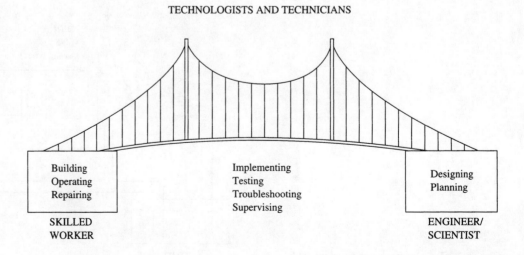

TECHNOLOGISTS AND TECHNICIANS

Building
Operating
Repairing

Implementing
Testing
Troubleshooting
Supervising

Designing
Planning

SKILLED WORKER

ENGINEER/ SCIENTIST

Figure 1.8 The technician acts as the bridge for the industrial team.

Figure 1.9 Staff (A) vs. line (B) relationships in an organization.

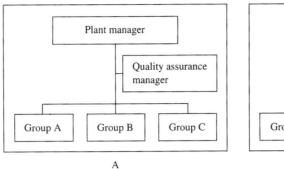
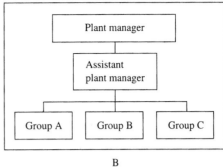

Technicians and technologists should be aware of both formal and informal decision-making structures in their organization. Understanding the concepts of *line* and *staff functions* from an organizational chart is a good first step.

For instance, consider Figures 1.9A and 1.9B. In Figure 1.9A, the quality assurance manager is in a staff position, reporting to the plant manager and coordinating quality assurance activities between the group managers. The quality assurance manager acts only in the capacity of an advisor and does not enjoy line authority. In Figure 1.9B, the assistant plant manager is in a line position, no longer simply an advisor, but in a position that may involve directing the group managers.

Confusing line and staff functions may result in serious misunderstandings in an organization. It pays for the organization to be clear about who manages whom and for each employee to be clear about whom to report to. Figure 1.10 is the organizational structure for a large manufacturing company. Can you identify the line and staff positions in the diagram?

If you are a member of a staff organization (many industrial engineering functions are staff organizations), you must be prepared to work differently with others in the organization. A staff department must work with, not direct, other managers. Top management should assist staff organizations to do their jobs by breaking down any barriers between departments.

Competition vs. Teamwork

Competition in manufacturing or service industries should be directed toward competitors and not between members of the same organization. Top management has a central role in setting the climate for eliminating unhealthy internal competition. Companies where there is bickering and backbiting between employees and between departments will not survive in today's global economy. Such an environment is too inefficient.

Teamwork is the business strategy of the twenty-first century. Teamwork is enhanced by freeing teams to make more decisions on their own. Employees at all levels working in teams that consist of people from many disciplines make decisions on equipment needs, production levels, staff support, and even financial support for a particular project. In this environment, engineers and technologists interested in simply being left alone to work with a certain piece of equipment cannot survive long. They must learn to work with others.

Your courses in psychology and sociology will be of great benefit to you in learning how to work with others. In your technical laboratory courses you will be expected to work with at least one other person. Your technical instructors will assign real-world projects that involve several students. Strive to understand others and your career will be greatly enhanced.

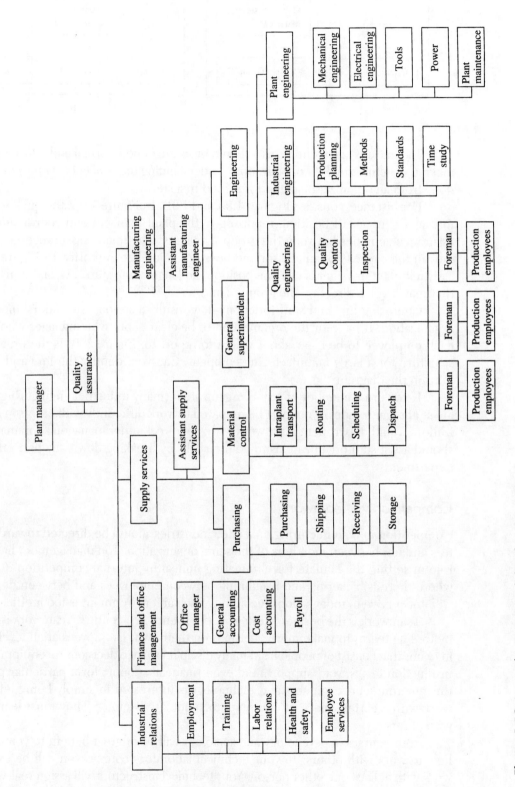

Figure 1.10 A typical organizational chart for a large manufacturer.

Service industries especially are looking for technicians and technologists who are flexible in dealing with customers. This means an ability to work with any client. Nontechnical clients are often put off by service technicians who can only use technical abbreviations and acronyms to describe what they do. Technologists and technicians must learn to explain what they do in popular terminology.

The greater the teamwork and the more personable the employees, the better will be the product or service. Technologists and technicians who can show they are willing to work with other people will be far more successful in obtaining a job. Companies used to hire on the basis of good grades. Now interviews are used to select graduates who can work with a team, have good communication skills, and have experience working on projects with others.

READING

Welcome to Cyberspace

[From *Literacy, Technology & Society*, G.E. Hawisher & G.L. Selfe (eds).]

Philip Elmer-DeWitt

In 1982, the computer was featured on the cover of *Time* magazine as the "Man of the Year." That article focused on the early and explosive growth of the microcomputer industry. In 1995, *Time* once again featured computer technology as a cultural phenomenon of interest in our society—this time with the Internet as a focus. The article that follows, because it was published in a popular news magazine aimed at a general and nonspecialist audience, provides a summary gloss of some of the issues connected with the Internet. It does not treat these issues in depth or provide more serious readers enough specific information to explore these issues thoroughly.

This contribution, however, authored by Philip Elmer-DeWitt, does provide a good space to observe how one reporter working for a mainstream news magazine portrayed the Internet in 1995, what knowledge the reporter (and the magazine's editors) assumed average readers had and did not have at that time, what topics were of interest to a general population of readers, and what level of sophistication discussions about the Internet had reached among a larger population. The article, in other words, provides a cultural snapshot of our society and its general understanding of technology—not a complete representation, by any means, but an interesting cultural image of one point in time.

It started, as the big ideas in technology often do, with a science-fiction writer. William Gibson, a young expatriate American living in Canada was wandering past the video arcades on Vancouver's Granville Street in the early 1980s when something about the way the players were hunched over their glowing screens struck him as odd. "I could see in the physical intensity of their postures how rapt the kids were," he says. "It was like a feedback loop, with photons coming off the screens into the kids' eyes, neurons moving through their bodies and electrons moving through the video game. These kids clearly *believed* in the space the games projected."

That image haunted Gibson. He didn't know much about video games or computers—he wrote his breakthrough novel *Neuromancer* (1984) on an ancient manual typewriter—but he knew people who did. And as near as he could tell, everybody who worked much with the machines eventually came to accept, almost as an article of faith, the reality of that imaginary realm. "They develop a belief that there's some kind of *actual space* behind the screen," he says. "Some place that you can't see but you know is there."

Gibson called that place "cyberspace," and used it as the setting for his early novels and short stories. In his fiction, cyberspace is a computer-generated landscape that characters enter by "jacking in"—sometimes by plugging electrodes directly into sockets implanted in the brain. What they see when they get there is a three-dimensional representation of all the information stored in "every computer in the human system"—great warehouses and skyscrapers of data. He describes it in a key passage in *Neuromancer* as a place of "unthinkable complexity," with "lines of light arranged in the nonspace of the mind, clusters and constellations of data. Like city lights, receding. . . ."

In the years since, there have been other names given to that shadowy space where our computer data reside: the Net, the Web, the Cloud, the Matrix, the Metaverse, the Datasphere, the Electronic Frontier, the information superhighway. But Gibson's coinage may prove the most enduring. By 1989 it had been borrowed by the online community to describe not some science-fiction fantasy but today's increasingly interconnected computer systems—especially the millions of computers jacked into the Internet.

Now hardly a day goes by without some newspaper article, some political speech, some corporate press release invoking Gibson's imaginary world. Suddenly, it seems, everybody has an E-mail address, from Hollywood moguls to the Holy See. Billy Graham has preached on America Online; Vice President Al Gore has held forth on CompuServe; thousands chose to celebrate New Year's this year with an online get-together called First Night in Cyberspace.

In Washington cyberspace has become a political hot button of some potency, first pressed during the 1992 presidential campaign by Al Gore and Bill Clinton, who rode to the White House in part on the promise that they would build the so-called information superhighway and route it through every voter's district—if not to his home. But the Clinton Administration lost the high ground of cyberspace, having, among other transgressions, come out on the wrong side of the privacy debate when it endorsed the Clipper Chip security device favored by its intelligence services. The Republicans were quick to grab the initiative. No sooner had incoming House Speaker Newt Gingrich taken office than he made his bid, staging a big press conference to unveil a new House computer system. At a Washington confab called "Democracy in Virtual America," attended by his old friends, futurists Alvin and Heidi Toffler, the Speaker talked expansively about wiring the world. "Cyberspace is the land of knowledge," proclaimed an information age Magna Carta issued in his name. "And the exploration of that land can be a civilization's truest, highest calling."

Corporations, smelling a land rush of another sort, are scrambling to stake out their own claims in cyberspace. Every computer company, nearly every publisher, most communications firms, banks, insurance companies and hundreds of mail-order and retail firms are registering their Internet domains and setting up sites on the World Wide Web. They sense that cyberspace will be one of the driving forces—if not the primary one—for economic growth in the 21st century.

All this is being breathlessly reported in the press, which has seized on cyberspace as an all-purpose buzz word that can add sparkle to the most humdrum development or assignment. For working reporters, many of whom have just discovered the pleasures of going online, cyber has become the prefix of the day, and they are spawning neologisms as fast as they can type: cyberphilia, cyberphobia, cyberwonk, cybersex, cyberslut. A Nexis search of newspapers, magazines, and television transcripts turned up 1,205 mentions of cyber in the month of January, up from 464 the previous January and 167 in January 1993.

One result of this drum roll is a growing public appetite for a place most people haven't been to and are often hard-pressed to define. In a *Time*/CNN poll of 800 Americans conducted in January by Yankelovich Partners, 57% didn't know what cyberspace meant, yet 85% were certain that information technology had made their life better. They may not know where it is, but they want desperately to get there. The rush to get online, to avoid being "left behind" in the information revolution, is tense. Those who find fulfillment in cyberspace often have the religious fervor of the recently converted.

These sentiments have been captured brilliantly in an IBM ad on TV showing a phalanx of Czech nuns discussing—of all things—the latest operating system from Microsoft. As they walk briskly through a convent, a young novice mentions IBM's competing system, called Warp. "I just read about it in *Wired*," she gushes. "You get true multitasking . . . easy access to the Internet." An older sister glances up with obvious interest; the camera cuts to the mother superior, who wistfully confesses, "I'm dying to surf the Net." Fade as the pager tucked under her habit starts to beep.

Cybernuns

What is cyberspace? According to John Perry Barlow, a rock-'n'-roll lyricist turned computer activist, it can be defined most succinctly as "that place you are in when you are talking on the telephone." That's as good a place to start as any. The telephone system, after all, is really a vast, global computer network with a distinctive, audible presence (crackling static against an almost inaudible background hum). By Barlow's definition, just about everybody has already been to cyberspace. It's marked by the feeling that the person you're talking to is "in the same room." Most people take the spatial dimension of a phone conversation for granted—until they get a really bad connection or a glitchy overseas call. Then they start raising their voice, as if by sheer volume they could propel it to the outer reaches of cyberspace.

Cyberspace, of course, is bigger than a telephone call. It encompasses the millions of personal computers, connected by modems—via the telephone system—to commercial online services, as well as the millions more with high-speed links to local area networks, office E-mail systems and the Internet. It includes the rapidly expanding wireless services: microwave towers that carry great quantities of cellular phone and data traffic; communications satellites strung like beads in geosynchronous orbit; low-flying satellites that will soon crisscross the globe like angry bees, connecting folks too far-flung or too much on the go to be tethered by wires. Someday even our television sets may be part of cyberspace, transformed into interactive "teleputers" by so-called full-service networks like the ones several cable-TV companies (including Time Warner) are building along the old cable lines, using fiber optics and high-speed switches.

But these wires and cables and microwaves are not really cyberspace. They are the means of conveyance, not the destination: the information superhighway, not the bright city lights at the end of the road. Cyberspace, in the sense of being "in the same room," is an experience, not a wiring system. It is about people using the new technology to do what they are genetically programmed to do: communicate with one another. It can be found in electronic mail exchange by lovers who have never met. It emerges from the endless debates on mailing lists and message boards. It's that bond that knits together regulars in electronic chat rooms and newsgroups. It is, like Plato's plane of ideal forms, a metaphorical space, a virtual reality.

But it is no less real for being so. We live in the age of information, as Nicholas Negroponte, director of M.I.T.'s Media Lab, is fond of pointing out, in which the fundamental particle is not the atom but the bit—the binary digit, a unit of data usually represented as a 0 or 1. Information may still be delivered in magazines and newspapers (atoms), but the real value is in the contents (bits). We pay for our goods and services with cash (atoms), but the ebb and flow of capital around the world is carried out—to the tune of several trillion dollars a day—in electronic funds transfers (bits).

Bits are different from atoms and obey different laws. They are weightless. They are easily (and flawlessly) reproduced. There is an infinite supply. And they can be shipped at nearly the speed of light. When you are in the business of moving bits around, barriers of time and space disappear. For information providers—publishers, for example—cyberspace offers a medium in which distribution costs shrink to zero. Buyers and sellers can find each other in cyberspace without the benefit (or the expense) of a marketing campaign. No wonder so many businessmen are convinced it will become a powerful engine of economic growth.

At this point, however, cyberspace is less about commerce than about community. The technology has unleashed a great rush of direct, person-to-person communications, organized not in the top-down, one-to-many structure of traditional media but in a many-to-many model that may—just may—be a vehicle for revolutionary change. In a world already too divided against itself—rich against poor, producer against consumer—cyberspace offers the nearest thing to a level playing field.

Take, for example, the Internet. Until something better comes along to replace it, the Internet is cyberspace. It may not reach every computer in the human system, as Gibson imagined, but it comes very close. And as anyone who has spent much time there can attest, it is in many ways even stranger than fiction.

Begun more than 20 years ago as a Defense Department experiment, the Internet escaped from the Pentagon in 1984 and spread like kudzu during the personal-computer boom, nearly doubling every year from the mid-1980s on. Today 30 million to 40 million people in more than 160 countries have at least E-mail access to the Internet; in Japan, New Zealand and parts of Europe the number of Net users has grown more than 1,000% during the past three years.

One factor fueling the Internet's remarkable growth is its resolutely grass-roots structure. Most conventional computer systems are hierarchical and proprietary; they run on copyright software in a pyramid structure that gives dictatorial powers to the system operators who sit on top. The Internet, by contrast, is open (nonproprietary) and rabidly democratic. No one owns it. No single organization controls it. It is run like a commune with 4.9 million fiercely independent members (called hosts). It crosses national boundaries and answers to no sovereign. It is literally flawless.

Although graphics, photos and even videos have started to show up, cyberspace, as it exists on the Internet, is still primarily a text medium. People communicate by and large through words, typed and displayed on a screen. Yet cyberspace assumes an astonishing array of forms, from the utilitarian mailing list (a sort of junk E-mail list to which anyone can contribute) to the rococo MUDS, or Multi-User Dungeons (elaborate fictional gathering places that users create one "room" at a time). All these "spaces" have one thing in common: they are egalitarian to a fault. Anybody can play (provided he or she has the requisite equipment and access), and everybody is afforded the same level of respect (which is to say, little or none). Striped of the external trappings of wealth, power, beauty and social status, people tend to be judged in the cyberspace of the Internet only by their ideas and their ability to get them across in terse, vigorous prose. On the Internet, as the famous *New Yorker* cartoon put it, nobody knows you're a dog.

Nowhere is this leveling effect more apparent than on Usenet—a giant set of more than 10,000 discussion groups (called newsgroups) distributed in large part over the Internet and devoted to every conceivable subject, from Rush Limbaugh to particle physics to the nocturnal habits of ring-tailed lemurs. The newsgroups develop their own peculiar dynamic as participants lurch from topic to topic—quick to take and give offense, slow to come to any kind of resolution.

But Usenet regulars are fiercely proud of what they have constructed. They view it as a new vehicle for wielding political power (through mass mailings and petitions) and an alternative system for gathering and disseminating raw, uncensored news. If they are sometimes disdainful of bumbling "newbies" who go online without learning the rules of the road, they are unforgiving to those who violate them deliberately. Many are convinced that the unflattering press accounts (those perennial stories about Internet hackers and pedophiles, for example) are part of a conspiracy among the mainstream media to suppress what they perceive as a threat to their hegemony.

The Usenet newsgroups are, in their way, the perfect antidote to modern mass media. Rather than catering to the lowest common denominator with programming packaged by a few people in New York, Atlanta, and Hollywood and broadcast to the masses in the heartland, the newsgroups allow news, commentary, and humor to bubble up from the grass roots. They represent narrowcasting in the extreme: content created by consumers for consumers. While cable-TV executives still dream of hundreds of channels, Usenet already has thousands. The network is so fragmented, in fact, that some fear it will ultimately serve to further divide a society already splintered by race, politics and sexual prejudice. That would be an ironic fate for a system designed to enhance communications.

The Internet is far from perfect. Largely unedited, its content is often tasteless, foolish, uninteresting or just plain wrong. It can be dangerously habit-forming and, truth be told, an enormous waste of time. Even with the arrival of new point-and-click software such as Netscape and Mosaic, it is still too hard to navigate. And because it requires access to both a computer and a high-speed telecommunications link, it is out of reach for millions of people too poor or too far from a major communications hub to participate.

But it is remarkable nonetheless, especially considering that it began as a cold war postapocalypse military command grid. "When I look at the Internet," says Bruce Sterling, another science-fiction writer and a great champion of cyberspace, "I see something astounding and delightful. It's as if some grim fallout shelter had burst open and a full-scale Mardi Gras parade had come out. I take such enormous pleasure in this that it's hard to remain properly skeptical."

There is no guarantee, however, that cyberspace will always look like this. The Internet is changing rapidly. Lately a lot of the development efforts—and most of the press attention—have shifted from the rough-and-tumble Usenet newsgroups to the more passive and consumer-oriented "home pages" of the World Wide Web—a system of links that simplifies the task of navigating among the myriad offerings on the Internet. The Net, many old-timers complain, is turning into a shopping mall. But unless it proves to be a total bust for business, that trend is likely to continue.

The more fundamental changes are those taking place underneath our sidewalks and streets, where great wooden wheels of fiber-optic cable are being rolled out one block at a time. Over the next decade, the telecommunications systems of the world will be rebuilt from the ground up as copper wires are ripped up and replaced by hair-thin fiber-optic strands.

The reason, in a word, is bandwidth, the information-carrying capacity of a medium (usually measured in bits per second). In terms of bandwidth, a copper telephone wire is like a thin straw, too narrow to carry the traffic it is being asked to bear. By contrast, fiber-optic strands, although hair-thin, are like great fat pipes, with an intrinsic capacity to carry tens of thousands of times as many bits as copper wire.

It's not just the Internet surfers who are crying for more bandwidth. Hollywood needs it to deliver movies and television shows on demand. Video game makers want it to send kids the latest adventures of Donkey Kong and Sonic the Hedgehog. The phone companies have their eyes on what some believe will be the next must-have appliance, the videophone.

There is a broad consensus in government and industry that the National Information Infrastructure, as the Clinton Administration prefers to call the info highway, will be a broadband, switched network that could, in theory, deliver all these things. But how it will be structured and how it will be deployed are not so clear. For example, if cable-TV and telephone companies are allowed to roll out the new services in only the richest neighborhoods—a practice known as "cream skimming"—that could exacerbate the already growing disparity between those who have access to the latest information and the best intelligence and those who must be content with what they see on TV.

An even trickier question has to do with the so-called upstream capacity of the network. Everybody wants to build a fat pipeline going into the home; that's the conduit by which the new information goods and services will be delivered. But how much bandwidth needs to be set aside for the signal going from the home back into the network? In some designs that upstream pathway is quite narrow—allowing just enough bits to change the channel or order a zirconium ring. Some network activists argue that consumers will someday need as much bandwidth going out of the home as they have coming in. Only then can ordinary people become, if they choose, not just consumers of media but producers as well, free to plug their camcorders into the network and broadcast their creations to the world.

How these design issues are decided in the months ahead could change the shape of cyberspace. Will it be bottom up, like the Internet, or top down, like broadcast television? In the best case, says Mitch Kapor, cofounder (with John Perry Barlow) of the Electronic Frontier Foundation, we could collectively invent a new entertainment medium, one that taps the creative energies of a nation of midnight scribblers and camcorder video artists. "In the worst case," he says, "we could wind up with networks that have the principal effect of fostering addiction to a new generation of electronic narcotics."

If Kapor seems to be painting these scenarios in apocalyptic terms, he is not alone. There is something about cyberspace that sets people's imaginations blazing. Much of what has been written about it—in the press and on the networks—tends to swing from one extreme to the other, from hype and romanticism to fear and loathing. It may be that the near-term impact of cyberspace is being oversold. But that does not mean that real change isn't in the works. As a rule of thumb, historians say, the results of technological innovation always take longer to reach fruition than early champions of change predict. But when change finally comes, its effect is likely to be more profound and widespread and unanticipated that anyone imagined—even the guys who write science fiction.

THINKING AND REREADING

1. In this article, Elmer-DeWitt mentions several indicators of the popular interest in, and knowledge of, the Internet. As you read, think about the indicators that the reporter has selected. Do they accurately reflect the American understanding of the Internet? What messages do these indicators portray to you? What concerns do they raise? Why?

2. As you read, consider who Elmer-DeWitt quotes in this article and why these people have been chosen as spokespersons on this issue. What are their qualifications? Why did Elmer-DeWitt select quotations from these particular people? If you consider this collection of people as a group, what impression does it give you of the Internet?

WRITING AND LEARNING

1. In a two- to three-page handout written for an informed group of ninth-grade high school students who have read this article, identify a collection of four to five textual images (metaphors, similes, images) that Elmer-DeWitt uses in this article to describe the Internet (e.g., "communication satellites strung like beads in geosynchronous orbit" or " . . . Usenet news-groups are . . . the perfect antidote to modern mass media."). In your handout—which should be aimed at enriching the ninth graders' understanding of the language used in this piece—discuss the implications of these specific images, the messages (both implicit and explicit) that they

convey, and the picture that they construct of the Internet. Taken as a collection, what is the overall picture that these images present? Why did the author select these images and not others? What overarching picture is communicated to readers? What parts of this picture seem most accurate? Least accurate? Explain why.

2. In a written response, choose one claim made within this article with which you disagree. In a letter to the editors of *Time*, explain why you disagree and use examples from your own life or from the lives of individuals you know to support your argument. Explain why this disagreement seems an important one to you, focusing on either the personal or the public implications of the claim, or on both if they are related. Your purpose is to persuade the editors that Elmer-DeWitt's representation of the Internet is faulty, inaccurate, incomplete, or misrepresentative in some way.

3. For your own insight and practice in citing material accurately, divide a piece of paper into three columns, lengthwise, or create a word processing file with three columns running lengthwise on a page. On the right-hand side of the page, summarize the major positive claims about the Internet that Elmer-DeWitt makes in this article. Use quoted material when possible but be sure to cite it correctly. On the left-hand side of the page, list the negative, or problematic, claims about the Internet that this article makes. If a negative claim relates directly to one of the positive claims, put these opposite one another on the page. If not, leave the other side of the page blank opposite the claim. In the middle column, identify stances on technology, drawn from your experience or from other readings that you have completed, that do not fall into this polarized scheme—stances that are neither negative nor positive, but maybe more complicated. Try to identify stances for this middle column that recognize *both* the positive and negative aspects of technology—all at once—or that identify aspects of technology that are *neither* simply good or bad. Your purpose in this exercise is to examine how the popular media frequently portray issues—as simplistically good or evil—and then to expand and complicate this portrayal to make it more accurate, complete, and fully representative.

PART II
Program of Study

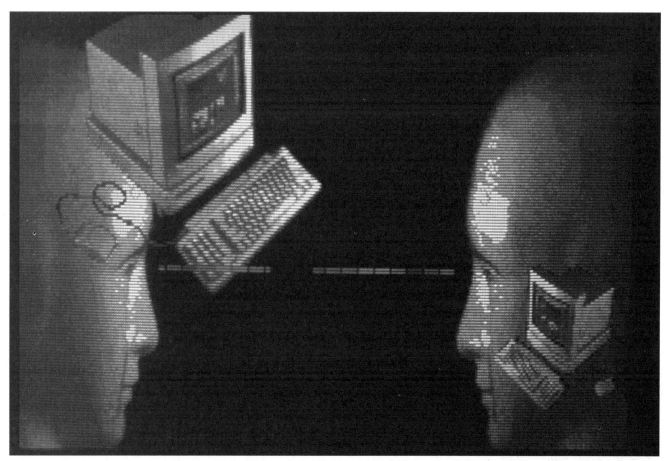

2

Studying Technology: The Keys to Success

WHY CHOOSE TO STUDY TECHNOLOGY?

The following statements are some of the reasons offered by first-year technology students as to why they chose to study technology:

"It's really interesting."
"Technology is practical."
"[It's] useful in life."
"I get to make a difference in society."
"To please my parents."
"I like to think."
"The money."
"[The] variety of challenging and exciting problems."
"[You] get to travel and meet lots of interesting people."
"If you can finish an technology degree, you can do anything."
"Prestige."
"Respect."
"[There's a] wide range of careers available within the technology profession."
"My parents told me I had to because it would get me a stable, secure job."
"To learn how to make practical and significant decisions."
"To train my mind and to give me confidence."
"Job security."
"Computer technology is an international subject. I can work anywhere in the world."
"I really enjoy applying math to physical, practical problems."
"Status in society."
"[It has a] well-defined career path and options."
"[There are] so many different types of study under the same umbrella."
"I have a knack for making things and understanding how things work."
"[You can] work on a team with engineers."
"It's a dynamic subject—new fields of technology are created every day!"
"My mom and dad are both practicing technologists—it seemed the natural thing for me to do."
"I love applying math and physics."

"I want to do something more than my parents did."

"I enjoy being creative."

The reason for this variety of reasons is that the rewards, benefits, and opportunities offered by an technology education are vast. A career as a professional technologist is just one of them. Priorities may be different (e.g., some may prefer the higher standard of living that comes with a technology career, while others might enjoy the challenges and the variety that are a part of studying technology), but most students agree on the following list of major reasons they chose to study technology (in no particular order):

1. Technology is really interesting and enjoyable.
2. Technology offers personal and intellectual development.
3. Technology is challenging—not just now and again, but every day.
4. Technology offers a variety of career opportunities.
5. Technology offers financial security.
6. Technology is being able to apply math and science to solve real-world problems and understand how things work.
7. The technology profession is respected and prestigious.
8. Technology offers the opportunity to be creative.
9. Technology offers the opportunity to do something good for society.

Your own personal preferences will dictate how you rank these different items. Most students agree, however, that the number-one reason for choosing a career in technology is job satisfaction. Many former students—now practicing technologists) tell the same story: After the honeymoon period of a new job (i.e., after the initial euphoria associated not only with obtaining an excellent salary and the corresponding increase to one's standard of living, but also with meeting new people, working in new surroundings, etc.), the number-one factor in sustaining you in your employment (and therefore in your career) is job satisfaction—how much you enjoy your job daily. Bright, inquisitive, intelligent people need to be challenged; they cannot spend their working lives in boring, routine, mundane occupations, no matter how high the material rewards. A career in technology challenges talented people to use all of their skills on a daily basis.

Consider the following questions:

- How much do you know about technology? Why did you choose to study technology?
- What reasons lead you to believe that you are *ready* and *equipped* to study technology?
- What are the main differences between studying at the post-high school level and studying in high school?
- What new *success skills* do you need to succeed in technology study?

Can you write down ten answers to each of the aforementioned questions? Go ahead and try.

This is an example of how a professor might begin a lecture to first-year technology students enrolled in an *introductory* technology class. After a little thought, most of them realize just how little they know about this subject called technology and (often despite excellent high school averages) how ill equipped they are to *study technology*.

Apart from the rewards, benefits, and opportunities afforded by a career in technology, you will find that a technology education will increase your confidence, your general analytical skills, your ability to communicate with people on all levels, and perhaps most of all, your ability to adapt to almost any new situation.

TECHNOLOGY OVERVIEW

In this chapter, we address the following questions:

1. What is technology?
2. What do technologists do?
3. Why choose to study technology?

The answers to these questions are not only interesting and informative, but will help you stay motivated along the long, hard road to a technology degree. Ability and hard work might get you through the initial states, but after that, you must have a driving force, something that will sustain you through the hard times. You must develop powerful motivation. The best way to do this is to learn as much as possible about the rewards of a technology degree. Perhaps write them out and pin them on your wall or paste them inside one of your texts. Keep them close at hand. They will keep you determined and strong. This is exactly what the most successful technology students do; they remain focused by keeping in mind the reasons they chose technology and the rewards associated with entering the technology profession. Make it a priority to keep learning about technology, so that you will become aware of all the opportunities and reward as they arise throughout your course of study. This will fuel your motivation and your desire to succeed. The more important it becomes for you to graduate, the more likely you are to do so.

WHAT IS TECHNOLOGY?

What does technology mean to you? Here are a few possible responses:

"A subject that reflects our understanding of things around us"
"The application of scientific knowledge to solve practical problems"
"Creative problem solving"
"The use of technology to perform tasks"
"The study of how to build things"
"The study of how things work and how we can make them work better"
"Creating, designing, testing, and improving systems"
"The application of the simplest and least costly method to solving a problem"
"Being creative and facing new challenges every day"

In fact, technology is all these things. The activities included in its definition are complex and varied. It is an ever-expanding subject area.

This is why technology is such a challenging and demanding field of study: It involves areas of expertise that continue to evolve independently, yet are required to perform together as part of the technology process. Thus, a technologist must be expert in many areas, must know how to communicate knowledge between those areas, and must apply that knowledge to study, research, run, and fix all kinds of things.

The early stages of a technology degree must be broad based. The initial emphasis on problem solving, mathematics, science, technology, and language arts is no accident: These are the building blocks for what will follow in the later years of specialization.

As we indicated earlier the technologist supports and works with the engineer, and we define engineering as follows:

> Engineering is a process that applies mathematics and physical science to the design and manufacture of product or service for the benefit of society. This process is illustrated in the following diagram.

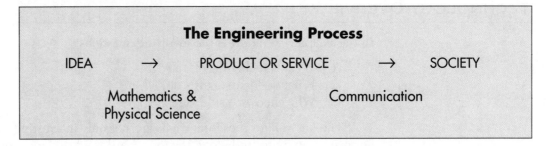

Because technologists participate in this same process, they must be able to understand and use the language of mathematics and physical science and communicate clearly in written form to move through the process.

TODAY'S ENGINEERING FIELDS

Today, demand has created over 30 different engineering fields from the original five main branches. Some of these new degree areas are

Aerospace	Electromechanical	Materials
Agricultural	Engineering science	Nuclear
Architectural	Environmental	Petroleum
Biomedical	Industrial	Systems
Computer	Marine	Welding

THE EMERGING NEED FOR TECHNICIANS AND TECHNOLOGISTS

With the launching of *Sputnik* by the former Soviets on October 4, 1957, the need for more specialized and more scientific engineers became apparent. By this time technology had become quite complicated, and new space systems offered almost overwhelming challenges. Four-year engineering schools were funded to upgrade curriculums and to produce engineering graduates with greater scientific skills.

Graduates of the engineering programs of the 1960s had more theoretical knowledge, but less practical knowledge and manufacturing experience. These new "engineering-scientists" achieved beyond expectations and allowed the United States to enter and win the space race of the 1960s and 1970s. New space systems planned for the twenty-first century promise to make space and other planets as much a home for humankind as earth is now. However, the practical engineer who could build and maintain traditional industrial systems became a rare commodity. Technological education was developed to bridge the gap. Technicians and technologist, graduates of technical programs, took responsibility for the more practical and less specialized scientific work.

Before going further, it makes sense to briefly discuss the engineering and technology professions. It is important to understand what an engineer does and what a technologist does and how the two professionals are interrelated.

Generally speaking, an engineer has the capability to develop an idea for a product that has never previously existed. The engineer is a practical designer who applies pure research, conducted by scientists, to the real world. The engineering technologist supports the engineer by helping him to develop, improve, and maintain products.

CAREER CHOICES IN THE ENGINEERING TECHNOLOGIES

This section includes the major technical areas used to classify technicians and the responsibilities of those positions. If you do not find your chosen technology listed, it is probably included as a part of one of the following four general areas. Your instructor may modify this list according to the particular classifications used in your college's service area. The major areas are:

1. Chemical engineering technician (CET)
2. Architectural engineering technician
3. Electronic engineering technician (EET)
4. Computer engineering technician (CEET)

Chemical Engineering Technician

Chemical engineering technicians (CETs) generally work in three major areas of industry: (1) research and development (R&D), (2) production, and (3) technical sales. Chemical engineering technicians and technologists work with little or no supervision in a team composed of research scientists and chemical engineers.

In R&D, the CET sets up and operates laboratory apparatus to test products for such characteristics as clarity, content of specific chemicals in the material, temperature sensitivity, and strength. The CET uses complex instrumentation to measure the effects of temperature change on materials, and to collect strength and hardness data. Often, he or she uses a computer to analyze the data. The R&D area also includes small production lines (pilot lines) that allow technicians to prove the feasibility of a manufacturing plan or process.

Example 2.1

Research a specific technology within the broader occupational area of Chemical Engineering Technology (CET) that is expected to expand within the next decade.

Solution The fastest growing industry in the whole economy in terms of output will be drug and pharmaceutical products, according to *Projections 2000,* a government source. According to the *American Technical Education Association Journal* (October-November 1995, page 21), several hundred experts agree that biotechnology will grow faster than all other emerging technologies. Other emerging technologies making the top five in the study were materials, electronics, and computers and telecommunications (discussed later in this chapter).

Environmental concerns about manufacturing have increased. The *environmental engineering technician* helps ensure that our air and water are protected. The Environmental Protection Agency (EPA) and other legislative bodies have recently enacted laws in defined areas such as air and water pollution, soil and groundwater pollution, toxic materials used in products (e.g., asbestos), and the use of pesticides. The environmental engineering technician's work is performed outside, collecting samples, and in the laboratory, analyzing the samples (Figure 2.1).

The *production technician* supervises or operates the manufacturing process in the plant and inspects the quality of the product or the amount of product produced per day. Often, the chemical engineering technologist directs skilled workers to adjust valves that regulate equipment, start pumps or compressors, or shut down a system if safety is questionable. (The 1979 incident at the Three Mile Island nuclear energy plant would not have occurred if operating personnel had been properly trained. At Chernobyl, operators were instructed to *disobey* standard operating procedures.) To verify process conditions, the technician bases most decisions on observing meters, gauges, or chart recorders.

Figure 2.1 A biotechnologist collects data on biomaterials in the laboratory.

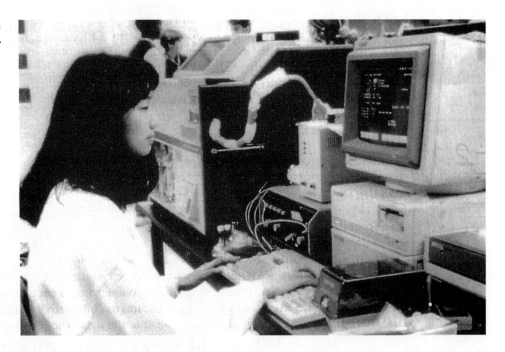

Technical sales and development (TS&D) technicians are concerned with identifying and meeting the needs of the customer. They test and determine characteristics of the product (e.g., color, taste, or durability) that will have an effect on sales, then sell the product to distributors and train them on the benefits and limitations of the product.

You may find the following list helpful in understanding the broad range of specialization in chemical engineering technology. Each specialty is usually needed in a particular geographical area. In these areas technicians may be trained for the specialty field. For example, a nuclear engineering technician program may be offered at colleges located near nuclear power plants.

- Materials engineering technology
- Ceramic engineering (i.e., glass) technology
- Plastics engineering technology
- Metallurgical engineering technology
- Biomedical/biological engineering technology
- Nuclear engineering technology
- Petroleum engineering technology
- Environmental engineering technology

Nuclear engineering technology is usually considered a separate technology—not a part of the chemical engineering technology area. All of the above technologies may be offered as specific two-year or four-year technology programs at your college.

Many chemical engineering technologists will be involved with composite materials (Figure 2.2). Formed of a combination of glass and plastic, composite materials are unbreakable, lightweight, corrosion-free, and easily repaired. Composites can be manufactured with attractive surface finish and high strength and flexibility. Some desirable properties of composites that can be controlled are electrical conductivity, vibration, damping, spring rate, and tribology (a quality characteristic used in bearings, gears, and computer disk drives). Within the next decade, composite materials will be manufactured as cheaply and quickly as plastics. Composite usage will then increase dramatically. Composite material advances in the near future will make chemical engineering technology a challenging and rewarding career field.

Figure 2.2 A computer displays a three-dimensional graph near a medical technologist performing an experiment. Copyright © William Taufic/The Stock Market, Inc.

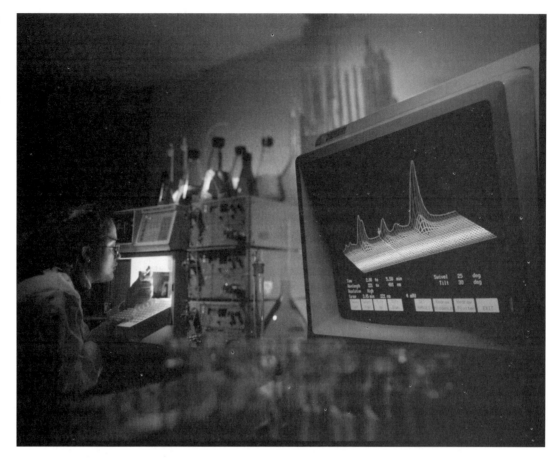

A 1994 report shows chemical engineering technologists in R&D were paid more than any other technical discipline. According to the study, CETs had a median income of $45,000. Projected employment growth through 2005 is moderate at 25 percent.

Personal qualities needed in order to achieve as a CET include

- an ability to work well with others as part of a team;
- an aptitude for science and mathematics;
- accuracy and patience when conducting laboratory tests;
- an ability to exercise care when working with toxic chemicals or disease-causing organisms.

Architectural Engineering Technician

Architectural engineering technology is offered in many technical colleges as *construction engineering technology.* The *Occupational Outlook Quarterly,* Fall 1993, reports that "Construction will add almost 1.2 million jobs between 1992 and 2005, an increase of 26 percent, as it recovers from the residential and commercial building slump of 1991–92."

Architectural design technicians select appropriate building materials and build structures that are safe, attractive, and efficient. They consult on repairs, prepare final drawings for private dwellings, and confirm compliance with building codes.

They are often design originators as well as acting always as the design producers—private dwellings may be designed by those who are not Registered Architects (RAs). Architectural design technicians are also energy technicians. They are responsible for specifying heating and cooling systems that conserve rather than waste energy.

Many architectural design projects involve the safety of large groups of people. Bridges and large buildings must be designed by the engineer approved for professional engineering (PE) or by an RA. Architectural technologists are the design implementors. They carry out the extensively researched and considered design of the professionally registered engineers. Concern for public safety and the need for improvements in construction quality will lead to faster than average employment growth for construction and building inspectors. Job prospects will be best for technologists with prior experience in construction industries.

The *Economic Research Institute* reported that the average starting salary was $23,000 in 1995 for a CET. The average starting salary was $27,500 for all working architectural engineering technicians, including new workers. Experienced workers earned $31,500.

Personal qualities needed in order to achieve as an architectural engineering technician include

- a willingness to work with others as part of a team and to direct others;
- an aptitude for science and mathematics;
- a need to exercise creativity and an ability to make decisions;
- an ability to think and plan ahead;
- a willingness to travel and work outdoors.

Drafting and Design Technician

Drafting and design is central to many industries, as well as architectural engineering technologies. Drafters produce the design drawings used to guide others who build structures or equipment. It is important to realize that their work is not simply to draw up the plans, but also to specify the right materials and establish suitable dimensions and tolerances. Drafters use handbooks, scientific calculators, and computers in their design work.

Manufacturing industries employ both electronic and mechanical drafting and design technicians. Electronics drafters must know the symbols and electrical concepts used to build suitable circuitry. Experienced electronic drafters are in demand and often command large salaries. Mechanical design technicians are discussed further in this chapter.

Drafting and design technicians using computer-aided design (CAD) systems are known as CAD technicians. The CAD system is a computer that allows designs drawn on a cathode ray tube (CRT) screen to be stored and easily modified later (Figure 2.3). For example, when designing a construction project, electrical and plumbing schematics may be layered on the system. Layering shows how the various elements will fit together and eliminates the necessity for many laborious drawings of the same building.

CAD must become more prevalent, and those who know how to effectively use such systems will remain competitive in the industry. It is especially important for students who aspire to owning their own contracting business to learn and integrate CAD systems in their operations.

Employment for both drafting and design CAD technicians is mixed. Because of the increased use of CAD systems, productivity increases may mean fewer jobs. However, many job openings are expected to arise as drafters are promoted, move on to other occupations, or retire. According to the *Occupational Outlook Handbook,* "Individuals who have at least two years of training in a technically strong drafting program and who have experience with CAD systems will have the best opportunities."

Electronic Engineering Technician

The abbreviation EET is most often used for the *electronic engineering technician.* EETs help develop, manufacture, and service equipment such as audio and video systems, radar and sonar systems, industrial instrumentation systems, and medical equipment. The EET is

CAD systems are rapidly changing the construction industry. (Courtesy Autodesk)

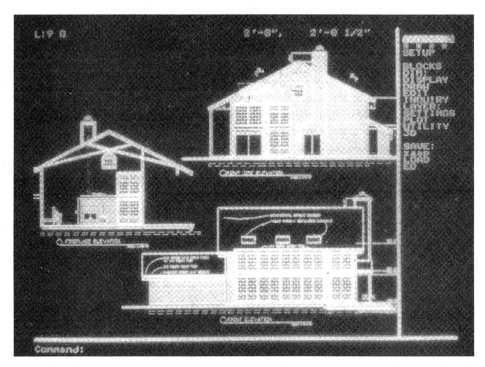

usually involved with computers and may be appropriately known as a computer engineering technician (CEET). The rapidly changing computer area is covered in the next section.

The best employment growth for EETs will be for *service technicians* and *field service representatives*. They install, maintain, and repair electronic equipment used in homes, offices, factories, and hospitals. The best growth is forecast for *office machine repairers*. This occupation will grow faster than the average through the year 2005 as the number of computer-based machines increases (also refer to the section on Computer Service Technologists).

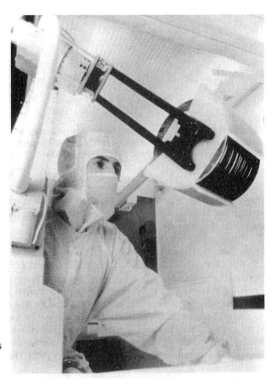

Instrumentation technicians control industrial processes. (Courtesy of International Business Machines Corporation. Unauthorized use not permitted.)

Perhaps one of the most rewarding long-range technical careers is instrumentation, which involves the control of manufacturing processes (Figure 2.4). *Instrumentation technicians* must understand such devices as electromechanical transducers that measure process characteristics such as heat and pressure, and the computer controller that keeps process characteristics under control. Instrumentation technicians work in sales, manufacturing, installation, and maintenance of all types of transducers and controllers.

Other electronic engineering technicians work in one of two major areas: (1) communication electronics or (2) computer electronics. This section will consider the communication electronics technician; another section will be devoted to the computer electronics technician.

More than 24 percent of the 2.5 million workers in the U.S. electronics industry are employed in producing communications equipment. Many *communications electronics technicians* are employed in radio and television broadcasting industries. Recently, cable TV systems have enhanced employment opportunities in this area. In a small station the technician is classified as a *chief technician*, is diversified, and performs tasks such as specifying (deciding what types of equipment to buy), connecting, and maintaining broadcasting or cable equipment. This equipment includes microphones, recording equipment, transmitters, receivers, sound and lighting control systems, television cameras, antenna towers, satellite receiving stations (dishes), and signal-processing equipment. In a large broadcasting station the technician may be specialized and concentrate in one or a few of these areas. The chief technician ensures the system's compliance with all federal, state, and local safety regulations and usually is required to be certified by the Federal Communications Commission (FCC). Students interested in entering the broadcasting industry should check with their instructor to determine whether their college prepares them for FCC examinations.

The U.S. Bureau of Labor Statistics reports that employment of broadcast technicians is expected to grow only 4 percent through the year 2005. This low employment growth projection is due to labor-saving technical advances such as computer-controlled programming and remote control transmitters. Strong competition for jobs will continue in major metropolitan areas, and prospects for entry-level jobs will be best in small cities.

A few ambitious communications technicians become entrepreneurs, building their own stations and managing them. The technician choosing this career should take courses in small business administration.

Closely related to communications electronics are radar and microwave. Both areas involve sophisticated electronic circuitry, and the technician must service these systems on a regular basis (perform preventive maintenance).

The *Economic Research Institute* reported that the average starting salary was $20,500 in 1995 for an electrical/electronics technician. The average salary was $34,000 for all workers, including new workers in this field. Experienced workers earned $63,500.

Personal qualities needed in order to achieve as an EET include

- a willingness to work with others as part of a team and to direct others;
- above-average mathematical ability;
- analytical ability;
- mechanical and science aptitude.

Computer Engineering Technician

The *computer engineering technician (CEET)* services, connects, and programs microcomputers or maintains the larger mainframe computer systems (Figure 2.5) used in both business and industry. In manufacturing, the microprocessor is the "brain" of the machine. In fact, the ability to automate in industry depends on the technician's ability to successfully interface (connect) the microcomputer to a specific machine or process.

Everyone is familiar with the rapid growth of the personal computer industry. Personal computers are now used extensively in business, industry, and homes. During the 1980s the proportion of industrial workers using computers increased from 18 to 28 percent. These computers must be serviced periodically by computer service technicians (often called field engineers or customer service engineers). *Computer service technologists* are usually assigned to several customers. This means they are often on the road. Also, they need strong public relations skills to deal with sometimes irate business customers who depend on their computers and suddenly find that the computers no longer work.

Figure 2.5 A male technician inspects data on two computer screens while sitting in front of a keyboard at a table of papers in an operations center of the New England Power Pool. Copyright © Hank Morgan Photo Researchers, Inc.

In all areas of computer troubleshooting and repair, the technician must be able to isolate the particular circuit board or, less likely, the malfunctioning component. Many times the diagnostic work can be done by the computer, but the technician must be able to understand the various computer operating systems and know how to use the system's software.

An interesting technology, linking the skills and knowledge of the communications electronics technician with those of the CEET is evolving. The *data communication technician* is responsible for building and maintaining specialized telecommunications equipment that transfers the enormous load of data that business and industry generate.

There is a great need for *network specialists*. It is one of the fastest growing occupations in the United States, second only to health care. As more companies depend on computer systems that are interconnected, trained network technologists will continue to be in great demand.

There is strong demand for computer technicians of all types. Companies report they are unable to fill all their openings in many cases. The job market for computer technicians will grow by 70 percent between 1994 and 2005. The U.S. Department of Labor lists computer and data processing services as the third fastest growing industry during this period.

Personal qualities needed in order to achieve as a CEET include

- a willingness to work with others as part of a team;
- problem-solving ability;
- a willingness to work long hours to meet deadlines;
- a constant drive to be retrained on new hardware and software;
- a willingness to travel.

THE TECHNOLOGY CURRICULUM

The major technology classifications represent only a few of the more specific curriculums offered by your community or technological college. These colleges will offer a large variety of programs geared to local needs. For instance, technical colleges in Maryland offer such programs as aviation maintenance, chemical technology, construction technology, and electrodiagnostic technology—all of which are well represented in the state's industrial base.

No matter how specific, all accredited programs will require a core curriculum of *general studies* courses (for instance, communications, psychology, and sociology. The difference between general studies in the two-year versus the four-year college is that the four-year liberal arts curriculum has more courses in general studies. Accredited programs must focus their much fewer credit hours on courses that teach students how to accomplish tasks essential to their fields. The few general studies courses you will be exposed to will be very important to your ability to advance in your career. Item number one in the following list should serve to illustrate the importance of general studies to your career.

A national dialogue concerning technical colleges (*National Roundtable on Economic Development,* July 1987) describes the characteristics employers are looking for when they hire technicians. These hundreds of employers interviewed required technicians who

1. have the ability to read, write, listen, speak, and work with others in technical teams, with others in the organization, and with customers;
2. have a strong base in applied math and science and are capable of learning new specialties as the technology changes;
3. are adept in the use of computers for data acquisition, storage, manipulation, and display; for automated control of machines; and for use in design;
4. possess a combination of knowledge/skills in mechanical, electronical, fluid, thermal, optical, and microprocessing devices; and
5. understand how electronic and mechanical systems and subsystems are interrelated. Your accredited curriculum will be based on these or similar requirements. See the following section for ITT Technology Curriculum sequences.

Clearly, if employers feel these skills are important, you need to focus your energies on mastering them. The first step in this process is reviewing your curriculum.

CURRICULUM SEQUENCES

Understanding the curriculum and its various components is part of understanding and mastering your chosen career path. Courses and the curriculums they are a part of are structured very carefully to have specific outcomes. If you understand these outcomes, their relationship to the overall curriculum, and the impact they will have on your employment prospects, it will help you to be a better and more motivated student. If you understand the curriculum and read syllabi carefully, you should be able to assess what you will need to know at the end of the given course and what you will need to do to achieve the necessary understanding.

Whether a course fits into the technical aspect of your major or is a general studies course like mathematics, English, or communication, it is there because it either establishes necessary prerequisites for later courses in the curriculum or is an issue of special import to potential employers.

Let's take a look at two curriculums—*Computer and Electronics Engineering Technology* and *Computer Drafting and Design*—in greater depth. The following are sample curriculums; you will need to look at your catalogue to review your own program.

Sample Program

Computer and Electronics Engineering Technology (CEET) Associate of Applied Science Degree

8 Quarters
96 Credit Hours

Program Objectives

This program helps students prepare for careers in entry-level positions in many fields of modern electronics and computer technology, such as aviation, communications, computers, consumer products, defense, and research and development. The program acquaints students with circuits, systems and specialized techniques used in electronics and computer technology fields and exposes students to a combination of classroom theory and practical application in a laboratory environment.

Equipment

In the laboratory, students typically work in teams. Students will use the following equipment throughout the program: computers, applications programs relevant to the field, standard hand tools, and various pieces of test equipment, including the multimeter, power supply, oscilloscope, and signal generator.

Sample Program Outline

Course Number	Course	Credit Hours
1st QTR		
CE 100	Computers in a Technical World	2
CE 110	Problem Solving	7
GS100	The Information Society	3
	Total	**12**
2nd QTR		
ET110	DC Electronics	4
ET120	PC Technology I	4
GS180	College Algebra and Trigonometry I	4
	Total	**12**
3rd QTR		
ET140	AC Electronics	4
ET150	PC Technology II	4
GS190	College Algebra and Trigonometry II	4
	Total	**12**
4th QTR		
ET210	Electronic Devices I	4
ET220	Networking Concepts	4
GS250	Physics	4
	Total	**12**

5th QTR		
ET240	Electronic Devices II	4
ET250	Intro to Computer Programming	4
GS120	Strategies for Composition	<u>4</u>
	Total	**12**

6th QTR		
ET270	Communications Systems I	4
ET280	Digital Electronics I	4
GS235	Social Problems	<u>4</u>
	Total	**12**

7th QTR		
ET310	Communications Systems II	4
ET320	Digital Electronics II	4
GS350	Group Dynamics	<u>4</u>
	Total	**12**

8th QTR		
ET340	Control Systems	4
ET350	Microprocessors	4
GS360	Art and Humanities	<u>4</u>
	Total	**12**
	PROGRAM TOTALS	**96**

ET = Electronics Technology, GS = General Studies,
CE = Basic Technology

COURSE DESCRIPTIONS

First Quarter

CE100 Computers in a Technical World
2 Quarter Credits

This course provides the student with practical experience using a computer to help manage resources, prepare documents, and explore technology.

CE110 Problem Solving
7 Quarter Credits

This course introduces students to problem-solving techniques and helps them to apply the tools of critical reading, analytical thinking, and mathematics to help solve problems in practical applications.

GS100 The Information Society
3 Quarter Credits

This course introduces the students to living, working, and learning in an informational society. Students will discover how to maximize their own learning style to learning in an ever-changing society and how to use a systematic approach to meeting challenges. Students will apply this approach to analyzing their course of study.

Second Quarter

ET110 DC Electronics
4 Quarter Credits

A study of electronic laws and components in DC circuits, emphasizing the study and application of network theorems interrelating voltage, current, and resistance. Students apply practical mathematics as it supports understanding the principles of electronics. A laboratory provides practical experience using both physical components and computer-generated simulations.
Prerequisites: CE100, CE110

ET120 PC Technology I
4 Quarter Credits

A study of microcomputer systems, including the functions of microcomputer main components and peripheral devices. Students study how systems are set up and configured. The course includes principles of operating systems, data storage, analyzing system performance, troubleshooting, and repair of computer systems.
Prerequisite: CE100

GS180 College Algebra and Trigonometry I
4 Quarter Credits

Students in this course will explore college mathematics through a detailed examination of practical applications. Learning activities will include solving problems and using appropriate technological tools.
Prerequisite: CE110

Third Quarter

ET140 AC Electronics
4 Quarter Credits

This course covers an analysis of reactive components as they relate to an AC sine wave. Transformers, filters, and resonant circuits are studied in this course. Laboratory supports the theory and continues use of both physical components and computer-generated models.
Prerequisite: ET110

ET150 PC Technology II
4 Quarter Credits

This course is a continuation of PC Technology I with an emphasis on interfacing with peripherals and troubleshooting.
Prerequisite: ET120

GS190 College Algebra and Trigonometry II
4 Quarter Credits

In this continuation of College Mathematics I, students will study college mathematics through a detailed examination of practical applications. Among the topics included are algebraic functions, exponential functions, matrices, and systems of equations.
Prerequisite: GS180

Fourth Quarter

ET210 Electronic Devices I
4 Quarter Credits

Students in this course study solid state devices, including diodes and transistors. Emphasis is placed on linear amplifiers and DC switching applications. Laboratory projects involve constructing, testing, and troubleshooting circuits using solid state devices.
Prerequisite: ET140

ET220 Networking Concepts
4 Quarter Credits

Computer network and internetworking concepts, such as standards, topology, models, protocols, devices, operating systems, and applications, will be explored. Students will have the opportunity to assemble a simple computer network and test its operations.
Prerequisite: ET150

GS250 Physics
4 Quarter Credits

Students in this course study the concepts of mechanical physics. Laboratory projects demonstrate the theory.
Prerequisite: GS190

Fifth Quarter

ET240 Electronic Devices II
4 Quarter Credits

Students study integrated circuits such as those used in communications and control systems. The circuits include, but are not limited to, amplifiers, timing circuits, summation amplifiers, active filters, and oscillators. Laboratory projects include constructing, testing, and troubleshooting circuits containing operational amplifiers.
Prerequisite: ET210

ET250 Introduction to Computer Programming
4 Quarter Credits

This course introduces a structured approach to computer software development. Students will have the opportunity to enter, run, and debug programs they have written. Emphasis will be placed on logical structures, arrays, and efficient programming.
Prerequisite: CE100, GS190

GS120 Strategies for Composition
4 Quarter Credits

This course covers all phases of the writing process with special emphasis on the structure of writing and techniques for writing clearly, precisely, and persuasively. Special emphasis is placed on critical thinking, reading skills, and elements of research in the information age.

Sixth Quarter

ET270 Communications Systems I
4 Quarter Credits

In this course, several methods of signal transmission and reception are covered, including such techniques as mixing, modulating, and amplifying.
Prerequisite: ET240

ET280 Digital Electronics I
4 Quarter Credits

This course is a study of the fundamental concepts of digital electronics. The focus in this course is on combinatorial logic. In lab, students construct, test, and troubleshoot digital circuits.
Prerequisite: ET240

GS235 Social Problems
4 Quarter Credits

This course involves an interdisciplinary study of social problems in an informational age. Students are required to apply social science techniques and critical thinking skills as they examine benefits and challenges of the ever-changing society.
Prerequisite: GS120

Seventh Quarter

ET310 Communications Systems II
4 Quarter Credits

A continuation of Communications Systems I, this course emphasizes digital techniques and the transmission and recovery of information.
Prerequisites: ET270, ET280

ET320 Digital Electronics II
4 Quarter Credits

This course continues the study of digital electronics. The focus in this course is on sequential logic. In lab, students construct, test, and troubleshoot digital circuits.
Prerequisite: ET280

GS350 Group Dynamics
4 Quarter Credits

In this course, students examine the elements of successful teams and small decision-making groups. Emphasis is on communications, critical thinking, and group process techniques.
Prerequisite: GS120

Eighth Quarter

ET340 Control Systems
4 Quarter Credits

Students examine the control of systems with programmable units. Applying digital logic to control industrial processes is emphasized. A final project in laboratory provides the students with the opportunity to apply knowledge of electronics gained in previous coursework.
Prerequisite: ET320

ET350 Microprocessors
4 Quarter Credits

Students study the architecture, interfacing, and programming of a microprocessor, including interfacing the microprocessor with memory and with input and output devices. In lab, students will write, run, and debug programs.
Prerequisite: ET320

GS360 Art and Humanities
4 Quarter Credits

This course focuses on the major artists, movements, and issues in painting, sculpture, architecture, and other media in the contemporary period. Using principles of critical thinking, clarity, and logic, students write critical analysis and research papers.
Prerequisite: GS120

CEET Prerequisites Flowchart

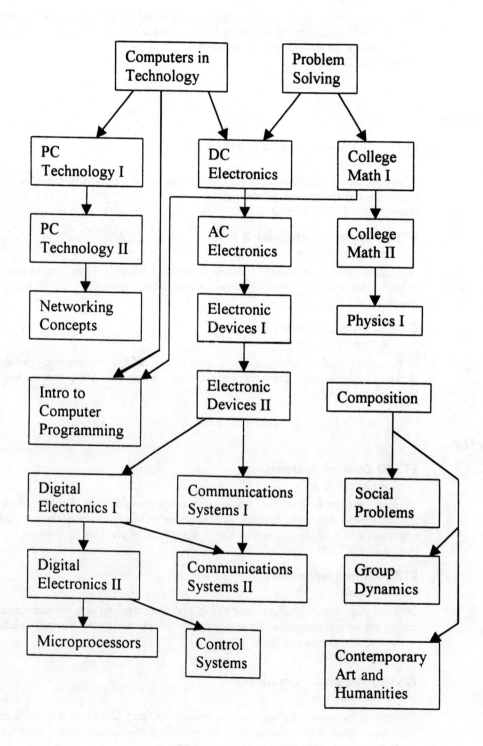

PROGRAM TECHNICAL OUTCOMES

This program offers the student the opportunity to accomplish each of the following outcomes. These do not include specific course objectives in math, physics, general education, or professional development.

Using Computers: Use a microcomputer to aid preparation of technical documents and diagrams, research information, manage resources, and explore technology. Evidence of achievement is indicated by the student's grades in the Computers in Technology course and in documentation generated in the course assignments.

Problem Solving: Demonstrate the ability to use the tools of analytical thinking, critical reading, and mathematics to help solve practical problems. Evidence of achievement is indicated by the student's grades in the Problem Solving course and in documented solution details.

DC Electronics: Demonstrate an understanding of and analyze DC circuits, including the application of algebra to aid the analysis of DC circuits using Ohm's Law, Kirchhoff's Laws, and network theorems. Prototype, test, and troubleshoot DC circuits in a lab. Evidence of achievement is indicated by the student's grades in the DC Electronics course.

AC Electronics: Demonstrate an understanding of and analyze AC circuits, including the application of trigonometry, vectors, and complex numbers to aid the analysis of AC circuits using circuit laws and network theorems. Prototype, test, and troubleshoot AC circuits in a lab. Evidence of achievement is indicated by the student's grades in the AC Electronics course.

PC Technology: Demonstrate an understanding of microcomputer operations and architecture. In lab, optimize the operation of a microcomputer system, and troubleshoot and repair faulted systems. Evidence of achievement is indicated by the student's grades in the PC Technology I & II courses.

Analog Circuits: Demonstrate an understanding of and analyze circuits containing diodes, transistors, and op amps. Prototype, test, and troubleshoot analog circuits in a lab. Evidence of achievement is indicated by the student's grades in the Electronic Devices I and II courses.

Computer Networking: Demonstrate an understanding of computer networking principles and practices. Assemble and test the operation of a simple computer network. Evidence of achievement is indicated by the student's grades in the Networking Concepts course and by proper operation of an assembled and configured computer network.

Computer Programming: Enter, run, and debug computer programs. Evidence of achievement is indicated by the student's grades in the Introduction to Computer Programming course and in the programs that the students develop.

Digital Circuits: Demonstrate an understanding of and analyze digital circuits, including the application of Boolean algebra to aid in the analysis of digital circuits. Prototype, test, and troubleshoot digital circuits in a lab. Design and implement a digital applications circuit in lab. Evidence of achievement is indicated by the student's grades in Digital Electronics I & II, plus documentation for the digital design project.

Electronic Communications: Demonstrate an understanding of electronic communications principles, circuits, and systems. Prototype, test, and troubleshoot electronic communications circuits in a lab. Evidence of achievement is indicated by the student's grades in the Communications Systems I & II courses.

Microprocessors: Demonstrate an understanding of microprocessors and their applications in industry, including programmable logic controllers. Prototype, test, and troubleshoot microprocessor applications in a lab, including writing and debugging programs. Evidence of achievement is indicated by the student's grades in the Microprocessors course.

Control Systems: Demonstrate an understanding of control systems and the principles of operation of programmable logic controllers (PLCs). Program and interface PLCs to inputs and outputs for the purpose of controlling some process.

Capstone Project: As part of the requirements in the Control Systems course, students work in teams to design, construct, and test an electronics application. Evidence of achievement is in the documentation for the project. The college typically has some operational prototypes of past.

CAREER OPPORTUNITIES

Graduates of this program may begin their careers in a variety of entry-level positions in various fields involving electronics engineering technology and computer engineering technology, such as technician, electronics technician, field service representative, salesperson, and computer technician.

Graduates who have difficulty distinguishing colors may not be able to perform the essential functions of various positions involving Computer and Electronics Engineering Technology.

Sample Program
Computer Drafting and Design (CDD)
Associate of Applied Science Degree

8 Quarters
96 Credit Hours

Program Objectives

Drafting is a graphic language used by industry to communicate ideas and plans from the creative-design stage through production. Computer-Aided Drafting and Design Technology is a new way to produce drawings in all traditional design and drafting fields. This program combines computer-aided drafting with conventional methods of graphic communication to solve drafting and basic design-related problems. The program will help prepare graduates to work in many diverse areas of technical drafting and design.

Students will be exposed to both classroom theory and laboratory projects. Students will be required to create a variety of drawings of various sizes on different drawing media, and will use conventional as well as computer-aided drafting equipment.

The goal of the Computer Drafting and Design program is to help the student acquire the skills to enter the workplace as a versatile draftsperson able to make basic design decisions and capable of meeting the challenges in the drafting and design profession.

Sample Program Outline

Course Number	Course	Credit Hours
1st QTR		
CE110	Problem Solving	7
CE100	Computers in a Technical World	2
GS100	The Information Society	3
	Total	**12**
2nd QTR		
CD115	Introduction to Design and Drafting	6
CD125	Drafting/CAD Laboratory	2
GS180	College Algebra and Trigonometry I	4
	Total	**12**
3rd QTR		
CD135	Architectural Drafting I	4
CD145	Rapid Visualization	4
GS190	College Algebra and Trigonometry II	4
	Total	**12**
4th QTR		
CD215	Engineering Graphics I	4
CD225	Materials and Processes	4
GS250	Physics	4
	Total	**12**
5th QTR		
CD235	Architectural Drafting II	4
CD245	Descriptive Geometry	4
GS120	Strategies for Composition	4
	Total	**12**

6th QTR			
CD255	Engineering Graphics II		4
CD265	Digital Information Management		4
GS235	Social Problems		<u>4</u>
		Total	**12**

7th QTR			
CD315	Civil Drafting and Intro to GIS		4
CD325	Basic Design Theory and Methods		4
GS350	Group Dynamics		<u>4</u>
		Total	**12**

8th QTR			
CD335	Project Planning and Portfolio Dev.		4
CD345	Physical and Computer-Aided 3D Modeling		4
GS360	Art and Humanities		<u>4</u>
		Total	**12**
	PROGRAM TOTALS		**96**

CE = Basic Technology, CD = Core,
GS = General Studies

COURSE DESCRIPTIONS

Technical Courses

CE100 Computers in a Technical World
2 Credit Hours

This course provides the student with practical experience using a computer to help management resources, prepare documents, and explore technology.

CE 110 Problem Solving
7 Credit Hours

This course introduces students to problem-solving techniques and helps them apply the tools of critical reading, analytical thinking, and mathematics to help solve problems in practical applications.

CD115 Introduction to Design and Drafting
6 Credit Hours

An introduction to graphic communication and its practices, including an introduction to the Design Process with an understanding of manual drafting and computer-aided drafting (CAD) techniques. The theory of geometric construction, sketching, detail drawing, various projections, sections, auxiliary views, dimensioning, lettering, dimension tolerances, and basic CAD procedures are presented in relation to the discipline of drafting and design. The course, being a theoretical foundation for the discipline of drafting and its application to various areas of design, has been developed to better acquaint students with concepts, processes, and skills required by professionals in the field.

CD125 Drafting/CAD Laboratory
2 Credit Hours

An application of graphic communications and its practices to practical experience in the use of drafting tools and CAD equipment. Hand-on projects include geometric construction, various projections, sections, auxiliaries, dimensioning, sketching, detail drawing, and lettering that is practiced and applied using both manual drafting and CAD procedures. Maintenance of CAD drawing files through the use of operating system commands is applied and stressed. This laboratory course has been designed to accompany and relate the theory course to corresponding practical applications.

CD135 Architectural Drafting I
4 Credit Hours

An introduction to the theory and practice of architectural planning and design. Fundamental design and methods and practices for the creation of architectural drawings are presented, with emphasis on the content of the drawings and the production skills. Topics include the development of floor plans, elevations, and perspective project principles of a single-level building project incorporating material specifications, legal, and building code requirements.
Prerequisites: CD115 and CD125

CD145 Rapid Visualization
4 Credit Hours

This course is an introduction to the technique of freehand drawing and its application to technical sketching and design visualization. Exercises include drawing of two- and three-dimensional shapes and objects, spatial thinking, and eye-hand coordination in relation to the practice of drafting and design.

CD215 Engineering Graphics I
4 Credit Hours

An introduction to the creation of pictorial, auxiliaries, sections, and orthographic working drawings incorporating developments, geometric dimensioning, and tolerance as they relate to mechanical topics. The fundamentals of weldments, threads, fasteners, springs, mechanisms, and symbol libraries are introduced in this course. Manual drafting and CAD techniques are used in the production of working drawings.
Prerequisites: CD115 and CD125

CD225 Materials and Processes
4 Credit Hours

This course is a survey of various materials, their applications, and production processes as found in the manufacturing and construction industries. Students will be introduced to various construction and manufacturing materials, machine tools, and tooling used in a variety of processes. Emphasis is placed on terminology and function.

CD235 Architectural Drafting II
4 Credit Hours

A continuation of Architectural Drafting I through the functional planning of a progressively complex project using light construction systems. Drawings incorporating foundations, elevations, wall sections, and roof framing details will be created using drafting and CAD techniques.
Prerequisite: CD135

CD245 Descriptive Geometry
4 Credit Hours

A study of spatial relations involving points, lines, planes, and solids. Students learn to solve for points and lines of intersections of different geometries and apply analytical graphics to solve design problems.
Prerequisites: CD115 and CD125

CD255 Engineering Graphics II
4 Credit Hours

An introduction to the layout, design, and drafting of mechanisms and machines using shafts, gears, fasteners, bushings, bearings, and couplings. Students will be introduced to the techniques necessary to complete solid models of appropriate assembly drawings.
Prerequisite: CD215

CD265 Digital Information Management
4 Credit Hours

This course introduces students to current technology in sending and receiving graphical data in digital form. Topics include file types, file conversions, file transfer, Web collaboration, and the interaction with different graphic-based information systems.

CD315 Civil Drafting and Introduction to GIS
4 Credit Hours

An introduction to site planning, civil engineering, plot plans, contour maps, map profile, highway layout, and basic Geographic Information Systems (GIS).
Prerequisite: CD235

CD325 Basic Design Theory and Methods
4 Credit Hours

This course is a study of the principles and element of basic design, which leads to the successful execution of form. Students demonstrate the uses of design as a creative and practical problem-solving and analytical tool.
Prerequisite: CD145

CD335 Project Planning and Portfolio Development
4 Credit Hours

An introduction to the theory and practical development, planning, management, and presentation of a drafting program from start to finish. Topics include techniques of project planning, project design and execution, documentation, and presentation. Students are required to apply theory to a hands-on project as well as the development of a professional portfolio through the compilation of drafting and design projects completed through the various courses in the program. Professional procedures, as practiced in the discipline of drafting and design, are among the topics covered.
Prerequisites: Quarters 1–7

CD345 Physical and Computer-Aided 3D Modeling
4 Credit Hours

Introduces the student to tools and skills used in the manipulation of two-dimensional materials to convert these into precise three-dimensional models of various forms, products, or architectural space layouts. Students will also use software to model objects and spaces with light, shadows, color, and textures that are placed in appropriate backgrounds.
Prerequisites: Quarters 1–7

General Studies Courses

GS100 The Information Society
3 Credit Hours

This course introduces the students to living, working, and learning in an informational society. Students will discover how to maximize their own learning style to learning in an ever-changing society and how to use a systematic approach to meeting challenges. Students will apply this approach to analyzing their course of study.

GS120 Strategies for Composition
4 Credit Hours

This course covers all phases of the writing process with emphasis on the structure of writing and techniques for writing clearly, precisely, and persuasively. Emphasis is placed on critical thinking, reading skills, and elements of researching the information age.

GS180 College Algebra and Trigonometry I

4 Credit Hours

Students in this course will explore college mathematics through a detailed examination of practical applications. Learning activities will include solving problems and using appropriate technological tools.

Prerequisite: CE110

GS190 College Algebra and Trigonometry II

4 Credit Hours

In this continuation of College Mathematics I, students will study college mathematics through a detailed examination of practical applications. Among the topics included are algebraic functions, exponential functions, matrices, and systems of equations.

Prerequisite: GS180

GS235 Social Problems

4 Credit Hours

This course involves an interdisciplinary study of social problems in an informational age. Students are required to apply social science techniques and critical thinking skills as they examine benefits and challenges of the ever-changing society.

Prerequisite: GS120

GS250 Physics

4 Credit Hours

Students in this course study the concepts of mechanical physics. Laboratory projects demonstrate the theory.

Prerequisite: GS190

GS350 Group Dynamics

4 Credit Hours

In this course, students examine the elements of successful teams and small decision-making groups. Emphasis is on communication, critical thinking, and group process techniques.

GE360 Art and Humanities

4 Credit Hours

This course focuses on the major artists, movements, and issues in painting, sculpture, architecture, and other media in the contemporary period. Using principles of critical thinking, clarity, and logic, students write analysis and research papers.

Prerequisite: GS120

Quarter 2
**Introduction to
Design and Drafting**

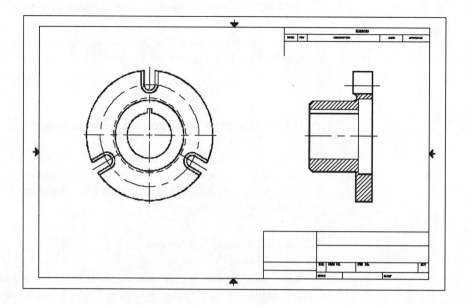

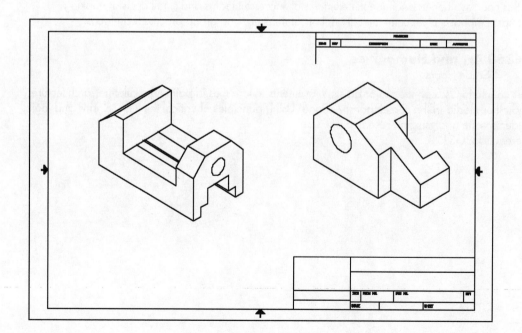

Quarter 3
Architectural Drafting I
Rapid Visualization

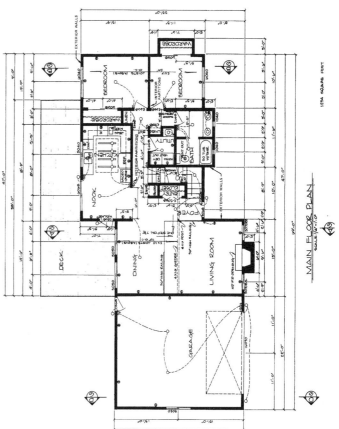

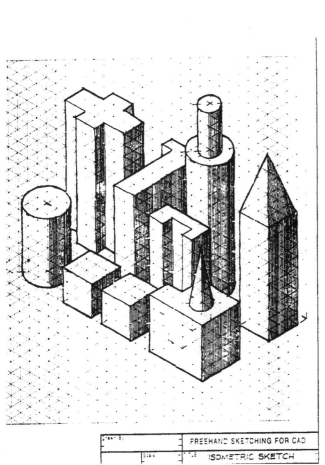

FREEHAND SKETCHING FOR CAD

ISOMETRIC SKETCH

Quarters 4 and 5
Architectural Drafting II
Engineering Graphics I

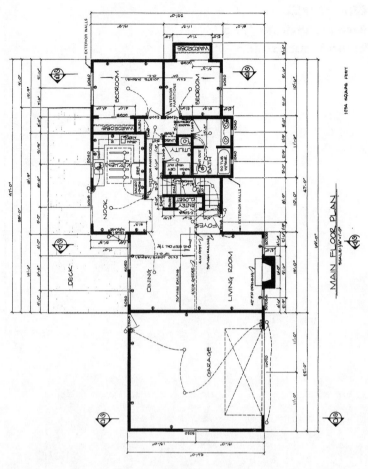

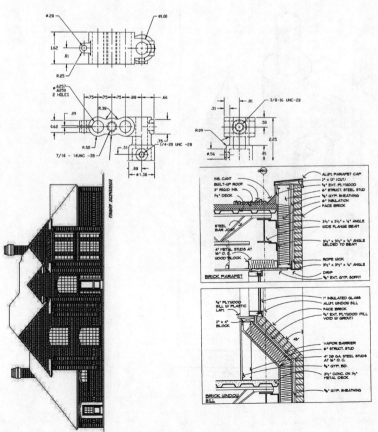

Quarter 6
Engineering
Graphics II
Digital Information
Management

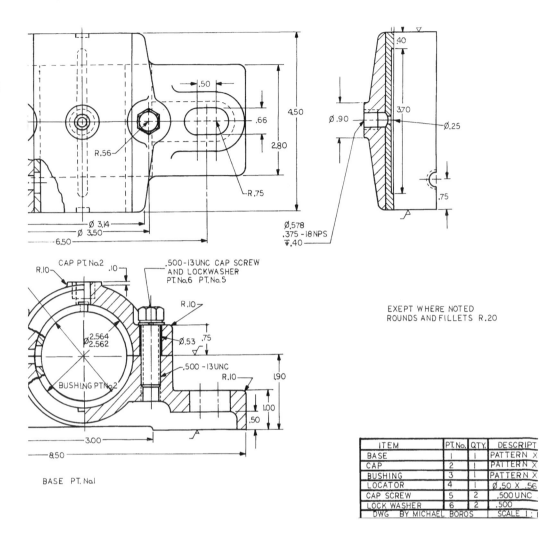

EXEPT WHERE NOTED
ROUNDS AND FILLETS R.20

BASE PT. No1

ITEM	PT.No.	QTY.	DESCRIPT
BASE	1	1	PATTERN X
CAP	2	1	PATTERN X
BUSHING	3	1	PATTERN X
LOCATOR	4	1	Ø.50 X .56
CAP SCREW	5	2	.500UNC
LOCK WASHER	6	2	.500
DWG BY MICHAEL BOROS			SCALE 1:1

CAREER OPPORTUNITIES

Most types of industry use drafters who can translate ideas, sketches, and specifications of an engineer, architect, or designer into complete and accurate working plans needed to make any product, engineered project, or structure. Graduates may begin their careers in a variety of entry-level positions in various fields involving drafting and design, some of which include mechanical drafting, piping, drafting, architectural and construction drafting, civil drafting, interior design, illustration, and design detailing. The availability of micro-CAD systems has enabled small drafting firms to utilize computer-aided drafting and design. Graduates who have difficulty distinguishing colors may not be able to perform the essential functions of various positions involving Computer Drafting and Design.

WHY TAKE GENERAL EDUCATION COURSES?

"I came to college to study technology. Why do I have to take liberal arts courses?"

This is a questions asked by many students—in particular, first-year technology students. They ask the question mainly because they are focused on the technical side of science and engineering and often don't understand why and where liberal arts courses belong in a technology education. They view these courses as risky (believing that their strengths lie only in the technical side of the engineering sciences) and as a distraction from their chosen field of study. This is unfortunate, since after all, the decision to include liberal arts courses in a technology education is made by experienced technology educators in collaboration with professional engineering technology organizations and practicing engineering technologists. In this section, we examine the reasons for taking liberal arts course and how they will benefit you as part of your technology education.

Liberal arts courses include a range of courses chosen from the arts, English, communication, and mathematics. There are two main reasons these courses are included in a technology curriculum.

TECHNOLOGY IS AN EDUCATION

When athletes train for a particular event, they don't just train the specific set of muscles required to excel in their chosen specialty; they train the whole body. For example, sprinters don't just sprint; they use weights to train their chest, arms and legs, they run long distances to improve their aerobic capacity, and they practice good nutrition. Athletes recogznize that the development of any specific skill is greatly influenced by overall strength and fitness. This is true also when it comes to intellectual skills. In particular, your performance in technology will be affected by your overall intellectual strength. Liberal arts courses contribute to that intellectual strength by exposing you to ideas, strategies, and practices in arts, communications, technology, economics, humanities, and management. The more you know, the more experience you obtain in as many areas as possible, and the better will be your appreciation of, and ability to use, technology. After all, you never know when an idea from what seems to be a totally unrelated area can be used to solve an engineering problem. (How many times have you used logical thinking and problem-solving procedures to solve everyday problems such as balancing your checkbook or dealing with a crisis at home?)

THE BIG PICTURE

In order to keep pace with a rapidly changing world, having strong technical skills is not enough. There is a need for lifelong learning, which also requires strong communication skills.

Practicing technologists often comment that new technology graduates are too focused on the technical aspects of technology and lack an appreciation for where technology fits into the big picture of society as a whole. Part of a technology education, therefore, is to understand that technologists cannot and do not work in isolation from the rest of the world. They function as part of a society that is made up primarily of nonengineers, such as economists, sociologists, lawyers, accountants, plumbers, poets, and writers. These same people create most of the demand for technology solutions, and they are the main consumers of the technology that engineers produce. Therefore, it is essential that technologists be able to communicate their expertise effectively to the many different sectors of society. This, in turn, requires an appreciation and understanding of different attitudes, ideas, procedures, beliefs, and opinions. For example, the design engineer technologist obtains ideas by collaborating with consumers who have little or no technical knowledge. Also, increasingly, technologists must compete in a global marketplace where business relationships depend significantly on the understanding of different cultures.

Liberal arts courses will help impress upon you the fact that technology is a valuable component of society by allowing you to step out of the technology domain and view your education in the context of its position on society.

DEVELOPING TECHNOLOGY SKILLS

Excellent technical skills are, in themselves, not sufficient to guarantee a successful career in technology. The following is a list of skills that employers are constantly demanding.

- The ability to communicate effectively, including
  —the ability to write clear, coherent, technical documents,
  —the ability to present well-researched, well-organized seminars confidently and competently.
- The ability to work effectively in teams with people from different backgrounds.
- The ability to demonstrate creativity in all aspects of the profession.
- The ability to manage personnel and resources in technology projects.
- The ability to keep up to date with development during one's years as a professional technologist.

These skills are highly prized by employers. Acquiring such skills will not only give you the edge in employability, but also allow you to go well beyond your training as a technologist toward an everexpanding number of exciting and challenging opportunities.

What can you do to give yourself a head start and acquire the foregoing skills before you graduate? *Teamwork and independent learning skills* can contribute to success in technology study. Practicing these skills as a technology student is an excellent way to equip yourself beforehand with at least three of them:

- *The ability to work effectively in teams with people from different backgrounds.* Your experience with teamwork as a technology student will make this skill second nature to you by the time you graduate. Not only will you know how to work as part of a team, but you will have the ability to organize and manage teams.
- *The ability to keep up to date with developments in technology.* As a technology student, you become well accustomed to learning and thinking independently. The ability to keep up to date with developments in technology requires that you find and assimilate information independently, as required. This is exactly what you do as a resourceful, committed technology student.
- *The ability to manage personnel and resources in technology projects.* Practicing teamwork and independent learning together means that you learn to manage not only your own resources (time, energy, money, etc.), but also the resources of those around you. You learn how to find information effectively, how to use that information to attain a defined goal, and how to communicate the information to other group members.

In this section, we concern ourselves with the remaining two technology skills:

1. *The ability to communicate effectively,* including the ability to write clear, coherent technical documents and to speak effectively
2. *The ability to demonstrate creativity* in all aspects of the profession.

COMMUNICATION SKILLS

Students seeking to become engineering technicians or technologists often lack communication skills. It has already been noted that employers regard good communication skills as a necessary element of technical positions. These managers know that a paraprofessional on the engineering team must be able to communicate ideas to others. This is why technology instructors require good report writing in technical courses.

Suppose after you graduate, you come up with a new idea—an earth-shattering idea for improving the way something is manufactured and produced. You spend months assessing the idea. What do you do next? Whatever it might be, one thing is sure: You will need to convince someone else, perhaps someone with little technical knowledge, that your idea is worthy of his or her time and money.

Basically, an idea remains just an idea until its essence and its implications are communicated to others. This means that, whether you work for yourself or for a major corporation, you need to be able to sell your genius, inspiration, enthusiasm, excitement, knowledge, and abilities to others, often people with time and money to invest, but with little patience and understanding for the technical beauty of the product.

Communicating is about *conveying information* concisely and effectively. As such, effective communication is also a vital aspect of acquiring understanding. (Trying to communicate your knowledge effectively in writing or discussion is an excellent way of reinforcing learning; any teacher will tell you *that teaching is the best way of learning anything!* Fortunately, you did not need to experiment with effective communication: People have been doing it for years. All you need to do is note what successful communicators do and do the same thing yourself. However, there is one essential ingredient that you cannot avoid: *practice*. Excellent communication skills, like most things, come from practice. Just remember that.

Practice results in improvement!

The two main methods of communication in technology are *written* and *oral communication*. As a technology student, you have many excellent opportunities to practice both. For example, you write the solutions to problems in lecture notes, term papers, reports, essays, assignments and tests, and so on. Similarly, your oral communication skills are used in oral presentations as part of team project debates or student seminars, interpersonal communications with fellow students and professors, and in technology student organizations, recreational programs, and student government. Whatever your experience of communicating information is so far, one thing is clear: Today's employers demand effective written and oral communication skills from all technology graduates.

In other words, there is no choice in the matter: Excellent communication skills are *necessary* for success in technology.

Your time in school is an excellent opportunity to work on and improve your communication skills. As previously mentioned, as a technology student, you are given many different opportunities to practice your communication skills, both written and oral. Take every one of these opportunities and use them to your full advantage to improve your abilities in both aspects of communication. The advantages will be not only immediate (the communication of well-organized, logical, coherent, and well-presented information), but, more importantly, long term, for when you enter the technology work world. If you don't take advantage of such opportunities now, you will bring your weaknesses in communication into your career, when you will have less time and opportunity for improvement and where you will be competing daily with people who have already mastered the necessary skills.

The price for waiting until after graduation to learn effective communication skills is much higher!

In this section, we will suggest different ways for you to develop your skills in each area of communication, written and oral.

DEVELOPING EFFECTIVE WRITING SKILLS

Effective writing skills develop slowly, over a period of time, with *practice*. That's why it's so important to begin the process as soon as possible. The following are a few suggestions for developing such skills:

- *Take Writing Classes.* Almost every post-high school in the country offers some form of supplementary noncredit (voluntary) writing classes. These classes are an excellent way for you to become more proficient in your writing. They are short, targeted, and to the point, focusing on the mechanics of writing rather than on an appreciation of the English language.

In addition, you can obtain help on an individual basis through private consultations.

- Write as much as you can. Apart from formal course work (e.g., assignments, tests, etc.), you can give yourself the following opportunities to practice your writing:
  —*Take lecture notes.* Regard each set of lecture notes as a writing assignment. Rewrite the notes as necessary until they are clear and concise. Have someone read them over and give you suggestions about how they can be improved. In particular, learn to incorporate mathematics into text using established procedures, as is done in technical books and journals.
  —*Write letters.* Write letters to friends and family back home, to newspapers, to magazines, and so on.
  —*Write summaries.* Summaries (of class notes, assignments, important theories, etc.) are extremely effective when you are reviewing, but they also provide an opportunity for you to practice your writing skills.
- *Read as much as possible.* Read newspapers, journals, novels, technical books, and magazines. Read at least a few pieces of work every day. There is no doubt that reading contributes to good writing skills, if only for the following reasons:
  —*Reading exposes you to professional writing.* This kind of writing serves as an example for your own writing and exposes you to techniques and procedures required for effective writing.
  —*Reading expands your vocabulary and grammar.* As you encounter new words, look up their meanings and use those same words yourself in conversation and in your writings.
  —*Reading increases your mental agility.* Reading exercises your mind.
- *Look for examples.* We have mentioned many times in this book how it is almost never necessary to "reinvent the wheel." The same is true in the case of writing a good report or proposal. Look at what other people have written. Go to the library, speak to people with experience, or surf the Web and seek out pieces of writing similar to the one you intend to write. Note the structure, use of language, headings, grammar, scientific notation, use of mathematics, how the mathematics is positioned with respect to text, and so on. If you know that a particular report or proposal was successful, then what you have in front of you is a winning combination. Use this information to help you prepare your own work. This procedure is commonplace even among professors who apply for funding. Usually the funding agency will issue what it refers to as "successful former applications" so that prospective applicants can see how to organize and present their proposals in the most effective manner.

- *Get lots of feedback; have other people read your work.* When you are faced with any writing assignment, get it done early, well ahead of time. That way, you can ask someone (e.g., your professor, a senior student, or a writing instructor) to look it over and provide some helpful suggestions. Then take the time to rewrite the assignment, incorporating all suggestions made by the reader(s). Remember, the effectiveness of your writing will be judged by how well someone else understands what you write. Consequently, whenever possible, take the opportunity to have someone else read and criticize your work. This serves the same purpose as a rehearsal.
- *Read your own work out loud to yourself.* Reading your own work out loud to yourself will allow you to hear what someone else will hear when you present your work. In this way, you can dramatically improve your work by yourself.
- *Elect to take courses that involve a strong writing component.* Whenever you are given a choice of which courses to study (electives), choose courses that involve extensive writing. They need not be technology courses. For example, you might choose economics, history, sociology, or a language course. Not only will you have the opportunity to write, but you will have available the skills of a trained professional to provide essential feedback on your writing.
- *Learn word processing.* The presentation of handwritten reports in a professional context is now uncommon. It is therefore essential that you become familiar with the use of a word processor. Popular packages now come with excellent, simple, on-line tutorials, making them extremely easy to learn. Add to that the many different tools available (e.g., automatic spell checking, an on-line thesaurus and dictionary, grammar checking, on-line editing, etc.) and you have an easy way to produce high-quality documents. Word processors also promote the effective use of layout: You have the ability to mimic styles already familiar to you from textbooks and technical journals. Since corrections are so much easier to achieve, word processing will allow you to concentrate on your ideas and understanding of the material to be presented.
- *Practice good spelling.* It must be stressed here that good report writing includes no spelling errors. This point is so crucial that a list of the most commonly misspelled words in engineering reports is offered in Table 2.1.

Good spelling, as well as good writing, takes discipline, dedication, and attention to detail. The conscientious student consults the dictionary or other resources whenever the spelling or usage of a word is in doubt. A report that has excellent content will not be seriously considered by most readers if they see misspelled or misused words in the report—especially if the words are technical in nature.

Table 2.1 The Most Commonly Misspelled Words in Technical Reports

1. recommend	11. hydraulic	21. discrepancy
2. vacuum	12. pneumatic	22. heat-treat
3. precede	13. proceed	23. humidity
4. basically	14. separate	24. materials
5. volume	15. inaccurate	25. procedure
6. proportional	16. maintenance	26. necessary
7. comparison	17. auxiliary	27. comparative
8. occurrence	18. develop	28. process
9. nozzle	19. mechanical	29. electromechanical
10. resonance	20. reservoir	30. receive

Effective writing is a complex skill and is developed over time. Following the foregoing suggestions and practicing whenever you can will make you not only more competent, but also more confident in your work and in the way you present it.

DEVELOPING EFFECTIVE ORAL COMMUNICATION SKILLS

One of the most rewarding aspects of my profession is being able to follow the careers of my former students as they enter professional technology in the *real world*. Each time one of them comes to visit me, I am amazed by just how much they have changed. They appear immaculately dressed, polished, confident, and extremely well-spoken. In addition, they are much more comfortable than they have ever been in one-on-one conversation—even those who used to sit at the back of the class and never utter a single word! I often remark, "How times have changed" from the days when they had to be constantly prompted for information and would often feel intimidated just being in the same room as me!

Most of them explain that their metamorphosis was more out of necessity than by choice: Within only a few weeks of beginning their careers, they would find themselves in formal meetings with clients, having lunch or dinner meetings with consultants, participating in conference calls, or explaining a new product line to an audience as part of a formal presentation. In other words, their interpersonal communication skills were now the deciding factor between success and failure. Being engineering technologists, my former students adapted as necessary, but not without a certain amount of anguish, frustration, and embarrassment. Consequently, their message to me is always the same:

"I wish I had paid more attention to my communication skills while at the university."

There are basically two different types of oral communication in which we engage: interpersonal communication and formal presentations.

INTERPERSONAL COMMUNICATIONS

Interpersonal communication includes the following:

- One-on-one informal conversations with a second party
- One-on-one formal meetings
- Group meetings in which you act as a participant or team leader
- Interviews in which you are the *interviewer* or the *interviewee*

Effective interpersonal communication involves many different skills, including:

- Listening skills
- The ability to define what you need from a meeting and how to ask for it
- The power of persuasion
- Sensitivity to the beliefs and perceptions of others
- The ability to understand and appreciate another's point of view
- The ability to present what you have to say in such a way that it appears attractive to the other party

These and many other aspects of interpersonal communication are discussed in the many different books dealing with personal empowerment and the psychology of success. These books make an excellent read and are full of extremely useful tips and suggestions for achieving your goals. They also serve as excellent motivators as you encounter the usual obstacles that are commonplace on the path to success in any discipline. Read these or related materials, and use the opportunities provided by your school environment to practice your skills, starting today.

FORMAL PRESENTATIONS

I have been giving formal presentations now for almost 15 years. To this day, as I am about to "go on stage," I still get nervous, my knees begin to buckle, and my mind goes blank. Despite all of this, I continue to give extremely effective presentations.

The fear of public speaking is perhaps the greatest fear of all. The symptoms I experience just before giving a presentation are not uncommon. To quote Mark Twain:

"There are two types of speakers: those who are nervous and those who are liars."

Everyone—even experienced speakers—has some anxiety when speaking in front of a group of people. This is perfectly normal. Accept this simple fact, and then take the necessary steps to make sure you give a superb presentation anyway. The key to doing this lies in preparation!

The following is the first of a list of simple suggestions I offer from my (many) experiences giving (extremely effective and not so effective) formal presentations in industry and academia:

1. *Prepare the technical aspects of your presentation properly and thoroughly beforehand.* Prepare all subsidiary materials (for example, slides, videos, handouts, and so on) meticulously. Make sure that:
   a. They are technically correct and contain no errors.
   b. They are clear and legible from anywhere in the room.
   c. You have the correct number of slides for the time allotted.
   d. You know all the material well enough to answer any question on any aspect of anything you present.
   e. Divide your talk into three parts:
      - *The beginning:* an overview of the presentation and background or motivational material
      - *The main body:* what you have to say
      - *The conclusion:* a summary of what you have said, together with suggestions for future considerations

2. *Rehearse, rehearse, rehearse!* This is an absolute must. You must rehearse the actual presentation. You would not believe how different it is actually giving the talk you have prepared on paper. I always go through any presentation, in its entirety, in the allotted time, out loud to myself (or to anyone willing to listen), at least twice before I actually make the formal presentation to the intended audience (once the day before and once again a few hours before the presentation). Usually I do this in my hotel bedroom, in an empty conference room, or in my office—anywhere I can talk out loud without disturbing other people. The confidence boost you get from such a rehearsal is incredible—plus, you get to remove awkward phrases and adjust the material so that it sounds better. Nothing will relax you more than knowing that you are well prepared and entirely confident about your presentation.

3. *Familiarize yourself with the room in which you will speak.* On the day of the presentation, arrive early and walk around the entire room (including where the audience will sit). Get familiar with the surroundings and your view during the presentation. Make sure all necessary equipment is in the room and in working order.

4. *Have a chat with someone in the room before the presentation begins.* Find someone in the room with whom you are acquainted, and have a friendly chat while the audience is seating itself. Not only will this relax you, but it will inform the audience that you are indeed relaxed, which adds to the appearance of a professional and polished presentation.

5. *Believe in yourself.* Get rid of any negative thoughts, and have nothing but 100-percent confidence in your abilities. Visualize the audience listening carefully to what you have to say and receiving your information with enthusiasm. Use the adrenaline rush as positive energy to project your voice and your personality throughout the room.

6. *Don't belittle yourself.* Don't say things that make you look unprofessional; for example, "You'll have to excuse me, this is only my second formal presentation," or "I don't know where this result came from. I just copied it out of a book. I'm not smart enough to do something like that," in an effort to make the audience feel better. It never works. All that happens is that the audience loses respect for your abilities and stops listening. Maintain 100-percent confidence and professionalism at all times. You are the expert; behave accordingly.

7. *The audience doesn't expect to be entertained.* In a technical presentation, the audience comes to learn something, not to be entertained. Don't try to tell jokes or try to make technical material funny. Concentrate on your message; that's what they want to hear above all else.

8. *Experience is unbeatable.* The more presentations you give, the more effective you will become as a speaker. Get involved in anything that will give you the opportunity to test yourself:

   - Take courses that allow you to make presentations.
   - Get constructive criticism from experts in public speaking. For example, ask your professor to criticize your performance and provide some tips to improve your effectiveness.
   - Lead your study group. Take the role of leader in your study group whenever you can.
   - Get involved in student government.
   - Join public speaking clubs.
   - Join debating clubs.
   - Read books and articles on giving formal presentations.

As with writing and interpersonal skills, formal presentation skills take time to develop, so use your time to make the most of every opportunity available to you to practice these skills.

DEVELOPING YOUR CREATIVITY

Creativity is basically defined as originality of thought or the ability to use the imagination to come up with new and innovative ideas. You can see why employers regard creativity as one of the most sought-after skills an engineering technologist can possess. If an engineering technologist is creative, not only is that technologist equipped (through his or her training) to turn ideas into reality, but also, the person is a source of new ideas, which often leads to improved products or services, which in turn keep companies in business.

Can a person learn to be creative? Some people say no, claiming that creative tendencies are inherited rather than learned. Modern-day evidence, however, suggests that this may not indeed to be the entire story—that creativity can, to a certain extent, be learned, developed, and continually improved.

The following are some general suggestions that you can implement today to develop your own creative-thinking skills:

- *Knowledge.* If you wish to be creative in technology, you must know your subject. Do all that is necessary to be most effective in technology study—to learn all that is offered you. This will equip you with the knowledge required to explore your ideas.
- *Maintain an interest in things outside technology.* Keep your mind sharp by staying up to date and challenging or debating people on other issues outside your area of interest; for example, politics, your views on social and religious issues, government, and so on. Exposure to other ideas is an excellent way of nurturing your creative side.
- *Ask yourself "What if . . .?"* Take a new look at old problems. Let your mind wander. Whenever you solve a problem (from, for example, an assignment or the textbook), ask yourself what would happen if you changed the conditions of the problem.
- *Play with ideas.* If you have an idea, no matter how ridiculous or impossible it might seem, go with it. Play with it, twist it around, work it a little, and see what you come up with.
- *Brainstorm.* Get together with a group of colleagues, and discuss existing ideas or brainstorm new ones. Talking about your ideas will make them clearer and help them develop further.
- *Allow your subconscious to play its part.* The answer to a challenging problem is almost never obtained at first thought. Most people let the idea sit in their subconscious while they do or think about something else. The brain then goes on "autopilot," bringing the idea to the conscious mind at different times (sometimes even during sleep). Allow yourself to do this. Don't expect the solution immediately; let things simmer in your head for a while—let the idea develop. You must have had the experience of moments of inspiration occurring in the most unusual places. For me, it's while I'm walking the dog or jogging—when my body is working and my mind is relaxing. This is just your subconscious communicating with your conscious mind!
- *Take time to recharge.* It has been said many a time that the most creative people are dreamers, people who can lose themselves in their own imaginations. Take the time to relax, to dream, to ponder, to engage in things that slow the pace down a little. If you're rushing about the whole day, your mind is in a state of constant activity. Let it do what it likes to at least some time each day.
- *Ask questions.* In each of my classes, the students who ask the most questions are almost always the most creative students. They reach beyond what I tell them into the realms of the unsolved. You should never be afraid to ask questions. Curiosity is what drives creativity.
- *Cut out irrelevant details and get to the heart of the matter.* Creative people don't worry about how things get done. (They believe this will come later, as they strive toward their goal). Instead they focus on the objective: what they would like to see happen, built, or developed.

The important thing to remember about creativity is that it is closer to a religious feeling than it is to science. It's more about belief, attitude, and approach than it is about facts and rules.

Problems

1. In a 500-word paper entitled "Why communication skills are an essential part of technology," explain why communication skills play such a vital role in technology.
2. What kind of documents do you think you will have to write as an engineering technologist? Make a list. From this list, identify which documents you can competently write now and which would require further development of your writing skills.
3. What are the strongest aspects of your writing skills? What are the weakest? Devise a strategy to deal with your weakest skills, and implement that strategy.
4. Look at your last (final version) set of class notes. Edit them for clarity, grammar, and punctuation. Give them to someone to read over. Use any comments you receive to improve that particular set of notes further. Decide to apply these improvements to all subsequent notes you take in class.
5. Write a letter to a local technology firm asking for a part-time job.
6. You need the use of a car for the evening. State how you would persuade one of your friends to lend you his or her car.
7. Write a summary of this section. Make your summary no more than two pages long. Let someone read it and tell you what they have learned from your summary. Does your summary capture the salient points of the section?
8. Have you ever given a formal presentation? If you have, write a one-page paper describing your experiences. If you haven't, write a one-page paper describing what you think it might be like to do so.
9. Plan a 20-minute seminar on a subject of your choosing. You should come up with the appropriate content for the allocated time, an opening statement, and a conclusion.
10. List your strengths and weaknesses in each of the following areas:
    * Interpersonal communication
    * Formal presentation
    Devise strategies for dealing with the weaknesses you have identified.
11. What are you going to do to ensure that when you graduate, you can perform effectively in meetings and conversation with professional clients?
12. Have you ever done something that you regard as being creative? Describe the experience.
13. What do you think makes for creativity in a technologist? What would you do to teach creative skills to a technology student?
14. Why is creativity so important to employers of technology graduates? Write a one-page paper that answers this question in detail.
15. Do you think you are creative? Why or why not?
16. Devise a strategy for improving your creativity. Implement the strategy.
17. How would you advise your professors to teach creativity? What do you think will work? Make some suggestions, and ask a particular professor if he or she would implement them in class.

READING

Strategies for Successful Writing
Written Communication in the Modern World 1st Edition

Compiled by Pamela J. Gurman

This reading is a compilation of necessary skills that employers require of engineering technologists. It includes both technical and non-technical skills expected for entry-level positions. As you read this selection, think about some of the skills we have been discussing, your curriculum, and how the skills and curriculum can work together to prepare you for your career.

Skills

Employers seek a variety of technical and non-technical skills. In 1992 the United States Secretary of Labor assigned a special commission consisting of employers and educators the task of identifying those skills necessary to achieve success on an entry-level job. The commission produced a detailed report outlining skills in the following three primary areas:

> The Three-Part Foundation
> The Five Competency Areas
> Qualities of High Performance

Since these skills have been accepted by a high percentage of employers, it is beneficial for you to assess your level of competency in each area.

The Three-Part Foundation

Sometimes these skills are referred to as general education skills because they are skills necessary for learning. In our rapidly changing technological world, it is imperative that you have these skills. The skills and knowledge that you are learning in college today must serve as a foundation for new information. The following outline the basic skills employers have determined are essential.

Three-Part Foundation
Basic Skills

Reading

Locates, comprehends, and interprets written information in prose and documents (manuals, graphs, schedules)

Summarizes written text determining the main idea and essential details, facts, and specifications

Determines accuracy, appropriateness, style, and plausibility of reports, proposals, or theories

Locates meanings of unknown technical vocabulary and determines the appropriateness

Writing

Checks, edits, and revises documents for correctness, grammar, spelling, punctuation, and correct information

Originates and appropriately responds to correspondence

Communicates thoughts and ideas logically and completely, providing factual support

Creates documents such as directions, manuals, reports, and proposals using graphs and flow charts

Determines language, style, organization, and format appropriate for the subject matter, audience, and purpose

Arithmetic/Mathematics

Performs basic computations using whole numbers, fractions, and percentages, in practical situations

Approaches practical problems by choosing from a variety of mathematical techniques

Makes reasonable estimates of arithmetic results without a calculator

Interprets graphs, diagrams, and charts to convey or obtain quantitative information

Uses quantitative data to construct logical explanations to real world situations

Interprets and expresses mathematical concepts orally or in writing

Understands the role of chance in the occurrence and prediction of events

Listening and Speaking

Receives, attends to, interprets, and responds to verbal messages and other clues such as body language and voice tone in ways that are appropriate to the purpose

Listens and summarizes speakers' messages

Listens and comprehends oral instructions

Organizes ideas and communicates oral messages appropriate to listeners

Selects vernacular language appropriate to audience

Participates in conversations and discussions in dyads or group situations

Selects the appropriate medium for conveying a message

Uses verbal language and other clues such as body language, style, tone, and complexity appropriate to the audience

Questions to obtain clarity, necessary information, or instructions

Gives and responds to feedback

Thinking Skills
Knowing How to Learn

Recognizes own learning style

Selects appropriate learning techniques and strategies to apply and adapt existing and new knowledge and skills

Asks questions and/or conducts research to obtain necessary clarity

Matches learning techniques and strategies to type of material

Problem Solving

Recognizes problem or perception of problem

States problem in a clear and concise statement

Analyzes problem in logical manner

Identifies possible causes and consequences of problem

Determines acceptable criteria or standard for solution

Identifies or develops possible solution to problem

Evaluates alternative solutions and determines consequences of each

Develops a plan of action or strategy to resolve the problem

Evaluates and monitors progress of tried solution

Creative Thinking/Mental Visualizations

Generates new ideas

Combines ideas by making nonlinear connections

Uses imagination freely to see abstract ideas

Sees things in the minds eye by processing and organizing symbols, pictures, graphs, objects, and/or other information

Reasoning/Decision Making

Discovers rule or principle underlying the relationship between two or more concepts and applies it to solve problems

Follows a logical process in reaching conclusions

Specifies goals and constraints of given situation

Evaluates facts, considers risks, and makes and supports decisions

Listens to new information that contradicts one's own set of assumptions or belief system

Personal Qualities
Self-Esteem
Believes in own self-worth

Maintains positive view of self

Demonstrates knowledge of own skills and abilities

Is aware of one's impression on others

Knows one's emotional capacity and needs and how to address them

Sociability
Relates to others with politeness and friendliness

Acts and responds appropriately to formal and informal situations

Asserts self in familiar and unfamiliar situations

Relates to others with understanding and empathy

Responsibility and Personal Integrity
Sets goals and develops strategy for accomplishment

Exerts high level of effort and perseverance to achieve goal

Maintains high personal standards

Completes assigned task even when unpleasant or tedious

Displays work ethic including punctuality, regular attendance, effort, and personal integrity

Displays enthusiasm, energy, and a high level of concentration toward task

Completes projects and tasks in a timely manner

Self-Management
Accurately assesses one's abilities and areas for improvement and designs and implements strategies for improvement

Sets realistic personal goals and motivates self to achieve it

Monitors progress and makes corrective adjustments as necessary

Exhibits self-control

Responds to feedback unemotionally and non-defensively

Five-Part Competency Skills
Allocates human resources

Realistically schedules time

Allocates material

Budgets financial resources

Allocates space and equipment

Interpersonal
Collaborates with teams toward common goal

Teaches others

Works well with others who are culturally diverse

Conscientiously and pleasantly serves customers

Demonstrates leadership skills

Manages personal conflict and effectively and fairly negotiates points of contention

Communicates effectively with all levels within the organization

Information
Acquires, organizes, and evaluates data

Uses computers to process information

Accurately interprets and reports data

Files and maintains a data system for efficient retrieval

Electronically researches information

Systems

Understands and effectively functions within social and organizational systems

Understands and effectively interfaces with technological systems

Designs and improves systems to accomplish set of tasks

Maintains monitoring systems and recommends corrective intervention

Technology

Selects equipment and tools that meet specifications

Uses technology to perform day-to-day tasks

Transfers technological skills to similar operations

Learns new technology in a timely manner

Maintains troubleshooting equipment

Appropriately uses electronic mailing systems

Qualities of High Performance

Maintains standards of monitoring for quality in process and product

Sets and preserves standards of excellence in product design

Sets and maintains standards of flawless production

Initiates and preserves standards of quality service focused on customer satisfaction

Commits to maximize the contribution of all employees

As you can see, the SCANS skills could be readily transferred from one position to another. These skills are known as transferable or adaptive skills. They can be discovered by selection of adjectives that best define you. Select the words that describe you from the list.

Adaptive Skills

Accurate, exact, correct

Adaptable, flexible, compliant

Affectionate, loving, warm

Aggressive, forceful, combative

Agile, dexterous, nimble

Agreeable, congenial, compatible

Analytical, logical, critical

Appreciative, thankful, grateful

Artistic, aesthetic, graceful

Aspiring, determined, ambitious

Assertive, emphatic, insistent

Assured, confident, self-confident

Athletic, strong, muscular

Attractive, beautiful, handsome

Benevolent, giving, charitable

Brave, bold, courageous

Businesslike, professional

Calculating, wary, astute

Calm, composed, serene

Careful, cautious, painstaking

Caring, understanding, empathetic

Cautious, deliberate, prudent

Cheerful, pleasant, joyful

Civilized, cultivated, urbane

Clear, explicit, definite
Clever, sharp, quick
Compassionate, kind, gentle
Competent, skillful, proficient
Competitive, combative, striving
Composed, self-controlled, poised
Conscientious, reliable, dependable
Considerate, kind, thoughtful
Consistent, steady, constant
Contemplative, serious, pensive
Convincing, influential, persuasive
Cooperative, agreeable, in accord
Courteous, polite, respectful
Creative, original, inventive
Dazzling, glowing, radiant
Definite, decisive, firm
Deliberate, purposeful, intentional
Delicate, tactful, sensitive
Democratic, equal, fair
Demonstrative, expressive, emotional
Dependable, trustworthy, reliable
Determined, steadfast, resolute
Discerning, insightful, perceptive
Discreet, tactful, considerate
Dominant, commanding, authoritative
Economical, frugal, thrifty
Efficient, work-saving, timesaving
Emphatic, strong, certain
Energetic, active, lively
Enthusiastic, eager, excited
Exact, definite, precise
Exemplary, good, virtuous
Expressive, vivid, powerful
Expressive, well-spoken, articulate
Factual, honest, truthful
Faithful, devoted, loyal
Farsighted, wise, foreseeing
Fashionable, stylish, chic
Firm, unsentimental, tough-minded
Frank, candid, truthful
Friendly, cordial, amiable
Friendly, sociable, warm
Genuine, natural, realistic
Gregarious, sociable, outgoing
Honest, truthful, straightforward
Humorous, comic, laughable
Impartial, fair, just
Impartial, fair-minded, unprejudiced
Impulsive, instinctive, spontaneous
Independent, self-reliant, free
Industrious, hardworking, busy
Initiative, resourceful, self-starting
Inquisitive, curious, eager to learn
Intelligent, bright, informed
Intense, earnest, passionate
Inventive, creative, imaginative

Chapter 2 Studying Technology: The Keys to Success   **71**

Kind, good-hearted, charitable
Lighthearted, fun-loving, playful
Literary, poetic, bookish
Lively, vigorous, active
Logical, rational, reasonable
Logical, rational, well-organized
Meditative, thoughtful, reflective
Modest, unassuming, simple
Neat, orderly, tidy
Nurturant, helpful, supportive
Observant, attentive, watchful
Optimistic, encouraging, hopeful
Optimistic, positive, forward-looking
Original, inventive, uncommon
Outgoing, gracious, sociable
Patient, persevering, uncomplaining
Perceptive, understanding, knowing
Persistent, constant, continuous
Persistent, firm, tenacious
Pliable, adaptable, flexible
Powerful, forceful, strong
Pragmatic, practical, useful
Precise, meticulous, perfectionist
Protective, watchful, defensive
Punctual, on time, timely
Purposeful, resolved, intentional
Reasonable, logical, well-founded
Receptive, open-minded, objective
Relaxed, easygoing, casual
Reserved, restrained, formal
Respectful, polite, proper
Responsible, mature, adult
Risk-taker, daring, adventurous
Scholarly, intellectual, cerebral
Sensible, careful, wise
Sentimental, moving, emotional
Serious, sober, earnest
Silent, quiet, noiseless
Sincere, genuine, authentic
Skilled, expert, proficient
Stable, steady, reliable
Studious, scholarly, academic
Sturdy, rugged, hardy
Sturdy, rugged, tough
Successful, accomplished, proven
Swift, rapid, quick
Sympathetic, humane, kind
Systematic, methodical, exact
Tactful, diplomatic, politic
Thorough, exhaustive, complete
Tolerant, broad-minded, liberal
Tolerant, charitable, lenient
Traditional, conventional, accepting
Tranquil, peaceful, serene
Trustworthy, reliable, dependable
Unique, distinctive, individual

Unselfish, generous, giving
Unwavering, firm, unbending
Useful, constructive, helpful
Versatile, many-skilled, handy
Vibrant, vigorous, assertive
Virtuous, ethical, moral
Zealous, eager, fervent

Functional/Transferable Skills

Administering
Analyzing
Anticipating
Applying
Arranging
Assembling
Assisting
Assessing
Budgeting
Calculating
Charting
Classifying
Coaching
Collecting
Communicating
Compiling
Composing
Computing
Conceptualizing
Confronting
Connecting
Consolidating
Constructing
Controlling
Coordinating
Copying
Corresponding
Counting
Creating
Cultivating
Deciding
Defining
Delivering
Demonstrating
Designing
Developing
Diagnosing
Discovering
Displaying
Drawing
Driving
Editing
Estimating
Evaluating
Expressing

Filing
Fine-tuning
Following
Foreseeing
Forging
Gathering
Goal Setting
Guiding
Handling
Identifying
Illustrating
Imagining
Implementing
Improving
Improvising
Influencing
Initiating
Inspecting
Inspiring
Installing
Interacting
Interpreting
Interviewing
Inventing
Inventorying
Judging
Learning
Leading
Listening
Loading
Locating
Maintaining
Managing
Manipulating
Measuring
Mentoring
Monitoring
Motivating
Moving
Navigating
Nurturing
Observing
Operating
Organizing
Persisting

Persuading
Planning
Preparing
Printing
Processing
Producing
Programming
Promoting
Proofreading
Questioning
Reasoning
Reconciling
Recording
Recruiting
Repairing
Reporting
Researching
Resolving
Retrieving
Reviewing
Scheduling
Setting up
Shaping
Sharing
Simplyifing
Speaking
Spelling
Steering
Summarizing
Supervising
Synthesizing
Tabulating
Teaching
Testing
Training
Translating
Troubleshooting
Tutoring
Typing
Upgrading
Verbalizing
Visualizing
Volunteering
Writing

Technical Skills

Technical skills are those skills related to a specific body of technical knowledge. As a student you are spending a great deal of time and energy learning and practicing the skills within your specialty. Not all of these skills are found in technical courses. For example, this text has covered writing instructions and descriptions. You may decide that you have reached a level of competence that would enable you to write instructions or descriptions. You may list one or both of the following:

> Write explicit technical instructions.
> Create graphic and verbal descriptions of manufacturing components.

The following lists of technical skills are some of the skills that have been covered or will be covered in your technical courses.

Chemical Technology Skills
Perform Routine Maintenance On

A gas chromatograph

A high pressure liquid chromatograph

A differential scanning calorimeter

A Fourier transform infrared spectrometer

An atomic absorption spectrometer

An UV-Visible spectrophotometer

Operate

A gas chromatograph in the analysis of a sample

Automatic acid/base titrators

A high-pressure liquid chromatograph in the analysis of a sample

A differential scanning calorimeter in the analysis of a sample

A Fourier transform infrared spectrometer in the analysis of a sample

An UV-Visible spectrophotometer in the analysis of a sample

Other

Set up and perform titrations

Determine correct parameters for and use a Karl Fischer titrator

Determine the flash point of a variety of materials

Measure viscosity using an Ostwald viscometer

Synthesize organic compounds using a variety of techniques

Obtain samples using standard sampling and methodology

Use ion-selective electrodes in the analysis of water and soil samples

Use statistical process control to determine the capability and then improve a process

Locate and use the appropriate standard method to analyze a sample

As part of a team, develop and perform a project based on an industrial problem

Computer-Aided Drafting Technology Skills

Use basic project management techniques that include planning, scheduling, documentation, and presentation of ideas and projects

Create geometric constructions

Create 3D and orthographic drawings that incorporate geometric tolerance concepts and auxiliary views

Demonstrate proficiency in creating surface models and 3D solid models using AutoCAD

Construct architectural elevation and perspective drawings

Create structural framing plans, plumbing plans, plot plans, and electrical plans

Use professional architectural office practices to complete code compliant drawings

Create steel framing plans; concrete framing plans, and structural detail drawings

Create electronic schematic diagrams, wiring diagrams, electrical power field drawings, logic diagrams and printed circuit diagrams

Apply proper standards and conventions to metric drawings

Apply and identify the proper symbols used to conform to AN51 and 150 standards

Create freehand technical sketches

Apply dimensioning standards to engineering drawings

Perform necessary research for the completion of projects

Edit existing drawings

Plot drawings on media using the proper conventions

Construct axonometric drawings, oblique drawings, and exploded assembly drawings

Create text using appropriate styles and size to annotate drawings

Complete wireframe models via data entry

Create objects from primitive shapes and features

Electronic Technician Skills
Perform

Construct circuits from diagrams

Install equipment per customer requirements

Initialize equipment per specification

Provide operational instructions and training

Set up and configure a microcomputer using available operating systems and software packages

Construct, test, and analyze power supplies of transistor components

Construct and assemble communication lab systems

Maintenance and Repair

Clean electrical connections

Calibrate as required

Tune process instrumentation and control systems

Test for correct operation

Repair and test electronic equipment

Customer Services

Communicate with customer

Instruct customer as to proper operation of equipment

Verify customer complaint

Develop estimate for customer

Demonstrate an Understanding of

Proper safety techniques for all types of circuits and components

Data books and cross-referenced technical manuals to specify and requisition electronic components

The interpretation and creation of electronic schematics, technical drawings, and flow diagrams

Construct, Test, Troubleshoot, and Repair

DC series circuits, DC parallel circuits, DC series-parallel and bridge circuits

DC voltage divider circuits DC RC and RL circuits

AC capacitive circuits

AC inductive circuits

AC circuits using transformers

AC differentiator and integrator circuits

AC series and parallel resonant circuits

AC, RC, RL, and RLC circuits

AC frequency selective filter circuits

AC phase locked loop circuits

Diode circuits

Optoelectronic circuits

Single stage amplifiers

Thyristor circuitry

Analog circuits

IF circuits

Linear power supplies and filters

Operational amplifier circuits

Audio power amplifiers

Regulated and switching power

Supply circuits

Active filter circuits

Sinusoidal and non-sinusoidal oscillator circuits

RF circuits

Signal modulation systems

Digital circuits

Linear integrated circuits types of logic gates

Types of registers and counters

Clock and timing circuits

Types of arithmetic-logic circuits

Types of multiplexer and demultiplexer circuits

Types of digital to analog and analog to digital circuits

Types of digital display circuits

Power distribution noise problems

Types of digital encoders and decoders

Digital display devices

Microprocessor interfaces

Types of microprocessor memory circuits

Microcomputer peripherals

Operate Equipment

Scientific calculator

Computer

Signal generators

Circuit Software Simulators

Logic probe

Multimeters (digital and analog)

Oscilloscope

Technical Mathematics

Compare, compute, and solve problems involving binary, octal, decimal, and hexa-decimal numbering systems

Convert, compare, and compute with common units of measurement, within and across measurement systems

Read scale on measurement device(s) and make interpolations where appropriate

Simplify and solve algebraic expressions and formulas

Determine slope, midpoint, and distance

Use Boolean algebra to break down logic circuits

Determine perimeters and areas of geometric figures

Determine surface areas and volumes of applicable geometric figures

Apply Pythagorean theorem

Identify basic functions of sine, cosine, and tangent

Graph basic functions using polar and/or Cartesian coordinate systems

Compute and solve problems using basic trigonometric functions

As you continue your education program, it is advisable to record new skills. Later, you may eliminate lower functioning skills, as you become competent in higher level skills. Not only will this give you a foundation for your resume; it will permit you to see your progress in the field. Often when we are focused on the details of learning specific skills, we are not aware of our progress. We may not remember how many different skills we have learned.

You will need to be able to provide demonstrations of your skills. Whether you keep this information on a data disk or a specific form, the list should be frequently reviewed. It is highly recommended that you review your list during each quarter. This will save you a great deal of time and effort when you are ready to write your resume.

EXPERIENCE

Another type of information that you will need for you resume is your employment history. It is imperative that this information be accurate. All names and addresses of companies and supervisors must be spelled correctly. Dates and salary information must be accurate. A graduating student had interviewed at her college for the position she wanted. She was given a second interview. When she arrived at the company, she was asked to fill out a detailed application. A few minutes after the receptionist took her application; she was told she could leave. The Director of Career Services later found out that a recent supervisor from another company was supposed to interview her. However, when he saw his name misspelled and the salary information incorrect, he decided that the position required someone who was more accurate. Most people change jobs and companies many times during their professional career. Get in the habit of keeping your files up to date.

PART III
Information and the Individual

3

What Is the Internet?

Today we are in the middle of an information revolution. We are witnessing the growth and evolution of a communication and information medium that is considered by many to be the fourth media positioned to take a place with print, radio, and television as a mass market means of communication. No one could have prophesied that the Internet of the 1970s and 1980s based at our educational institutions would become the fastest growing communication medium of all times.

In 1965 Gordon E. Moore, cofounder of Intel, predicted that the processing power of integrated circuits will double every 18 months for the next ten years. Moore's law has governed Silicon Valley for over 30 years. Moore's observation still holds today and is the basis for many performance forecasts. In 24 years the number of transitions on processor chips has increased by a factor of almost 2,400, from 2,300 on the Intel 4004 in 1971 to 5.5 million on the Pentium Pro in 1995 (doubling roughly every two years). In December 1996 Intel announced yet another processing gain with the introduction of the MMX Pentium. The MMX has set multimedia performance records, making the new computer chip the fastest ever. Consumers have been told to expect performance increases of between 50 to 500 percent. Since 1996, chip processing power has continued to grow.

The history and background of what has driven Moore's law is both interesting and fascinating. In this history one sees predictive forecasts of our future. A future that is rapidly moving to a digital world where the way we live, work, and play is about to be changed forever. Those who want to be successful in this world are learning about the digital tools and resources that are transforming our lives. Those who do not join this webolution will be left behind.

This chapter contains information on Internet research tools and tips, Internet search techniques, and links to electronic websites.. Also presented are a number of new vocabulary words, new jargon, and acronyms that have emerged. Learning this new medium will enable you to be more successful in your career.

WHAT IS THE INTERNET?

In.ter.net (n)

1. world's largest information network **2.** global web of computer networks **3.** internetwork of many networks all running the TCP/IP protocol **4.** powerful communication tool **5.** giant highway system connecting the computer and the regional and local networks that connect these computers *syn* **information superhighway, infobahn, data highway, electronic highway, Net, cyberspace**

The term most frequently used to refer to the Internet is *information superhighway.* This superhighway is a vast network of computers connecting people and resources around the world. The Internet is accessible to anyone with a computer and a modem.

The Internet began in 1969 when a collection of computer networks was developed. The first network was sponsored by the United States Department of Defense in response to a need for military institutions and universities to share their research. In the 1970s, government and university networks continued to develop as many organizations and companies began to build private computer networks. In the late 1980s, the National Science Foundation (NSF) created five supercomputer centers at major universities. This special network is the foundation of the Internet today.

Computer networks were initially established to share information among institutions that were physically separate. Throughout the years these networks have grown and the volume and type of information made available to people outside these institutions has also continued to evolve and grow. Today we can exchange electronic mail, conduct research, and look at and obtain files that contain text information, graphics, sound, and video. As more and more schools, universities, organizations, and institutions develop new resources, they are made available to us through our computer networks. These networks make it possible for us to be globally interconnected with each other and to this wealth of information.

For more detailed information on using the Internet, See Appendix B in this book and the Internet coverage in your *Tools for Problem Solving* reference.

FINDING INFORMATION AND RESOURCES ON THE INTERNET

This section provides an introduction on how to find information and resources on the Internet. Additional information on Internet searches is also covered in the section "Understanding the Research Process," presented later in chapter 4. You will be using search directories and search engines to find information of interest to you, your career, and your field of study. You will also learn about the following search tools:

- Yahoo (search directory)
- Magellan (search directory)
- Excite (search engine and search directory)
- Alta Vista (search engine)
- Infoseek (search engine and search directory)
- Open Text (search engine)

The Internet contains many tools that speed the search for information and resources. Research tools called "search directories" and "search engines" are extremely helpful.

Search Directories

Search directories are essentially descriptive registries of Web sites. They also have search options. When you connect to their page, you will find a query box for entering in key words. The search engine at these sites searches only for keyword matches in the directories' database.

Search Engines

Search engines are different from search directories in that they search World Wide Web sites, Usenet newsgroups, and other Internet resources to find matches to your descriptor key words. Many search engines also rank the results according to a degree of relevancy. Most search engines provide options for advanced searching to refine your search.

Basic Guidelines for Using a Search Engine

Search engines are marvelous tools to help you find information on the Internet. However, none of these engines delivers consistently accurate and relevant information to your search query, and they provide a high proportion of irrelevant information. Therefore, it is essential that you use several search tools for your research.

Although there are many kinds of search tools, the basic approach to finding information with each is similar:

1. Determine one or more descriptive words (key words) for the subject you are researching. Enter your key words into the search dialog box.
2. Determine how specific you want your search to be. Do you want it to be broad or narrow? Use available options to refine or limit your search. Some search engines permit the use of boolean operators (phrases or words such as "and," "or," and "not" that restrict a search). Others provide HELP for refining searches, and some have pull-down menus or selections to be checked for options.
3. Submit your query.
4. Review your list of hits (a search return based on a keyword).
5. Adjust your search based on the information returned. Did you receive too much information and need to narrow your search? Did you receive too little information and need to broaden your key words?

YAHOO

Yahoo is one of the most popular search tools on the Internet and is an excellent place to begin your search. Although Yahoo is more accurately described as a search directory, this Web site has an excellent database with search options available.

Yahoo can be accessed from the Netscape Search Directory button, or by entering this URL http://www.yahoo.com

There are two ways to find information using Yahoo: search through the subject index, or use the built-in search engine.

Yahoo Subject Index

When you connect to Yahoo you will see a list of subjects or directories. Select the topic area that best fits your search needs. Follow the links until you find the information you are searching for.

Using Yahoo to Search for Information

Follow these steps to use Yahoo to search for information:

1. Begin by browsing the subject directory. For example, if you were searching for information on "the use of lasers in medicine," you would first

Figure 3.1 Yahoo search form and subject index in which the key word *laser* has been entered.

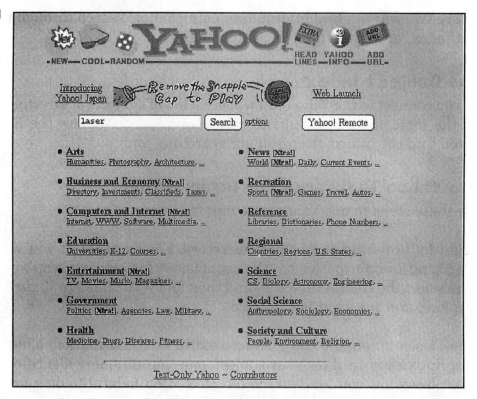

select the *Health* directory and then follow the links to *Medicine*. Explore, and see what is available.

2. Yahoo's search engine can also be used to find information. Enter a descriptive keyword for your subject, one that uniquely identifies or describes what you are looking for. It is often helpful to do a broad search first, though results often provide information on the need to change descriptive key words or to refine your query.

Enter the word "laser" (see Figure 3.1).

3. Click on the **Search** button and review your results (see Figure 3.2).
4. You may now want to refine your search. Most search engines have options for advanced searching using boolean logic or more carefully constructed database queries. Review the search page for **Options** or **Advanced Options**. When using Yahoo, click on the **Options** button.

If you are using two key words, do you want Yahoo to look for either word (boolean **or**), both key words (boolean **and**), or all words as a single string? For example, in the search for "use of lasers in medicine" select boolean **and** because you want to find

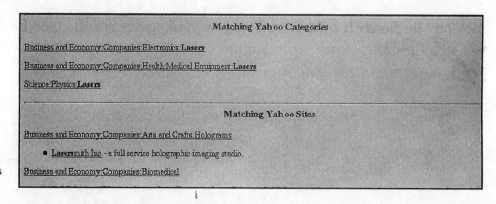

Figure 3.2 Yahoo search results from the keyword *laser*.

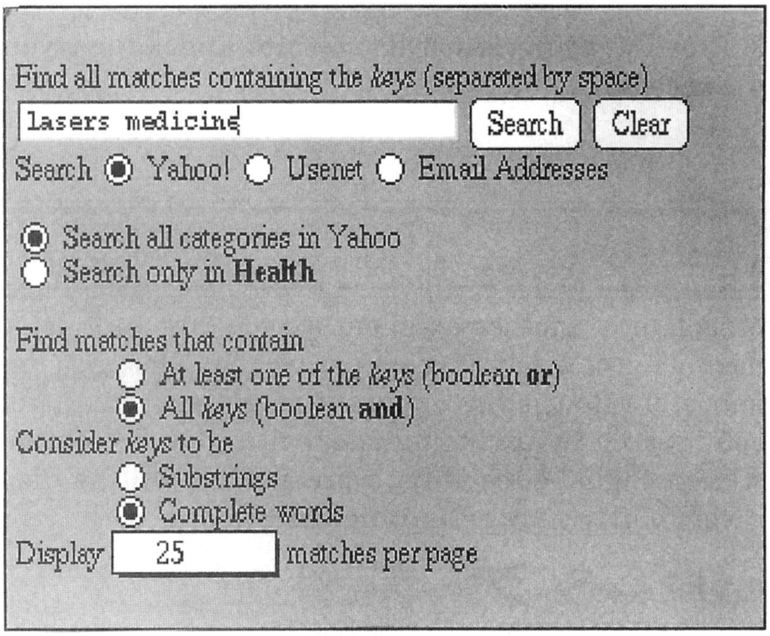

Figure 3.3 Yahoo **Options** for refining a search.

Find all matches containing the *keys* (separated by space)

`lasers medicine`   [Search] [Clear]

Search ◉ Yahoo! ○ Usenet ○ Email Addresses

◉ Search all categories in Yahoo
○ Search only in **Health**

Find matches that contain
　　　　　○ At least one of the *keys* (boolean **or**)
　　　　　◉ All *keys* (boolean **and**)
Consider *keys* to be
　　　　○ Substrings
　　　　◉ Complete words
Display　[25]　matches per page

resources that contain both words "laser" **and** "medicine" in their titles (see Figure 3.3). Otherwise the search would be too broad and would find all resources that contained either of the key words "laser" **or** medicine."

5. Further limit or expand your search by selecting Substrings or Complete words. For example, with your *lasers medicine* search, you would select the search option for *Complete words,* or Yahoo treats the word as a series of letters rather than a whole word. A research return using substrings would include all incidences where both the words *lasers* and *medicine* appeared in any form.
6. Determine the number of matches you want returned for your search.
7. Submit your query.
8. Review your return list of hits and adjust your search again if necessary.

Magellan

Magellan is another excellent search directory. It provides options for narrowing or expanding your search by selecting sites rated from one to four stars (four stars being the most

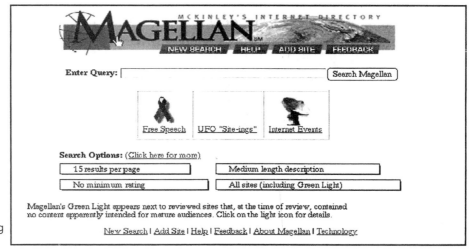

Figure 3.4 Home page for Magellan with options for specializing your search.

restricted). You can also restrict your search by excluding sites with mature content by searching for "Green Light" sites only (a green light will be displayed next to the review). http://magellan.mckinley.com

Excite

Excite provides the fullest range of services of all the search tools. Excite searches scanned Web pages and Usenet newsgroups for key word matches and creates summaries of each match. Excite also provides a Web directory organized by category. Excite consists of three services:

- **NetSearch:** comprehensive and detailed services
- **NetReviews:** organized browsing of the Internet, with site evaluations and recommendations
- **Excite Bulletin:** an on-line newspaper with reviews of Internet resources, a newswire service from Reuters, and its own Net-related columns

Excite provides to different types of search options: concept-based searching and key word searching. The search engines described thus far have used keyword search options. Keyword searches are somewhat limited due to the necessity of boolean qualifiers to limit searches.

Concept-based searching goes one step beyond keyword searches—finding what you mean and not what you say. Using the phrase use of "lasers in medicine", a concept-based search will find the documents that most closely match this phrase. Excite is available at http://www.excite.com.

Searching with Excite

1. Type in a phrase that fits your information need. Be as specific as you can, using words that uniquely relate to the information you are looking for, not simply general descriptive words. For example, for your laser search enter the following phrase: *use of lasers in medicine.*
2. If certain words in your search phrase are critically important to the search, you can give them special emphasis by repeating them. For example, if I wanted to find information on the research in the use of lasers in medicine, I would enter in these words: *research research lasers medicine.* By adding these extra words, the search engine focuses on the double key words; in this instance, the word "research."
3. If you are not sure how to spell a word, type in multiple spellings in your search phrase.
4. There are two ways to have your search results displayed:

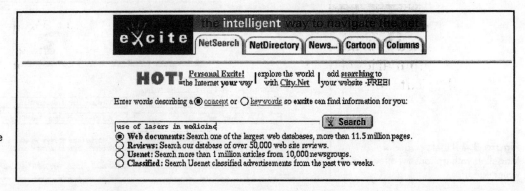

Figure 3.5 Excite Web page displaying concept-based search using the phrase "Use of lasers in medicine".

Figure 3.6 Search results for "use of lasers in medicine" (concept-based search) with a percentage of confidence rating for finding relevant information.

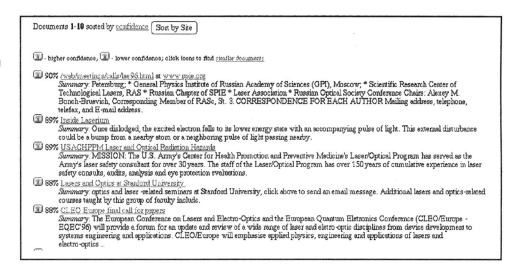

Figure 3.7 Excite search using critically important words.

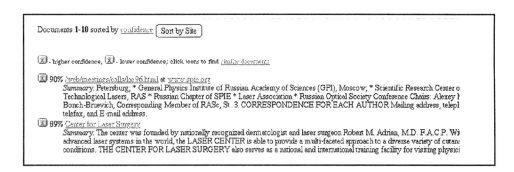

- **Grouped by confidence:** listed in the order from highest calculated relevance down (see Figure 3.6).
- **Grouped by site:** shows you where your items in the result list come from (from what physical location) (see Figure 3.7).

Alta Vista

Digital's Alta Vista is considered one of the best search engines currently available, with one of the largest Web-search databases. Alta Vista's searches are consistently more comprehensive than any of the other search tools. Although you will spend a great deal of time browsing you search results, you will be provided with as much information as possible on a search query. http://altavista.digital.com

We will use Alta Vista to search for information on "the use of solar energy for electricity." We will conduct two searches using Alta Vista: a simple query and an advanced query.

1. A simple query is conducted by entering in key words or phrases. Do not use AND or OR to combine words when doing a simple query. For this query we will type in the phrase: "solar energy to produce electricity."
2. Alta Vista's advanced options use the binary operators AND, OR, and NEAR and the unary operator NOT. For more information on the advanced options, click on the Help for Advanced Options.

   We will conduct a more refined search using Alta Vista's advanced options. We enter the following words: *solar and energy and electricity and produce.*

Figure 3.8 Alta Vista Home page.

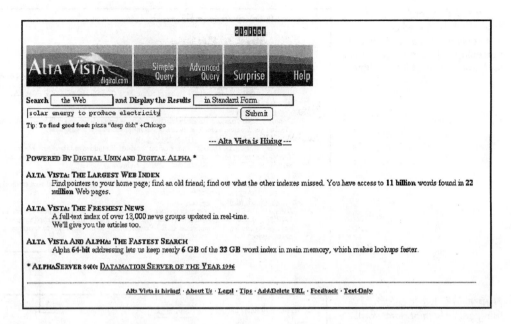

InfoSeek

InfoSeek is a professional service provided by InfoSeek Corporation. In 1995, InfoSeek introduced their easy-to-use search services to subscribers for a monthly subscription fee. Because of its popularity, the services have been expanded to include two new options: InfoSeek Guide and InfoSeek Professional.

InfoSeek Guide is the free service that integrates the latest search technology with a browsable directory of Internet resources located on World Wide Web sites, Usenet newsgroups, and other popular Internet resource sites. Users can choose to use the search engine and enter key words or phrases, or browse the navigational directories. Visit the InfoSeek Guide site and try these tolls for finding Internet information and resources. http://guide.infoseek.com

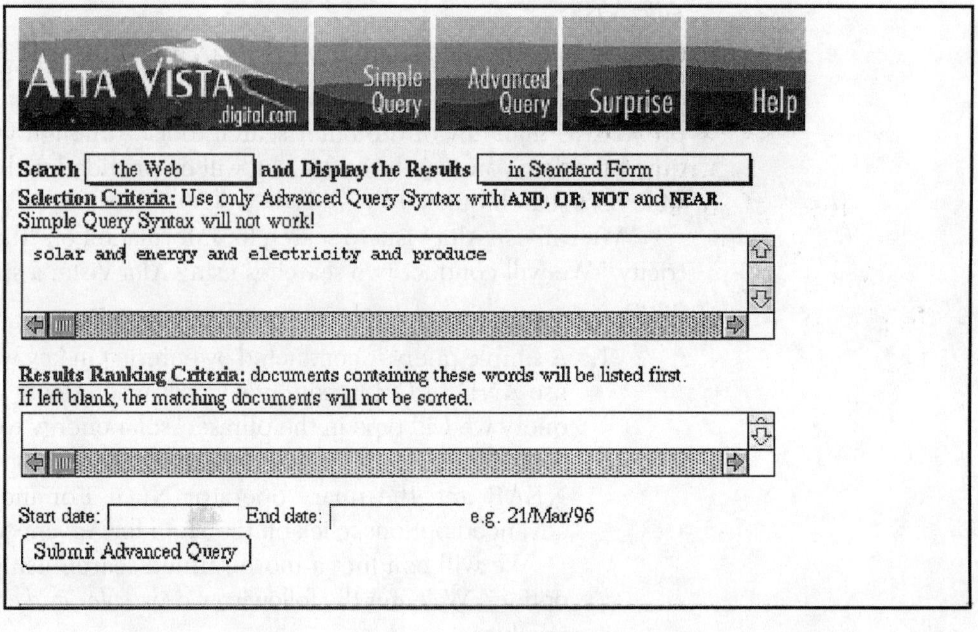

Figure 3.9 Alta Vista advanced options search using the binary operator AND.

Figure 3.10 InfoSeek guide
for information and resources.

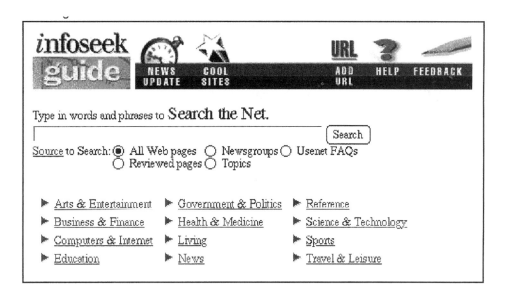

InfoSeek Professional is a subscription-based service that offers individuals and business professionals comprehensive access to many Internet resources such as newswires, publications, broadcast programs, business, medical, financial and government databases. The difference between InfoSeek Guide and Professional is the capability to conduct more comprehensive searches and to have options for refining and limiting your searches. For example, you can conduct a search query by just entering in a question such as "How do I get information on ISDN?" You can also limit your query to just the important words or phrases that are likely to appear in the documents you are looking for: information on the best "ISDN hardware".

By identifying the key words or phrases (**ISDN** and **hardware**) with quotes, your search accuracy is greatly enhanced.

Professional offers a free trial period. To learn how to perform the most efficient search, Link to InfoSeek's information on search queries and examples.

http://professional.infoseek.com

Open Text

Open Text has one of the most comprehensive collections of search tools and is one of the best designed search engines on the Internet. http://www.opentext.com

Open Text offers many search options:

* Simple query on words

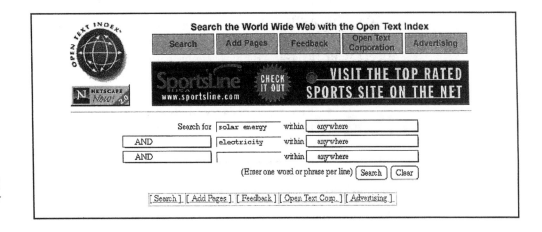

Figure 3.11 Open Text
page showing query entered
with two search terms: "solar
energy" and "electricity".

- A power search using up to five operators between terms (*and, or, not, but not, near,* and *followed by*)
- Options to create your own weighted search
- Results scored by relevancy
- An option to show a report of where Open Text found your search matches

Open Text produces better returns on your search if you break up a phrase into key words. For example, when "use of solar energy to produce electricity" was entered, Open Text reported "no matches." When the query was changed into individual search terms "solar energy" and "electricity," a large number of results were displayed.

Search Tips

- When you find a resource that you may want to return to, make a bookmark or add the page to your hotlist.
- Avoid using common words such as articles and prepositions in your searches. These words are frequently ignored by search engines. Use words that describe or are very specific to your search topic.
- Use boolean qualifiers such as "and" or "or" to limit your search.
- If your search result is too limited using boolean qualifiers, resubmit the search with these qualifiers.
- Evaluate your search of key words and the types of results you obtain using different search engines.
- Look for key words displayed with your search results that better describe your topic. Resubmit your search using these new key words.
- Each search engine provides a slightly different type of search. For one type of search, one engine might be more appropriate than another. For example, in the past you may have used different resources for your searches such as an encyclopedia, periodicals, or books. Each resource is good for a different type of information. The same is true with search engines.
- Use more than one search engine because each search site has its own database resources. Some sites may have information that others do not.
- Make a bookmark for each of the search engines described here. Add others that you might find useful.

COOL ELECTRONIC AND ELECTRICAL WEB SITES

In this section, you will find a plethora of electronic resources on the Internet. Explore how Electronics Technology is using the Internet. Categories include:

- Links to Electronic and Electrical Web Sites
- Technical Societies and Publications Web Sites
- Circuit Archives, Technical Information, and Projects
- Universities and Government Sites
- Electronics Companies
- Electronic Listserv Mailing Lists
- Electronic Usenet Newsgroups

LINKS TO ELECTRONIC AND ELECTRICAL WEB SITES

Journey into the cyberworld of Electronic Engineering and explore many of the best electronic and electrical sites.

Best Electrical Engineering Site: EE/CS Mother Site

The EE/CS Mother Site is a starting point when looking for Electrical Engineering and Computer Science related information. It is sponsored by the Stanford IEEE. Companies and product information are listed,
http://www.ee.standord.edu/soe/ieee/eesites.html

Cool Electronics Stuff

Links to electronic resources.
http://pasture.een.purdue.edu/-laird/Electronics/index.html

Circuit World On-line Services

This provider of information and commercial services to the Electronics Manufacturing Industry has more than 500 links. Major categories include Electronic Assembly and Packaging, Printed Circuit Fabrication, Electronic Components and Semi-Conductors, Design and Engineering, Industry Associations, OEM Manufacturers, and much more. This comprehensive site takes you through the entire spectrum of electronics.
http://www.circuitworld.com

Electronic and Computing Links

This site, maintained by Ben Shirley, School of Electronics, UCS, has links to sites that he has found useful or fun. http://www.uscsalf.ac.uk/-bens/eleclink.htm

Yahoo

Learn about how your electronics education can open doors to the future. At Yahoo's Engineering Web page, you will find links to aerospace, agricultural, automotive, biomedical, chemical, electrical, environmental, industrial, mechanical, naval, nuclear, optical, petroleum, reliability, software, and structural and welding engineering.
http://www.yahoo.com/Science/Engineering

Technical Societies and Publications Web Sites

These sites offer the new engineering technologist an opportunity to join with other engineering technologists to share knowledge and discuss real-world problems. Trade magazines and newsletters keep abreast of constant changes in the world of electronics and electrical engineering.

CAD Electronics

A newsgroup with lots of articles relating to CAD in electronics. Links to shareware CAD, RF Mosfet Models, and Document Conversion Resource Center are some of the subjects covered. News:sci.electronics.cad

Computing Research Association

An association of more than 150 North American academic departments of computer science and computer engineering as well as industrial laboratories. http://cra.org

The Directory of Engineering and Scientific Trade Technical Magazines

One of the most useful sites to locate trade publications on any technical subject. Links are provided to those who have on-line sites and addresses. http://www.technexpo.com/tech_mag.html

A Directory of Engineering and Science Societies and Organizations

Links to and addresses of technical and scientific organizations of every imaginable subject. A great place to explore. http://www.technexpo.com/tech_soc.html

EDN Magazine

This technical magazine is published every two weeks and keeps electronics professionals up to date on the latest products, design techniques, and emerging technologies. View the latest issue on-line or subscribe on-line to review your own copy. http://www.ednmag.com

EE Times

The latest news for electrical and electronic engineers. http://techweb.cmp.com/techweb/eet/current

EIA Electronics Industries Association

An established trade organization representing U.S. electronics manufacturers. It is a multifaceted group with interests in technical standards, market analysis, government regulations, trade shows, and seminar programs. http://www.eia.org

Electronics and Electrical Engineering Laboratory

A government lab to promote standardization in many field of electronics and electrical engineering. http://www.nist.gov/item/About_NIST_Electronics_ and Electrical_Engineering_Labroratory.html

Institute of Electrical and Electronics Engineers (IEEE)

Institute of Electrical and Electronics Engineers, Inc. The world's largest technical professional society. Its mission is to promote the development and application of electrotechnology. It provides Technical Societies in 37 fields of special interest ranging from Aerospace to Vehicular Technology. Technical conferences are listed as well as the IEEE Bookstore for all your technical publication needs. Industry Standards for the electronic industry also can be ordered. The Student Activities Committee's Home Page will be of interest to students and educators alike. Membership information and student web pages are listed. The latest in fashion wear, the IEEE T- shirt, can be the smartest addition to your wardrobe.

IEEE Publications includes the on-line Spectrum magazine and The Institute, the IEEE monthly newspaper. Information to become a Professional Engineer, help with career planning, self study courses, teaching opportunities, women in engineering home page, and much, much more make this a MUST VISIT site. http://www.ieee.org

ISO International Organization for Standardization

The premiere group promoting standardization in the world today consisting of a federation of national and local organizations from more than 100 countries. http://www.iso.ch/welcome.html

ITU International Telecommunication Union

An organization headquartered in Geneva, Switzerland that coordinates global telcom networks and services for the government and the private sector. http://www.itu.ch

PC/104 Magazine

This on-line journal of Controlled Systems focuses on PC/104 embedded control systems and the products that make them work. Also check out their jobs database for something of interest. You can also fill out a form to list yourself as wanting a job. http://www.controllercom/pcl04

Professional Organizations and Government Labs of Interest to Electrical Engineers

A site maintained by the Department of Electrical Engineering at the University of Missouri-Rolla. http://www.ee.umr.edu/orgs

Stanford Center for Integrated Systems

A cooperative venture between Stanford University and member industrial firms. http://snf.stanford.edu/cis

Telecommunications—The Telecommunications Library

Here is a wealth of information about the telecommunication field sponsored by LDDS WorldCom Network. Visit the Telecom Digest, one of the oldest and most respected forums on the Internet. In its 12-year history, the Digest has covered every imaginable issue of telecommunications. Telecomreg is the source for the latest on regulation in the telecommunications industry. Academic papers are published through the Research Institute for Telecommunications and Information Marketing (RITIM). The Insight Research Corporation provides trend analysis and comparative market research in the wireless, voice, data, and video communications field. In addition, jobs that are available at LDDS are published. An excellent site for engineers interested in the telecommunications field. http://www.wiltel.con/library.html

Circuit Archives, Technical Information, and Projects

Every engineering technologist needs reference material and never has enough. These sites offer thousands of circuits and technical information to construct your own projects and research many subjects. This is the great advantage of the Web because new technology is being added daily and it is there for the taking. Log on now!

Beast 95

Bucknell Engineering Animatronics Systems Technology is an ongoing senior design project with the goal of creating a fully interactive animatronic figure. This figure is interactive, which means it can sense, for instance, how many people are in the room and modify its performance based on that data, such as begging you to stay. A block diagram of the animatronic system shows an overview of the microcontrollers and sensors. The components used to build the Beast are listed along with photos and details of the project. Beast 96 has already been started so check it out!
http://www.eg.bucknel.edu/~beast96

Berkeley Sensor & Actuator Center

Learn about the latest in sensor and actuator technology.
http://www-bsac.eecs.berkeley.edu

The Center for Compound Semiconductor Microelectronics

Funded by the National Science Foundation, this University of Illinois facility seeks to address research in optoelectronic integrated circuits. New high-speed communications and data processing technology is a goal of the group.
http://www.ccsm.uiuc.edu/ccsm

Chaos

Since the mid-1970s, the Chaos Group of Maryland has done extensive research in various areas of chaotic dynamics ranging from the theory of dimensions, fractal basin boundaries, chaotic scattering, and controlling chaos. It is hoped tha their knowledge will be useful to others.
http://www-chaos.umd.edu/chaos.html

Circuit Archive

The circuit archive at the University of Washington site contains many circuits for applications, including IR related circuits, PC circuits, telephone circuits, and miscellaneous circuits. You are encouraged to submit your own designs to the archive.
http://weber.u.washington.edu/d99/pfloyd/ee

The CPU Info Center

This site contains various CPU related information and with special focus on CPU architecture. Comparisons between types of CPUs are given. Technical papers, embedded microprocessor information, the history of CPUs, and a die photo gallery can be found here. http://infopad.eecs.berkeley.edu/CIC/about.html

Electrical Engineering Shop

Lots of unusual electronics projects that have not been seen on the Web. Everything you could want to know about PC Serial Communication, signals used on ISA Buss, a Binary-to-IntelHex Conversion utility, and prototyping tips and pitfalls are listed at this University of Nebraska server.
http://engr-www.unl.edu/ee/eeshop/miscinfo.html

The Electronic Cookbook Archive

Sponsored by the University of Alberta's Department of Electrical Engineering, this circuit "cookbook" archive covers audio, computers, digital, power, RF, software, telecommunications, video and wave shaping.
http://www.ee.ualberta.ca/html/cookbook.html

Electronics In Music

A music electronics archive containing circuits for many electronic music effects. Delay based effects, distortion, overdrive, and fuzz-tones are some of the circuits shown. A very interesting site for the musically inclined electronics engineer.
http://rowlfcc.wwu.edu:8080/~n9343176/schems.html

How Semiconductors Are Made

A step by step look at the manufacturing process used to make semiconductors.
http://rel.semi.harris.com/docs/lexicon/manufacture.html

Lexicon of Semiconductor Terms

A site where you can look up an unfamiliar technical semiconductor term and find out its meaning. http://rel.semi.harris.com/docs/lexicon/preface.html

MICAS: Medical and Integrated Circuits and Sensors

http://www.esat.kuleuven.ac.be/micas

Microelectronics

Engineers interested in microelectronic circuit design will want to check out the newsletters at this University of Tennessee site. Subscribers are notified when a new issue is published. Integrated circuit prototyping via MOSIS, as well as microelectronic systems, are discussed. http://microsys6.engr.utk.edu:80/ece/msn

Microelectronics Research Center (MRC)

A NASA Space Engineering Research Center for VLSI, ASIC, and device modeling.
http://www.mrc.uidaho.edu:80/

NASA Electronic Packaging and Processes Branch

This site at the Goddard Space Flight Center is set up to implement new packaging technologies and address problems in older technologies.
http://package.gsfc.nasa.gov/package.html

The National Nanofabrication Users Network

With the motto "No Job Too Small," this site is devoted to share research in nanoscale science. http://snfstanford.edu/NNUN

Ohm's Law

Check out the Ohm's Law experiment from California State. You can make measurements directly on equipment linked to their server.
http://plabpc.csustan.edu/physics/expt/ohmslaw.htm

Optoelectronic Computing Systems Center

The mission of the Colorado Advanced Technology Institute is to provide cross-disciplinary research and education in optoelectronic technology.
http://ocswebhost.colorado.edu

QuestNet

A site where the engineer can search for information on semiconductor and integrated circuit devices. http://www.questlink.com

Research In Analog IC Design

University of California-Berkeley projects and research with a focus on the design of analog circuits for high integration. A monolithic CMOS RF Transceiver is described as well as High Speed, Low Power CMOS ADCs. http://kabuki.eecs.berkeley.edu

Robotics

Links to robotics. http://www.yahoo.com/Science/Engineering/
Mechanical_Engineering/Robotics

Semiconductor Subway

The Semiconductor Subway site maintained by the Massachusetts Institute of Technology. Links to other sites with a focus on semiconductor related sites. Upcoming conferences relating to semiconductor manufacturing can be found.
http://www-mtl.mit.edu/semisubway.html

Signal Processing Information Base (SPIB)

Digital information including data papers, software, newsgroups, and bibliographies that are relevant to signal processing and research. http://spib.rice.ecu:80/spib.html

Signal Processing URL Library

Links to web sites with a focus on signal processing. http://www-sp.rice.edu/splib

Solid State Lab

The University of Michigan department of Electrical Engineering and Computer Science Solid State Electronics Laboratory. The latest technology for semiconductor design, including materials, devices and integrated circuits is discussed. Ongoing projects are reviewed, as well as group efforts between students, technicians, and engineers.
http://www.eeecs.umich.edu/dp-group

Spreadsheets

A number of spreadsheets dealing with various aspects of teaching basic electricity have been compiled. Click "batteries" for a spreadsheet containing graphics that teach about batteries in series. "Resistors" provides practice for computing resistors in series. Click "circuits" for a spreadsheet that uses simple circuits to teach about Ohm's Law. http://192.239.146.18/SS/Spreadsheets.html

The Tech

A hands-on museum of technology located in the heart of Silicon Valley. Explore this site on your next trip to San Jose or logon the site and explore from your computer. http://www.thetech.org/about.html

Theremin Home Page

What is a Theremin? A theremin is an electronic musical instrument based on the theory of beat frequencies. Learn more about theremins by visiting this interesting Web site. http://www.ccsi.com/-bobs/theremin.html

Turbulence Links Around the Web

Here are some links to a variety of turbulence modeling and related WWW sites. http://stimpy.ame.nd.edu/gross/fluids/turbulence.html

VLSI Engineering

VLSI design, free CAD shareware, conferences—and best of all—job opportunities are here. Interesting links to other VLSI educational projects and educational courses in VLSI are listed at this University of Idaho site. http://www.mrc.uidaho.edu/vlsi/vlsi.html

Weird Science

"It is not uncommon for engineers to accept the reality of phenomena that are not yet understood, as it is very common for physicists to disbelieve the reality of phenomena that seem to contradict contemporary beliefs of physics."—H. Bauer http://www.eskimo.com/~billb/weird.html

UNIVERSITIES AND GOVERNMENT WEB SITES

Many universities and colleges have sites maintained by the Department of Electrical and Electronic Engineering. Teaching opportunities, graduate and post graduate programs, research projects, and courses are listed. Government sites also have research programs and provide the direction for implementation of Standards in the Electronic and Electrical Industry.

Alabama Microelectronics Science and Technology Center (AMSTC)
http://www.eng.auburn.edu/department/ee/amstc/amstc.html

CalTech Department of Electrical Engineering
http://electra.micro.caltech.edu

Carnegie Mellon Department of Electrical Engineering
http://www.ece.cmu.edu

Cornell University School of Electrical Engineering
http://www.ee.cornell.edu

Duke University Department of Electrical and Computer Engineering
http://www.ee.duke.edu

Electrical Engineering Programs
Listed here are links to home pages of Electrical Engineering academic programs throughout the world. A great way to see what's happening in academic electronics world wide.
http://www.ee.umr.edu/schools/ee_programs.html

Johns Hopkins University Electrical and Computer Engineering Department
http://www.ece.jhu.edu

Kansas State Department of Electrical and Computer Engineering

http://www.eece.ksu.edu

COMPANIES' WEB SITES

The bulk of the job opportunities are with private industry. Companies that would be of interest to electrical and electronic technicians are listed. Many have employment pages where job openings are listed. Some have the capability for you to submit your resume on-line. This is a great way to learn about a specific company or industry before your job interview.

Allied Signal

An 88,000 employee company that services the aerospace, automotive, chemical, and advanced materials industries. Many opportunities are available to the electrical/electronic engineer or technician in a company as diverse as this one. Check out the site for an overview of its activities. http://www.alliedsignal.com E-mail: address not given

AT&T

This company is one of the oldest and best known in the telecommunications field. AT&T's Bell Telephone Labs is a premiere company devoted to research and innovation and has distinguished itself with seven Nobel prize scientists. While visiting this site review the job links for college students. http://www.att.com E-mail: webmaster@att.com

Compaq Computer Corp.

This well-known computer manufacturer has supplied products to the computer industry for many years. Visit the site to see what's new at Compaq. http://www.compaq.com E-mail: webmaster@compaq.com

Dallas Semiconductor

A diversified manufacturer of silicon products such as digital thermometers, microcontrollers, silicon-timed circuits, and more. Check out employment opportunities at the site and submit your resume. http://www.dalsemi.com E-mail: recruiter@dalsemi.com

Delco Electronics

A worldwide manufacturer of automotive and consumer-related products. With 28,000 employees, many opportunities are available for the electronic and electrical engineer and technician.
http://www.delco.com/recruitment.html#employment or view the home page at: http://www.delco.com E-mail: address not given

Digital Equipment Corporation

Worldwide supplier of network computer systems, software, and services. This site provides career opportunities for students in the electronic engineering field.
http://www.dec.com E-mail: jobs-us-servers@digital.com

Dolby Laboratories

This well-known maker of audio products has some interesting career opportunities for the electronic engineer. Visit the career page: http://www.dolby.com/carops.html and check out the company page at: http://www.dolby.com E-mail: address not given

Fujitsu

This high technology electronics manufacturer of drives, mobile telephones, radios, and other equipment offers many job opportunities in the United States and abroad. Check out the job site of your choice. http://www.fujitsu.com E-mail: webmaster@fujitsu.com

General Electric

General Electric Company is a worldwide diversified technology, manufacturing, and services company. http://www.ge.com E-mail: good.things@corporate.ge.com

General Motors

Excellent opportunities are here at the world's largest auto manufacturer. Career opportunities in their engineering matrix chart list divisions where electrical and electronic engineers and technicians would fit. While you are there check out this huge site and its links to various GM divisions as well as taking a Virtual Reality trip through the newest cars: http://www.gm.com/edu_rel/careers.htm#Engineering Visit the corporate site at: http://www.gm.com/index.htm E-mail: address not given

GTE

One of the largest telecommunications companies in the world with $20 billion in sales. Many opportunities exist for the recent college graduate as well as the seasoned professional. Check out the recruitment site at: http://www.gte.coni/Working/Campus/campus.html or look at the corporate site at: http://www.gte.com. Several E-mail addresses for human resources sites can be found at: http://www.gte.com/career/contact.html

Harris

A worldwide company doing business in electronic systems, semiconductors, communications, and Lanier Worldwide Office Systems. With 27,000+ employees, many job opportunities exist for the college graduate. http://wwwharris.com
E-mail: webmaster@harris.com

IBM

An international computer manufacturer. IBM has an excellent employment page at: http://www.empl.ibm.com and a lot of information about the company and its programs: http://www.ibm.com E-mail: askibm@info.ibm.com

Intel

Logon to Intel for a look at the company's latest technologies. Also drop off your resume at its Employment Office. http://www.intel.com/intel

Lockheed Martin

The combined companies of Lockheed and Martin Marietta, best known for their aerospace history, offer many opportunities for the aspiring engineer or technician. http://www.Imco.com E-mail: webmaster@Imco.com

Motorola

A $27 billion company with job opportunities worldwide. Visit the job matrix to see where you might like to work and follow up with a link to the business unit of your choice. A leading provider of semiconductors, cellular, telephones, two-way radios, automotive products, and much more. http://www.motorola.com/UR/introl.html

For overall information visit the corporate site at: http://www.mot.com E-mail: webmaster@mot.com

Motorola Semiconductor Products Group

Find the latest product information from the Analog Microcontroller Division, Analog IC Division, MOS Digital-Analog IC Division, RF Products-Communication Semiconductor Division, Digital Signal Processors (DSP).
http://design-net.com/home/prodgroups/html/prod_groups.html

Okidata Corp.

A manufacturer of semiconductors with job opportunities for the college graduate. http://www.okisemi.com/index.html E-mail: webmaster@obd.com

Panasonic–Matsushita Electric

This $7 billion company employs over 16,000 people in 21 manufacturing sites in North America alone. The range of products manufactured is exceptionally wide with a focus in consumer electronics. http://www.mitl.research..panasonic.com/pana.html E-mail: webmaster@research.panasonic.com

Philips Semiconductors

The tenth largest supplier of semiconductors in the world in wireless communications, micro controllers, audio, video, and more. Employment information is at:
http://www.semiconductors.philips.com/ps/philipsl9.html
Visit the corporate site at: http://www.semiconcuctors.philips.com
E-mail: webmaster@semiconductors.philips.com

Texas Instruments

A supplier of electronic and scientific calculators, printers, notebook computers, electrical controls, etc. http://www.ti.com E-mail: address not given

Videonics

A video editing company with opportunities listed at this Web site.
http://www.videonics.com/employment.html E-mail: helpline@videonics.com

LISTSERV MAILING LIST FOR ELECTRONIC TECHNOLOGY

Chemical Engineering

Discussion of Interfacial Phenomena
Mail to: LISTSERV@WSUVM1.CSC.WSU.EDU

Engineering

Discussion of engineering and construction
Mail to: MAILBASE@MAILBASE.AC.UK

Nuclear Engineering

Discussion of nuclear energy, research, and education
Mail to: LISTPROC@MCMASTER.CA

Technology

I-TV
Discussion of two-way interactive television used for education and community development
Mail to: LISTSERV@KNOWLEDGEWORK.COM

INFO-FUTURES

Discussion of the effect of technology in industry
Mail to: INFO-FUTURES-REQUEST@WORLD.STD.com

PHOTO-CD

Kodak CD products and technology
Mail to: LISTSERV@INFO.KODAL.COM

SATNEWS

Satellite television industry newsletter
Mail to: SATNEWS-REQUEST@MRRL.LUT.AC.UK

USENET NEWSGROUPS FOR ELECTRONIC TECHNOLOGY

Electronics Newsgroups

sci.electronics
This newsgroup evolved from the *sci.electronics basic* group in January of 1996.

sci.electronics.basics
A forum for the discussion of electronics, where there is no stupid question. A place to ask elementary questions about electronics

sci.electronics.cad
A forum for the discussions of Computer Aided Design software for use in designing electronic circuits and assemblies.

sci.electronics.components
Discussions of integrated circuits, resistors, capacitors.

sci.electronics.design
Discussions on electronic circuit design.

sci.electronics.equipment
Information on test, lab, and industrial electronic products.

sci.electronics.misc
General discussion of the field of electronics.

sci.electronics.repair
A forum for discussing the fixing of electronic equipment.

misc.industry.electronics.marketplace
Electronics products and services.

OTHER ELECTRONIC TECHNOLOGY AND NEWSGROUPS

alt.cad
alt.cad.autocad
alt.electronics.analog.visi
alt.energy.renewable
alt.sustainable.agriculture
alt.solar.photovoltaic
alt.solar.thermal
clari.tw.aerospace
comp.cad.autocad
comp.cad.microstation
comp.robotics.misc
comp.robotics.research
sci.bio.misc
sci.bio.technology

sci.chem
sci.energy
sci.engr
sci.engr.biomed
sci.engr.chem
sci.engr.civil
sci.engr.heat-vent-ac
sci.engr.lighting
sci.engr.manufacturing
sci.engr.mech
sci.engr.semiconductors
sci.engr.television.advanced
sci.engr.television.broadcast
sci.environment
sci.geo.satellite-nav
sci.life-extension
sci.materials
sci.med.physics
sci.military.naval
sci.nanotech
sci.optics
sci.optics.fiber
sci.research

4

Critical Analysis of Information

Critical thinking is becoming more necessary as vast quantities of new information become available through electronic sources. You need to explore the concept of truthfulness and what is "right" in relationship to the information you will be discovering from cultures around the world. Evaluate your own views as you work through this chapter.

EVALUATING SOURCES ON THE INTERNET

The information age is progressing so rapidly that frequently we are required by our career or educational opportunities to jump into the middle of something new without really knowing what we are doing. While you still will do research in traditional libraries, you will also do research on the Internet. Before you use the information you find on the Internet, however, you need to go back a few steps and see what you are exploring.

The Internet is actually an enormous collection of computers linked together in order to share their resources. Initially the people who had access to the Internet were scientists, computer programmers, and government officials who were sharing top-secret information. The computers ran constantly so that users could connect to it at any time. As more people became aware of the Internet and as access became easier, more people found ways to become linked, first through the government and educational institutions and now through businesses and the private sector. Now anyone with the necessary hardware can connect to the Internet by using an Internet provider. America On-line and Microsoft Network are two of the many commercial providers. Your community may have other smaller providers you can use. You also may have access to a provider through your university or business. You will want to choose the service you use on the basis of factors such as cost, reliability, and special features. While most of the Internet is based in the United States, access to it is now becoming more readily available in other countries.

As the Internet grew, a global service known as the World Wide Web (WWW) developed. Web pages or home pages are written in Hypertext Markup Language (HTML). These pages use hypertext links to allow the user to easily move from one location to another with the use of a browser such as Netscape. Searching through the pages, you can discover an endless wealth of information. Since the World Wide Web has become enormously popular, Web sites are popping up everywhere.

Before you start to use the Internet and the World Wide Web for researching, you need to learn how to critically analyze the information you will discover there. Since people can post just about anything on the Web, much valid, current, exciting information is available, but lots of "garbage" is also available. A professional-looking Web page can be posted by a novice, so it's easy to be fooled. But before you can critically analyze information, you need to be aware of how to think critically. All of us think all the time, but most of that time is spent with practical functioning, random thoughts, and daydreaming. Critical thinking involves much more than the usual thoughts rambling around in our heads.

Critical thinking occurs when you take the time to *observe* what you look at. Have you ever tried to describe something you have just seen, but you do not remember enough detail about how it looked to be able to convey your thoughts? Critical thinking is also analyzing what you observe. When you try a new entree at a gourmet restaurant, do you savor the flavor and taste the different ingredients so that you can replicate the recipe at home? Critical thinking involves reasoning about and evaluating information. Is the new information consistent with what you already know? Do you need more information? Do you fully understand what you have found? Challenge all ideas you formulate; don't accept them at face value. Carefully and deliberately analyze all the information you find. Be willing to recognize when you do not have enough information to make a decision, and be prepared to change your mind.

Traditional research methods required hours in the library, and that provided the advantage of dealing with materials that had been carefully chosen for purchase. Scholars and librarians carefully researched printed materials to determine which of them had significant value. Money was not spent on supermarket tabloids and unreliable sources, so you could be relatively safe in assuming that your source was likely to be valid if you discovered it in a reputable academic library. The Internet removes that safety net. When you search the Internet and the Web, you are on your own to evaluate what is true, accurate, and/or valuable.

When you use the Internet to do research, you need to decide what approach you will take to evaluate the information you discover. You need to consider first what information you already have. Then you need to decide what additional information you hope to find in your search. If you already are knowledgeable in the field in which you are doing research, evaluation will be easier for you. You will have some idea of who the authorities are in the field, the direction current research is taking, and where your most promising sources will be located. If you are a novice in the field you are exploring, you need to take the time to plan a strategy before you start to search, so that you will have a general idea of what you need to know. Spending hours on the Net is easy to do when you allow yourself to jump from site to site using the hyperlinks you discover. Be cautious of allowing your research time to slip away while you explore.

Evaluating the sites you find is a complex process, and there are several different areas you will need to assess to determine the usefulness of anything you find. Before you start your evaluation, though, you need to decide how discriminating you will be. Here's an analogous situation to think about: When the jury deliberated in the O. J. Simpson murder trial, they were instructed by the judge that the evidence had to prove *beyond a reasonable doubt* that O. J. had committed the crime. The jurors must have had enough doubt so that they could not be positive that he killed Nicole Brown Simpson and Ron Goldman. However, when the judge in the later civil trial gave instructions to the jury, he told them the law required *a preponderance of evidence,* a more than 50 percent probability that O. J. had committed the murders. The jurors had access to much of the same evidence in both trials, but the *parameters* for making the decision were different.

What you need to do before you start your search is decide on your own research parameters. How certain do you need to be that the information you find is true and accurate? If you were attempting to discover a cure for cancer, your standards would have to be high to protect and to help the cancer patients who would benefit from your findings. If you were attempting to prove that a program to help the homeless in your community is the best of those being suggested, you would need a preponderance of evidence rather than absolute certainty. A difference would also be noted between proving that something has happened historically as opposed to predicting that something will happen based on the information you find. Factors like these must be taken into consideration as you set your research goals and objectives.

After you have decided that you have sufficient ideas and you have set your research parameters, you still need to assess your own critical thinking skills before you actually start evaluating your sources. You should critically evaluate all the sources you discover, whether on the Internet, in print, or in any other form. Be honest with yourself. Assess what you do and do not know—not only about your subject but also about the sources you are discovering. Not admitting that you don't understand material written in an elevated academic style will only hurt you if you misunderstand the information or misquote what you discover.

Be objective in your evaluations. When doing research, controversial issues should be a challenge. Allow your curiosity to lead you to explore new and different ideas. Don't let personal bias or prejudices taint your evaluation. For example, if you oppose the wearing of fur and you discover that an authority you want to quote has a fur coat, don't automatically discount what that person has to say about an entirely different subject. Realize your limitations. Although you may have witnessed something you consider of value to your research, what you think you observed may not be what you actually did observe. Be sure you check it out before you accept it.

Take your time with your research. Don't write a ten-page research paper the night before it is due. You are setting yourself up to fail; it's impossible to objectively analyze your sources in such a short time, let alone write the paper. Have patience, plan your writing project, and take your time.

As you do your research, base judgment on evidence and facts. A fact is something real, something that has been or is. Never assume that what you are reading must be true. The easy way to "research" would be to merely accept at face value anything written, but that would be doing yourself a great disservice. Carefully read what you discover, whether you agree or not. You may discover that what you expected to find is not true. Really observe what is going on around you. Careful observation will make the unfamiliar become familiar to you. Learn facts firsthand by actually seeing the evidence. And listen cautiously to what people say. Many times when we think we are having a conversation and learning something new about a subject, we are just planning what we want to say next in the conversation. Joe Thornton, a respected reflective thinker, once said, "You never learn anything with your mouth open." Pay attention to what people have to say; then make up your own mind on the basis of the facts you discover, not your feelings.

Thoughts

As you search for "facts," you must identify which claims about them are "true." Write in your journal your definition of "truth." What are the necessary components in your definition? Do you believe that your love is true? Do you believe that your church is true? Do you believe that your teachers tell the truth? How can you tell whether information is true or not? Do the "facts" in a statement have to be absolute, or is there room for interpretation?

Truth, Knowledge, and Belief
Truth and Events or Occurrences

You need to distinguish carefully between events and occurrences that exist in reality, either within us or outside of us, and claims or assertions we make about such events.

Essentially, it is the difference between the sun *actually* shining or not shining and our *claims* that the sun is shining or not shining. Truth does not apply to the events or occurrences; they either are actual or not actual. Truth applies only to the claims or assertions we make. That is, truth and falsity apply only to claims *about* events or occurrences, not to the events or occurrences themselves. The term *fact* can be confusing because when people use this term, sometimes they mean a true claim and at other times they mean an actual occurrence. Be sure that when you use the word *fact* you either clarify how you are using it or use other terms such as *claims, occurrences, or events.* (Philosophers also use the terms *proposition and state of affairs to* describe claims and events or occurrences.)

As you can see, the word *true* may be used to mean "real," as in "My love is true," or "My church is true," or "This is true coffee, not a substitute." You should, however, be concerned with the truth of claims or assertions such as "It is true (or false) that the sun is shining" or any other claim a source is making.

Truth and Falsity

How do we know when a claim is true or false? Many theories have been put forth by philosophers; however, to simplify, we can say that a claim is true if it describes an event or occurrence that is actually happening, has actually happened, or will actually happen. For example, if the sun is actually shining (event or occurrence) and I make the claim "The sun is shining," my claim is true; if you claim, "The sun is not shining," your claim is false.

Knowledge and Belief

Distinguishing between knowledge and belief or opinion is also very important. Three requirements must be met before you can say whether you know that a claim is true (or false).

1. The subjective requirement: You must believe it is true (or false).
2. The evidence requirement: You must have good grounds for your belief.
3. The objective requirement: Evidence must indicate that your belief is indeed true (or false).

Obviously, just to believe a claim is true (or false) doesn't make it so. Furthermore, a claim can be true or false whether one believes it or not or whether one has evidence. For example, in the early 1900s, someone might have claimed, "One day human beings will go to the moon." The person who believed it was right, and it was actually true, but there was no evidence. When astronauts actually landed on the moon, however, the claim was *known* to be true—the evidence requirement had been met.

Perception and Truth

All that we consider true is shaped by our own personal way of seeing. The perception of individuals varies. Imagine interviewing the witnesses to a traffic accident involving a truck and two cars. Each witness saw the accident from a different perspective. The driver of the truck says, "The driver of the red car was going too fast." The driver of the red car insists, "The truck driver ran the stop sign." The driver of a blue car says, "The red car ran into my car." A witness standing on the sidewalk insists, "The truck was not involved in the accident—the driver just stopped to help." Each person was there and watching, but each person saw something different. The police investigation shows that the truck driver did run the stop sign, hitting the red car and pushing it into the blue car. Who was telling the truth? How could the officer investigating the accident determine the truth on the basis of what the witnesses said?

Sometimes a part of some information you discover is accurate. But don't guess whether the rest of the information is true. You might be right, but you also might be wrong. Sometimes the information is incomplete. You might need one more piece of evidence to show what really happened. Sometimes information may be true only for a certain point in time. If an accident happened in a rainstorm, the conditions would be different from the conditions later.

When you have strong opinions about ideas, differentiating them from evidence can prove difficult. Opinions can be valuable, especially in new areas where the claims are not well established yet, but to be valuable, they must be *informed* opinions. Too often people form an opinion when they do not have adequate information. An uninformed opinion can be misleading as well as untrue. Once someone has formed an opinion or heard some information, it can be difficult to convince that person otherwise. Resistance to change is a strong barrier. Researchers come up against this problem when they try to convince their audience of claims or values that are contrary to what has traditionally been accepted. For example, physicians in the United States still will not use methods of pain control proven and used for years in Europe because that is not the way they do things here. They seem to be afraid in the case of terminal patients to give them pain medication that is too strong because the patients might become addicted or die. Opening their minds to try something new could be advantageous to the audience, but their resistance to change is great.

Another trap the noncritical thinker can easily fall into is stereotyping. This comes into play with prejudicial thinking, like tall women are not sexy or short men are not masculine. Be sure to base your conclusions on true claims rather than beliefs or opinions. With any thinking and evaluating you do, be careful to avoid the extremes. Supporting radical ideas at either end of the spectrum is difficult at best. Finding the balance in any situation will make supporting your ideas easier and more likely to succeed.

Logical Fallacies

Philosophers have identified many fallacies in logic that are regularly used by the non-critical thinker. Becoming aware of these can help you to identify fallacies in your own thinking and in others' thinking and conclusions. There are a myriad of fallacies; only the ones most frequently encountered are included here. Before you start your research, examine these *informal fallacies*, which will help you evaluate the sources you find to determine their objectivity and truthfulness. As you read through these fallacies, think of examples you can identify in your own thinking and research or in the ideas other people have shared with you.

Either/Or

This form of thinking is seldom reasonable. With either/or thinking, the argument is made that something must be either one way or the other—that it cannot be both ways or fall between extremes.

Example: Either people have to graduate from college or they are not educated.

Analysis: This statement implies that anyone who does not graduate from college is not educated, or that a college degree ensures education, neither of which is necessarily true.

Attacking the Person

The person who presents the information is attacked instead of the information that is presented.

Example: A school board member suggests a proposal for ensuring adequate nutrition for low-income schoolchildren, and other board members argue against his proposal because the person suggesting it is overweight.

Analysis: This argument is a personal attack on the school board member rather than on his proposal.

Burden of Proof

The person arguing a position should be prepared to offer the evidence to prove the point. When that process of showing the evidence is shifted to another party, the burden of proof is shifted also.

Example: Maria says that God exists. Alberto says that He does not. Maria says, "You cannot prove He does not." She has shifted the burden of proof.

Analysis: This particular example is also sometimes called argument from ignorance. That is, we cannot argue that since God's nonexistence cannot be proved, He must therefore exist. He may, but this argument does not prove it.

False Cause (post hoc, ergo propter hoc)

This fallacy assumes that because one event happened before another, the first event caused the second. The possibility of coincidence is ignored.

Example: The death of the man was caused by the full moon that occurred the night before.

Analysis: Just because the full moon occurred prior to the death does not mean that the lunar event was the cause of death.

Straw Man

This is an argument without substance. When someone ignores the actual position of an opponent and instead presents a distorted representation of the opponent's argument, this person has created a straw man.

Example: In a political campaign with national defense as an issue, a woman candidate is criticized by a male opponent who feels that women are too weak or emotional to make decisions that would send young people to war.

Analysis: Here, the straw man argument is that women are weak and emotional; the real issue is national defense.

Smoke Screen/Red Herring

These are two different names for the same fallacy, in which a person changes the focus of the conversation to something unrelated to the argument.

Example: Juan argues that animals should be used for testing of pharmaceutical products. Sophia states that she does not agree. Juan is quick to retort that animal rights activists burn down research centers and always have complaints.

Analysis: Juan's descriptions of what animal rights activists do is not related to his original argument.

Subjectivist

In a subjectivist argument, two positions are stated that may both be true, but they are based on people's opinions rather than facts.

Example: Lourdes says that she needs to exercise every day to maintain good health. Joe says he never exercises, yet his doctor said that he is in perfect health.

Analysis: These statements are each true for the person who said them, but neither is necessarily true for people in general.

Bandwagon/Peer Pressure

These are two names for the same fallacy. Such an argument states that because everybody believes it, it must be valid.

Example: At a party, all the people except Sonia are drinking tequila shots. They encourage her to drink with them, saying they all feel fine. She does, only to become very ill.

Analysis: Sonia yielded to peer pressure ("jumped on the bandwagon"). Nobody else got sick, but she regretted the outcome for herself.

Wishful Thinking

Wishful thinking occurs when facts are ignored in favor of hopes.

Example: Hans tells Vanessa he loves her. Even though she knows he has a wife and children, she agrees to have sex with him. When she becomes pregnant, he breaks off the relationship.

Analysis: Vanessa realizes that Hans did not love her; rather, it was her wishful thinking that led her to believe him.

Scare Tactics

Fear can cause a person to succumb to an argument. What is said rarely has anything to do with the actual issue.

Example: Diane is negotiating with a real estate agent but is undecided about whether she wants to buy a house. The agent tells her untruthfully that another prospective buyer has made an offer.

Analysis: The real issue is whether Diane wants to buy a house, but the agent is trying to scare her into making a quick decision about a particular property.

Apple Polishing

Flattery can be used to influence people.

Example: Geraldo wants to sell his new line of lawnmowers, so he goes to lunch with the owner of a hardware business. He tells the owner, "Your business is the most attractive one in town, and you're a great golfer."

Analysis: The looks of the shop and the golfing ability of the owner do not relate to the essence of Geraldo's desire to make a sale.

Hasty Generalization

This fallacy occurs when people jump to a conclusion based on too little information.

Example: All lawyers are dishonest. Therefore, you should never hire one.

Analysis: This generalization is not valid because not all lawyers are dishonest.

Slippery Slope

Also known as the ripple effect or the domino theory, this fallacy argues that one action will necessarily lead to another action.

Example: Sex education will encourage students to experiment, and there will then be more teenage pregnancies and more mothers and children living on welfare.

Analysis: Having sex education in school doesn't mean students will have babies and go on welfare.

Fallacies of Relevance

Appeals require us to decide whether what is being said is reliable or unreliable. We need to question whether the appeal is presented in an objective fashion or based on faulty reasoning. The premises in a fallacious argument are irrelevant to the conclusion, though they may be relevant emotionally. The following list of appeals demonstrates what to watch for.

Appeal to Authority

The opinion of an expert may be valid.

Example: Retired General H. Norman Schwarzkopf says in his autobiography, "The purpose of our armed forces is to protect our national interests and defend our country. Before we allow deep cuts in our forces, we should be sure that we have made a thorough analysis of what our national interests will be for the next twenty years."

Analysis: Because of Schwarzkopf's rank and experience, he is qualified to make such an appeal to the American public.

If a newly elected senator whose background is in finance states that national defense cuts would be a good idea to help balance the budget, constituents need to remember that defense is not the senator's field of expertise. You should remember three things about authority as a source of knowledge.

1. The authority must be an expert in the subject under discussion.
2. When authorities differ, judgment should be deferred.
3. Any authority's claims must be verifiable.

Appeal to Common Sense

When we say, "Everyone knows that" about a subject, we are appealing to their common sense, a quality not all people have.

Example: It is common sense not to drink and drive.

Analysis: Many people drink and drive without considering the consequences. An appeal based on common sense has no effect on them.

Appeal to Belief

Saying that every one believes a claim does not make it true, nor does everyone necessarily believe it.

Example: Prior to 1492, many Europeans believed that a boat that kept sailing toward the horizon would fall off the end of the world.

Analysis: When Columbus sailed to America and returned, he proved that stating or believing a claim did not make it true.

Appeal to Tradition/Common Practice

This fallacy assumes that because something has always been done in a certain way, it must be right.

Example: Fourteen-year-old Tasha wants to get her eyebrow pierced, so she argues that everyone else in her class has a pierced eyebrow.

Analysis: Even if everyone else in her class has one, which is doubtful, that does not support her argument that she should get her eyebrow pierced.

Appeal to Pity

Pity is evoked in order to get us to do something.

Example: A celebrity cries on television, encouraging us to adopt starving children all over the world for just a small contribution every month.

Analysis: Contributing may be a good thing, but we should not make the decision to do so because someone is shedding tears.

Begging the Question

Begging the question is sometimes also called circular argument because the person presenting it argues in circles.

Example: Tiffany states that God exists. When Lori asks her to prove it, Tiffany states, "The Bible says it's so." When Lori asks why she should believe the Bible, Tiffany answers, "Because the Bible is inspired by God."

Analysis: Tiffany is arguing in circles, first citing the Bible to prove that God exists, then saying the Bible is true because God inspired it.

How Critical Is Your Thinking?

Create a critical thinker profile of yourself by writing the answers to the following questions. Take the time to carefully evaluate your answers as you write them to identify your strengths and weaknesses as a thinker.

- Do you dismiss positions opposed to yours without considering them?
- Do you accept your own beliefs without evaluating them?
- Can you change your beliefs?
- As you observe your own thinking, what are your strengths?
- What are your weaknesses?
- Identify the logical fallacies you frequently use in your writing. How do you use them? Why do you use them?

As you become aware of your critical thinking style, take the time to look more carefully at items you choose to evaluate. Listen thoughtfully to what people say, and record your thoughts and ideas when you first think them. Do not trust your memory to retain the good details that come to you by conscientious examination, reasoning, thinking, and observation. Evaluation skills are especially important when you look at materials on the Internet.

Definitions

Knowing the meanings of terms used in evaluation will help you to better describe your discoveries. The following terms are generally used in critical assessment.

Innuendo—an indirect or subtle implication of something derogatory

Inference—to arrive at a conclusion based on reasoning from evidence

Implication—an incriminating suggestion

Event or occurrence—something that either happens or does not happen

Claim—a statement describing an event or occurrence

Judgment—an inference expressing approval or disapproval

Implicit—something unsaid yet understood

Explicit—something clearly stated

Opinion—something somebody believes, which may or may not be true

Issue—a matter in dispute

Vague—something not clearly expressed

Hyperbole—exaggeration used for effect

Sensing—perceiving things with your sense organs

Perceiving—to receive, catch, or hold

To know—to be certain that a claim is true (or false)

Objective—something actually real or reliable outside of you

Subjective—something within you

Verifiable—something that can be proved

Reliable—something that can be depended on

Plausible—something likely to be valid

Probable—something likely but uncertain

Plagiarism

How would you define *plagiarism?* Have you ever committed plagiarism, either intentionally or unintentionally? Have you known someone who plagiarized? What were the results of the plagiarism? Do you think plagiarism is ever acceptable? Why or why not?

Thoughts

The definitions listed on the previous page may vary some from the way you are accustomed to using or hearing these words. Take some time now to analyze what you have learned from reading this section and evaluating your thinking style. Write in your journal your own personal definitions for the following words.

- Truth and falsity
- Knowledge
- Belief
- Claim
- Event or occurrence
- What something is if it is neither true nor false
- Thinking

Plagiarism is theft, plain and simple. If you steal another person's idea, research, thinking, or writing, it is theft. To plagiarize is to give the impression you wrote something that someone else actually wrote. Plagiarism is easy to do, even inadvertently, but it is also easy to avoid. All you have to do to avoid it is consistently give credit for all quotations, summaries, and paraphrases of other people's work that you use when you are writing. Of course, you must carefully follow the guidelines of the documentation style you are using, but that is all there is to it.

Sometimes, when you are on the Net for hours reading information about a subject you are researching, your mind starts to mix what you have read with what you are thinking, and you may confuse your ideas with someone else's. Because of this problem, you must start your research by setting clear guidelines for yourself, recording what you already know and what you need to discover. Doing this will help you to differentiate your ideas from the ideas of the author of your source.

Even though plagiarism is common, it is always unacceptable. When caught, a student faces dire consequences-ranging from failing an assignment, to failing a class, to expulsion from school. One of the biggest problems that students face in trying to avoid plagiarizing is that cheating has never been so easy. With the computer's copy and paste functions so easy to use, many students don't think about copyright laws. But the fact that a crime is easy does not make it acceptable.

Plagiarism is a relatively new crime in the history of society. Copying or rewriting other people's work and ideas was common until the early 1700s. Chaucer did it; Shakespeare did it; most writers did some form of sharing or borrowing of work and ideas. But as the printing and distribution of the written word became easier and printed materials became more accessible to the public, writers started to earn income for what they did. Thus, the concept of *intellectual property* was created. The first patent law was implemented in 1623, and the precursor to copyright, the Statute of Anne, was introduced in 1710. Since that time, many countries have embraced the idea that writers should be remunerated for their ideas, research, thinking, and writing. This concept, however, has not been adopted or accepted worldwide. Many Asian and African cultures teach students that until they are scholars themselves, their ideas are not good enough to share, so they are required to copy the good ideas of experts and authorities in their writing. Students who have been trained that way find the concept of intellectual property to be unreasonable at best.

Intellectual Property Versus Intellectual Value

The current school of thought differentiates between intellectual property and intellectual value. *Intellectual property* is something that can be replicated. If intellectual property can be replicated, it can be easily stolen. For instance, you could find an essay on the Internet you really liked and cut and paste it into your own file. Then you could put your name on it and turn it in to your instructor. After all, how can somebody own words, and are not ideas just words? Yet this action is still a theft, just as if you stole that writer's car instead of an essay.

Intellectual value is different from intellectual property in that it requires an agent. If there is intellectual value, the written material still exists, but the writer must be there for it to work. The writer could express something in writing that could be stolen, but the thief would not be able to use the information without the expertise of the writer. Most writing is intellectual property; ideas and thoughts, however, are more likely to have intellectual value.

The shifting attitudes toward intellectual property have caused businesses to reevaluate how they operate in the realm of computers and the Internet. For instance, much software is now given away to get people to use it. The software required to use many on-line services is a good example of this. New computers come with preinstalled software for several services—and if you did not get it then, it will soon be coming in the mail.

This attitude of sharing has caused many people to be concerned because they feel that property rights are essential to creation. They say that without the incentive of being paid for what they do, nobody will create anything. History proves this wrong. Much of the best literature ever created was written before the age of the copyright and royalties. The new school of thought is that writers can be paid for other things they can do using the intellectual value of their ideas. Money can be earned for consulting, support, performance, and service; writing is just a by-product of these intellectual endeavors. Some of the best writing today is published in scholarly journals, but scholars and researchers are not paid by the journals. The writers simply strive for the honor of being published. They are paid for their work at the college or university where they are employed. Researching and publishing their writing is considered a professional responsibility and exists without financial reward from the journals. Scholars are rewarded by their universities for their intellectual value in other ways, such as promotion and tenure.

The rapid expansion of the Internet brought with it a similar attitude among the initial participants of the democracy of the Internet. These users felt that the Internet offered a new society in which everyone would truly be equal. You cannot tell age, ethnicity, sex, social status, education, or abilities by reading what someone writes on the Net. This fact led to an attitude of freedom-all users were free to create and publish anything they wanted on the Net. Nothing was more important than anything else. The concept of "owning" information does not fit in to this philosophy. In this new culture, the members could own their hardware, but they freely chose to share their ideas. Ideas did not cost the creator anything, and the creator did not gain or lose by sharing them. Thomas Jefferson reflected this idea when he said, "He who lights his taper at mine receives light without darkening me." However, as wonderful as all this sounds, somebody has to pay to support the everexpanding Internet and World Wide Web.

Copyright Laws

Copyright laws have changed over the years. In 1989, copyright became automatic. All an author has to do now to protect what is written is to include a statement such as "This document cannot be distributed in its entirety without permission of the author" and include the copyright symbol © and the date. Now if an author wants to put something on the Internet, it can easily be copyrighted. But who pays for its placement there? Many Web pages are created by faculty and students who have access to school-based servers, and the authors do not pay directly to publish their information. But whoever pays the school's bills has to pay for that privilege. Some servers, such as America On-line, allow their members to post a personal Web page, but while the members may not pay directly for the page, they do pay for the service that, in turn, is paying for the page.

Many Web pages now sport advertising, some so much that it almost obliterates the pages. Other sites on the Web have gone to pay-per-entry service: if you want to look at their information, you have to pay each time you access them, or you have to pay to receive the information they have. CarlUnCover is an example of this. You can search for articles on the subject you are researching, but when you discover which articles you want, you can't download them. Rather, you have to pay a service fee and a fax fee and the articles will be faxed to you. Another way that information on the Web is starting to cost the user is the 'Zine, the Web version of a magazine. You can pay for subscriptions to these just as you do for the old-fashioned magazines delivered by "snail mail" to your home. There are also services now that will search for articles from sources you define on subject areas of your interest. They will find the articles and deliver them directly to your E-mail account, for a fee of course. So, while many of the users of the Internet would like to consider the Net a free and equal culture, it is rapidly becoming commercial.

Computer Ethics

With all these changes, a new field of study in computer ethics and social responsibility has developed. Computer scientists and philosophers have joined forces to explore ideas and create guidelines for Internet users to follow. An example of this is "The Ten Commandments of Computer Ethics," as prepared by the Computer Ethics Institute:

1. Thou shalt not use a computer to harm other people.
2. Thou shalt not interfere with other people's computer work.

3. Thou shalt not snoop around in other people's computer files.
4. Thou shalt not use a computer to steal.
5. Thou shalt not use a computer to bear false witness.
6. Thou shalt not copy or use proprietary software for which you have not paid.
7. Thou shalt not use other people's computer resources without authorization or proper compensation.
8. Thou shalt not appropriate other people's intellectual output.
9. Thou shalt think about the social consequences of the program you are writing or the system you are designing.
10. Thou shalt always use a computer in ways that ensure consideration and respect for your fellow humans.

An irony about these commandments is they can be found in many locations on the Internet, some giving credit to the Computer Ethics Institute, some not.

Term Paper Services

In your research, you may come across term paper sites. Don't use them! These sites are like fraternity and sorority files of the past, where previously used term papers were kept on file for the use of the members. Now term papers are posted at various Web sites, either free to download or available for a fee. Some papers are good, some not so good. Some are obtained by paying students for A papers. Some are obtained by paying people to write papers on certain subjects. Some are just copied from other sites. There is no standard of quality. Using one of these papers is not a guarantee of a good grade.

Sometimes even accessing one of these Web sites from an academic address will create a "flame war" overloading your E-mail account with angry messages from the people who maintain the term paper sites—they don't want instructors snooping in their sites. Most sites of this nature have some form of disclaimer such as the one used at Term Papers for Free:

"Welcome to the TERM PAPER site. This site is for research only. This is NOT to cheat on your term papers. This is to use as a possible guide for your own or to make sure that you have covered all issues on your paper. I personally take no responsibility if you fail, get suspended, or are expelled for using this link." (http://www.openix.com/~bytor/)

Term papers found at these sites are easy for instructors to spot. If the instructor is suspicious, all he or she has to do is type a sentence from the paper into a search engine and see if it shows up on a Web address. Using these sites for anything other than seeing how someone else writes a paper is not a good idea.

Computer Ethics Electronic Resources

Here are some interesting Web sites on the topic of computer ethics.

Introducing Ethics into the Computer World
http://www.freedommag.org/english/vol2704/ethics.htm

Professional Ethics and Computing
http://www.efa.org.au/Issues/Ethics/Welcome.html

Sex, Cats, and Computers: Ethics for a New Communication Medium
http://wings.buffalo.edu/computing/Publications/interface/
vol-25/iss-6/.html/ethics.html

Computer Ethics Institute listserv
http://tile.net/listserv/ceil.html

Avoiding Plagiarism

With all these admonitions of what not to do so that you can avoid plagiarism, what do you *need* to do? Use the following checklist while doing your research:

1. Make sure you will be able to get back to your original source. For a World Wide Web site, keep track of
   - the URL (Uniform Resource Locator) of the site,
   - the name of the organization providing service, and
   - the title of the site (this may be the first line of the content if a title is not listed).
2. When using a source that contains a copyright notice, always get permission to quote the source if you are going to use more than 40 words. You can do this by E-mail, asking the author of the source how it should be cited.
3. Remember that facts can be copied without permission. No one can claim authorship of facts such as "Bill Clinton was reelected President in 1996."
4. Check to see if your source is in the public domain. If so, it is not protected by copyright. The work may have been written before copyright laws, or its copyright may have expired.
5. When taking notes on your computer, always distinguish quotations, notes, summaries, and paraphrases from your own original material.
6. When writing a document that will be posted on the World Wide Web, get permission from copyright holders before posting their material on your page or before linking other sources to your document.

Thoughts

How have your ideas about plagiarism changed after reading this information? What will you do differently now when you write and research?

Finding Sources on the Internet

Doing research in the libraries of the past was slow, tedious, and cumbersome. That kind of research is as obsolete as the record player, and it went out of date much faster. The uses of technology are expanding so rapidly that what seems a great new concept today is old news tomorrow. To do research today, you must keep up with the most recent developments. For example, your campus library may have developed an on-line catalog that works only for the students of your university. If it is there, you need to know about it. Of course, with these rapid advances come opportunities for misinformation and inaccuracy. Your responsibility as a researcher is to do enough research to verify the correctness of what you find. Finding information from one source does not guarantee that it is true, so you must learn to evaluate your sources and be discriminating in their use. All research sources must be evaluated, but this is especially crucial with Web sources because of the lack of a filtering process. No editor, peer reviewer, or librarian has checked the material on the Internet, so it is up to the researcher to judge the accuracy of statements and sources and judge the reasoning that leads the authors to conclusions.

When working on the Internet, you must first decide which sources are worth evaluating. Don't waste your time on sources that cannot help you. Do a preliminary search to discover what sources are available on your subject; then determine what information is available about the document you find. Always carefully take notes electronically or by hand as you search. Don't count on finding sources again unless you have good records of where you found them initially. When searching on your home computer, use the Bookmark or Favorite Places option, or the equivalent on your browser. These tools save the URLs of the sources you find, making it easy to go back to the sites you want. As you collect bookmarks, develop a filing system so that you can organize the information you are discovering. URLs are not like titles; you can't readily determine the content of the source by reading the address. Keep track of which URLs go with which area of your research to save time and keep yourself organized as you work through the research process.

Many students do not have the luxury of working on their own computers. If you don't, make an accurate list of the URLs you discover. Whenever possible, download good sources onto your own disk and/or print hard copies. Be sure as you are doing this to record information essential to cite the source and to find it again.

Evaluating Web Sites

Each Web site should be evaluated in nine key areas:

1. Accuracy
2. Authority
3. Completeness
4. Content
5. Cost
6. Design
7. Propaganda
8. Reliability
9. Scholarliness

While most of these areas must be evaluated when doing any research, some of them refer only to research on the Internet. They are vital in assessing the reliability of available information. As you approach each source you discover, write in your notes comments about each of the nine areas, considering all the issues listed.

Accuracy

- Does the author expect you to accept the information in the source at face value, or is there information on the page indicating its validity?
- Has the page been refereed, rated, or evaluated in some manner? If so, who did the evaluation? Was it a scholarly evaluation, or was it done by a business? Some ratings indicated on Web pages are like a popularity contest for flashy presentation rather than well-developed, accurate content.
- Is the author's point of view clear and sound? Does it leave room for question? Some pages merely list links to other sources, so you can't tell what the author is trying to accomplish.
- Is there a bias—political, ideological, or cultural? Biased writing may be true and accurate, but because it is skewed, distinguishing fact from opinion is difficult at best.
- When was the site produced? Is the page updated regularly? Timeliness is everything in this era of instantly available information. Sometimes yesterday is too long ago.
- How up to date are links? Even if the page is updated, its value is significantly decreased if many of the links are inaccessible or dated.

- Is the page well edited? Sloppiness is an indicator of inattention to detail that can also mean inaccuracy.
- Does the site describe the limits of its research? If not, are the limits clear from the content? Does the site attempt to cover too much or too little? If it tries to cover too much, it will be difficult to wade through as well as unlikely to be complete. If it covers too little, it may not be of much use.
- Are accurate alternative views included?

Authority

- Are the qualifications of the site's author or producer indicated on the page? Is the author's status or position in the field or profession clearly indicated? Is the author experienced in the field discussed on the site? Is the author an acknowledged expert?
- Is there a link to a biography page or home page of the author?
- If there is a question about the author's identity or credentials, can you find information by doing a search?
- Is the author the original creator of the information, or is he or she reporting what others have discovered?
- Are sources for the information on the page clearly stated?
- Is this source cited by other sources (Web pages or scholarly journals)?
- Is the source available in other formats, such as print or CD-ROM?
- Who sponsors the site? Is it a commercial or educational site, or does it appear to be created by an individual?
- Are the links from the site primarily commercial or educational?
- If the source is commercial, does the sponsor appear to be a reputable company?

Completeness

- How well and thoroughly is the subject covered?
- Are there any inexplicable omissions?
- If hyperlinks are used, is the selection criterion indicated?
- Are the hyperlinks appropriate, relevant, and comprehensive?
- Are there hyperlinks to a range of sources, such as gopher sites and newsgroups, or only to Web pages?
- Does the page cite other sources?
- Does the page provide links to search engines?
- Is the E-mail address or phone number of the author included on the page? Is the E-mail address a hyperlink?
- Is evidence presented to indicate the accuracy and validity of the page?

Content

- Does the site contain documentation for all sources indicated?
- Does the content appear to be the truth or the author's opinion? How can you tell?
- Does the site contain original information, or does it provide only links?
- Is the site the original source for the information included, or is the information abstracted from another source? Is the purpose of the site clearly stated? Is the purpose fulfilled? The purpose of the page is likely to be either to inform, to explain, or to persuade.

- Does the page encourage debate, comments, and/or criticism?
- How many items are included on the page?
- In what country is the site published?
- In what language is the site written? If appropriate, is it available in translation?
- Does the page contain search options?
- Is a copyright notice indicated on the page?
- Does the site include a bibliography?
- Is the page unique?
- Is the information on the site available in other forms (gopher, print, or CD-ROM)?
- What are the advantages of this site over others?
- What kinds of links are there to other types of sites? (Often, repetition is not desirable, but the more often a site is linked to other sites, the more valuable it is likely to be.)
- Can the site work with a variety of equipment?

Cost

- Most sites are currently free. If the site is not free, who collects the fee?

Design

- Is the site aesthetically pleasing? Are the colors and backgrounds annoying, or is the text difficult to read?
- How long is the waiting time while graphics load? Is it so long that the researcher is not likely to wait?
- Are graphs and charts clearly labeled and easy to understand?
- Is the response time of the site reasonable?
- Is there a "hit count" telling you how many people have viewed the site? If so, is the site frequently visited?
- Is the site easy to use?
- If special services are needed to view the site, are they available for download at the site? Are they easy to use? Do you have to pay for them?
- Is the site frequently unavailable or off-line?

Propaganda

- Does the site indicate that it supports the only one "right" view?
- Does the author attack or ridicule other perspectives?
- Is the writing overly emotional?
- Are there logical fallacies in the reasoning the author presents?
- Does the page include undue bias?
- Does the author's use of language to suit his or her needs obscure the truth?
- Does the author use the site as a "virtual soapbox"?

Reliability

- Can the information on this site also be found in a book or journal?
- Is there contact information for the author, such as an E-mail address or a phone number?

- Is there advertising? Is it differentiated from the content?
- Is the page a public service?
- Is the site reasonably permanent?
- Does the address contain *.edu*, indicating that it originates from an educational source?
- Is a tilde (~) included in the address, meaning that the site is an individual's home page or personal Web directory?
- Is the site linked to a home page? If so, what kind of home page is it—for instance, a commercial site, a nonprofit organization's home page, or an educational site?

Scholarliness

- Does the author describe the limits of research or data?
- Does the author present accurate descriptions of alternative views?
- What else on the topic is available in both print and nonprint sources?
- Is the scope stated, indicating limitations of subject area and time period?
- Are all aspects of the subject covered?
- Is the level of detail appropriate for the subject?
- Has the page had a peer review?

Has the information you read in this section caused you to reevaluate your approach to evaluating the sources you use? Can you see the importance of and reasons for evaluating Internet sources? How will you use this information in your research?

Resources on Evaluation of Web Pages

These Web sites deal with evaluation of Web pages.

"Thinking Critically About World Wide Web Resources" by Esther Grassian UCLA, College Library
http://www.library.ucla.edu/libraries/college/instruct/critical.htm

"Criteria for Evaluation of Internet Information Resources" by Alastair Smith
http://www.vuw.ac.nz/-agsmith/evaln/index.htm

"The UTC Lupton Library Guide to Information Literacy" by Marea Rankin
http://www.lib.utc.edu/info.html

"Evaluating Web Sources" Widener University, Wolfgram Memorial Library by Jan Alexander and Marsha Tate
http://www.science.widener.edu/~withers/webeval.htm

"Using Cybersources" DeVry Institute of Technology by Nancy L. Stegall
http://www.devry-phx.edu/lrnresrc/dowsc/integrty.htm

"Evaluation of Information" by Lisa Janicke Hinchliffe
http://alexia.lis.uiuc.edu/-janicke/Eval.html

"Evaluating Quality on the Net" by Hope N. Tillman, Director of Libraries, Babson College, Babson Park, MA
http://www.tiac.net/users/hope/findqual.html

Review

Now that you have read about using critical thinking, avoiding plagiarism, and evaluating Web sites, summarize what you have learned. How will using the information in this section make your writing process different from what it is now?

UNDERSTANDING THE RESEARCH PROCESS

What Is Research?

While doing research is generally associated with colleges and universities, most people do some form of research daily. Research can be as simple as deciding what brand of breakfast cereal to purchase based on the calories, the fat content, the price, and the sodium content of the cereal. People also do research when they decide which candidate to vote for, which school to attend, or which route to take to their destinations. Research is a normal, everyday function. Don't let the idea of doing research intimidate you. The key to successful research is to allow adequate time to find the information you require.

Most writing you do calls for some form of research. Sometimes your research is informal; for example, you might talk with a parent or sibling about an incident you recall from your childhood that you want to recount in a paper you are writing. Most of the time in higher education, your research will take on a more formal perspective. You will need to discover what the authorities in the field have to say about your subject, and you will need to find what others have already said. Whatever you choose to research, be sure you can feel passionate or excited about your subject. Your research should present you with a challenge to discover new information or to see things in a different light. A research project should not be an exercise in simply transferring information from the sources you find into the paper you write. Rather, as you research you should discover new and different ways to interpret the information you find.

Thoughts

Think about the kinds of research you do every day apart from school. What kinds of questions do you ask? How do you find answers? How can you improve the research methods you have applied in the past? What techniques from your everyday research can you incorporate into your academic research practices?

Recording Information

After you have developed a preliminary thesis statement and a research strategy, you now need to decide how to record what you learn about your subject and then most efficiently incorporate that evidence into your writing. As you research, consider what controversies may come up about your subject and how you will handle them when they arise. Stay objective while you research because you may find enough evidence to sway your own view on the topic you have chosen.

Before you start looking for sources, decide how to record the information you discover. Traditionally, researchers have used note cards or recorded their information in notebooks, but computers now make notes easy to store, sort, and retrieve. If you do not have a laptop to carry to the library or wherever you will be doing your research, take your notes by hand, and then transfer them to your computer as soon as you get a chance. The ease in managing the information you record by using a computer is well worth transferring your notes. Whichever way you decide is easiest for you, you need to develop a format to ensure that you consistently keep track of all the information you need not only to document your sources but also to quote, summarize, paraphrase, or synthesize the materials you find. For each source, record the following information:

- Author(s)
- Title of the article
- Title of the book, magazine, newspaper, or other source
- Publication information, including the publishing company and the location of publication
- Date of publication or copyright (for an Internet source, the date the site was created or revised, if available, and the date of access)
- URL for an Internet source
- Page numbers of the material
- E-mail address of the author of an Internet source

Do not count on returning to the source later to get this information—it may not be available. A site you find on the World Wide Web, for example, may no longer exist.

Resources

When you are recording source information for an electronic document done in frames, be sure to get the URL for the part of the document you need. The URL in the location window is not necessarily the URL for your reference. To find the URL for the file you are viewing within a particular frame, click on the frame with the file you want and choose View, then Frame info. This will show you the URL for that individual frame.

When you record source information, also describe the content of the document. Include the following kinds of data:

- **Facts.** Record facts—items that will not vary from source to source, such as names, dates, and technical data.
- **Quotations.** Record the exact information stated in the source, including all punctuation and spelling. In your notes, put quotation marks around exact quotations, and double-check to be sure that you copy the information accurately.
- **Summaries.** Condense the essence of the information you find into your own words.
- **Paraphrases.** To paraphrase, restate the material in your own words, using about the same number of words and giving the same amount of detail.
- **Synthesis.** Bring together the ideas of two or more sources.

To simplify this process, you can create a template in your word-processing program (see Figure 4.1). Each time you want to add notes about a new source, open your template and save it under an identifying name, such as the name of the author or the title of the article or book. Then just fill in the blanks. To indicate whether your note is a fact, quotation, summary, paraphrase, or synthesis, delete the words that do not apply. Make a separate note for each type of information so you will not get confused. Create a folder for each of your research projects.

By keeping this information on your computer, you will be able to retrieve valuable information as you write. You can also make photocopies of printed sources, but don't rely on these copies instead of writing your own notes. You can easily be overwhelmed by keeping copies of all the documents you find on-line, too, so take careful notes about information you may want to use.

Figure 4.1 Template for
recording information.

Author:

Title:

Source:

Location of publisher:

Publisher:

Date of publication, copyright, or Internet access:

URL:

Page numbers:

E-mail address:

Fact, quotation, summary, paraphrase, or synthesis:

Resources

Browsers offer a mechanism to save the addresses of sites you discover as you search. Netscape Navigator has bookmarks, Microsoft Internet Explorer has favorites, and America On-line has favorite places. When **you** discover a site you want to be able to return to, add the URL to your own list so that you can easily get back to it. You can also organize these URLs by putting them in folders. For example, add all related URLs to a folder with the name of your research project. If you are not working on your own computer, you can save your bookmark file onto a disk.

When you use Netscape Navigator 3.01 or higher, you can use the bookmark Properties option to save notes along with an URL (see Figure 4.2). Type in the name of the location, then write notes. This process enables you to create electronic note cards for your research.

Problems

Choose a Web site or article you will be using as a source for your research paper and complete the following exercise:

1. Make a list of all the **facts** you note in the Web site or article. Remember, facts are statements that can be verified. They will remain consistent in the different sources.

Figure 4.2 Netscape Bookmark Properties.

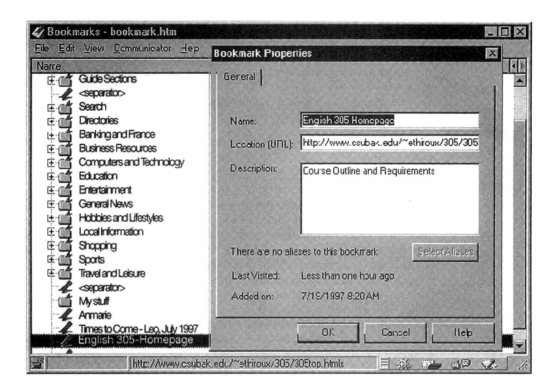

2. Chose an important part of the article to **quote.** Remember not to quote arbitrarily just for the sake of using your source. You need to have a specific purpose for including quotations in your research.

3. Write a **summary** of your source. Clearly state the author's purpose for writing. Also state the author's thesis and the points the author uses to support that thesis. One way to do this is to list the topic of each paragraph. In your summary, be clear and precise and do not copy information from the source.

4. Choose a paragraph out of your source to **paraphrase.** A paraphrase is a restatement in your own words of the original text. A paraphrase is generally as long as the original. Use paraphrasing for parts of your source that are particularly difficult to understand, for example, to clarify jargon or technical terms.

5. Find another Web site or article on the same topic and write a **synthesis** of the two sources. Find out what they agree on and what seems to be the most important information. When you write a synthesis for your research projects, compare what all the authors of your sources agree and disagree on. You may gain insight into the validity of your own thesis.

Using Information

As you do your research, consider how you can use the information you find to support your thesis, suit your purpose, and appeal to your audience. Kenneth Burke developed what he called a *pentad,* or five questions, which can help you decide what you need to look for and help you analyze your data and fit it into your project. These questions are similar to the five journalist's questions that can also help you use your sources. Burke suggests that you ask questions using *agent* (referring to "who"), *action ("what"), agency* ("how"), *scene* ("when" and "where"), and *purpose* (referring to "why"). For example, consider the escalating costs of higher education:

- **Agent:** Who is causing the higher costs? The legislators? The administrators? The public? Who is affected by the higher costs? The students? Their families? The public? The faculty?
- **Action:** What is the problem? The higher costs? Paying for the higher costs? Who is paying for the higher costs?
- **Agency:** How are the students affected? How are the institutions affected? How is the public affected? How are the administrators and the faculty affected?
- **Scene:** When will the higher costs go into effect, or have they already? Where will the effects be noticed?
- **Purpose:** Why have the costs risen? For what purpose will the additional funds be used? Will the higher costs just enable the institutions to maintain the status quo, or will they actually allow improved services?

To these five questions Burke added two elements: *circumference,* which refers to the background of the subject, and *ratio,* which identifies the most important area of the pentad in regard to the argument being considered:

- **Circumference:** What have the costs been in the past? Are the institutions performing effectively without the increase? Why have the increases been implemented?
- **Ratio:** What is the most important issue in the implementation of the higher costs? Will fewer students be able to obtain a higher education? Will the public bear the burden of the increased costs? Will the value of the advanced degree be lessened, stay the same, or increase?
- **Perspective:** The answer to the question of ratio will depend on the perspective of the researcher and the evidence available to support the tentative thesis.

When you do your research, identify unique information that you discover. Maybe you will even find that your argument is unique. A unique argument provides the opportunity for you to prove something new. In addition, assess what information you will need in order to prove your thesis. If you cannot find this information, you may need to redefine your thesis. Consider how your ideas fit into previously documented research. If you discover that your thesis is old news and has already been proved or argued to death, you will want to reconsider your direction and redefine your thesis.

Sources of Information

You should have already created a research plan that encouraged you to develop a strategy by making a list of all the things you need or want to do so you can explore and write about your subject. You probably wrote a list of everything you know about the subject, what you need to know, and where you think you can find what you need to know. On your timeline, you noted deadlines for yourself based on the list you wrote and the tasks you need to accomplish. Take time now to adjust and evaluate your plan so you can do your best work on your project.

Now, we will explore how to search for information. To be prepared to start this research, you need to decide what you want to find. Most information falls into general categories such as these:

- Business
- Government and politics
- Humanities
- Law

- Life sciences
- Physical sciences
- Social sciences

Make a note of which of these categories are most likely to contain information related to your thesis. You can search these categories using several approaches:

- By subject
- By author
- By title
- By key word

Make a list of all the subjects, authors, titles, and key words you can think of related to your thesis. Have this list of items available when you start your search.

When you do a search, you are likely to encounter more information than you could possibly process, so you need to keep in mind ways to narrow your search. Electronic searches give you options in search strategies. One simple way to narrow a search is to limit the dates of the materials you are searching. You may also choose to view citations sequentially by publication date to assess what the most current ideas are. You may be inspired to start a new search based on what you find in your initial search.

Primary Sources

When you research, you will find primary and secondary sources. A *primary source* is firsthand information and is likely to be more valuable than a secondary source. Primary research may be published or unpublished and can be discovered in different types of sources:

Autobiographies	Personal papers	Observations
Diaries	Interviews	Lectures
Notes	Oral histories	Surveys
Letters	Recordings	Questionnaires

The results of experiments are also considered primary information. A report on an experiment includes the methods used and a discussion of its significance.

You can also do original research on your own that can be a meaningful addition to your project. When you do original research, be sure to clearly define your problem and search strategy or method. Consider both sides of a controversial issue, or find a source that addresses the opposing view. Be sure to include sufficient evidence to support your findings. Also, be sure to use statistics accurately and interpret them fairly. You can use data from someone else's research in a primary research project of your own. Just be sure to give credit to the source of the data while clarifying that you did the interpretation of the results.

Field Research

Field research is primary research and can take the form of interviews, observations, oral histories, and surveys or questionnaires. Much useful information can be obtained from these methods, and the key to all of them is your preparation. You have to decide what information you need and base your preparation on that. After you clearly define the purpose of doing your field research, decide which method or methods are most appropriate for you. Make a list of who your most significant sources will be and where you will be most likely to find the information you need. For example, if your topic is domestic violence in your community, you might want to interview the following people:

- A victim of domestic violence
- A worker at a local women's shelter
- A prosecutor in the district attorney's office
- An emergency room worker
- A law enforcement officer
- A child from an abusive home
- A counselor who runs a support group for victims of domestic violence
- A reporter who writes about domestic violence
- A person who has been convicted of domestic violence

You could consider making observations in places such as these:

- The waiting area of a hospital emergency room
- A courtroom during a trial in a domestic violence case
- A ride-along with a local law enforcement officer

When doing field research, be sensitive to the privacy and confidentiality issues that may arise.

Once you have decided whom you are going to talk to, where you will observe, or whom you will survey, then become prepared.

For an interview or oral history project, follow these steps:

1. Make an appointment. Be sure to ask whether you can bring a tape recorder.
2. Do some preliminary research, considering what kinds of questions to ask.
3. Create a specific list of questions.
4. During the interview, assess whether your interviewee is biased, and if so, what the significance of that is to your project. Observe body language and infer what it may mean. Take notes. Don't assume you will remember everything. Confirm anything you want to quote directly, and make sure you understand important assertions your interviewee makes.
5. As soon as the interview is over, write your reaction to it in your research log. Include everything you saw, thought, or experienced that is of significance to your thesis.
6. Follow up with a thank-you note or call, or maybe even a copy of your research paper.

For doing observations in fieldwork, follow these steps:

1. Make an appointment if necessary.
2. Do some preliminary research so you will know what to look for.
3. Create a list of things you are looking for.
4. When doing your observation, take specific notes. Don't assume that you will remember what you see or that you can come back and see the same thing later.
5. Assess whether your observation supports or challenges your thesis.
6. Write your reaction to your observation in your research log, including everything you saw, thought, or experienced that is related to your thesis.

If you are doing a survey, follow these steps:

1. Decide on the purpose of your survey.
2. Decide what kind of information you want to gather in the survey.
3. Identify the people who are most likely to provide you with the information you need.

4. Decide how to do your survey. Will it be a telephone survey, a written questionnaire, or some other method?
5. Make a list of the questions you want to ask.
6. As soon as you compile your results, write your reaction to them in your research log.

These instructions take a traditional approach to doing field research, but you have more options. For instance, if you subscribe to a Usenet newsgroup, you could ask other members to answer a few questions for your research project. You would probably be deluged with responses. Or you could simply post a question to your newsgroup and assess the response. If you subscribe to an on-line service such as America On-line, which schedules interviews with famous people, you may be able to directly ask questions of a professional. You also might do a people search on specific directories dedicated to locating individuals to find authorities in the field and then E-mail them directly. Examples of this type of directory include Big Yellow at http://www.bigyellow.com and Four 11 at http://www.four11.com. Be sure if you do any of these things to be well prepared. Know exactly what you want to ask and what you need to learn.

Secondary Sources

Secondary sources include everything that isn't original information. Most of the information you will find is in secondary sources such as newspaper reports, commentaries, reviews, journals, biographies, and other books. They are about somebody or somebody's accomplishments, describing or analyzing their work. Secondary sources are good for background information, but you should quote and refer to them sparingly.

In our multimedia society, sources are no longer confined to the written word. Much valuable information can be gained from a vast variety of sources. Watching and listening to the "I Have a Dream" speech of Martin Luther King, Jr., has a much greater impact than just reading it. His facial expression, his vocal intonation, and the power of his presentation give you a whole different perspective than if you merely read the words. For literary research, you can watch and compare different video productions adapted from works by famous authors like Jane Austen. When you start to research, make of list of what you may find about your source in nonprint sources such as these:

Films	Records	CD-ROMs
Slides	Tapes	Lectures
Movies	Radio	Public debates
Videos	Television	Speeches

Electronic Searches

Definitions

Before you start your research, you need to become familiar with terms you will encounter. If you learn what these terms mean in regard to electronic research, you can be productive from the start.

- **Search:** To look for information on the Internet.
- **Search engine:** A program that uses key words to provide a searchable index of electronic sites. Alta Vista is a search engine.
  http://altavista.digital.com

- **Directory:** A list created by people who search Web sites and assign them to categories. Some directories have searchable indexes of the World Wide Web and/or the Internet. Yahoo is a directory. http://www.yahoo.com
- **Hybrid search engine:** A search engine with an associated directory, such as Excite. http://www.excite.com
- **Metasearch:** A search strategy that submits your query to many search engines and/or directories at the same time. Some metasearch engines allow you to choose your own combination of search engines to search. http://www.dogpile.com/
- **Browse search:** A search strategy in which the user enters a word that best describes the topic and the browser displays a list of sources that include the word. The list can be huge and will include many irrelevant items.
- **Keyword search:** A search strategy that retrieves records that include the keyword(s).
- **Command search:** A search strategy in which parts of subjects are searched first and then their results are combined.
- **Concept search:** A search strategy that finds sites related to key words.
- **Boolean logic:** A search method that uses the words *and, or,* and *not* to combine terms in order to narrow or broaden a subject.
- **Truncation:** A search method that looks for all forms of a root word.
- **Fuzzy logic:** A search method that finds plurals and different tenses of a keyword.
- **Natural language processing (NLP):** A method that uses English sentences for a search inquiry.

Search Engines

There is no single clear, definitive way to find information on the Internet. Many search engines are available to help you with your research, but none of them lists all the sources out there. If you enter the same subject in a variety of search engines and directories, you may come up with completely different results. Using a hybrid search engine or a metasearch may be of great advantage to you.

A browse search is the easiest form of searching available. You start with one word or a short phrase, such as "Ebonics" or "teen pregnancy." Figure 4.3 shows a search for the topic "Ebonics" on WebCrawler.

You can do a keyword search to find more specific information by listing the name of an author or the title of a book or article you are looking for or the subject you are using. When you submit a word, you will retrieve a set of records that include the word(s) you search. Depending on the search engine you choose, words are either considered separately or automatically joined by "and." Also, depending on your search engine, your search can be limited by specifying these qualities:

- Location (e.g., one library in a system)
- Format
- Language
- Publication type
- Year

In a command search, you search parts of a subject and then combine the results. You can do a command search in indexes such as these:

Figure 4.3 Search Example for "Ebonics."

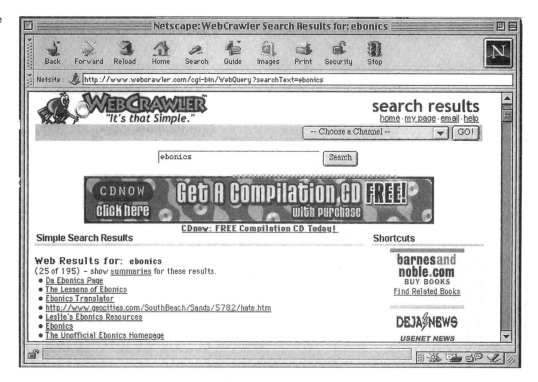

> *Business Periodicals Index and Abstracts*
> *Education Index and Abstracts*
> *General Science Index and Abstracts*
> *Humanities Index and Abstracts*
> *Readers' Guide to Periodical Literature*
> *Social Science Index and Abstracts*

Command searching works well for longer subjects like "pornography and censorship on the Internet." To do this search, you first break the subject into short topics:

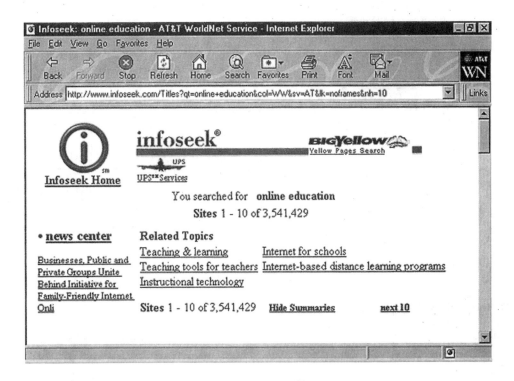

Figure 4.4 Shows the results of an InfoSeek search for "online education."

"pornography," "censorship," and "Internet." Then you search for each part separately, linking different word forms or synonyms with or-for example, "censorship or censoring," "pornography or pornographic." After you do your initial search, you instruct the search engine to compare the lists of the items you found. You will get a new list of sources that include words from all the lists.

A concept search looks for more than just the word you enter. Using a process called intelligent concept extraction (ICE), a search engine like Excite will find words that are closely associated with the words you enter. For instance, if your search topic is "effects of welfare reform on children," you will retrieve items related to "fatherlessness," "poverty," "AFDC," and "Personal Responsibility and Work Opportunity Act of 1996." None of these items includes the specific phrase you searched for, but they are all related to the concept. (See Figure 4.5.)

Using Boolean Operators

George Boole founded "symbolic logic," which is a field of mathematical and philosophical study. Boolean logic, named after him, is a type of symbolic logic that is used to construct database queries. Boolean logic is the process of combining terms to narrow or broaden a subject using the words AND, OR, and NOT and sometimes others. Being familiar with the basic principles of Boolean logic will help you assess the best ways to do searches.

Searching with the Boolean operator AND will find only sources that include all the key words. Say you are doing a project on voluntary euthanasia and want information about the role of the physician.

Example: physician AND assisted AND suicide

Some systems use a plus sign instead of the word AND:

physician + assisted + suicide

The search engine finds all sources with these three words and then combines them and shows you only the sources that have all three words. In the study of logic, the Venn diagram is used to indicate this principle.

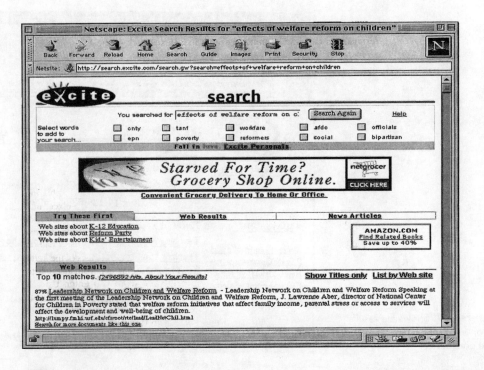

FIGURE 4.5 Search Example for "Effects of Welfare Reform on Children."

The Venn diagram in Figure 4.6 illustrates the operation of AND. The small shaded area where all three circles intersect represents the material you would find in this search.

When you use OR, or a minus sign in some searches, you will find sources that include either one or both of the words. You might want to start with a wide-ranging search if you are working on a big topic such as the early detection of cancer.

Example: cancer OR radiology

The operator NOT indicates words you do not want to find in your search (see Figure 4.7).

Example: pets NOT cats

For instance, you may want to find out about all pets other than cats. The Venn diagram in Figure 4.8 shows that sources about cats have been eliminated from your search about pets.

There are other operators as well. WebCrawler is one search engine that uses ADJ, W/n, and NEAR operators. ADJ, which stands for "adjacent," means that two words must be next to each other, in the order in which they are written, to be selected in your search. Yahoo, another search engine, uses quotation marks to mean the same thing as the ADJ operator.

Example: United ADJ States

In this case, only items that include *United States* will show up, not items such *as United Farm Workers or states of consciousness.*

Using the proximity operator, W/n, you can find words within a certain distance of each other. Replace the n with the number you want to use.

Example: drugs W/5 arrests

This search finds records that include the word *drugs* followed within five words by the word *arrests.*

The NEAR operator operates in much the same way except that it is bidirectional— it will find the words in either order.

Some of the Boolean search methods can be combined. For instance, in Excite you can use parentheses around word groups to indicate certain exclusions or additions.

Example: (college OR university) AND courses

With this search you would get anything that includes the terms *college courses* or *university courses,* but you would not get *go@(courses).*

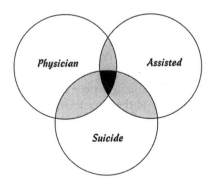

Figure 4.6 Venn Diagram illustrating the Operation of AND

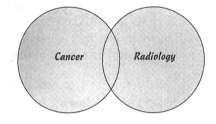

Figure 4.7 Venn Diagram Illustrating the Operation of OR

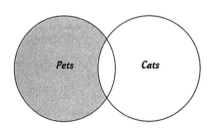

Figure 4.8 Venn Diagram Illustrating the Operation of NOT

Using Other Search Features

When you use the truncation feature, you type the first part of the word and then a symbol that tells the search engine to find all forms of that word. Different search engines use different symbols.

Search System	Symbol	Example	Result
Yahoo, MLA, Psychlit	*	diabet*	diabetes, diabetic
Lexis/Nexis	!	legal!	legally, legality
Wilson	:	pollut:	pollution, polluting, pollute
Lycos	$	teen$	teenager, teenage

Most search engines have some way to rank the relevancy of their sources. Although they may find thousands of sites, you probably will only want to look at the most relevant ones. Many search engines also rate their sources, so look for "reviewed sites" or other indicators of assessment.

Natural Language Processing

Natural Language Processing (NLP) is a kind of intelligent text processing that allows you to write out what you want to research in "natural language." Then it will search the different elements in what you write in a logical manner that will discover information which Boolean searching will not. However, Boolean still can discover items that NLP will not, so there is value in using both systems. With NLP, you can enter your query in full sentences or even in full paragraphs. DR LINK is an example of a searchable database that uses NLP. Its URL is http://www.mnis.net.

Netiquette

When you start working on the Internet, you will need to learn *netiquette*—the accepted, expected, and polite way to navigate the Net. Netiquette is a social agreement that allows a diverse range of people and personalities to function effectively on the Internet. If you keep in mind that you are sending your messages to *people* rather than just into cyberspace or to other computers, then you can keep grounded in the human world. Remember that the use of the network is a privilege, not a right. Unlawful or abusive conduct may result in your privileges being temporarily revoked, and illegal activities can be prosecuted. But basically, etiquette just helps keep you from embarrassing yourself.

Review

If you have not been using the Internet, now is the time to start. Using a graphical browser such as Netscape Navigator, do a Web search on your topic and see what you discover based just on what you have learned so far.

SEARCH TECHNIQUES

Research Agenda

Technological innovation speeds the research process. Print-based periodical indexes, library card catalogs, and CD-ROM databases are resources common to libraries. However, as the digital revolution of the end of the century expands our access to reference materials available on the World Wide Web, it also complicates the process by which we conduct research, evaluate the findings, and document the material. Traditional forms of

Figure 4.9 *Music Therapy FAQ.* Reprinted, by permission, from the American Music Therapy Association, Inc.

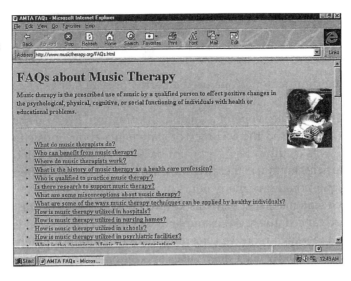

Figure 4.9 *Music Therapy FAQ.* Reprinted, by permission, from the American Music Therapy Association, Inc.

research involve settling on a topic, narrowing the topic into a search question, and then locating reference materials related to the subject matter. Transcribing notes from printed material often means hours of copying words from printed sources, followed by more time figuring out how to fit hand-recorded notes into the paper.

The critical thinking involved in deciding on a topic and then formulating a research question remains the same with electronic research methods. Dana Morris, a sophomore honors student, knew immediately that she wanted to research some aspect of music. As a toddler, she loved to sing. Now as a college student, she enjoyed singing in a choir. Thinking about how music helped her to relax, she looked in the library for ways that music changed people's behavior. Finding few sources on her topic, she used a search engine to find Internet sources on music and behavior. Among the sites in her Internet search, she found a credible site sponsored by the American Music Therapy Association, FAQs about Music Therapy (see Figure 4.9). This site led to music therapy programs at the University of Kansas and other links to professional and personal sites. As a result, she narrowed her topic to music therapy and her research question to: How is music therapy used to treat mental patients?

From a mix of conventional and electronic re-sources, Dana developed a mind map, similar to the one in Figure 4.10, to help her organize her thoughts from her notes on traditional and electronic resources. She put the narrowed topic at the very heart of the essay.

Relevant Resources
Finding Relevant Sites

To continue gathering information, Dana used an array of search engines to find more Internet sources. As she examined these sources, she noted the site's sponsor and assessed the scope of available information. Because she knew about music, she checked the accu-

Figure 4.10 *Mind Map for Music Therapy.*

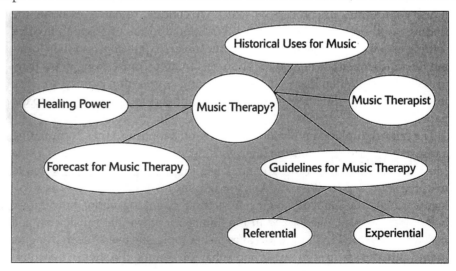

racy of statements about music to determine if the site was credible. She also went back to the library to find specific books and articles on music therapy. Dana found that a well-crafted query to a search engine could save many hours of research time.

A **query** is a search statement that contains key words or complex expressions written as an advanced query. An example of a keyword expression is *music therapy*. When the search requires screening a large amount of potentially unnecessary data, an advanced query uses special operators to show how the key words are related to one another. These **Boolean operators** are: *and, or, not*. Another operator, *near*, may also be used to indicate that a keyword should be found near another keyword. Said another way, a search statement consists of a **character string** formed by key words with some relationship established by operators in the string.

The following sample statements illustrate a query strategy to gather information about music therapy. Italics denote key words in the sample expressions, which appear in various combinations suited to the most popular search engine. When query phrasing can use shortcuts with symbols, these shortcuts appear in brackets as an alternate query phrase. Meant to be a general list, some search engines allow for finer distinction than this list suggests.

Query Phrase	Search Results
music [*"music"*]	Finds and publishes all URLs that have *music* in the title or in the content. Using the quotation marks around the phrase can sometimes narrow the list of sites.
mus*	With the wildcard symbol (*), finds and publishes a list with music, muse, musical, etc.
music or therapy [*music/therapy*]	Finds all URLs that have *music*, and then finds and publishes all the URLs that have *therapy*.
music therapy *music and therapy* [*+music+therapy*]	Lists Web documents that contain *music* and therapy. Both key words *music and therapy*.
music and not *entertainment* [*music -entertainment*]	Finds all the Web documents that have *music* excluding those documents dealing with *entertainment* before publishing the final list.
music near therapy	Publishes a list with sites which have *music* mentioned within 10 words of *therapy*.
music therapy or (*music and healing*) [*music therapy or* (*+music+healing*)]	Looks for *music therapy* and then looks again for any documents that contain both key words *music and healing*. The results are published as a list.
(*not entertainment*) *and* *music*	Finds all Web documents with the keyword *music* and without any mention of *entertainment*.
title: *music* [t:music]	Finds and lists all the documents on the WWW with *music* in the title.
url: *music therapy*	Finds and lists all the URLs having information about *music and therapy*.

RESEARCHING

Using Libraries

Technology is wonderful, but traditional libraries will be here for a long time to come. They offer a vast wealth of information not readily available yet on Internet sources. Before you jump into the new ways to do things, it is important to be grounded in the established methods the new methods are based on. Consider the library for your research carefully. Three main types are available:

- Public libraries open to the general public
- Academic libraries located at educational institutions
- Professional libraries, such as a medical library at a local hospital or a law library in the district attorney's office

Knowing how to use the library is essential to doing thorough research. Before you start a research project, take a walk through your library to become familiar with the layout and the location of materials. Find out about special features in your library. When you explore your library, locate the following areas:

- **Circulation desk.** This is where you check books in and out. You may also be able to ask for directions, pay fines, and arrange for interlibrary loans of materials not available in your library.
- **Reference room.** This room contains basic, general background materials that can help you start your research. Reference books usually cannot be checked out, so be prepared to take good notes. Reference materials include dictionaries, encyclopedias, bibliographic information, biographical indexes, periodical indexes, and indexes to government documents.
- **Reserve desk.** Instructors may reserve materials for student use. You can often check these materials out for a few hours.
- **Stacks.** The stacks are the shelves where books are located. Some library stacks are closed, and a librarian has to retrieve what you need. In open stacks, you can browse in the area where the books related to your research topic are shelved.
- **Interlibrary loan desk.** Although libraries have vast quantities of books, no library has them all. If you need a volume that is not available in your library, you may be able to borrow the book from another library. This service may take ten days or longer.
- **Nonprint sources**. Video- and audiotapes are often available. The modern library stores much more than just books, so be sure to look for alternatives to traditional resources when doing your research.
- **Librarians.** Librarians are the most valuable resource in the library. They are there to help you and can be a tremendous support. You just have to ask for help. Remember, be prepared—don't waste their time. Tell them what you have done so far, tell them what you need to know, and tell them what kinds of sources you think you need.

Catalogs

Libraries used to have rows and rows of file cabinets for their card catalogs. Now most libraries use computerized catalogs or Public Access Catalogs (PACs). A PAC may even be available from your computer at home. PACs list items such as these:

Books	Video recordings
Periodicals	Audiovisual sources
Government documents	Electronic media sources
Maps	Computer files and software
Musical scores	Rare books and manuscripts
CDs	Microforms

A PAC is easy to use. You just need to follow the directions on the computer screen. There are several ways you can typically search a PAC:

- Browse search
- Title search
- Keyword search
- Subject search
- Reserve list search
- Number search

Choose the way you want to search, and then follow the directions. You oftenwill have a choice of display options:

- Brief display: call number, location, and current status of the material
- Full display: complete bibliographic information
- Index display: a list of authors or subjects

You can do a browse search by author, title, or subject. Just enter what you are looking for and browse through the results until you find something you want to explore. From there you can choose a brief or full display. If your initial search is too broad, state more specifically what you are looking for. When you find what you need, you can usually print the information or copy it to a disk, or you can copy the information onto a note card, being sure to include all you will need to locate your source.

If you know the title of the item you are searching for, a title search can quickly find results. You can search for the titles of journals and series as well as articles and books. Keyword searches will look for items containing the keyword, using the delimiters you choose. For instance, a subject keyword search will list all the articles containing your keyword with subjects that match the standard Library of Congress subject heading you chose. A title keyword search will find all the titles that contain the keyword.

A subject search will search the standard Library of Congress subjects. A reserve list search will indicate which materials are on reserve in the library. Frequently instructors put materials on reserve in the library that are not readily available to their students in other ways. And a number search is good if you know a number assigned to the source you are trying to find:

ISBN: International Standard Book Number
ISSN: International Standard Serial Number
OCLC: On-line Computer Library Center number
MPK: Music Publisher Keyword

Mixed searches can be done by combining different search elements. For instance, if you are using a PAC from a university campus and you know the campus has several libraries, you can limit your search by using a keyword search and combining the word you want to search and the name of the library in which you wish to search. Or if you know the name of the author you want to find and you know that the materials this author has published are primarily stored on CD-ROMS, then you could search by author and format (CD). You can combine any of the key words to make a search more specific, and some PACs support the use of Boolean search techniques. As with most computerized services, the directions are usually there on the screen. You just need to read them carefully and follow them.

Of course, the Library of Congress or Dewey decimal call number system is still used in most libraries. College and university libraries generally use the Library of Congress system. In your library, locate the map that shows you how things are stored in accordance with this system. Then you can go browse in the stacks. Pick up the books and look at their tables of contents or indexes to see what they have or where they can lead you.

Problems

Do a preliminary search on your subject at the University of Texas Public Access Catalog, UTNetCAT. Its address is http://dpwebl.dp.utexas.edu/lib/utnetcat/

After you do this search, try your search in another PAC at the following URL. http://sunsite.Berkeley.EDU/Libweb/

This address provides access to different libraries all over the world. At the top of the Web page, you will see a menu option labeled "Keyword Search." This is not for looking up key words as in a PAC; rather, it is for library locations. Enter your city or county and see what appears. Libraries in your area that have PACs will be listed, and you can do your searching right from your computer at home or school. Many of the libraries restrict privileges—for example, you may need to be a student at a school in order to use its library.

Try looking for your subject in libraries close to home. Then try looking for your subject in libraries in other parts of the world. Remember to bookmark any page that will be of use to your research, or carefully copy down the URL and a description of the page if you are not working on your own computer.

Library and Related Electronic Resources

Here's a list of libraries and related sources you can access on the World Wide Web:

University of California, Los Angeles Libraries and Collections and Internet Resources
http://www.library.ucla.edu/cird/index.htm

Oxford University Alex Catalog of Electronic Texts
gopher://rsl.ox.ac.uk/11/lib-corn/hunter

Consortium of University Research Libraries in the United Kingdom (COPAC) National On-line Public Access Catalogue
http://copac.ac.uk/copac/

Yale University Library
http://www.library.yale.edu/

New York Public Library
http://www.nypl.org/

Library of Congress
http://www.loc.gov/

Library of Congress Machine-Assisted Realization of the Virtual Electronic Library (MARVEL)
gopher://marvel.loc.gov

Harvard University
http://hplus.harvard.edu/

Columbia University
http://www.cc.columbia.edu/cu/libraries/index.html

The Carnegie Mellon Electronic Books and Other On-line References
http://www.cs.cmu.edu/Web/books.html

Periodical Indexes

Periodical indexes are where you will find articles and their page numbers from magazines, journals, serials, and newspapers. Magazines are generally commercial and are not necessarily written by experts. Journals publish scholarly research written by people considered to be experts in their fields. Before being published, journal articles are generally reviewed by other people considered to be experts in the same field. *Serials* are journals appearing in successive parts, frequently published by organizations. Newspapers are also covered in periodical indexes.

Periodical indexes can be found in print, on microform, on-line, or on CD-ROM. Consider which ones will most likely have the most information about your subject.

Magazine Indexes

Readers' Guide to Periodical Literature (on-line and CD-ROM) *Magazine Index*

Journal indexes

America: History and Life
Accountant's Index (on-line)
Applied Science and Technology Index (on-line and CD-ROM)
Architectural Periodicals Index (on-line)
Art Index (on-line and CD-ROM)
Biological and Agricultural Index (on-line and CD-ROM)
Business Periodicals Index
Computer Literature Index
Criminal Justice Periodical Index
Combined Retrospective Index Set to Journals in History, 1838-1974 (CRIS)
Cumulative Index to Nursing and Allied Health Literature (on-line and CD-ROM)
Dissertation Abstracts International (DAI; on-line and CD-ROM)
Dramatic Criticism Index
Education Index (on-line and CD-ROM)
Engineering Index (on-line and CD-ROM)
Educational Resources Information Center (ERIC)
Current Index to Journals in Education (CIJE; on-line and CD-ROM)
Resources in Education (RIE; on-line and CD-ROM)
Essay and General Literature Index (on-line and CD-ROM)
General Science Index (on-line and CD-ROM)
Humanities Index (on-line and CD-ROM)
Index Medicus
Index to Legal Periodicals
InfoTrac (provides access to several databases; on-line and CD-ROM)
Magazine Index (on-line and CD-ROM)
MLA International Bibliography of Books and Articles on the Modern Languages and Literature (on-line and CD-ROM)
Music Index
Philosopher's Index (on-line)
Physical Education Index
Psychological Index
Public Affairs Information Service Bulletin (PAIS)
Recently Published Articles

Religion Index (on-line and CD-ROM)
Social Sciences Index (on-line and CD-ROM)

Newspaper Indexes

New York Times (on-line)
http://www.nytimes.com/subscribe/help/sources.html
Wall Street Journal Index
http://ptech.wsj.com/html3/on-line.html
Boston Globe
http://www.boston.com
San Francisco Chronicle
http://www.sfgate.com/
Washington Post
http://washingtonpost.com/

Other Indexes

American Statistical Index (microfiche)
Vertical File Index (pamphlet index)

Citation indexes are a form of index that will tell you where the author you are researching has been quoted in print: books, journals, magazines, and newspapers. This is a good way for finding authoritative sources on your subject. Citation indexes are divided into four parts:

- **Citation index**: shows who has cited the author you are researching
- **Source index:** shows where the author you are researching has been cited
- **Permuterm subject index:** searches by pairing significant related words in article titles
- **Corporate index:** shows what has been published in a certain geographical area

There are three major citation indexes.

Social Sciences Citation Index (on-line and CD-ROM)
Science Citation Index (on-line and CD-ROM)
Arts and Humanities Citation Index (on-line and CD-ROM)

Bibliographies

Printed and electronic bibliographies are a good place to start your research. If you are doing research on a current topic, you will want to use an up-to-date electronic source such as a bibliographic database. If you want a historical perspective, then a printed bibliography is what you need. If you are still not committed to your subject, you may want to use a general bibliography to help you get started. If you are committed, then go to a specialized bibliography in the field you are researching. In either case, the bibliographies can give you information about what has been written about your topic. Many printed bibliographies in a wide variety of subject areas can be found in the reference section of your library. You may wish to explore some of these bibliographies:

Annotated Bibliography of Health Economics
Bibliography of Bioethics

Bibliographic Guide to Business and Economics
Bibliographic Guide to Education
Bibliographic Guide to the History of Computing, Computers, and the Information
    Processing Industry
Bibliographic Index: A Cumulative Bibliography of Bibliographies
Geographical Bibliography for American Libraries
International Bibliography of Political Science
Native Americans: An Annotated Bibliography
Omega Bibliography of Mathematical Logic
The Literature of Journalism: An Annotated Bibliography
World Philosophy: A Contemporary Bibliography

Your library is also filled with other sources to explore. Encyclopedias, for example, are a good place to find summaries of information on subjects, but because they try to summarize just about everything, their coverage is too brief to base your research project on them. They do, however, often point to useful sources and may have good bibliographies.

You will also find sources that contain abstracts of articles, theses, and books. Abstracts are merely concise summaries of sources. Use these only to lead you to whole sources. Abstracts generally are not written by the original authors, so do not quote from them. Dissertation Abstracts International (DAI) is a good source for abstracts. This provides a good place for you to look to see what others have already argued on your subject.

Another source you will find in the library is reviews. Reviews are written about books, plays, and works of art and as commentary on articles in scholarly journals. While reviews can help you determine the reliability of a source, they are not ordinarily cited in a research project. Go to the primary sources for your real research. Here are some indexes that will help you find abstracts:

Book Review Digest
Book Review Index (on-line and CD-ROM)
Book Review Index to Social Science Periodicals
Index to Book Reviews in the Humanities (on-line and CD-ROM)
Choice (American Library Association monthly publication; contains short reviews and bibliographic essays)

Microforms can also help you discover sources. Many national newspapers, weekly magazines, and dissertation abstracts come on reels of microfiche. You can make copies of sources you find right on the reading machines.

Government Documents

The Unites States government generates an amazing quantity of written material. Check to see whether your library is a government document depository. If it is, you will find a wealth of information waiting for you. If what you need is not there, check the U.S. Superintendent of Documents, which is a monthly catalog of the U.S. government publications. It is published by the Government Printing Office (GPO) and includes materials from 1895 to the present. It has an index ("Title Keyword") that makes it easy to use. The GPO Access address is http://www.access.gpo.gov/su-docs/. *The Public Affairs Information Service Bulletin* (PAIS) is another good source for government publications. You can order government documents, most for free, from the Superintendent of Documents.

Superintendent of Documents
Government Printing Office
Washington, DC 20402

The Congressional Record is the key publication of the legislative branch of the government. It contains Senate and House bills, documents, and committee reports. You can order copies of specific legislation from these addresses.

Senate Documents Room
SH-BO4 Capitol Building
Washington, DC 20510

House Documents Room
B-18 Ford Building
Washington, DC 20515

Government Document Electronic Resources

Many Web sources are available to provide you quick and easy access to government documents.

GPO Gate (University of California)
http://www.gpo.ucop.edu/

University of Michigan Document Center
http://www.lib.umich.edu/libhome/Documents.center/ govweb.html

Government Information, University of Texas Library On-line
http://www.lib.utexas.edu/Libs/PCL/Government.html

Resources for Government Documents Librarians
http://www.lib.berkeley.edu/GODORT/#GPO

Indiana University School of Law U.S. Government World Wide Web Virtual Library
http://www.law.indiana.edu/law/v-lib/us-gov.html

CD-ROM Databases

Some indexes are available on CD-ROMs that can be accessed only in the library. Check with your librarian to see which CD-ROM databases are available in your library. They are easy to use. When you open the database, choose a general subject and scan to see what is available. These databases generally have abstracts for you to read. Some have full texts available. Either print your sources or take good notes as you work.

CD-ROM Electronic Resources
The URLs listed below will guide you to Web sites for these sources. These sites give further information about the CD-ROM sources, but you will have to go to your library to actually use the CD-ROMs:

InfoTrac
http://www.iacnet.com/-lib/libhome.html

UMI-ProQuest
http://www.umi.com/hp/Products/PDQlntro.html

SilverPlatter
http://www.silverplatter.com/

ERIC (Educational Resources Information Center)
http://www.ed.gov/databases/ERIC-Digests/index/

On-line Databases

On-line databases may be located in your library. They are available by subscription and can be costly. You may need librarian assistance in order to use them, and you may have to pay from $1 to $60 an hour or a flat fee of $5 to $100. Charges depend on several factors:

- Library used
- Computer time required
- Database searched
- Time of day

If you choose to do this kind of search, have your search strategy prepared to save time. Your library may have a form for you to fill out before you start, so you will need to have this information ahead of time:

- Subject
- Titles
- Key words or descriptors: synonyms, closely related topics, alternative spellings, names, technical terms
- Range of dates or years

Annotated Bibliography Electronic Resources

Most databases print out an annotated bibliography with brief abstracts. The list below indicates some resources to ask for at your library. URLs about the sources are included when available. The other resources listed are available on CD at libraries.

Business Periodicals Index
350 business periodicals, including scholarly journals
http://info.exeter.ac.uk/~ijtilsed/lib/datasets/buspers.html

Chemical Abstracts Service (CAS)
http://www.cas.org/

Cumulative Index to Nursing and Allied Health
http://www.tau.ac.il/medlib/nurs.html

Dissertation Abstracts International (DAI)
DataStar Web (multiple database source)
http://www.krinfo.com

DIALOG@Carl (information retrieval services)
http://dialog.carl.org

Disclosure (business use and commentary)
http://www.disclosure.com

DR-LINK (general searches)
http://www.mnis.net

Education Index (400 journals for teachers)
Educational Resources Information System (ERIC)
http://www.ed.gov/databases/ERIC-Digests/index/

General Science Index (150 science journals)
http://www.cc.columbia.edu/cu/libraries/clio_Plus/user_guide/392.html

GeoRef (published research in geology)
http://www.agiweb.org/agi/georef.html

*Humanities Index (350 scholarly journals) Lexis
(commercial, full-text legal information service)*
http://www.lexis-nexis.com:80/lncc/about.html

Medline (index for published medical research)
http://eee.uci.edu/w3m3/anesthesiology/msg00027.html

*MLA (Modern Language Association; 3,000 journals; literary criticism,
research on language and folklore)*
http://www.pitt.edu/~refquest/LI/MLA.html

Nexis (news and public affairs)
http://www.lexis-nexis.com:80/lncc/about.html

NewsEDGE/WEB (current and recent news)
http://www.desktopdata.com

National Technical Information Service (NTIS)
http://www.ntis.gov/

Profound (market analysis)
http://www.profound.com

ProQuest Direct (full-text documents)
http://www.umi.com

Psychlit (research in psychology)

Social Sciences Index (350 important scholarly journals in the social sciences)

Readers' Guide to Periodical Literature (about 250 popular sources)

Using Your Computer to Do Research

You can accomplish many research tasks without going to the library. By planning ahead, you can save valuable time when you do make a trip to your library. In this section you will learn how to use your computer to do on-line research.

In addition to doing keyword searches on the World Wide Web, you can join listservs and newsgroups to gather information on your research topic.

Virus Protection

Be sure the computer you are using to do your research has virus protection. Your computer needs to be protected whenever you download an Internet file. Viruses can range from just pranks to programs that can destroy data. Virus protection software such as Norton Antivirus or McAfee can be invaluable to you. You can find other information on virus protection by doing a Web search or by checking with your Internet service provider.

Listservs

As described earlier in this chapter, *listservs* are electronic mailing lists that deliver messages to and from all the members of the list. Some listservs are relatively private and may serve a group as small as one class. Other listservs deliver a huge volume of messages every day. The number of available listservs increases daily. You can join lists that are of personal interest to you, or you can find lists that may help you with your research.

Finding Listservs

Try these URLs to find listservs that might interest you:

http://tile.net/tile/listserv/
http://www.iti.org/staff/
http://www.liszt.com/

When you discover a list you are interested in, there will be directions for how to subscribe to that list. Be sure to follow the directions carefully. Upon acceptance to the list, you will receive a notification that you need to save. This document will include information on how to unsubscribe to the list as well as information about the list. Often a list of frequently asked questions (FAQs) will help acclimatize you to the list. Be sure to read messages from the list for a while before you post anything.

Newsgroups

Newsgroups are similar to listservs. Listserv mail, however, is delivered to your E-mail account. In contrast, when you post something to a newsgroup, the information is stored on the computer where the newsgroup resides. It will not stay on the host computer forever, so if you want to use information you discover on a newsgroup, be sure to save it on your own computer. Most of what you find in Usenet groups and listservs will not help you with academic research, but sometimes you can find worthwhile information you could not get elsewhere. Always remember, though, that newsgroups are not a place to get definitive answers or facts; they are mostly a hodgepodge of individual ramblings. Newsgroups are listed by general topics. These are some of the most frequently used headings that identify topics:

Heading	Topic
alt.	Alternative 11; anything from coffee to romance to yoga
bionet.	Biology
bit.	A list that redistributes BitNet ("Because It's Time") mailing lists
biz.	Business related
clari.	Commercial news; requires a fee
comp.	Computers
gnu.	Set up to promote shareware
humanities.	Literature, music, or language
ieee.	Institute of Electrical and Electronics Engineers
kl2.	Kindergarten through high school education
misc.	"Miscellaneous," from books, to education, to health, to legal, to writing
news.	Usenet news information
rec.	Recreation, art, hobbies
sci.	Any of the acknowledged sciences
soc.	Social issues and socializing
talk.	Debate and discussion

Newsgroup Resources

Here are URLS for some sites that can help you find newsgroups:

Alta Vista (search for Usenet)
http://www.altavista.dligital.com/

Deja News
http://www.dejanews.com/

Reference.Com
http://www.reference.com/

Usenet Newstand
http://www.criticalmass.com/concord/

Web Searches

New Web search mechanisms are introduced frequently. Each one tries to be bigger or better or different than the rest. Many Web pages have a "Help" or "Tips" link that will give you much more detailed information. Read and follow the instructions for each search carefully.

Carefully choose the words and phrases you search for to save time while you are searching. The more specific you are, the more likely you will be to find what you need. The more distinctive a word is, the more likely you are to find results. Remember to watch your spelling. The spelling must be exact for matches to be possible.

You may find a search engine you really like, but don't limit yourself to using just one. You always find different sources when you use different search engines. No service can do everything.

Electronic Search Engines

The following is by no means a complete listing of search engines, but it will get you started on the World Wide Web.

All-in-One Search Page
http://www.albany.net/allinone/
All-in-One is a metasearch page you can use to initiate searches using 150 different search engines.

Alta Vista
http://altavista.digital.com/
Alta Vista is the preferred search engine for Yahoo! (a directory). Use quotation marks to search for phrases, and use an asterisk for truncation; Boolean logic is supported in advanced searches.

You can do a Usenet search from Alta Vista. A pull-down menu allows you to search either "The Web" or "Usenet."

Archie
http://web.nexor.com/public/archie/archieplex.html
This Archieplex can do Archive searches to locate anonymous FTP sites on the Internet.

Argus Clearinghouse
http://www.clearinghouse.net/
This site offers a good selection of reviewed search sources.

CUSI (Configurable Unified Search Interface)

http://abyss.idirect.com/

CUSI allows you to search the Web for files, other search tools, people, documents, and dictionaries.

DejaNews

http://www.dejanews.co.uk/

DejaNews is one of the most popular search methods for locating newsgroups.

Dogpile

http://www.dogpile.com

Dogpile is a metasearch engine that allows you to search 23 search engines at the same time. It also allows you to search multiple Usenet and FTP site sources. It even allows you to set the order in which it will send your query out to the search engines. Using this kind of search can save you a lot of time.

Excite

http://www.excite.com/

Excite is a search engine that searches for ideas and concepts as well as key words. It looks for relationships between words. Boolean operators and symbols such as + and - can be used to narrow your search. Excite will also find recent news articles. Usenet newsgroups also can be accessed through Excite.

Galaxy

http://galaxy.einet.net/

Galaxy lists only Web sites that have been submitted and reviewed. Started in 1994, it is one of the oldest Web directories.

Gopher

http://galaxy.einet.net/gopher/gopher.html

This site allows you to search Gopher sources. Many Gopher sources can still be reached by telnet or FTP (file transfer protocol), but the World Wide Web is becoming the most common navigational tool for Gopher sources. Gopher menus and directories contain a multitude of valuable text-based documents. Veronica is the main search engine for Gopher sources.

HotBot

http://www.hotbot.com/index.html

This search engine supports a variety of Web and Usenet searches. A pull-down menu allows you to search for any or all of the words in your query, for exact phrases, for a person named in your query, or for links to an URL. You can use the standard Boolean operators.

InfoSeek

http://www.infoseek.com

InfoSeek allows you to browse using Ultrasmart or search using UltraSeek. Separate names and titles in your queries with commas. Put quotation marks around or hyphens between words that must appear together. The symbols + and - are used as Boolean operators. InfoSeek allows you to narrow the scope of a search by searching again within the results of the previous search.

Internet Sleuth

http://www.isleuth.com/

Internet Sleuth allows you to use many different Web search engines and to search by phrases. Boolean operators are not recognized.

Jughead

http://pine.shu.ac.uk/~eitrgh/ntiwk8.html

Jughead is a Gopher search mechanism that is usually limited to searching within its own system. This site gives an in-depth explanation.

Lycos

http://www.lycos.com

Lycos is a search engine that picks from the most popular Web sites. Searching in Lycos, use a period to indicate that you want a word matched exactly, use a - sign to screen out words, and use $ for truncation. The Lycos custom search page offers the option to match specified numbers of words.

Magellan

http://www.mckinley.com

Magellan provides a powerful search engine and a directory of rated and reviewed sites. It includes Web sites, FTP and Gopher servers, newsgroups, and telnet sessions. Reviewed sites are rated on a point system, and sites listed with a green dot indicate that at the time of the review there was no content intended for mature audiences. Magellan uses + and − signs as Boolean operators and ranks search findings by relevancy.

MetaCrawler

http://www.metacrawler.com/

MetaCrawler searches seven major search engines at once, checking as it goes to be sure that each source it finds is still accessible.

Open Text

http://index.opentext.net/

Open Text supports full Boolean searching, but its database is small and incomplete.

SavvySearch

http://www.cs.colostate.edu/-dreiling/smartform.html

SavvySearch is a metasearch tool that allows you to search 25 search engines at once. More search engines may be added to its list. You can obtain the number of results you want from each search engine, and SavvySearch will display the results in brief, normal, or verbose format.

Search Tools

http://www.bright.net/~genensuz/search.html

This is a source for a variety of search engines not found on most metasearch pages.

Veronica

gopher://veronica.scs.unr.edu/11/veronica

Veronica indexes titles of Gopher items and allows you to search them using key words. The site listed here explains how to use Veronica.

WebCrawler

http://www.webcrawler.com

WebCrawler offers "natural language searching," which allows you to describe your search topic in your own words. Of course, the more specific you are, the better your results will be. WebCrawler supports full Boolean operators and has a Boolean quick-reference chart you can print out to help facilitate your search.

Yahoo!

http://www.yahoo-com/

Yahoo is a Web site directory that uses concept searching and allows both browsing and searching. Alta Vista is its preferred search engine. Search results are listed by category.

Yahoo supports the use of + and - as Boolean operators, uses quotation marks for matching sets of words, and uses an asterisk for truncation. If you want a certain word in your search phrase to be given extra consideration, repeat the word three times.

Review

Summarize the information you learned in this chapter. Create a list of words and short phrases that best express your research topic. Use several of the Internet tools listed in this chapter to search for these words, and compare the results. Try some advanced searches using Boolean logic and truncation.

READING

[From *Reading with Confidence,* Joan Monahan, Allyn and Bacon.]

Purpose

Probably you have discovered (or soon will) how easy it is to find interesting material on the Internet. However, it is important to evaluate the material you find there as to its timeliness, accuracy, and validity. The article that follows describes an Internet hoax that was believed for a time by many people. Read it as a warning to evaluate Internet sources carefully.

Preview

The article is short. Skim first sentences and check the questions and the vocabulary at the end.

Anticipate/Associate

1. Have you, or has someone you know, ever had problems with material found on the Internet?
2. How can you verify the accuracy of material found on the Internet? What checks might you use before citing an "authority" on the Internet?

Internet Writing Can't Be Believed

Howard Kleinberg

That settles it! If it happened on the Internet, I won't believe it. Someone's going to have to prove to me that anything on the Internet is true, even the baseball scores and weather report. If I run across a scientific claim that the sky is blue, I'm going to think it's green.

It's all because of Ian Goddard, and people like him.

If there is an Ian Goddard.

See? I don't even believe that.

A keystroker who says he is Ian Goddard recently admitted that his earlier claim on the Internet that a U.S. Navy missile shot down TWA Flight 800 was false. "Reckless and a mistake" was the language he used in explaining it, and apologizing.

"Malicious and criminal" are the words I would use in rejecting his apology.

It apparently was a person identifying himself as Ian Goddard who influenced former John Kennedy press chief Pierre Salinger to make a fool of himself last spring in not only accepting the missile theory but in claiming he had irrefutable evidence—which he did not. Salinger's involvement created widespread media coverage and promoted the theory of a deadly military blunder and subsequent cover-up.

Goddard is a mystery to me and to others with whom I spoke. In seeking anything about him on the Internet, we find only his <u>conspiracy</u> theories, as well as his <u>hoaxes</u>.

When the Goddard missile theory first found its way to the Internet, CBS's *60 Minutes* belittled it, causing Goddard to bellow back that whatever he puts out is true and <u>verifiable</u>.

In a March 17, 1997, Internet site report, a man calling himself Goddard boasted: "The portions of the Salinger Report that are derived from my world—hence my status as co-author—are derived from carefully researched and referenced reports I have posted publicly on the Internet."

Now, in a written statement to Cable News Network, the alleged Goddard admits to making a reckless and mistaken accusation about the Navy missile and confessed that he pursued and promoted his claim because he "wanted to give the government a black eye by any means that looked <u>opportune</u>."

In doing so, he cost the taxpayers millions of dollars in investigative pursuit of his counterfeit claim, brought greater <u>anguish</u> to the families of those lost on TWA 800 and rendered <u>implausible</u> anything you might see on the Internet.

The Goddard character certainly is not the sole practitioner of electronic treachery; it is widespread throughout the Internet as well as in television commercials (Fred Astaire and the vacuum cleaner), in the printed word, and in doctored photographs, film and graphics that pretend to be truthful but are, in fact, <u>callous distortions</u>.

Seein' ain't believin' any more.

Check Your Understanding

Review

Without further research, you cannot be sure of the events that caused Howard Kleinberg to distrust the Internet, but it is helpful to place the following events recounted in the article in a probable chronological (time) order. Place the following events in their probable sequence by numbering the first event 1, and so on.

—Goddard admits a "reckless and mistaken accusation about the Navy missile."
—Pierre Salinger accepts Goddard's accusation as fact.
—CBS's 60 *Minutes* discounted Goddard's report.
—Goddard wanted to give the government a black eye.
—Goddard defends his work as "carefully researched."

Multiple Choice

Select the letter of the answer that best completes the statement.

1. The main idea of this selection is that
   a. Ian Goddard is a hoax.
   b. you can't believe everything you read on Internet.
   c. you can't believe anything anymore.
2. The writer's primary purpose is to
   a. entertain.
   b. persuade.
   c. inform.
3. Kleinberg
   a. exaggerates to make his point.
   b. will never believe anything on Internet.
   c. finds only the Internet guilty of providing misinformation.

4. The paragraph beginning, "In doing so," is organized by
   a. examples.
   b. comparison/contrast.
   c. cause-and-effect.
5. The writer's tone is
   a. ironic.
   b. angry.
   c. sad.

True/False

Label the following statements as true or false according to the article.
1. The identity of Ian Goddard remains a mystery.
2. A Navy missile shot down TWA Flight 800.
3. Goddard's hoax cost millions of dollars.
4. Goddard's purpose was to seek the truth about TWA Flight 800.
5. The program 60 *Minutes* exposed Goddard as a fraud.
6. The cause of the flight's crash was covered up by the military.
7. The Internet is the only source that presents fantasy as fact.
8. Goddard finally admitted that his reports on the Internet were false.
9. Goddard admitted that his false claims were "malicious and criminal."
10. Sophisticated electronic devices cause misinformation.

Vocabulary

Use the words from the list to complete the following sentences.

malicious	irrefutable	conspiracy	hoax	verifiable
opportune	anguish	implausible	callous	distortion

1. My source of information was an authority, so I knew the information was _____.
2. He had a hardened or _____ indifference to my plea for forgiveness.
3. Usually an encyclopedia is a(n) _____ source for factual information.
4. The death of a great leader is usually the cause for sorrow and _____
5. It seemed like the _____ moment to request a loan.
6. Spreading false rumors is considered an evil and _____ activity.
7. A political plot to destroy a reputation is called a(n) _____
8. His misrepresentation of the accident was a(n) _____ of the facts.
9. A(n) _____ is a deliberate attempt to mislead someone.
10. Jerry's excuse for missing the study group was far-fetched and _____

Writing

1. Write a paragraph defending, condemning, or taking a middle position on the use of electronics to doctor photographs and other data, as mentioned in the next-to-last paragraph of the article. Cite reasons and examples to support your point of view.

2. What do you think would be a just punishment (if there should be one) for Ian Goddard if he is ever identified? Again, defend your point of view in a paragraph.

Critical Thinking

1. Discuss what might be done to control Internet abuse by individuals. Should laws be passed? (Brainstorm this one. It's difficult, but solutions need to be developed.)
2. Discuss whether you think Kleinberg overreacted to this situation. What reasons might he have for overreacting?
3. Are there examples of biased words used in this selection?

PART IV

Education and the Individual in an Information Society

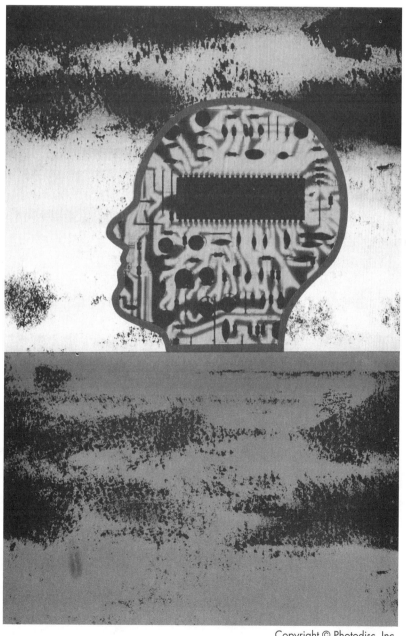

5

Cultural and Economic Impact of Technology on the Individual

TECHNOLOGY AND TECHNOLOGY PRACTICES

As we have established in earlier chapters, we currently live in the age of technology and information, which is everchanging and affects every area of our lives. As a future technologist, your career success will depend on how well prepared you are to keep up with the fast-changing world of technology, and to use your technological creativity to offer solutions to problems as they arise.

The technology that has the most transforming effect on us is the computer. It impacts many areas of social life, including employment and the quality of work performed, the distribution of power in businesses, and their ability to quickly adapt to the rapid changes in today's economy. Your ability to control information and knowledge will enable you to make effective on-the-job decisions.

This chapter offers an overview of the psychological and cultural effects of technology on society and on the individual. It offers valuable insight into the areas of technology that have the greatest effects on us. You should integrate this knowledge into your own education. As John Sculley states, "A diverse educational experience will be the critical foundation for success. You should be more like researchers actively exploring [your] environment." Utilize the information presented here to help you determine the career opportunities available to you.

Technology can be defined as the systematic application of ideas to produce some desired outcome by manipulating the material world. This definition points to the fact that technology is rooted in the immaterial (ideas, wants, values) but finds expression in the material world, including our bodies. The goal of any technology is a desired state of affairs or condition, such as the production of material goods or good health.

A **technology practice** is the complex set of social and cultural patterns in which a society's technologies are embedded. It includes the organized individual and group activity that applies scientific and other knowledge to solving practical tasks (Drengson, 1995). A basic component of a technology practice is a given society's fundamental model of "reality," or the larger context in which human action occurs. This reality is often expressed in the stories and myths members of a given society cherish. Of special importance in a society's technology practice are the organized groups that promote specific technologies and the ideas and values underlying these groups. For example, during the 1970s agribusiness (massive business firms that operate for their own profit through the production and distribution of agricultural products and the implements and chemicals used to produce them; today these businesses often operate globally) supported efforts of leading U.S. research universities to develop products such as tough, juiceless (and largely tasteless) tomatoes that could be picked by machines without bruising. The underlying value in this instance was not the production of high-quality food, either in terms of nutrition or taste, but increased profits and reduced labor costs.

Natural systems survive and thrive only by means of self-correcting processes that enable them to resist the forces of disorder in the physical universe. Technology practices intervene in natural systems that are self-organizing structures. For example, the use of chemical insecticides has disturbed the natural balance between predators and the insects that eat many of our crops. This has resulted in increased crop losses resulting from insect pest populations that grow much larger without the restraints of natural predators. Human technology takes advantage of natural processes and redirects them toward human ends. The laws of nature dictate that imposing human order (novelty) comes at a price, which inevitably involves greater disorder (referred to as *entropy*) somewhere in the environment. This, too, is an aspect of technology practice. In contemporary times we are learning much more about the limits or boundaries of ecological systems in which we participate and are coming to understand the need to respect those limits.

All of this has led philosopher Frederick Rapp to describe our present age as the age of technology, which he sees as involving "constant technological alteration of the natural world; substantial alteration of daily human life through technology; and the continuous global expansion of Western technological processes" (quoted in Drengson, 1995:86-87). More than any previous people, we define ourselves in terms of technological processes. This age of technology, then, is dominated by the corporation-based, science-driven development of technology.

INFORMATION TECHNOLOGY

Information technology is the technology of communication and information, including computers and satellite television, and is increasing the frequency of human interactions at an exponential rate. The speed of social change is itself partly a function of the speed and ease of these interactions. Therefore, the present technology is hastening social change.

The technology that is currently transforming social life and the way we think about ourselves and the world most directly is the computer. Fierce debates will probably continue for some time about the impact of computers on employment, and about the nature and quality of the jobs that people will have in a world dominated by computers. Whether the computer will create more jobs than it eliminates is at present an open question. Still, a crystal ball is not required to realize that the answer depends largely on whose values and interests shape present and future choices. The democratic participation of employees and of citizens in these decisions is critical if we are to counteract the effect that the concentration of power in the hands of huge multinational corporations and First World nations may have on the elimination of jobs.

Work

The quality and content of work and work relationships are also related to the use of computers. Some argue that the long-range trend of capitalism has been to replace the worker's thoughts, choices, and practical wisdom with management-controlled technological processes. Computers can and do aid management in accomplishing such an end. But a study of 24 U.S. plants using computer-controlled manufacturing showed that the majority had upgraded worker's skill levels, increased workers' flexibility and commitment to the job, and improved relationships between management and unions. The introduction of computers apparently redistributes skills more often than it replaces them. This research suggests that computers have the capacity to enrich jobs and to give workers more influence as well as more flexibility about when and where they work (Barbour,1993).

Business

How will information technology change the distribution of power in businesses and corporations? Control of information and knowledge has always been one source of management power; there will probably be considerable resistance to sharing information and knowledge with those lower in the workplace hierarchy. The first computers were large devices that centralized information and groups of experts. Today's information technology, in contrast, involves networks of small personal computers that can be most effectively used in flexible and decentralized ways. Too much top-down control will tend to interfere with the creativity, efficiency, and effectiveness of the new technology. If such a situation develops, it may hamper a corporation's ability to adapt to the rapid changes in today's economy (Pes 1987). Efforts to use computers more creatively may also lead to new approaches to management and decision making that will reduce hierarchical structures (Senge, 1990); However, such changes will have to be introduced within the context of strong managerial power, which will be difficult.

Political

Direct voting by citizens made possible by cable hookups and computers has been proposed as one contribution that information technology can make to the political process. But someone will still have to define issues and choices, and these can be subtly manipulated. Citizens may be uninformed, deceived, and easily swayed by emotional factors during the process. Many poor people will not have access to the channels of information necessary to register their opinions. Voting may be monitored by "Big Brother," and so forth.

Professor of history and critic of contemporary culture Theodore Roszak (1994) notes that for the average citizen desirous of more democratic participation and discussion, Citizen Band radio offers an even better means of achieving this goal than do computer hookups. Yet that has not been the use to which CB radio has been put. To some extent, the computer has been used to connect citizen interest groups, not only across the country but also around the globe. Such a use is particularly vital for environmental groups and/or groups concerned with empowering Third World people who are otherwise isolated. Connecting these groups to each other and to the peoples of the Third World may turn out to be a far more effective and democratic use of computer technology than direct voting. Such connections can be two- or three-way exchanges of information and services. But of course the peoples of the Third World would have to gain greater access to computers. Still, having said this, we need to point out that there is also a potential political "downside" to computers—they may allow governments or other groups to engage in surveillance and to compile information about citizens and citizen groups for the purposes of manipulating them, undermining their power, or otherwise harming or deterring them.

Geographical

Information and information technology have been monopolized by the developed world for some time, but that too, is changing. In 1984 Brazil banned the import of computers. Less than ten years later, 270 Brazilian companies had entered the computer business (Barbour, 1993). This situation is obviously not typical of Third World countries, but it does suggest what is possible in some cases. A report made in 1987 to the UN by a commission to study environment and development (called the Brundtland Report) maintained that microelectronics could facilitate sustainable development, and the International Labor Office (ILO) proposes the integration of computers with traditional methods of agriculture and production (Barbour, 1993). International agreements now make it possible for every nation to have orbital positions available if and when they have their own communication satellites on the principle that space is the common heritage of humankind.

Still, what is transmitted via much of the cable and satellite media is not the "common heritage of humankind," but largely Western commercial mass media fare. Beamed into Third World and tribal cultures, these programs sometimes have devastating effects. For example, television viewing among these peoples disrupts traditional patterns of transmitting culture from elder to younger generations and undermines the elders' authority (Macionis, 1996). Furthermore, the content of these messages replaces traditional values with the consumerism, moral relativism, and individual self-indulgence that abound in the Western media. Traditional people may have, if anything, less resistance to the persuasiveness of these media than do the members of the developed countries.

Other issues about the effects of computers focus on the availability of and access to information, as well as its content and quality. When access to databases and information networks requires a fee, information is available only to those who can afford it. When access is too available, or simply free as a public service, the quality of the information and communications may tend to become degraded, as some critics of the Internet, the leading public access computer network, suggest (Stoll, 1995). The promise of an "information superhighway" will probably never be fully realized for many reasons. The main reasons are seemingly unresolvable issues of property rights over information and ideas and lack of control over the quality of what is available. Moreover, most books and journals will never be placed on computers, and most readers of books and journals will probably never want them to be, mainly because people like and find it convenient to hold a book or magazine in their hands. A particularly frequent problem may turn out to be the on-line traffic jams that result as the participation of people in the network increases (Stoll, 1995). The box, "Contemporary Discussion: Information Technology," debates the upside and downside of the new information technology.

CYBERNOMICS

In the following material, you will explore the new world of cybernomics (the application of economic analysis to human and technological activities related to the use of the Internet in all of its forms). You will find out about the growing world of electronic commerce, banking, and finance. In addition, you will find out about the changes it is bringing in the theory of the firm, monopoly, and labor markets.

A WORLD OF CONTINUOUS CHANGE

As with all technological changes, there are losers and winners. The cyberspace revolution is creating many winners and, of course, some losers. That is not new. Decades ago, when elevator control systems were automated, elevator operators lost their jobs. When

Contemporary Discussion

Information Technology

No reasonable person today denies the immense value that information technology has in contemporary life. Computers are indispensable in monitoring and modeling changes in the atmosphere caused by pollution, for example. The space program would be impossible without computers, as would be many forms of new medical technology. Information technology also has many business applications, including allowing increasingly sophisticated record keeping. Nevertheless, a lively dialogue is shaping up among those optimists who see information technology as a largely positive force and those less optimistic about it.

The Upside of the Information Age

We are essentially the first generation to live in the information age—a transformation of society and culture as great or greater than those wrought by the shift from nomadic hunting societies to agricultural societies and the onset of the industrial revolution. Today the most important new resource is "information" or "knowledge," which is different from other resources such as money or land because it is the one resource that can be increased by our sharing it. Power and influence will pass to those who possess this "social" resource. Already we see the impact of information technology on businesses, which are shifting from hierarchical structures to "flatter" structures based on the sharing of information among flexible work teams.

Access to global networks of information will probably enhance democracy. People who have access to information tend not to be easily manipulated, and the ability to communicate issues globally will help to focus public and professional opinion about the plight of groups previously exploited simply because they were isolated. In addition, increased access to technical, scientific, and medical information; to social and political skills; and to national and international markets will empower people around the globe. The net result of these ongoing changes is most likely to be enhanced participation and the formation, for the first time, of a truly worldwide community.

Moreover, information technology and the perspectives it generates are altering our assumptions about the very nature of reality. Many sciences are finding that the concept of "information" is necessary to explain the organization of natural systems (a system is a set of interacting components that produces an overall effect, i.e., that act as a "whole") and this recognition is leading to the "dematerialization" of our worldviews, according to some observers. Thus we think less and less about the material components of systems and look more and more to the information content and processes of those systems. Matter and energy flow into and out of living organisms at a rapid rate, yet they maintain their stability and basic structure because of information processes, for example. Perhaps the following example will make this clear. After seven years all of the matter and energy in a human body has been replaced (while many organs and tissues replace themselves in a matter of months or even days). Yet if you meet a friend you haven't seen for seven years, you can still recognize her because her body has a genetic information "blueprint." This blueprint is a set of instructions (information) that directs the matter and energy flowing into and out of her body, so that from day to day and year to year, her body and face continue to display a familiar pattern. Even our economic production seems dematerialized because of the new reliance on information, and its wider and faster spread has resulted in our using fewer materials to meet our needs. Increasingly, we rely on information to serve this purpose. Finally, our reexamination of the nature of reality and of the mind and of the relationship between them has led to the recent introduction into our language of terms like" cyberspace" and "virtual reality." New concepts like these themselves open up new conceptual possibilities and stimulate creativity. We are more able to think in terms of dynamic systems (e.g., living organisms or human groups, whose present activity is based in part on their own past activity; thus, they change over time in response to their own activity), which is precisely what the "real" world is all about.

The Downside of the Information Age

People cannot eat, wear, or drive information. Information technology will not enable us to transcend our need for basic resources, no matter how valuable information or knowledge becomes. Moreover, some applications of information technology (e.g., genetically engineered grains) are not delivering all that they promised in areas of basic needs. In addition, power has not shifted from transnational corporations and the developed societies to smaller companies and less developed societies; nor does it show signs of doing so in the near future. Besides, the sorts of knowledge that are truly useful in the world require extensive university education and access to scientific research, communication skills, and languages, which are not generally available to most of the world's people. Indeed, the reduction in the need for raw materials in this "information age" will have devastating effects on poor countries that depend almost entirely on the export of one or two natural resources.

Moreover, within the developed world, the chief impact of information technology may be the elimination and deskilling of jobs. Mental functions and decision making that used to require human beings are now routinely taken over by machines, reducing even the little mental skill once necessary. Just as the demand for factory labor has been greatly reduced by the introduction of "smart" machines, clerical and service (e.g., health care aides, fast-food attendants) jobs continue to decrease, with no new types of work in sight to absorb those seeking jobs. To whose advantage is it to deskill or eliminate jobs? In such a situation, owners and managers will benefit by gaining their share of higher profits engendered by the smaller labor force needed to produce and sell products. The future will bring relatively few jobs, and even those few new jobs created will require high levels of education and mental skills. The majority of people will thus become an "information proletariat," a group lacking the information skills and knowledge base necessary for success in contemporary society. In addition, because most people in developing nations will lack access to information technology and to information networks altogether, the new technology will only reinforce the growing gap between many of these nations and the developed world.

The much-hyped Internet will be used chiefly for the trivial pursuit of pleasure. It is already being exploited by commercial interests, not to mention pornographers and others of questionable motives. The suggestion of some that being "on-line" will encourage grassroots democracy is not likely to be realized. Although, obviously, some people will make good use of the Internet to expand grassroots democracy, others will use it to indulge in escapist behavior.

Indeed, the concepts of the new information sciences and technology tend to debase rather than to elevate the human spirit by confusing knowledge and meaning with information and information processing, and with the more creative process called thinking. Further, the new information sciences and technology confuse the rather depersonalized and often dishonest interactions via the computer with true human communication. In face-to-face settings, and even over the telephone, we reveal a great deal of our identity and social status—age, sex, and race—and to an extent display our intentions. These important social markers are absent when we use electronic communications in which persons can easily misrepresent who and what they are by disguising their identity. The Internet makes it much easier to manipulate or exploit others (e.g., adults have used the Internet to seduce children). Indeed, what is real may come to be confused with the computer-enhanced fantasy of "virtual reality." The effects on human identity (at least for some people) may be unfortunate, leading to greater isolation and mental difficulties.

optical character recognition systems were perfected, bank employees who manually sorted checks were laid off. As word processing systems have become easier to use, the demand for typing specialists has diminished. Technological change will almost always reduce the demand for traditional labor services, but at the same time it will increase the demand for new types of labor services. The fear of technological change has been around for centuries, as you can see in Example 5.1.

Example 5.1

International

Luddites Unite Against Automated Textile Machinery

In the vicinity of Nottingham toward the end of 1811, an organized band of English crafts-men started riots with the aim of destroying the textile machines that were replacing them. The members of the band were called Luddites, named after an imaginary leader known as King Ludd. Bands of Luddites were generally masked and operated at night. They were often supported by the local townspeople—but certainly not by threatened employers. One employer, a man named Horsfall, ordered his supporters to open fire on a band of them in 1812. The Luddite movement eventually lost steam by 1817, when prosperity again reigned in England.

   For Critical Analysis: *What are some other technological changes that have created job losses?*

THE AGE OF INFORMATION

Let there be no mistake, the information age is here. What is one of the most important industries in the United States? The answer is information technology, or IT. Sales of the American computing and telecommunications industry have doubled during the 1990s, to exceed $1 trillion a year. IT is the largest American industry—ahead of food products, automotive manufacturing, and construction. The share of IT in American firms total investment in equipment was a mere 7 percent in 1970 and is now about 45 percent. If you add software investment, current U.S. business spending on IT exceeds investment in traditional machinery. Employment in the IT sector now accounts for around 6 million workers and is growing. The average IT worker earns wages that are about 60 to 70 per-cent greater than the average wage in the private sector. The American Electronics Asso-ciation wants to call this the "new economy." This so-called new economy consists of high-tech companies that are generating new work practices and new challenges in pub-lic policy.

HOUSEHOLD AND BUSINESS USE OF THE INTERNET

Panel (a) of Figure 5-1 shows the rise in the percentage of households with a link to the Internet. At the beginning of the 1990s, the number was virtually zero; the estimate for the year 2005 is over 50 percent. In panel (b), you see average hours per week spent on-line per household connected to the Internet. At the beginning of the 1990s it was almost nothing, whereas today it is over eight hours per week.

   For the moment, the greatest use of the Internet is electronic mail, or **E-mail**.

   U.S. businesses alone send about 10 billion E-mail messages a year, and that figure is likely to increase. The number of Internet hosts has increased from a few thousand in 1988 to about 20 million today. Worldwide, about 200 million global citizens are con-nected to the Net. Some estimates for the year 2030 put that number well over a billion.

Figure 5.1 *The Internet Invades America*
Perhaps no other innovation has caught on so quickly in America. Not only are more people connecting to the Internet, but they are also using it more.
Source: Consumer Electronics Manufacturer's Association. Figures after 1998 are predictions.

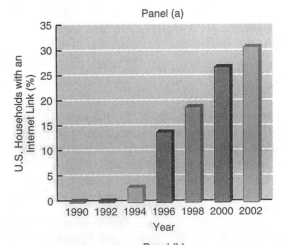

Panel (a)

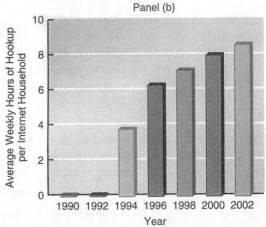

Panel (b)

EFFICIENCY, TRANSACTION COSTS, AND E-COMMERCE

Individuals turn to markets because markets reduce the costs of exchange, which are called transaction costs. These are defined as the costs associated with finding out exactly what is being transacted, as well as the cost of enforcing contracts. Entrepreneurs since the beginning of time have attempted to make markets more efficient by figuring out ways to reduce transaction costs.

A big part of transaction costs is the cost of obtaining information. Buyers need information about sellers—their existence, the goods and services they offer, and the prices of those goods and services. A stroll through one's local mall may be a pastime for some, but it is a costly activity for all—time usually does not have a zero opportunity cost. The advent of mail-order shopping reduced transaction costs for many. It also introduced additional competition for retailers located in remote cities. After all, one no longer had to rely solely on the local camera store once camera ads from stores in New York City and elsewhere started appearing in nationally available print publications.

The Web as a Reducer of Transaction Costs

Enter the Internet and the World Wide Web. The existence of information about numerous goods and services, such as automobiles and cameras, via the Web simply means that transaction costs are being further reduced. This should make the market work more efficiently and should lead to less variation in price per constant-quality unit for any good offered for sale.

Business-to-Business E-Commerce

The first place that e-commerce (the use of the Internet in any manner that allows buyers and sellers to find each other and can involve business selling directly to other businesses or business selling to retail customers) has been extensively used is for the sale of goods between businesses. A good example is Cisco Systems, Inc., a major producer of Internet computer routers. It estimates that over 40 percent of its orders are already handled through the Internet—to the tune of about $5 billion a year. The benefits to Cisco by taking orders on-line are many: faster service for its customers, quicker production cycles, and savings on labor and printing charges. Cisco believes that it has reduced overall costs by more than $500 million a year by relying so heavily on e-commerce.

As can be expected, the first companies to take full advantage of the ease of ordering through the Internet have been those involved in information technology, particularly computers and computer parts. In any event, business-to-business Internet commerce is not highly visible, and this may explain why the government underestimated annual on-line sales for 1997 at $5 billion when they were probably closer to $25 billion. If current trends continue, e-commerce should account for almost $1 trillion of sales in the year 2002.

"E-'Tailing"

While the growth rate in e-commerce at the retail level has been impressive, the total dollar volume is still a mere drop in the bucket compared to retail sales through normal retail outlets. An increasing proportion of Internet users are willing to purchase via the Net, but they do not do so on a regular basis. One issue that retail customers are concerned about is security. They worry that it is too easy for their credit card number to be stolen off the Net by individuals who wish to use it for fraudulent purposes. The real problem area, though, involves Internet merchants, particularly those selling software for immediate download, for these people have been the victims of cybercrimes much more than consumers who have had their credit cards "lifted" out of cyberspace.

Cybershopping Crooks

The ease of selling software over the Internet also makes it easy for cybershoppers to defraud Internet sellers of software provided on-line, occasionally. CyberSource, the owner of the on-line retail source Software.Net, experiences more fraudulent sales than legitimate ones. Cybercrooks use someone else's credit card number to order the software. CyberSource downloads the software almost instantaneously. By the time the seller discovers the fraud, the buyer has a copy of the software and can resell it.

On-line software sellers have struck back. They have developed a computer model that looks at 150 factors to calculate the risk of fraud for any particular purchase. Any on-line company can pay 50 cents to have a pending credit card request run through the model. There is also an ever more complete name-fraud database that can be used as a reference point.

Better Encryption

Encryption software systems that prevent anyone else from obtaining information provided on-line are getting better all the time. Both Netscape's Navigator and Microsoft's Internet Explorer browsers have built-in encryption systems. On-line retailers are developing even better ones. Given the demand for a system that is totally secure, we can predict that concerns over losing a credit card number in cyberspace will virtually disappear over time. In any event, even current encryption systems are much more secure than a telephone conversation with a mail-order company operator to whom you give your credit card number in order to have goods shipped to you.

Using Intelligent Shopping Agents

Intelligent shopping agents are software programs that search the Web to find a specific item that you specify. Using these agents saves the time you might have to spend searching all potential sites through your browser. Suppose that you wanted to order a pair of pants. An intelligent shopping agent would ask you for essential descriptions and then go searching on the Web.

A new software program called XML—for "extensible markup language"—will assist intelligent shopping agents. Preparing a Web home page in XML makes the Web site smart enough to tell other machines what is inside in great detail. In essence, XML puts "tags" on Web pages that describe bits of information. Each group of on-line businesses (travel, stocks and bonds, and so on) will have its own set of agreed-on tags. This will allow searching intelligent shopping agents to "flip through" all of the Web sources for a particular item more easily.

Suppose that you are considering the purchase of some airline tickets in the middle of a fare price war. You are not sure how low the ticket prices are going to go. In the near future, you will be able to tell your intelligent shopping agent to keep looking for a lower fare as the airlines change prices on a daily basis. When the agent finds the best price, it can automatically order the tickets on your behalf.

The development of XML along with better intelligent shopping agents is crucial for the most efficient utilization of the Web. Currently, there are over 450,000 commercial sites selling products on-line, and the number is sure to increase rapidly. In the meantime, certain search engines, such as Excite, offer services to compare listed prices from various cyberstores for a desired product.

The Trend Away from Mass Merchandising

Electronic retailing may reverse the trend toward mass merchandising that we have seen over the past 50 years. This reversal has already taken place in the computer industry. Computer mail-order pioneer Dell does not even start the production of a computer until the customer selects all the features—size of hard drive, amount of memory, processor speed, modem speed, and so on. Over 10 percent of Dell's orders are now through the Internet. Dell asks the customer each feature it wants and gives a menu. Apple is doing the same thing on a full selection of its latest computers. Levi Strauss and Company has a customized jeans site on the Internet—a type of on-line fitting room. A similar plan has been put forth by Custom Foot, a large shoe retailer.

Example 5.2

Buying a Car on the Net

They said it could never be done—selling cars in cyberspace. After all, the thinking went, before purchasing such an expensive item, consumers would want to "kick the tires." For most consumers, that is still true. But a growing number now use the Internet to search for the best price on exactly the car they want. And many more have discovered that the most painless way to start looking for a car is on the Net. You can go to Microsoft's Car-Point site at www.carpoint.msn.com. You will even find videos that display car interiors. This allows you to take a look at all your options in order to narrow your choices. You can go to Kelley Blue Book at www.kbb.com to get exact dealer invoice prices including destination charges. This tells you what the dealer paid for the basic car wholesale. All you have to do is add the prices of optional equipment that you want. These prices are also available at the Kelley Web site. (From the total price listed, you should deduct about 3 percent, which is what the dealer gets from the manufacturer when the car is sold this is known as the "holdback.")

Once you know what you want, you can start shopping for the actual car via the numerous Web sites for dealers throughout the country. Some dealers are making more than 10 percent of their total sales via the Web. You can also use an on-line car-buying service that processes orders and forwards them to dealers. Detroit's Big Three—Chrysler, General Motors, and Ford now have their own on-line selling sites.

For Critical Analysis: *Car dealers argue that on-line auto shopping will destroy customer bonds. Why should this matter?*

The Advent of the Internet Shopping Mall

Perhaps the wave of the future in Internet retail shopping is the equivalent of today's shopping mall. The biggest player in on-line shopping malls is netMarket.com. Sales for 1997 were $1.2 billion, and the company anticipates that its sales will more than double every year into the foreseeable future. The netMarket site sells everything from books and videos to cars, travel, CDs, and kitchen appliances. Within the next several years, net-Market will sell about 95 percent of the goods purchased by a typical household. The on-line firm netMarket is like a club warehouse, for it charges a $49 annual fee. In effect, though, netMarket is not a mall. Rather, it's a megastore that uses the best specialized retailers' efficiencies and discounts. Unlike the typical megastore, such as Wal-Mart or a club warehouse, such as PriceCostco, on-line megastores carry no inventory. They simply pass the orders on electronically to distributors or manufacturers, who then ship the goods from their own warehouses directly to the buyers.

Reduction in the Demand for Retail Space

If more shopping will be done over the Internet in the future, less shopping will be done in traditional retail outlets. Even in those retail outlets that exist, customization may be the order of the day because of new digital scanning and manufacturing systems. The Levi's store in Manhattan allows customers to be scanned electronically to order perfectly fitting jeans. There are a few stores where customers' feet are scanned electronically for custom-made shoes. If more consumers opt for such custom-made items, retail stores will carry much smaller inventories, keeping on hand only samples or computerized images.

The result will be a reduced demand for commercial retail space. Moreover, there will be a reduced demand for trucking to haul inventory, for electricity to light and heat retail space, and for the paper that is used for all the ordering.

THE INCREASING IMPORTANCE OF BRANDS

Brands have value because they indicate to potential purchasers of a branded item that a strong and successful company stands behind it. Successful companies typically have well-recognized brands—think of Microsoft, IBM, Levi's, Mercedes Benz, Sony, Nike. In the world of e-commerce, cybershoppers will increasingly look for branded items to satisfy their purchase desires. Why? Because there will be no salesperson extolling the virtues of a perhaps lower-priced but less well known item.

Brands Created on the Net

That does not rule out new brands establishing themselves on the Net. A case in point is Amazon.com. The most successful virtual bookseller, Amazon.com didn't even exist before it went on-line. Nonetheless, it has established its brand name as a reputable place to purchase books. Amazon offers incentives to other Web site owners to link with it. If you link your Web site to Amazon, you get a 3 to 8 percent commission on each book purchase made by anyone who follows that link and buys that book from Amazon. Because Amazon orders only books that customers have agreed to buy, the return rate is less than one-quarter of 1 percent, versus 30 to 40 percent for the industry overall.

Reputation on the Web is crucial for success. Jeff Bezos, CEO of the company, makes it clear: "This is the Web. If people feel mistreated by us, they don't tell five people—they tell 5,000."

Example 5.3

Selling CDs On-line

While Amazon.com and Barnes & Noble are busily selling books on-line, the music industry has had a slower start. According to Juniper communications, on-line music purchases represent less than a half a percent of the U.S. industry's $13 billion total sales. Some small companies are nonetheless doing well. Internet Underground Music Archive at www.iuma.com started in business by selling CDs of bands that were not yet under contract. Today, it carries over 1,000 bands, gets a quarter of a million "hits" (visitors to its site) a day, and is selling CDs at the rate of $1 million a day. The on-line CD purchaser gets a sample song before purchase and also typically spends less than at a regular retail CD store. Many minor artists are starting their own Web sites to publicize their works and sell them, too.

The real future in on-line CD sales will begin when Web surfers can quickly and easily download entire albums in digital quality onto blank CDs.

For Critical Analysis: *Who will be affected most by the digital on-line downloading of CDs?*

MARKETING AND ADVERTISING ON THE NET

If you are marketing a product and you have 20 potential purchasers, you can use the phone to call them. If you want to reach 20 million potential purchasers, you take out a TV ad during the Super Bowl. What do you do if you want to reach 10,000 people? Typically, you engage in direct-mail advertising, at a cost of 50 cents to $1 per person targeted. But now you've got the Internet. In principle, the Net makes it easier to reach more finely targeted audiences and to communicate with them. Consider an example. You are using the search engine InfoSeek, and you enter the keyword "airline tickets." When you do so, a banner ad for American Express's travel services will appear on top of the resulting list of potential Web sites.

The key difference between a similar-looking ad on a TV screen and one on your computer is important—you can click on the one on your computer for an instant response. For TV advertising (and space ads in newspapers and magazines, too), there is no way of really knowing how many people's behavior is truly changed. With Internet advertising, all you have to do is count the number of "click-throughs." If American Express finds out that its travel service ad on InfoSeek has only a 1 percent click-through rate, it will rethink that particular type of advertising.

The future of Internet advertising is impressive. America On-line already has more "viewers" than any single cable television network and more "readers" than most popular magazines. As Internet service providers, browsers, home pages, and the like attract larger and larger audiences, the potential for more extensive advertising is dramatic. Currently, Internet advertising revenues represent only a few percent of the annual $35 billion spent on television advertising. But that proportion will change.

TAXES AND THE INTERNET

The United States has some 30,000 tax jurisdictions. In addition to the 50 states, there are thousands of municipalities as well as other taxing districts. Not surprisingly, many of these tax jurisdictions are looking covetously at e-commerce. It represents a potential boon as sales of products and services on the Internet grow. But there is a big potential problem: taxation confusion.

A single Internet transaction does not just go from one entity to another. The nature of the Internet is such that servers may be located virtually anywhere in the world, and the transaction from one end point to the other may be routed through half a dozen servers in numerous tax jurisdictions. Virtually every tax jurisdiction in the United States has different fees and regulations. If all jurisdictions started imposing their tax structures on every Internet transaction, the result would be total confusion. This chaos would inhibit firms from getting involved in electronic commerce and would slow the growth of the use of the Internet.

A bill is in Congress, a draft of the Internet Tax Freedom Act. The bill proposes a five-year moratorium on any new taxes and regulations in cyberspace. The underlying reasoning is simple: A uniform policy must be developed for on-line transactions to ward off confusion. Governors and mayors are fighting vigorously against enactment of the Internet Tax Freedom Act. They want to be able to tax Internet sales. Under current law, the Constitution has been interpreted as prohibiting the states from taxing interstate commerce. They can tax the activities only of companies that have a physical presence in the same state as the consumer. What if states argued that Internet and on-line service providers, such as America On-line, are really just acting as independent agents of any company doing business on the Internet? If this interpretation were to be accepted by the courts, every company selling anything over the Internet would have a taxable telecommunications nexus in every state in the union and could owe dozens of taxes on each transaction.

Even if we assume that uniformity of taxation does not apply to transactions on the Net, the market will still punish governments that attempt to apply relatively high taxes on cybertransactions. When Tacoma, Washington, decided to subject on-line service providers to its 6 percent telecommunications tax, the companies immediately threatened to move elsewhere. The city reversed its decision.

Example 5.4

Avoiding Taxes by Setting up Offshore

If you are willing to break the law, you can set up an Internet business in a Caribbean tax haven. One such place is Anguilla. All you have to do is send your name, phone number, E-mail address, and a proposed Web address for your business to www.offshore.com.ai. You will have a Web site set up, and an Anguillan lawyer will register your corporation. You can open a corporate bank account with the Anguillan branch of Barclays Bank or the local National Bank of Anguilla. You can transfer the $1,500 fee using DigiCash, Inc.'s e-cash—which is untraceable. Anguilla does not impose any taxes on your venture. It does not cooperate with the U.S. Internal Revenue Service, either. You can get a corporate credit card and spend your money anywhere you want. Remember, though, that as a citizen or legal resident of the United States, you owe federal income taxes on your worldwide income. On Schedule B of your tax form 1040, there is a box to check if you have an offshore bank account. If you do not check it when you have such an account, you have committed a felony.

For Critical Analysis: What types of businesses would individuals seeking to avoid taxes most likely set up on an offshore Web site?

E- TRADING AND CAPITAL MARKETS

Gone are the days when all stock market transactions had to be run through a licensed broker. The Internet has transformed the industry—from two angles. First, anybody can trade on-line from virtually anywhere in the world for as little as $8 a trade no matter what the size of the transaction. Second, small companies can now find financing through the Internet.

On-line Trading

A few years ago, on-line trading seemed to be a fantasy. You had to call your broker, usually at a full-service brokerage firm, and pay hundreds or sometimes thousands of dollars in commissions, depending on the number of shares you bought or sold. Discount brokers then entered the fray. Commissions were slashed to half or less. Now on-line retail brokerage firms offer commission rates that "can't be beat." One of the first and biggest is E*Trade. You can buy or sell 200 shares of a $20 stock on-line and pay less than $15 in commissions. You can buy or sell 3,000 shares of a $10 stock and pay less than $75.

Fierce Competition

During the first half of 1998, average daily on-line financial trades increased by more than 50 percent over the previous six months. Currently, there are about 3.5 million on-line investing accounts. Forester Research, Inc., of Cambridge, Massachusetts, predicts 15 million by the year 2002.

Datek Securities, Ameritrade, and Suretrade offer a fixed-price commission. The commission prices are incredibly low compared to what people were paying just a few short years ago in fact, none of those companies charges more than $10 a trade.

The bright future of on-line trading does not bode well for the future of regular retail securities brokers in the industry. The demand for their services should shift leftward through time.

Seeking Capital on the Web

For very small firms, it has always been difficult, if not impossible, to obtain public financing for expansion. The costs of reaching potential investors, filing with the various state and federal regulatory agencies, and dealing with all the other red tape have been just too great.

In 1996, the U.S. Small Business Administration, working with the federal Securities and Exchange Commission (SEC), helped privately financed Angel Capital Electronic Network launch its first Internet site (ace-net.sr.unh.edu/). The goal of this Web site is to have small business entrepreneurs provide information to investors about promising small businesses that wish to raise from $250,000 to $5 million in equity financing. What's more, it is now possible to go public on the Internet—to sell initial shares of stock to the public directly, as you can see in the following example.

Example 5.5

Going Public Via the Net

History was made when Spring Street Brewing Company became the first company to conduct an initial public offering (IPO) over the Internet in 1995. In March 1996, the company again made history when the SEC allowed Spring Street to trade its shares via its Web site without registering as a broker-dealer—provided that the company modified its program. Among other things, the SEC required Spring Street, which had been directly processing the funds received from buyers, to use an independent agent, such as a bank or escrow agent, to receive such funds.

> ***For Critical Analysis:*** *Why would the SEC give up control over public offerings?*

Advantages of Using the Web

According to the government, going public via the normal route takes about 900 hours, most of it devoted to preparing a prospectus prior to the sale of stock. It also involves hiring specialized lawyers and using an underwriter, who takes 10 percent of the IPO as a fee. The alternative is to buy a computer program called CapScape, which automates the process of compiling the offer documents. Then the shares can be sold directly to investors over the Internet.

Who will ultimately benefit from Internet IPOs? Small businesses. Who will lose? Lawyers, accountants, and financiers who specialize in raising money for small companies. The demand for their services should drop over time.

Example 5.6

$500 Million of Bonds Through the Internet?

One of the first major uses of the Internet in the capital market was to aid General Motors Acceptance Corporation (GMAC) in selling $500 million of bonds. It used Chicago Corporation, a regional investment bank, to get the job done. What Chicago did was unusual, though. It used a Web-based bulletin board called Direct Access Notes. Investors were able to download the prospectus for the bond offering and an interactive bond calculator. GMAC also developed a multimedia "dog and pony show" for its Web site. This allowed more investors to view the road show personally than would have otherwise. They bought bonds directly off of Chicago's Web site. Investors even participated in chat room discussions about the bond offering.

> ***For Critical Analysis:*** *Who benefits most from such Internet activities?*

THE MICRO THEORY OF BUSINESS BEHAVIOR WITH THE INTERNET ADDED

The theory of the way firms make decisions was developed well before the Internet became even a pipe dream. How has the advent of the Internet changed the theory of the firm? To understand the answers to this question we look at several areas, including pricing and cost of entry.

Pricing

In a competitive market, the perfect competitor has no control over price—the perfect competitor is a *price taker*. The market price simply equals the price at which the market demand curve intersects the market supply curve. A firm with any market power, however, is a *price setter*. The profit-maximizing price occurs at the quantity at which marginal revenue equals marginal cost, with the price being read off the market demand curve.

Marginal Cost for Software

Consider the issue of marginal cost. Once a software program is developed, the marginal cost of providing one more unit to the world via the Internet transmission is very close to zero. Moreover, this marginal cost is probably constant over all of the potential demanders throughout the entire world (at least with respect to the cost incurred by the offering firm). What, then, is the correct pricing decision for a software company that can provide millions of users with its product at a virtually zero marginal cost?

Such a pricing strategy cannot, however, provide revenues to compensate for the initial development costs of the program. So some software providers have come up with different ways to obtain revenues, even while "selling" their programs at a zero price. Microsoft Corporation has offered its Internet Explorer at no charge for years now. It obtains revenues from the advertising that it sells on the Explorer pages. Netscape went one step further at the beginning of 1998 and opened up its entire Navigator program free to the world. Anybody can modify Navigator now to suit a particular environment. The share of Netscape's total revenues from its Navigator browser program had already fallen to 13 percent when it made this policy change. The other 87 percent was obtained from the development of corporate intranets and the like.

Many software firms have offered their programs free of charge simply to "capture" the names of users to whom it might later sell upgraded versions. This is true, for example, of the free E-mail program Eudora. Some accounting software has also been given away free. The best-known example among game players is Doom. The first few levels of the game are given away free on the Net. Once "hooked," though, players pay extra to get to more difficult levels. Several million copies have now been sold.

Cost of Entry

One thing the Internet has certainly done is reduce the cost of entry, at least for companies willing to sell goods via the Internet. Amazon.com has no inventory, only an Internet site, programmers, and a small staff. Numerous CD retailers on the Internet carry no inventories. The megamalls on the Internet carry no inventories. Entry and operating costs cover simply development of the software retailing programs, paying for the server, and other relatively modest outlays.

Example 5.6

Your Business on the Net for $25,000

If you have an existing retail business, you can set up on the Net for an initial investment of $25,000. The offer to do so was announced by Pandesic at the beginning of 1998. For the $25,000 fee, a small to midsized company can obtain everything it needs to put its business on the Net—and do so in less than six weeks. This includes computer hardware (a server) plus software programs to handle finance, shipping, and inventory. In addition, however, once the retailer is on the Net and up and running, Pandesic takes a fee of 1 to 6 percent of monthly sales. In return, Pandesic provides all of the installation, training, upgrades, and maintenance of the system. This approach has been taken by Thin Blue Line, Inc., a small mountain-bike maker in Canada that has stormed the U.S. market via its Web site.

For Critical Analysis: To make a profit, what else must a company do besides get on the Net?

The Global Connection

One thing is certain: Because anybody can set up an e-commerce site from anywhere in the world, the Internet is easing entry into any retailing or wholesaling business. Moreover, foreigners can operate Internet sites just as U.S. citizens can. Thus worldwide competition is a given on the Internet. Software that can be downloaded from anywhere is a clear example.

READING

The Relationship Between Business and Higher Education: A Perspective on the 21st Century

John Sculley

> As might be expected, John Sculley, the former CEO of Apple Computer, is also interested in the intersection between computers and education, in this case higher education. In his article, first published in 1989 by the Association of Computing Machinery, Sculley argues that as we move toward the twenty-first century, three electronic technologies are essential for new learning environments: hypermedia, simulation, and artificial intelligence. In presenting what he calls a "new paradigm for lifelong learning," Sculley outlines educational priorities that many of you will recognize in your own experience with schooling. He also presents an example of a particular kind of software, or courseware, that begins to assimilate the three. He ends his piece with the observation that in the twenty-first century there is the possibility of creating a second Renaissance heralded by the new technologies.

We are privileged to live during an extraordinary time. It is the turning of an era. The world is in passage from the industrial age to the information age. This is a time of profound changes, in which the key economic resources in the world will no longer be capital, labor, and raw materials, but rather knowledge, individual innovators, and information.

Technologies which are emerging today will give us the ability to explore, convey, and create knowledge as never before. This has enormous implications for us as individuals, as well as for our institutions. Our colleges and universities will take on especially heavy responsibilities as we make this transition.

We have an opportunity that is given only to few generations in history. I believe that if we respond with our best creative energies, we can unleash a new Renaissance of discovery and learning.

In our global economy, we are moving from a hierarchical order to one of interdependence. Not long ago the United States stood unchallenged at the top of the world's economic hierarchy. Drawing on the consuming power of an affluent population, this country built a strong industrial base. Our manufacturing companies added value to natural resources through technological know-how. Economies of scale favored the development of large, highly structured institutions.

Today, however, we are not at the top of a pyramid, but rather one node along a network. Our once exclusive know-how is available in many newly industrialized nations, such as Korea, Taiwan, Singapore, Mexico, and Brazil. What is at risk, as the United States loses economic primacy, is not simply our own standard of living, but also the health of the world economy. The global economic system functions like a biological ecosystem. An unbalance in one sector can affect the whole.

A good analogy can be found in the shrinking rain forests of Brazil. Eighty percent of the world's oxygen comes from the Brazilian rain forest. Yet we lose every year, through the cutting of trees and the clearing of land, a land mass the size of the state of Nebraska. If we keep doing that long enough, the decreasing amount of oxygen in the atmosphere will alter the entire ecosystem of the planet.

The United States participates in the world economy not simply as a producer, but also as a marketplace. If our population loses the ability to afford our own products, it also will not afford Japanese automobiles, electronics from the Pacific Rim countries, and so forth. And that would have a tremendous impact on the macroeconomic ecosystem of the world.

Yet it is clear that as a nation, we are living beyond our means. We are no longer creating enough value to sustain our lifestyle, we are falling deeper into debt. There is a compelling need to find new ways to continue to create value in the world.

I believe that in order to do that our businesses and universities must be designed to foster innovation. Yet innovation has never come through bureaucracy and hierarchy. It has always come from individuals.

There is a dangerous timelag built into even the most successful institutions. They are created at one time in response to some particular opportunity in a given historical context. And then as the context shifts, the institution finds itself carrying excess baggage that is no longer useful.

How will the organizations designed to thrive in the 19th and early 20th centuries learn to contribute to the 21st? Only by reinventing themselves through refocusing on *individuals*.

The key strength of 21st-century organizations will be not their size or structure, but their ability to simultaneously unleash and coordinate the creative contributions of many individuals. Unleashing and coordinating may sound like contradictory actions and in older models they would be—but we must develop new patterns of organization that promote alignment and collaboration while avoiding rigidity and stagnation.

A Lifetime of Learning

Communication in the new organization will be more fluid, action more spontaneous. Think of the speed and agility of basketball versus the massed force of football. Think of a jazz combo trading solos, versus a marching band in lock step. The individuals who will succeed as contributors in these new organizations also need to change. In fact, change will be the one constant in their careers.

Over-specialization and a limited perspective can be a dead-end trap. Students today cannot count on finding one smooth career path because jobs that exist today will change radically (by the millions) tomorrow. Individuals will need to have tremendous flexibility to be able to move from one company to another, or from one industry to another. Those who are best prepared to do that will be the most successful.

We used to talk of "taking a position with the firm." Those are revealing words: *position* and *firm* belong to a static model of rigid hierarchy. If you are only going to take one position, you can get by on only one point of view. In the information age, however, a diverse educational experience will be the critical foundation for success. What tomorrow's student will need is not just mastery of subject matter, but mastery of *learning*. Education will be not simply a prelude to a career, but a lifelong endeavor.

Let me list some of the requirements of this new paradigm for lifelong learning:

- It should require rigorous mastery of subject matter under expert guidance.
- It should hone the conceptual skills that wrest meaning from data.

- It should promote a healthy skepticism that tests reality against multiple points of view.
- It should nourish individual creativity and encourage exploration.
- It should support collaboration.
- It should reward clear communication.
- It should provoke a journey of discovery.
- And above all it should be energized by the opportunity to contribute to the total of what we know and what we can do.

Higher education has traditionally defined itself in terms of two missions: instruction and research. In the past, these have been seen as very different activities. Research, which is primarily the domain of faculty and graduate students, is the process whereby we increase the world's store of knowledge. Instruction, which involves all students, is the process whereby we transfer some subset of that knowledge to *individuals*.

But, as we have seen, it is no longer enough simply to transfer knowledge to students. It is thought we can give young people a ration of knowledge that they can draw on throughout their careers. Instead, we need to give them access to the unbounded world of knowledge. That means we must prepare all students, not just professional scholars, to embark on a lifetime of learning and discovery. Which means that our students will not simply be passively absorbing subject matter . . . but be more like researchers actively exploring their environment.

To work in research is to recognize that knowledge does not reside privately in individual minds, or text books, or journals, or libraries, or laboratories, or databases. Knowledge resides in a complex web that encompasses all of these. To work in research is to recognize that knowledge is not static. Everyone in the research community shares the responsibility to test our knowledge and to enlarge it.

The challenge for higher education will be to find ways of bringing to the process of instruction the passion for discovery that drives research. Students today should master the skills and tools of research as part of their basic education. To give our students this mastery, we must create a learning environment in which research and instruction are integrated.

I believe we all can make important contributions to that process. If we succeed we will have found new ways of empowering individuals—not in isolation from each other, but with pathways for rich communication and effective collaboration.

A Lesson in History

The transformation I am calling for—shifting focus from the institution to the individual—has a close parallel in history. In medieval Europe people were subservient to the institutions of the church and feudal hierarchies.

Then came the Renaissance, which redefined the individual as the epicenter of intellectual activity. It did more than change people's perspective of the world, it literally invented perspective. The medieval painter depicted great religious events with the most important figures appearing the largest. Composition reflected ideology. Then drawing styles changed. The Renaissance artist drew figures and buildings in perspective, the way they appeared to an individual observer. For the first time, point-of-view came into the world.

The many forces which converged to bring about the Renaissance galvanized around one key technology: printing. The rise of printing led with astonishing speed to an explosion of literacy. The result was a new self-esteem for the individual. A wealth of invention. An excitement of the power of wonderful ideas. Today, we are in need of a second Renaissance, which like the first can also be galvanized by technology.

We are on the verge of creating new tools which, like the press, will empower individuals, unlock worlds of knowledge, and forge a new community of ideas. These core technologies and the tools they support will help create a new environment of lifetime learning.

We believe the tools that show the most promise for the new learning environment build on three core technologies: hypermedia, simulation, and artificial intelligence. Each of these technologies alone can enrich the educational process. Each gains additional strength when learners can share resources over networks. And when these technologies are fully integrated with each other, they will fuel a 21st-century Renaissance—an outpouring of new learning and achievement.

Technological Tools

Hypermedia is a new word for many of us. Yet this term and its definition will become increasingly important the more we rely on personal computers to store, manage and retrieve information.

In broad terms, hypermedia is the delivery of information in forms that go beyond traditional list management and database report methods. More specifically, it means that you do not have to follow a predetermined organization for information. Instead you can make instant choices about where to go next. What this means for instruction and research is that content is not bound by particular choices of organization. Instead content and organization become complementary tools that act on each other to deepen our understanding of the world around us.

Hypermedia lets us use a type of cross-reference that can be used to span courses that present related material, like physiology or microbiology. It gives us the capability to explore deeper, linking one idea with another as the student or researcher pursues his own personal learning path.

In a sense, hypermedia is nothing new at all. A researcher using a card catalog and reference materials traditionally had the opportunity to pursue ideas according to insight and interest. Hypermedia does not change that process, it merely *accelerates* it.

It's a natural way of working, but until recently, personal computers were too limited to address it. Today, however, desktop computers can have more information on line than the largest mainframe managed 10 years ago. We are coming to expect high-capacity magnetic hard disks, optical media such as CD-ROM, and high-speed networks as standard in our installations.

Once we have experienced hypermedia, established methods of finding related pieces of Information seem cumbersome. Hypermedia can also be seen as a new form of publishing. There are now readily available tools that enable faculty in any discipline to create richly branching presentations. The major obstacles still to be cleared are not technological, but social and economic. We have not yet devised licensing procedures for the electronic formats of the textbook or journal abstracts.

We must all work together to address such issues as copyright and royalties, and access and security in the information age. Just as hypermedia offers a new paradigm for exploring vast amounts of information, the second core technology, simulation, pushes the boundaries of experimentation. Simulation takes us beyond the "what" to the "how and why." We move from a static picture to dynamic visualization—from limited experience to diverse, multiple experiences.

The excitement in educational simulations today comes from generalized programs which allow professors and students to design their own simulations in particular disciplines, simulations that permit virtually all dynamic phenomena to be modeled and visualized.

Just as the spreadsheet allowed us to ask "what if" questions about financial calculations, this new class of software allows those "what if" questions to act on a dynamic graphic system, whether in physics, chemistry, electronics, or economics.

Another new application of simulation is in the humanities and social sciences, not normally what you would think of as computer-intensive disciplines. At Stanford University, a toolkit built on HyperCard has been designed in deference to a traditionally non-programming group: the humanities and social sciences faculty. (See box.)

Using this toolkit, called ALIAS, professors or students in anthropology, history, or sociology can model a culture or period of history by entering their data into the toolkit. ALIAS will in turn create a HyperCard stack that allows students to play the role of an individual of that culture. It is an approach that combines simulation and hypermedia.

In fact, this very simulation has been developed by Stanford Professor Harumi Befu. It's called SHOGAI, which means life course. To Professor Befu, SHOGAI means a new territory for his anthropology students; one in which they can explore the richness of Japan's people, its customs, and events, by assuming the roles of characters profiled in the simulation.

Using this simulation, students can make some critical decisions about school, social activities and work that will collectively dictate the character's niche in Japanese society. The point is to understand how and why the choices they make for him will determine the career opportunities he will have and the social status he can achieve. As different choices are made, different results will unfold.

Simulation and hypermedia tools exist today. As they come into more widespread use we will find two things happening. First, authors and publishers will continue to enrich our libraries of linked subject matter. And second, developers will continue to make the underlying tools more powerful. We will have full, three-dimensional motion graphics, and stunning images on CD-ROM. But perhaps the most spectacular advance will not be in the presentation level, but will lie deeper in the programming.

Sooner Than We Think

Just a short way into the future, we will see artificial intelligence (AI) emerge as a core technology. Combined with our core technologies, AI will boost simulations and hypermedia to new levels of realism and usefulness. For example, we will move from building

---

Sculley Envisions Life by 2001 P.C.

By the turn of the century, John Sculley predicts personal computers will house the type of technology and interface design that will seem like descendants of today's UNIX and Macintosh systems. He calls this futuristic PC the Knowledge Navigator and has described in several recent speeches the five key technologies crucial to its success.

The first feature is advanced communications technology that can link processors and databases around the world, thus providing better vehicles and broader information pathways. Secondly, real-time, 3-D color animations will become commonplace as users rely more on graphic simulations. Such capabilities will allow scientists to visualize complex numerical models with the same ease with which they now graph a column on a spreadsheet.

Improved database technology—element number three—is the key to creating intuitive and responsive information systems. One approach that Sculley claims shows great promise involves mapping and storing information into object-oriented structures.

Fourth is hypermedia, which will give future PC users more intuitive ways of navigating through enormous collections of information: combining text, graphics, sound, and motion. Rounding out the essentials is artificial intelligence technology—critical to the future vision of personal computing. All will allow future users to create agents that can recognize and anticipate strategies and preferences as well as increase productivity.

molecules into two-and three-dimensional space, to building the environment in which they combined where each molecule understands the structure and behavior of the other.

Another important contribution of AI will be intelligent agents that can learn a user's preferences and search strategies. These agents will transform the nature of academic computing. Agents will be sent to prowl among remote databases and bring back the specific information and citations that the user requires.

These future systems are not that far away. Soon, faculty and students will be using systems that enable them to drive through libraries, museums, databases or institutional archives. These tools will not just take you to the doorstep of these great resources, as sophisticated computers do now; they will invite you deep inside its secrets, interpreting and explaining—converting vast quantities of information into personalized and understandable knowledge.

In a (previous) keynote address, Dr. Herb Simon, professor of computer science and psychology at Carnegie Mellon, reminded, "We think of revolutions as being sudden events, producing far reaching changes in a very short period of time. But the revolution launched by the steam engine took, by any reasonable account, 150 years." Changes in computing have been like a whirlwind in the last 40 years. But I think we have only begun to see what innovation and creativity can produce in this industry.

The personal computer could become as galvanizing as the printing press in stimulating change in the world, in creating an environment for innovation and new ideas. Let us remember that the printing press never wrote a single book. Authors write books. So, too, with the new technologies that I have described. This will only be achieved if we work together—universities, corporations and government—and if we recognize the role of the creative individual within these organizations.

We all have a role in making this vision of the future a reality. The technologies I have talked about are only platforms that represent opportunities and possibilities. They are, however, the tallest of platforms, the richest of opportunities, and the broadest of possibilities that I know of.

They will allow us to set loose an avalanche of personal creativity and achievement. Once we have thousands of ideas to harvest, we may have the chance once again to create a second Renaissance, perhaps every bit as important as the first, in the early part of the next century. It would represent a rebirth and revival of learning and culture unleashed by new technologies. It would bridge the gaps between the arts and sciences. And it would signify the emergence of an integrated environment for instruction and research.

It is an exhilarating time to live. I cannot think of any other time in history in which such profound change has gripped each decade. It is destined to be an eventful journey to the 21st century. And there is no place that journey will be more exciting than in higher education.

THINKING AND REREADING

1. As you reread, take notes on how Sculley sees education as changing this coming century. What does he see as one of the more important changes that occurred in the historical period commonly referred to as the Renaissance? Why does he think that in the early twenty-first century "we can unleash a new Renaissance of discovery and learning"? Give examples that support his view from the reading and from your experience. What changes in learning does he see as characterizing what he calls the second or twenty-first century Renaissance?

2. The title of Sculley's article talks of "the relationship between business and higher education." List the changes he sees as occurring in business settings. How does his twenty-first-century notion of the "individual" differ from the "individual" he writes of as emerging in the original Renaissance?

3. In what ways do Strassmann and Sculley agree about the future priorities of education? Disagree? What educational activities might be appropriate today that were not possible when Sculley was writing his article?

Writing and Thinking

1. Think back on your educational experiences in high school, and jot down the different ways in which computers were used in a variety of your classes. Imagine now that your high school is considering revamping its curriculum and has asked its alums for help in setting priorities. Choose one area of your high school education and write a letter to the administrators and teachers, suggesting changes to the curriculum based on Sculley's article and your own educational experiences. In your letter, describe one particular use of computers that you find particularly promising for students. What kinds of learning would this activity have that you and your classmates missed out on? Why is such learning important in your opinion? You might begin your letter by first praising or thanking your teachers for the activities and learning experiences they offered that you have come to value.

2. Set up an interview with a college professor or high school teacher whom you regard as being particularly knowledgeable about teaching with the new information technologies. Construct an interview based on Sculley's, and your own views of the current priorities for education. Share these with another member of your class until both you and your classmate are satisfied with the questions you will ask. If it is acceptable to the person you are interviewing, tape-record the interview, all the while taking notes as well. Write up a report of the interview in which you compare your interviewee's thoughts about technology and education with those you've encountered in the readings, and share it with others in your class.

Will Our Future Be Workable?

William Raspberry

William Raspberry began his career in journalism in Indiana before joining the *Washington Post*. He now writes one local column and two syndicated columns each week, usually focusing on urban or race problems or issues regarding the poor, as this June 5, 1995, column on work reveals.

Prepare

1. From what you know about the author and the selection, what can you predict about purpose and format or style?
2. State briefly what you expect to read about.
3. What do you already know about the topic?
4. Use the title to pose questions about the reading selection.

5. Preread the selection. Then read and annotate the article. Finally, complete the comprehension and vocabulary checks that follow and answer the questions for discussion and reflection.

There is something about us human beings that doesn't like work. We look forward to weekends and vacations and retirement. We speak disparagingly of those who love work—workaholics, we call them. Sometimes we think it almost blasphemous to like work; after all, wasn't work God's punishment for the sins of Adam and Eve? Our futuristic musing are virtual hymns to anti-work; machines run everything, make everything, do everything.

And yet we value work—very nearly worship it. We assign it great dignity and moral power. We look down on those who don't (or won't) work, counting them as less than full contributing member of society. In our ideal world, everybody would have a job.

Is there any way to reconcile these two contradictory ideas?

The question is not merely philosophical. It has deep implications for our society; particularly as machines (robots, computers, and the entire range of information Age technology) take over more of the work that humans used to do. It's something Jeremy Rifkin has been thinking a great deal about.

"On the micro level," he said the other day, "every business leader and CEO is determined to replace bodies with thinking machines. The machines are more reliable and more productive; they make fewer demands and work longer hours. Using them gives a company a major advantage.

"But on the macro level, if everybody uses machines to replace human beings, the obvious question is: Who will buy their products?"

It's a point he made in his new book, *The End of Work*, and in a fascinating interview. "I recently talked to the Young Presidents' Organization, and I asked these young executives how many of them are re-engineering and downsizing and letting people go, and most of them raised their hands. How many of them saw fewer employees in their corporate futures? All of them. But when I asked them what they were going to do with these people—their customer base as well as their work pool—they had no idea.

"They are smart enough to see that they are building tremendous inventories in the face of falling purchasing power, but they haven't seen the connection—that both have the same source."

There are other similar dilemmas on the man vs. machine landscape. For example, says Rifkin: "We already have near-workerless factories in such industries as insurance and bank—and not just because the machines are more efficient. There are advantages to having a small, highly trained work force that go beyond efficiency or even health insurance costs. Pensions, for instance, are a big chuck of employer costs, and the fewer workers you have the smaller the outlays for pension plans.

"But as corporations let people go, the pension funds dwindle, and then you discover that it is the pension funds that have kept the economy going; they are the main form of savings for the capitalist system, a third of the bond and stock markets, worth more than the commercial assets of all the banks in America. They are, in fact, the main source of funds for the shift to the Information Age."

There's a third dilemma. As much as companies love low-cost production and high profits, they fear instability. But the same forces that produce the one threaten to produce the other. The incipient instability is not immediately obvious, as it might be in periods of high unemployment. But look at the nature of much of today's employment: part-time work, contingent work, sporadic work—erstwhile employees transmogrified into "independent contractors," which is to say workers without security and the fringe benefits we had come to expect.

Not only do insecure workers buy fewer of the goods businesses want to sell, which tends to destabilize markets, but they also tend to earn less, thereby accelerating the polarization of rich and poor. The very economic changes that make entrepreneurs rich also create the instability and uncertainty that threaten their economic survival.

The issues Rifkin raises seem so obvious that you wonder why we haven't spent more time talking about them. Most of our future-of-work conversations explore only the edge of his concerns. We recognize that work is becoming more technical, but take little notice of the fact that there will be less of it. We talk about the growing gap in real earnings between the elite workers and the blue-collar class, but we delude ourselves into believing that the answer lies in periodical retraining. We accept the idea that work is the solution to welfare dependency—indeed we are ready to accept two-years-and-out as a reasonable way of nudging people back into the world of work.

But to do *what*? It's a question worth exploring.

THINKING AND REREADING

1. As you reread this piece, identify Raspberry's topic. State it so that you indicate the structure/strategy that he uses.
2. Briefly explain the three economic consequences of companies downsizing.
3. What response to the situation (or solution to the problem) does Raspberry dismiss?

WRITING AND LEARNING

1. Raspberry says that most of us have conflicting views of work. Do you share his view? Do you think that many Americans hold these conflicting views?
2. What group of people is Raspberry especially concerned about as he sees the trends to employ machines rather than people?
3. If his view of the future workplace is accurate, what should we as a society be doing? What solutions do you have?

6

The Individual as a Successful Technology Student

The last chapter focused on the effects of technology on society and on the individual. You learned about the impact of change and how important it is to be well-equipped to adapt to our everchanging world. In order to prepare yourself for a successful career in such an environment, you need to maximize your educational performance in college to ensure the best outcome.

This chapter focuses on learning in the college environment, and how to identify and apply your own particular learning style to make class and study choices that are in sync with your personal style.

HOW TO BE SUCCESSFUL IN TECHNOLOGY

What does it take to be successful in technology? The good news is that we *know* the answer to these questions: Thousand of students have been doing it for years. As a first-year student, your biggest advantage lies in the fact that many people have already done what you have decided to do, namely, graduate in technology. To find out what you need to do, you need only draw from the experiences of the many *successful* technology students who have gone before you. That is what this chapter is about: the tried *and* tested techniques that will guarantee you success in technology study.

The most successful technology students exhibit common key characteristics in their approach to technology study. The following table lists those characteristics, along with actions typically associated with each.

In the sections that follow, we discuss each of the preceding characteristics and how they will guide you to success as a technology student.

Commitment

When you chose technology as your career, did you *decide* to be successful, or did you simply *prefer* to be successful? There is a significant difference between the two approaches, particularly when applied to engineering study. When you decide to succeed in technology:

There is no alternative: Failure is not an option.

Characteristic	**Actions**
Commitment	*Decide* to be successful.
	Set appropriate *goals.*
	Stay *focused.*
	Stay *determined* to succeed.
	Continually remind yourself of the *reasons* you chose technology.
Application	*Apply* yourself fully to attain your goals.
	Work hard.
Strategy	*Work* smart.
	Maximize effectiveness.
	Learn the rules and play the game.
Perseverance	*Don't* give up after the first, second, or third try.
	Keep going.
	Stay focused on your goals.
	Use *power thinking*!
Associations	Associate with people who maintain a positive
	attitude, people who will help you attain your goals.
	Avoid underachievers and those who do not share your objectives.

When you simply prefer to succeed in technology:

You allow yourself the option of failure.

Each approach has significant consequences for your performance as a technology student.

When you decide to be successful, you become focused, determined, and committed to success. Graduating in technology becomes your top priority. You do *not* allow yourself the option of failure. Your mind responds accordingly, allowing you access to the full range of your abilities. This, in turn, maximizes your effectiveness and subsequent performance as a technology student.

By merely preferring to succeed in technology, you allow yourself the option of failure: You believe that there is always an alternative, for example, a career in science or business, or perhaps in the "real world." The message your mind gets is that it's okay to fail. Consequently, you become reluctant to apply yourself, you don't try as hard, you lose focus, and you become less determined to succeed. All of this results in less-than-satisfactory performance.

Committed students had no *inner conflict*—they never fight themselves. They know what they want, and they go after it. In doing so, they refuse to lose.

Your level of *commitment* is one of the most important factors in deciding your performance as a technology student.

Commitment = Deciding to Succeed

Start your path to success by deciding that you will graduate in technology. Make this your major goal and commit to it. This will equip you with maximum power to achieve that goal. To maintain this commitment, keep in mind the following:
1. You chose technology for definite *reasons.* Stay focused and determined by reminding yourself of these reasons frequently.
2. Believe in yourself—go for it!

Application

Some people find it easy to get good grades in high school without working too hard. This is usually attributed to the fact that they are endowed with some sort of natural academic ability (i.e., they are smart). There is one undeniable fact about technology study at the post-high school level:

You cannot be successful without hard work!

Many of the so-called smarter first-year technology students are lulled into a false sense of security, primarily because of their high school experience. They believe that they can carry on as they left off in high school and achieve the same level of success with the same level of application. This belief is always destroyed around midterm time, when grades begin to tumble and they find themselves scrambling to recover. This, of course, is wasteful, counterproductive, extremely stressful, and completely unnecessary.

There are no hard-and-fast rules for how many hours you should spend studying per day, per week, or per semester. Application is more about *productivity* than hours spent. If you spend six hours in the local cafeteria with a group of "study buddies" and devote perhaps 20 percent of this time to doing anything meaningful, then you haven't studied for six hours. So don't fool yourself! The best way to approach technology study is to accept the fact that you must study as hard as is required of you. In this respect, professors are there to guide you. Relevant and necessary material is presented in lectures, seminars, and laboratories, and assigned as homework. It makes sense to ensure that, at a minimum, all assigned work is:

1. Completed accurately, thoughtfully, and in accordance with the requirements.
2. Understood entirely.
3. Recorded clearly for later review—it is always better to *review* than to *relearn* (see next section).

Any additional work, over and above that required and recommended by the professor, is a bonus—like money in the bank!

The very best technology students are always well aware of the fact that their performance is entirely dependent on how hard they choose to work. At the heart of this is the following belief:

"I'm doing this for me—not for my professor, but for me!"

That's right: Your professors are wonderful people, but at the end of the day, if you perform below your capabilities because you didn't apply yourself, you suffer the consequences, not your professors. Many first-year technology students believe they are doing their professors a favor by attending classes, completing assignments on time, and applying themselves fully to attain their goals. You are the primary beneficiary of all your hard work—not your professors—*you!* Whenever you feel reluctant to sit down and tackle a difficult assignment or attend an early lecture, repeat the following to yourself:

"This is for *me!* I'm doing this for me!"

The road to a technology degree is long and hard; if it were easy, the profession would never command the respect it enjoys today. Only very special people are successful in technology, and never forget that! Take time to remind yourself of the rewards of the profession, but *expect* and *accept* the discipline and hard work required to get there. After all, for the next two years or so, studying technology is your job, your mission, and your reason for being.

Strategy

Most of us drive a vehicle of some sort. To be able to drive that vehicle on public roads, there are basically two requirements:

1. To learn how to drive.
2. To pass a driving test.

Most of you will agree that knowing how to drive is necessary, but not sufficient, to pass a driving test. A driving test has certain specific requirements. For example, you must be able to execute selected maneuvers in certain ways (as required by an examiner) and demonstrate knowledge on all areas related to the driving experience. When preparing for a driving test, we do not simply spend time driving. That is not enough. Rather, we learn exactly what is required in the test and practice those *specific requirements*. We *rehearse* the actual test over and over again. Let's face it, many excellent drivers would not pass a driving test today without the necessary targeted preparation. Another way to look at this is, in deciding to pass a driving test, we:

1. Set the appropriate goal, i.e., to pass the driving test.
2. Discover the rules of the test, i.e., learn exactly what is required to pass the test.
3. Practice the specific requirements of the test.
4. Rehearse the test itself.
5. Pass the test.

Similarly, in studying technology, there are two basic requirements:

1. To learn all that is required to obtain a technology degree.
2. To be successful on a (large) number of tests and examinations.

Like it or not, tests and examinations continue to dominate as indicators of student performance at technical schools. For this reason, they will occupy much of your time and energy over the course of your degree. *Examination technique* (preparing for and writing examinations) is therefore extremely significant in determining your overall performance in technology. For example, as in the case of driving a car, it is not sufficient to know the course material (even 100 percent) to demonstrate excellence on a test. The reason is that the latter is a *time-constrained* examination of your abilities. Because of this, there are many additional factors at play that will affect your performance in an examination (e.g., *exam anxiety*). To deal with these additional factors, effective test preparation must include, among other things, the following two strategies:

1. Find out, learn, and practice the *specific* requirements of the test. (*Target* your review.)
2. Rehearse (and dress rehearse) the test. (Work through sample or past examinations.)

These form the basis of an effective examination technique.

Perseverance

When you try something new, a certain amount of trial and error is inevitable. Consequently, as you strive toward your major goals of graduating in technology, you *will* be faced with setbacks, disappointments, and frustrations. Adversity is inherent in technology study; It's part of the process. How you deal with adversity, however, will determine, to a large extent, whether or not you are successful in technology. Consider Example 6.1.

Example 6.1

John has a big problem with one of the homework questions in Descriptive Geometry CD240. He has been working on this problem for hours. Not only is it an important assignment problem, but also, it illustrates a key concept that John simply must understand. He consults his professor during office hours. The professor scribbles some equations on John's page and tells John that this should fix his problem. There are other students waiting to see the professor, so John leaves, sits in the hallway, and tries to understand what the professor has told him, but is not convinced. He returns to his professor, who politely and persistently continues to give John the same explanation. John listens respectfully, but keeps coming up with reasons the explanation does not make sense. He once again adjourns to the hallway. Recognizing the urgency of his situation, John returns again to his professor. Politely and professionally, he once more presents the same problems to his professor. By now, John knows the problem intimately, so he knows exactly what to ask. He persists with his counterarguments, but this time he gets what he wants. He leaves the professor's office knowing that he has achieved his immediate goal. John hung in there, pursuing his desired outcome.

The key to John's success was *perseverance*. He had to have the information. This was his immediate goal, and his perseverance allowed him to achieve that goal.

Perseverance is what drives committed individuals to success.

The previous scenario has been played out many times. The advantages for the student are numerous:

1. The student now knows how to solve the problem.
2. The student now knows that he or she can always come to the professor for help—without feeling intimidated.
3. The professor is impressed with the student's ability to communicate ideas and with the student's enthusiasm for and commitment to his or her work.

Adversity is not what prevents people from achieving their goals; it's what people do in the face of adversity that counts. Successful technology students persevere whenever they encounter adversity—they don't give up. They hate the idea of not being able to achieve their goals.

Perhaps the most important reason to persevere in technology study is to develop an effective problem-solving technique, as illustrated by Example 6.2.

Example 6.2

Linda encounters a really challenging problem. She consults her notes and looks for something "similar." This allows her to make a start on the solution. Soon, however, the solution path diverges considerably from any of the examples in the class notes and course textbook. She's stuck! What does Linda do next? It's the middle of the evening, so she cannot see her professor until the next day. She can leave it until then, or she can take a break and try again. The latter is what she does. She sits for a while and tries different things, such as inventing, adjusting, and experimenting with the solution technique. Adversity begins to creep in, but she perseveres. Soon she is very well acquainted with what will work and with what won't work in this particular problem. Then, all of a sudden it hits her! Bingo! She solves the problem.

Have you ever had such an experience? Many students have told me of similar experiences and compared them to air travel. That is, to solve the problem, they had to move up a level of thinking. As in air travel, moving up a level meant that it was necessary to go through the inevitable turbulence (adversity). Once they had fastened their safety belts (analogous to perseverance) and passed to the next level, they entered into the *power-thinking* zone, which enabled them to solve the problem. Entering the power-thinking zone may not be sufficient (i.e., you may have to ask for outside help eventually), but it certainly is necessary to learn how to solve the problem yourself.

We summarize effective problem solving in the following three stages:

Stage 1   Acquaint yourself with the details of the problem, define the goal, and decide that nothing will stop you from achieving that goal.

Stage 2   Try some obvious solutions. Use class notes or the course textbook. This is where adversity begins to creep in. You become frustrated with each setback.

Stage 3   Here, you are well acquainted with all details of the problem. You know more or less what doesn't work, and you have narrowed down the search to a few alternatives. You may seek some help, but you are highly focused nonetheless. This stage allows for power, *or* deep thinking. The problem is solved here.

Perseverance is what allows you to progress to Stage 3. In addition, the following are true of perseverance:

1. *Ingenuity increases with perseverance.* As you move from stage to stage, you try smarter or more informed solutions, you really hone your problem-solving skills, and you *learn* from the experience.
2. Perseverance is necessary to *warm up* your thinking so that you may enter the *success zone,* i.e., so that you may proceed from Stage 1 to Stage 3.
3. Perseverance allows you to break through into *power thinking.*

Associations

Have you ever noticed how you tend to pick up the habits of the people with whom you associate the most? For example, you may find yourself:

- Using the same words or phrases.
- Believing the same things.
- Enjoying the same things.
- Doing the same things.
- Finding the same things distasteful.
- Developing the same attitudes.

You may do all of these things just by association.

If you are committed to achieving your goal of graduating in technology, your choice of friends and colleagues is extremely significant when it comes to progressing toward that goal. Imagine for a moment that your best friend:

1. Always missed the 8 o'clock class in favor of an extra snooze.
2. Almost never handed in assignments on time.
3. Was part of a study group for the sole reason of copying solutions to assignments.
4. Made a habit of leaving everything to the last minute in favor of more important things such as movies, football games, nightclubs, and parties.
5. Retained certain high school attitudes, including the belief that it was *cool* to fail.
6. Talked or read the newspaper during lecture.

At best, a friend like this will distract you sufficiently to ensure that you never perform to your full potential. At worst, you will inherit similar characteristics and begin the downward spiral to failure!

In studying technology, it is *essential* that you align yourself with people who:

- Share your objectives.

- Will stretch you and *push* you toward your goals.
- Share your attitudes on studying technology.
- Strive for excellence.
- Are positive.
- Are suitable role models—share your hopes and dreams.

Your technology education represents a considerable investment in time, money, and effort. This is your *job* for the next two years or so, and you should do everything possible to maximize the effectiveness of your learning environment.

Begin by making a list of all the people who are significant in your life. Ask—do they contribute to or detract from your goals, the most important of which is graduating in technology. Then, systematically get the negative people out of your life. It takes a lot of time and energy to achieve your goals; you do not need the added burden of people who will slow you down and prevent you from realizing your dreams. Fill your life with positive, energizing people, people whom you admire and who are what you want to be.

Summation

Commitment, application, strategy, perseverance, and associations are all characteristics of successful students. If you practice and internalize these characteristics, you will be well on your way to success.

You can accelerate that success by examining some common assumptions about learning. In the next section, we address learning styles and help you to analyze your personal learning style.

WHAT ARE SOME COMMON ASSUMPTIONS ABOUT LEARNING?

The human mind is a powerful tool. Each person has a unique capacity to take in and process information. Certain common assumptions about learning, however, can prevent people from making the most of their abilities. Here are three such assumptions.

1. **There is one "best" way to learn, and the most successful people are those who learn that way**. It may seem that the educational system favors the verbal learner, and that the workplace favors the organized, detail-oriented worker. A design course might emphasize the visual, however, and a psychology course might emphasize interpersonal interaction. Furthermore, success in the workplace is not limited to one kind of learner. A software salesperson may use communication savvy to ride the wave to success, and a hospice worker may be valued most for personal integrity and caring.

2. **Everyone has a set capacity for learning**. The way people are often labeled reinforces the idea that everyone has the same capacity for learning. You go through your educational experience being given a place in line (97th in your class, a C on a scale of A to F), or being categorized (learning disabled, gifted and talented, developmental English, Advanced Placement History), based on your performance. These labels can lead you and others to form assumptions about your learning capacity. Such assumptions, however, can limit students to levels far below what they actually can achieve. Winston Churchill (Prime Minister of England during World War II) failed the sixth grade, for example, and Louis Pasteur (master chemist) was a poor student in chemistry.

3. **If you don't have a clear talent for something, you shouldn't pursue it**. It might seem that people who have certain talents don't even have to lift a finger to find success. Remember, though, that the information you receive about successful people sometimes is limited to what the media want to communicate. You might not hear about how hard these people work each day or the tough road that they traveled to get where they are. Ask questions of the people around you whom you consider to be successful. Did they have an immediate aptitude for what they do? What obstacles did, or do, they have to overcome? What kind of day-to-day hard work and learning lies behind the more visible side of what they do?

Think critically about these assumptions and any others you know of. Ask questions: What examples support or negate this statement? Does what I already know support it or not? Is it fact or opinion? What positive or negative effects might result from assuming this to be true?

There are many ways to learn, and different strategies are suited to different tasks and situations. Each person's learning style is unique. Like any other personality trait, learning style is part of your individual set of personal characteristics.

HOW CAN YOU DISCOVER YOUR LEARNING STYLE?

Many different assessments—by exploring strengths and weaknesses, abilities and limitations—help people discover how they learn. This chapter focuses on one assessment. You also can find information about other assessments, such as the widely used Myers-Briggs Type Indicator (MBTI) and the Keirsey Sorter (a shorter version of the MBTI), through your career or counseling center or even on-line.

After you complete the assessment, you will read about strategies that can help you make the most of certain aspects of your style, both in school and beyond. Knowing how you learn will help you to improve your understanding of yourself—how you function at school, in the workplace, and in your personal life.

Multiple Intelligences Theory

There is a saying, "It is not how smart you are, but how you are smart." In 1983, Howard Gardner, a Harvard University professor, published his theory of multiple intelligences and changed the way people perceive intelligence and learning. Gardner believes all people possess at least eight distinct intelligences, and that every person has developed some intelligences more fully than others. Most people have at one time learned something quickly and comfortably. Most also have had the opposite experience: No matter how hard they tried, something they wanted to learn just would not sink in. According to the multiple intelligences theory, when you find a task or subject easy, you probably are using a more fully developed intelligence; when you have more trouble, you may be using a less developed intelligence.

Following are brief descriptions of the focus of each of the intelligences. Study skills that reinforce each intelligence are described later in the chapter.

The multiple intelligences reach beyond helping you understand how you learn. They help you to see how you operate in every arena of life: how you think, how you relate to others, how you understand yourself, and more. Because this chapter focuses on learning styles, however, your collective set of scores will be referred to here as your "learning style." Elsewhere in the text you will find references that illustrate how the intelligences influence other skills and life areas.

Multiple Intelligences

Intelligence	Definition
Verbal-Linguistic	Ability to communicate through language (listening, reading, writing, speaking)
Logical-Mathematical	Ability to understand logical reasoning and problem solving (math, science, patterns, sequences)
Bodily-Kinesthetic	Ability to use the physical body skillfully and to take in knowledge through bodily sensation (coordination, working with hands)
Visual-Spatial	Ability to understand spatial relationships and perceive and create images (visual art, graphic design, charts, and maps)
Interpersonal	Ability to relate to others, noticing their moods, motivations, and feelings (social activity, cooperative learning, teamwork)
Intrapersonal	Ability to understand one's own behavior and feelings (self-awareness, independence, time spent alone)
Musical	Ability to comprehend and create meaningful sound (music, sensitivity to sound, understanding patterns)
Naturalistic	Ability to understand features of the environment (interest in nature, environmental balance, ecosystem, stress relief brought by natural environments)

Pathways to Learning

The following assessment of your multiple intelligences, *Pathways to Learning*, will help you determine the levels to which your intelligences are developed. Don't be concerned if some of your scores are low (that is true of almost everyone, even your instructors and the authors). To rate each statement, think critically. Evaluate how similar or different to your own behavior you consider the statement to be. The more closely you can see who you are today, the more effectively you can set goals for where you want to go from here.

The Reasonable Approach to Learning Style

No learning style assessment can give you the final word on who you are and what you can and cannot do. It's human to want an easy answer—a one-page printout of the secret to your identity—but this kind of quick fix does not exist. You are a complex person who cannot be summed up by a test or evaluation.

The most reasonable way to approach any assessment of learning style is as a reference point rather than a label. There are no "right" answers, no "best" set of intelligences scores. Instead of boxing yourself into one or more categories, which limits you, approach your learning style assessment as a tool with which you can expand your idea of yourself. Think of it as a new set of eyeglasses for a person with somewhat blurred vision. The glasses will not create new paths and possibilities for you, but they will help you see more clearly the paths and possibilities that already exist. They give you the power to explore, choose, and move ahead with confidence.

You will continually learn, change, and grow throughout your life. Any evaluation is simply a snapshot, a look at who you are at any given moment. The answers can, and will, change as you change and as circumstances change. They provide an opportunity for you to identify a moment and learn from it by asking questions: Who am I right now? How does this compare to who I want to be?

Pathways to Learning Assessment

Directions: Rate each statement as follows: rarely 1; sometimes 2; usually 3; always 4. Write the number of your response (1–4) in the box next to the statement and total each set of the six questions.

☐ 1. I enjoy physical activities.
☐ 2. I am uncomfortable sitting still.
☐ 3. I prefer to learn through doing.
☐ 4. When sitting, I move my legs or hands.
☐ 5. I enjoy working with my hands.
☐ 6. I like to pace when I'm thinking or studying.
☐   **TOTAL for Bodily-Kinesthetic**

☐ 7. I use maps easily
☐ 8. I draw pictures/diagrams when explaining ideas.
☐ 9. I can assemble items easily from diagrams.
☐ 10. I enjoy drawing or photography.
☐ 11. I do not like to read long paragraphs.
☐ 12. I prefer a drawn map over written directions.
☐   **TOTAL for Visual-Spatial**

☐ 13. I enjoy telling stories.
☐ 14. I like to write.
☐ 15. I like to read.
☐ 16. I express myself clearly.
☐ 17. I am good at negotiating.
☐ 18. I like to discuss topics that interest me.
☐   **TOTAL for Verbal-Linguistic**

☐ 19. I like math in school.
☐ 20. I like science.
☐ 21. I problem-solve well.
☐ 22. I question how things work.
☐ 23. I enjoy planning or designing something new.
☐ 24. I am able to fix things.
☐   **TOTAL for Logical-Mathematical**

☐ 25. I listen to music.
☐ 26. I move my fingers or feet when I hear music.
☐ 27. I have good rhythm.
☐ 28. I like to sing along with music.
☐ 29. People have said I have musical talent.
☐ 30. I like to express my ideas through music
☐   **TOTAL for Musical**

☐ 31. I like doing a project with other people.
☐ 32. People come to me to help settle conflicts.
☐ 33. I like to spend time with friends.
☐ 34. I am good at understanding people.
☐ 35. I am good at making people feel comfortable.
☐ 36. I enjoy helping others.
☐   **TOTAL for Interpersonal**

☐ 37. I need quiet time to think.
☐ 38. I think about issues before I want to talk.
☐ 39. I am interested in self-improvement.
☐ 40. I understand my thoughts and feelings.
☐ 41. I know what I want out of life.
☐ 42. I prefer to work on projects alone.
☐   **TOTAL for Intrapersonal**

☐ 43. I enjoy nature whenever possible.
☐ 44. I think about have a career involving nature.
☐ 45. I enjoy studying plants, animals, and oceans.
☐ 46. I avoid being indoors except when I sleep.
☐ 47. As a child I played with bugs and leaves.
☐ 48. When I feel stressed, I want to be out in nature.
☐   **TOTAL for Naturalistic**

Developed by Joyce Bishop, Ph.D., and based upon Howard Gardner, *Frames of Mind: The Theory of Multiple Intelligences.*

Below are eight empty bars, corresponding to the eight intelligences. For each intelligence, draw a line at your score and fill in the bar below the line.

	Bodily/ Kinesthetic	Visual/ Spatial	Verbal/ Linguistic	Logical/ Mathematical	Musical	Interpersonal	Intrapersonal	Naturalistic
24								
23								
22								
21								
20								
19								
18								
17								
16								
15								
14								
13								
12								
11								
10								
9								
8								
7								
6								
5								
4								
3								
2								
1								
0								

This chart will help you see visually which of your intelligences are most developed. You may have obvious strong and weak areas, or your chart may reveal a relative balance among the intelligences. There is no right answer—your strengths are simply your strengths! Take advantage of them!

In addition, you may change which multiple intelligences you emphasize, depending on the situation. For example, a student might find it easy to take notes in outline style when the instructor lectures in an organized way. If another instructor jumps from topic to topic, however, the student might choose to use the Cornell system or a think link.

Now that you know a little more about which of your intelligences are strongest, you can apply that knowledge to your learning environment. First, it is important to avoid labeling yourself based on one intelligence, such as saying, "I'm no good in math" because your scores were lower in the "logical/mathematical" intelligence. Anyone can learn math, but perhaps you can learn math more easily using one of your other intelligences. For example, if you have a more developed visual-spatial intelligence, you may want to draw diagrams of a math problem to help you understand it.

Remember that there is no general benefit to one type of intelligence over another. People are a blend of all the intelligences, in proportions unique to them. No person fits exclusively into one category or another. When material is difficult or when you are feeling insecure about learning something new, use your most developed intelligences. When something is easy for you, try using one of your less developed intelligences to learn in new ways. The following tips can help you develop study habits based on your multiple intelligences to make learning easier.

Visual/Spatial

- Use visuals in your notes such as timelines, charts, graphs, and geometric shapes.
- Work to create a mental or visual picture of the information at hand.
- Use colored markers to make associations or to group items together.
- Use mapping or webbing so that your main points are easily recognized.
- When taking notes, draw pictures in the margins to illustrate the main points.
- Visualize the information in your mind.

Verbal/Linguistic

- Establish study groups so that you will have the opportunity to talk about the information.
- Using the information you studied, create a story or a skit.
- Read as much information about related areas as possible.
- As you read chapters, outline them in your own words.
- Summarize and recite your notes aloud.

Musical/Rhythm

- Listen to music while studying (if it does not distract you).
- Write a song or rap about the chapter or information.
- Take short breaks from studying to listen to music.
- Commit the information being studied to the music from your favorite song.

Logic/Math

- Strive to make connections between subjects.
- Don't just memorize the facts; apply them to real-life situations.
- As you study the information, think of problems in society and how this information could solve those problems.

- Create analyzing charts. Draw a line down the center of the page, put the information at hand in the left column and analyze, discuss, relate, and synthesize it in the right column.
- Allow yourself some time to reflect after studying.

Body/Kinesthetic

- Don't confine your study area to a desk or chair; move around, explore, go outside.
- Act out the information.
- Study in a group of people and change groups often.
- Use charts, posters, flashcards, and chalkboards to study. When appropriate or possible, build models using the information studied.
- Verbalize the information to others.
- Use games such as chess, Monopoly, Twister, or Clue when studying.
- Trace words as you study them.
- Use repetition to learn facts; write them many times.
- Make study sheets.

Interpersonal

- Study in groups.
- Share the information with other people.
- Teach the information to others.
- Interview outside sources to learn more about the material at hand.
- Have a debate with others about the information.

Intrapersonal

- Study in a quiet area.
- Study by yourself.
- Allow time for reflection and meditation about the subject matter.
- Study in short time blocks and then spend some time absorbing the information.
- Work at your own pace.

Naturalistic

- Study outside whenever possible.
- Relate the information to the effect on the environment whenever possible.
- When given the opportunity to choose your own topics or research projects, choose something related to nature.
- Collect your own study data and resources.
- Organize and label your information.
- Keep separate notebooks on individual topics so that you can add new information to each topic as it becomes available to you.

LEARNING STYLES THEORY

Another way that educational psychologists have attempted to understand learning and intelligence is to examine how individuals actually learn or process information. This is called learning styles theory. While this may seem similar to the theory of multiple intelligences, learning styles focuses more on the process of learning (how you absorb, think about, and evaluate information) rather than on your natural talents and abilities as described in the eight areas of intelligence. Think of multiple intelligences and learning styles as two different approaches to the same things—helping you better understand yourself so you can improve your learning and career choices.

I vividly remember my first job after graduation; I was assigned to work as part of a team developing instrumentation for use in military aircraft. The project leader was an ex-air-force commander called Stan. He was an electrical engineer by training, but had extensive experience in aerodynamics and applied mathematics. My job was to develop a mathematical model for the aircraft in flight, so that we could test onboard measuring instruments in the lab. To do this, I needed to know how the various motions of the aircraft would affect the different variables used in my model; I knew more about vectors and geometry than I did about aerodynamics, so I took my mathematics to Stan's office and asked him how I should adjust the equations so that my model adequately represented the aircraft's motion. Stan pulled out a diagram of the aircraft and began to describe how air resistance, sideslip, and aircraft flutter contributed significantly to the overall motion of the aircraft. He waved his hands and arms about a lot and, at one point, picked up a model of an aircraft he had on his desk and began to demonstrate the different motions and how they are influenced by the aircraft's design and orientation. I left the office about an hour later and none the wiser. It was as if Stan and I spoke completely different languages. I enjoyed speaking to him, and his explanations were clear and extremely interesting, but I just couldn't see the connection between what he was *telling me* and what I *needed to know*.

The problem was not one of communication (I had understood what Stan had told me), but rather one of a mismatch between Stan's *teaching style* and my *learning style*. Stan was very much a *visual person*. He preferred to use demonstrations, pictures, and diagrams. He wrote down very little and avoided abstraction whenever he could—he preferred to stay in the real world at all times. I, on the other hand, had spent four years learning in the typical classroom situation, where the external information is presented in the form of written and spoken words. I was accustomed to lectures, equations, and theory written either on the overhead, on the chalkboard, or in my textbook. In other words, I was mainly *verbal* in my learning. The information Stan presented to me was indeed what I needed, but it was in the wrong form for me to use. Immediately after the meeting, I reviewed and expanded the notes I had taken during the previous hour. I then began to try to translate them into my language using various books, reports, and articles and talking to different engineers. It was hard work, but eventually I succeeded. I learned a lot that afternoon. In particular, I learned that if I was to be successful in engineering, it would be up to me to make information fit into my particular mode of learning. I couldn't expect others to change for me. How about you? What is your preferred mode of learning? For example, would you rather see a video demonstrating how the flow of air over an aircraft wing allows an aircraft to fly, or would you prefer to read about Bernouilli's equation and the theory of flight? Do you learn more effectively from *visual* or from *verbal and written* information? It is important to know as much as possible about how you learn most effectively. That way, if there is a mismatch between your *learning style* and your professor's *teaching style* you can take the necessary steps to make up for the shortfall.

Your *learning style* is determined largely by how well you *receive, respond to, and process* different forms of external information. For example, there are a number of different groups of learners:

1. Active/Reflective

Active learners understand and retain information better after they have applied the information to something concrete in the external world.

Reflective learners retain and understand information better after they have taken time to think about it.

2. Factual/Theoretical

Factual learners prefer concrete and specific facts, data, and detailed experimentation. They like to solve problems with standard methods and are patient with details. They don't respond well to surprises or unique complications that upset normal procedures. They are usually good at memorizing facts.

Theoretical learners prefer innovation. They are good at grasping new concepts and big picture ideas. They dislike repetition and fact-based learning. They are comfortable with symbols and abstractions, often connecting them with prior knowledge and experience.

3. Visual/Verbal

Visual learners remember best what they can see—pictures, diagrams, flow charts, time lines, films, and demonstrations. They tend to forget words and ideas that are only spoken. Although words on paper or in books are something you see, visual learners learn best from pictures and symbols that don't involve words. *Verbal learners* remember much of what they hear and then say. They benefit from discussion, prefer verbal explanation to visual demonstration, and learn effectively by explaining things to others. Verbal learners learn well through reading.

4. Linear/Holistic

Linear learners find it easiest to learn material presented in a logical, ordered progression. They solve problems in a linear, step-by-step manner. They can work with sections of material without fully understanding the whole picture. They tend to be stronger when looking at the parts of a whole rather than understanding the whole and dividing it into parts. They learn best when taking in material in a progression from easiest to most complex.

Holistic learners learn in fits and starts. They may feel lost for days or weeks, unable to solve even the simplest problems or show the most rudimentary understanding, until they finally "get it." They may feel stupid and discouraged when struggling with material that other students learn easily. Once they understand, though, they tend to see the big picture to an extent that others may not achieve. They are often highly creative.

Knowing your particular learning style can help you find success in school and on the job. In school, you'll need different strategies to deal with the different ways instructors present the material. At work, you'll have a much easier time if you understand the type of thinker you are and can apply that to your contributions in the workforce.

A mismatch between *learning and teaching styles* can have drastic effects on your performance in the classroom, For example, you may find yourself becoming increasingly bored, inattentive, or perhaps disruptive to those around you (in particular, those with learning styles that do match the professor's teaching style). As a result, you may do poorly on assignments and examinations, and perhaps begin to lose enthusiasm and the all-important motivation required to be successful in technology.

So what can you do if you find yourself in a situation where your learning style does not match the professor's teaching style? What follows are a few simple suggestions based

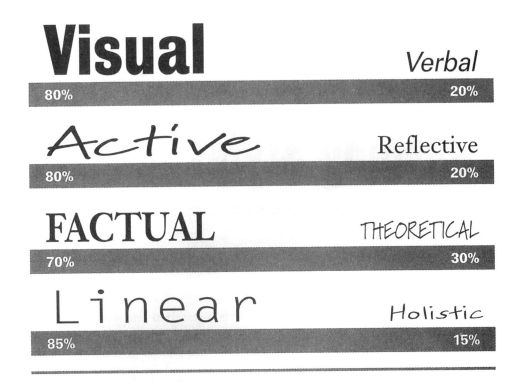

on my experiences as both a student and an instructor:

1. ***Don't*** label the professor as a "bad teacher" and then blame him or her for all your problems. Complaining will do very little to help you. Remember, the professor is not responsible for your learning. *You are!* Instead, take matters into your own hands and use your energies constructively, as follows:

2. ***Find out*** what you need to make the course material more compatible with your particular learning style. For example, do you need more pictures, more demonstrations, more worked-out examples, more real-world applications, more theory, more formulas, or more corroborating evidence? Find out what you need.

3. ***Talk*** to your professor about the difficulties you are experiencing. Suggest ways in which the professor could help you get more out of the lectures. For example, you might ask the professor to:
   a. Add more worked-out examples to the lectures.
   b. Illustrate important concepts with real-world applications.
   c. Provide some demonstrations of how a particular theory works in practice.
   d. Suggest any additional resources that might help you process the necessary information more effectively (e.g., books, articles, videos, Web page addresses, etc.).

   Remember, your objective here is not to persuade the professor to change his or her teaching style (which would be almost impossible). Rather, it is to ask the professor to provide you with the necessary information to translate the course material into a form more *compatible* with your learning style and to fill in any gaps (as I did with Stan).

4. ***Talk,*** discuss, and collaborate with people who are likely to know what you need to know (e.g., graduate teaching assistants, bright or resourceful classmates, former professors with whom you have enjoyed a good work-

Figure 6.2 Typical college class.

Having problems in a class? Don't panic—get help!

ing relationship, etc.). Sometimes an alternative explanation delivered from a different point of view will make things clearer. For example, I would often ask my mathematics professors to explain difficult concepts from engineering mechanics. This worked for me because I was more *intuitive* in my learning and I needed to *see* certain concepts through the eyes of a mathematician. (For instance, to me, relative motion analysis was an exercise in vector geometry with applications to mechanics. To others, relative motion analysis was an exercise in mechanics with applications to vector geometry.)

5. ***Consult*** sources that will *supplement* or provide alternative explanations of information from the lectures. Seek out other references on the same subject matter (e.g., other textbooks, journal articles, videos, CD-ROM, and anything that gives alternative explanations of the points that confuse you). Colleges and universities are information centers that provide knowledge, both new and old. Usually, if you look hard enough, you can find what you need.

Following these simple steps will not only maximize your effectiveness in class, but will also dramatically develop your ability to *learn independently*—in all aspects of your life, not just academics.

Learning Styles Assessments

"Learning effectively" and "tailoring studying to your own needs" means choosing study techniques that help you learn. For example, if a student responds more to visual images than to words, he might want to construct notes in a more visual way. Or, if a student learns better when talking to people than when studying alone, she might want to study primarily in pairs or groups.

The following learning styles inventory has four dimensions, within each of which are two opposing styles. At the end of the inventory, you will have two scores in each of the four dimensions. The difference between your two scores in any dimension tells you which of the two styles in that dimension is dominant for you. A few people score between the two styles, indicating that they have fairly equal parts of both styles. Following are brief descriptions of the four dimensions.

1. ***Active/Reflective.*** Active learners learn best by experiencing knowledge through their own actions. Reflective learners understand information best when they have had time to reflect on it on their own.
2. ***Factual/Theoretical.*** Factual learners learn best through specific facts, data, and detailed experimentation. Theoretical learners are more comfortable with big-picture ideas, symbols, and new concepts.
3. ***Visual/Verbal.*** Visual learners remember best what they see: diagrams, flowcharts, timelines, films, and demonstrations. Verbal learners gain the most learning from reading, hearing spoken words, participating in discussions, and explaining things to others.
4. ***Linear/Holistic.*** Linear learners find it easiest to learn material presented step by step in a logical, ordered progression. Holistic learners progress in fits and starts, perhaps feeling lost for a while but eventually seeing the big picture in a clear and creative way.

Learning Styles Inventory

Please complete this inventory by circling "a" or "b" to indicate your answer to each question. Answer every question, and choose only one answer for each question. If both answers seem to apply to you, choose the answer that applies more often.

1. I study best
   a. in a study group.
   b. alone or with a partner.
2. I would rather be considered
   a. realistic.
   b. imaginative.
3. When I recall what I did yesterday, I am most likely to think in terms of
   a. pictures or images.
   b. words or verbal descriptions.
4. I usually think new material is
   a. easier at the beginning and then harder as it becomes more complicated.
   b. often confusing at the beginning but easier as I start to understand what the whole subject is about.
5. When given a new activity to learn, I would rather first
   a. try it out.
   b. think about how I'm going to do it.
6. If I were an instructor, I would rather teach a course
   a. that deals with real-life situations and what to do about them.
   b. that deals with ideas and encourages students to think about them.
7. I prefer to receive new information in the form of
   a. pictures, diagrams, graphs, or maps.
   b. written directions or verbal information.

8. I learn
    a. at a fairly regular pace. If I study hard I'll "get it" and then move on.
    b. in fits and starts. I might be totally confused, and then suddenly it all "clicks."
9. I understand something better after
    a. I attempt to do it myself.
    b. I give myself time to think about how it works.
10. I find it easier
    a. to learn facts.
    b. to learn ideas or concepts.
11. In a book with lots of pictures and charts, I am likely to
    a. look over the pictures and charts carefully.
    b. focus on the written text.
12. It's easier for me to memorize facts from a
    a. list.
    b. whole story or essay with the facts embedded in it.
13. I will more easily remember
    a. something I have done myself.
    b. something I have thought or read about.
14. I am usually
    a. aware of my surroundings. I remember people and places and usually recall where I put things
    b. unaware of my surroundings. I forget people and places. I frequently misplace things.
15. I like instructors
    a. who put a lot of diagrams on the board.
    b. who spend a lot of time explaining.
16. Once I understand
    a. all the parts, I understand the whole thing.
    b. the whole thing, I see how the parts fit.
17. When I am learning something new, I would rather
    a. talk about it.
    b. think about it.
18. I am good at
    a. being careful about the details of my work.
    b. having creative ideas about how to do my work.
19. I remember best
    a. what I see.
    b. what I hear.
20. When I solve problems that involve some math, I usually
    a. work my way to the solutions one step at a time.
    b. see the solutions but then have to struggle to figure out the steps to get to them.
21. In a lecture class, I would prefer occasional in-class
    a. discussions or group problem-solving sessions.
    b. pauses that give opportunities to think or write about ideas presented in the lecture.
22. On a multiple-choice test, I am more likely to
    a. run out of time.
    b. lose points because of not reading carefully or making careless errors.

23. When I get directions to a new place, I prefer
    a. a map.
    b. written instructions.
24. When I'm thinking about something I've read
    a. I remember the incidents and try to put them together to figure out the themes.
    b. I just know what the themes are when I finish reading and then I have to back up and find the incidents that demonstrate them.
25. When I get a new computer or VCR, I tend to
    a. plug it in and start punching buttons.
    b. read the manual and follow instructions.
26. In reading for pleasure, I prefer
    a. something that teaches me new facts or tells me how to do something.
    b. something that gives me new ideas to think about.
27. When I see a diagram or a sketch in class, I am most likely to remember
    a. the picture.
    b. what the instructor said about it.
28. It is more important to me that an instructor
    a. lay out the material in clear, sequential steps.
    b. give me an overall picture and relate the material to other subjects.

Table A.1 Learning Styles Inventory Scoring Sheet

Active/Reflective			Factual/Theoretical			Visual/Verbal			Linear/Holistic		
Q#	a	b	Q#	a	b	Q#	a	b	Q#	a	b
1			2			3			4		
5			6			7			8		
9			10			11			12		
13			14			15			16		
17			18			19			20		
21			22			23			24		
25			26			27			28		
Total			Total			Total			Total		

Scoring Sheet: Use Table A.1 to enter your scores.

1. Put 1's in the appropriate boxes in the table (e.g., if you answered **a** to Question 3, put a **1** in the column headed **a** next to the number **3**).
2. Total the 1's in the columns and write the totals in the indicated spaces at the base of the columns.
3. For each of the four dimensions, circle your two scores on the bar scale below and then fill in the bar between the score. For example, if under "ACTV/REFL" you had 2 **a** and 5 **b** responses, you would fill in the bar between those two scores, as this sample shows:

ACTV   ———————————   REFL

7a 6a 5a 4a 3a 2a 1a 0 1b 2b 3b 4b 5b 6b 7b

LEARNING STYLES SCALES

ACTV   REFL

7a 6a 5a 4a 3a 2a 1a 0 1b 2b 3b 4b 5b 6b 7b

FACT   THEO

7a 6a 5a 4a 3a 2a 1a 0 1b 2b 3b 4b 5b 6b 7b

VISL   VRBL

7a 6a 5a 4a 3a 2a 1a 0 1b 2b 3b 4b 5b 6b 7b

LINR   HOLS

7a 6a 5a 4a 3a 2a 1a 0 1b 2b 3b 4b 5b 6b 7b

If your filled-in bar has the 0 close to its center, you are well balanced on the two dimensions of that scale. If your bar is drawn mainly to one side, you have a strong preference for that one dimension and may have difficulty learning in the other dimension.

Personality Spectrum

Joyce Bishop developed a system that simplifies learning styles into four personality types. Her work is based on the Myers-Briggs and Keirsey theories. The *Personality Spectrum* will give you a personality perspective on your learning styles. Please complete the following assessment.

Step 1. Rank all four responses to each question from most like you (4) to least like you (1). Place a 1, 2, 3, or 4 in each box next to the responses, and use each number only once per question.

1. I like instructors who
   □ a. tell me exactly what is expected of me.
   □ b make learning active and exciting.
   □ c. maintain a safe and supportive classroom.
   □ d. challenge me to think at higher levels.
2. I learn best when the material is
   □ a. well organized.
   □ b. something I can do hands-on.
   □ c. about understanding and improving the human condition.
   □ d. intellectually challenging.
3. A high priority in my life is to
   □ a. keep my commitments.
   □ b. experience as much of life as possible.
   □ c. make a difference in other's lives.
   □ d. understand how things work.
4. Other people think of me as
   □ a. dependable and loyal.
   □ b. dynamic and creative.
   □ c. caring and honest.
   □ d. intelligent and inventive.
5. When I experience stress, I am most likely to
   □ a. do something to help me feel more in control.
   □ b. do something physical and daring.
   □ c. talk with a friend.
   □ d. go off by myself and think about my situation.
6. I would probably NOT be close friends with someone who is
   □ a. irresponsible.
   □ b. unwilling to try new things.
   □ c. selfish and unkind to others.
   □ d. an illogical thinker.
7. My vacations could best be described as
   □ a. traditional.
   □ b. adventuresome.
   □ c. pleasing to others.
   □ d. a new learning experience.

8. One word that best describes me is
   ☐ a. sensible.
   ☐ b. spontaneous.
   ☐ c. giving.
   ☐ d. analytical.

Step 2. Add up the total points for each column.

Total for (A)	Total for (B)	Total for (C)	Total for (D)
☐	☐	☐	☐
Organizer	Adventurer	Giver	Thinker

Using Learning Styles

Most students want to learn as much as possible while minimizing frustration and study time. Just as you can use knowledge of your multiple intelligences to help you learn more effectively, if you know your particular learning style, you can make class and study choices that are in sync with your personal style. For example, say you perform better in smaller, discussion-based classes. When you have the opportunity, you might choose a course that is smaller and taught by an instructor who prefers group discussion. Figure 6.3 provides suggestions for your natural or primary style of learning and offers techniques for strengthening less developed styles of learning.

Problems

1. Consider the following table:

Learning Style	Your Preference
Visual	
Verbal	
Active	
Reflective	
Intuitive	
Sensing	

Mark the styles that most adequately describe how you learn.

2. Using the results from Problem 1, identify your preferred learning style.
3. Consider the following table.

Teaching Style	Prof. 1	Prof. 2	Prof. 3	Prof. 4	Prof. 5	Prof. 6
Visual						
Verbal						
Active						
Reflective						
Intuitive						
Sensing						

Mark the teaching styles that most adequately describe each of your professors' teaching styles.

4. Using the information in Problem 3, identify those courses in which your learning style does not match the professor's teaching style. List the consequences of each of these mismatches and what you have done to try to make up for them.

Figure 6.3

Learning Style	Definition	If This Is Your Natural Style, Use These Learning Techniques	If This Is Not Your Natural Style, Use These Learning Techniques
Active	Apply information to real world and experience it in their own actions. Remember more easily if there is movement or rhythm.	☐ Give real world examples for concepts. ☐ Relate learning to own experiences ☐ Make up "cheers" or songs about material. ☐ Act out material. ☐ Use flash cards. ☐ Review material while walking or exercising.	☐ Write down a real-world example. ☐ Study in quiet place. ☐ If role play or computer simulations are used, write out conclusions.
Reflective	Retain and understand information better after they have taken time to think about it.	☐ When you are reading, stop periodically to think about what you have read. ☐ Don't just memorize material, think about why it is important and what it relates to, considering the causes and effects involved. ☐ Write short summaries of readings or class lectures in your own words. It may take additional time, but writing can help you retain the information more effectively. ☐ Study in quiet setting.	☐ Keep a journal to strive to become aware of thoughts. ☐ Apply ideas to things you have done. ☐ Create games or activities that illustrate concepts.
Factual	Prefer concrete and specific facts, data, and detailed experimentation.	☐ Ask the instructor how ideas and concepts apply in practice. ☐ Ask for specific examples of the ideas and concepts. ☐ Brainstorm specific examples with classmates and by yourself. ☐ Think about how theories make specific connections with the real world.	☐ Write down what makes the details and facts important. ☐ Relate the examples to experiences in your own life. ☐ Ask the instructor to give an overview of the main ideas.
Theoretical	Learn best when they can understand big picture. Often become impatient with details.	☐ Try to think of concepts, interpretations, or theories that link the facts together. ☐ Because you become impatient with details, you may be prone to careless mistakes on tests. Read directions and entire questions before answering, and be sure to check your work. ☐ Look for systems and patterns that arrange the facts in a way that makes sense to you. ☐ Spend time analyzing the materials.	☐ Write or give orally the big picture. ☐ Outline and fill in facts and details that support the concepts. ☐ Relate major points to subpoints.
Visual	Remember best what they can see; pictures, diagrams, symbols, flow charts, times lines, films videos, and demonstrations.	☐ Add diagrams to your notes whenever possible. Dates can be drawn on a time line; math functions can be graphed; percentages can be drawn in a pie chart. ☐ Connect related facts in your notes by drawing arrows. ☐ Color-code your notes with highlighters so that everything that relates to one topic is the same color. ☐ Organize your notes so that you can easily see main points and supporting facts and how things are connected. ☐ Rewrite notes. ☐ Use concept mapping or think-link	☐ Verbally explain all diagrams, charts, flow charts, time lines, and graphs. ☐ Summarize in writing or orally, videos. ☐ Use outlines and margin notes instead of color code. ☐ Number main points instead of highlighting.

Verbal	Remember much of what they hear and then say. Benefit from discussion and verbal explanation.	☐ Explain concept to others. ☐ Read material saying main points out loud. ☐ Record main points and play back to review. ☐ Work in study groups. ☐ Outline chapters.	☐ Use visual aids in presentations. ☐ Draw diagrams of lecture material. ☐ Use videos and computer simulations. ☐ Take notes of observations.
Linear	Find it easiest to learn material presented in a logical, ordered progression. They solve problems in a linear, step-by-step manner.	☐ If you have a class where the instructor jumps from topic to topic or skips steps, ask the instructor to fill in the skipped portions or help you connect the topics. ☐ When you study notes from a class where the information has been given at random, don't read your notes as they are. Take time to rearrange the material according to what logic helps you to understand it best.	☐ Be patient. ☐ Ask questions about how each piece relates to the whole. ☐ Outline the main points before filling in the details.
Holistic	Learn in fits and starts. May feel confused at first until they finally see the big picture and how everything relates.	☐ Before you study a chapter in a book, read all of the subheadings to try and get an overview of where the chapter is going. ☐ Try to relate subjects to other things you already know. Keep asking yourself how you could apply the material. ☐ Instead of studying a short time on many subjects each day, immerse yourself in one topic at a time. ☐ Don't lose faith in yourself. You will get it, and once you do, you may be able to do even more than you can imagine.	☐ Number main points. ☐ Create an outline of the material. ☐ Discuss specific examples with classmates that illustrate ideas. ☐ Draw diagrams and flow charts.

READINGS

The first article suggests some other strategies or "keys" that can help you become a more successful college student. Your purpose for reading is to discover more ideas to make you a more confident reader.

Preview

1. Skim the article, noticing in particular the six italicized strategies or keys.
2. Skim the end questions and the vocabulary.
3. (Anticipate) Which ideas sound like new ideas to explore?
4. (Associate) Have you used any of these skills in learning before?
5. What ideas in these keys are related to strategies discussed earlier in this chapter?

Six Keys to Quicker Learning

Patricia Skalka

A friend of mine was at a dinner party where two men she knew were discussing *The Right Stuff*, a book about the Mercury space program. While Ted went on and on about the technical details he had picked up from the book, Dan offered only a few tentative comments. "Ted got so much more out of the reading than I did," Dan later said to my friend. "Is he much smarter than I am?"

My friend, an educator, was curious. She knew the two men had similar educational backgrounds and intelligence levels. She talked with each and discovered the answer: Ted just knew how to learn better than Dan did. Ted had made his brain more <u>absorbent</u> by using a few simple skills.

For years, experts had believed that an individual's ability to learn was a fixed <u>capacity</u>. During the last two decades, however, leading psychologists and educators have come to think otherwise. "We have increasing proof that human intelligence is <u>expandable</u>," says Jack Lochhead, director of the Cognitive Development Project at the University of Massachusetts in Amherst. "We know that with proper skills people can actually improve their learning ability."

Moreover, these skills are basic enough so that almost anyone can master them with practice. Here, gathered from the ideas of experts across the country, are six proven ways to boost your learning ability.

1.   *Look at the big picture first.* When reading new, unfamiliar material, do not <u>plunge</u> directly into it. You can increase your comprehension and <u>retention</u> if you scan the material first. Skim subheads, photo captions, and any available summaries. With reports or articles, read the first sentence of each paragraph; with books, glance at the table of contents and introduction.

All this previewing will help anchor in your mind what you then read.

2.   *Slow down and talk to yourself.* While speed-reading may be fine for easy material, slower reading can be much more effective for absorbing complex, challenging works. Arthur Whimbey and Jack Lochhead, co-authors of the high-school and college handbook *Problem Solving and Comprehension*, have <u>isolated</u> three basic differences in how good and bad learners study:

- Good learners <u>vocalize</u>, or voice, the material, either silently or aloud. They slow down, listening to each word as they read.
- Good learners, when <u>stymied</u>, automatically reread until they understand the material. Poor readers, by contrast, just keep going if they don't get it the first time.
- Good learners become "actively involved" with new information. They think about what they read, challenge it, make it their own.

In 1979, Whimbey introduced a slow, vocalized reading method into a five-week, pre-freshman program at Xavier University in New Orleans. Many of the 175 students using this technique jumped two grade levels in comprehension, and their college-aptitude test scores rose by as much as 14 percent.

3.   *Practice memory-<u>enhancing</u> techniques.* When I was eight and couldn't spell *arithmetic,* a teacher taught me a sentence that has remained locked in my mind for decades: "A rat in Tom's house may eat Tom's ice cream." The first letters of each word spell *arithmetic.*

All such memory-enhancing techniques, called <u>mnemonics</u>, transform new information into more easily remembered formulations.

Other first-letter mnemonics include "Homes" (the names of the Great Lakes—Huron, Ontario, Michigan, Erie, and Superior); "George Eaton's old granny rode a pig home yesterday" (for spelling *geography*); and "My very educated mother just served us nine pickles" (the planet system in order—Mercury, Venus, Earth, Mars, Jupiter, Saturn, Uranus, Neptune, Pluto).

Mnemonics can also work with images. The trick is, to invent visual clues that will make unfamiliar material mean something to you.

In studying Spanish, for example, you might learn that the word for "duck" is *pato. Pato* sounds like the English word pot. To link the two, imagine a duck waddling about with a large pot over its head. You will have a clear image that reminds you pot = *pato* = duck.

Once dismissed by researchers as a mere <u>gimmick</u>, mnemonics are now considered an effective means of boosting memory-doubling or even tripling the amount of new material that test subjects can retain. "A good memory is the key to all <u>cognitive</u> processes," according to William G. Chase, professor of psychology at Carnegie-Mellon University in Pittsburgh. "And it is something we can all have with practice."

Cognitive research shows that we have two kinds of memory: short-term and long-term. Short-term memory (STM) lasts for about 30 to 60 seconds. We call directory assistance for a phone number, dial the number, and then forget it. Long-term memory (LTM), however, can last a lifetime. The secret to developing a good memory, say Francis S. Bellezza, author of *Improve Your Memory Skills*, is learning how to transfer useful information from STM to LTM and how to <u>retrieve</u> that information when needed.

Mnemonics can be the key that puts data into LTM and gets the information back out again. Remember, the mind and memory are like muscles—the more you use them, the stronger they get.

4. *Organize facts into categories.* In studies at Stanford University, students were asked to memorize 112 words. These included names of animals, items of clothing, types of transportation, and occupations. For one group, the words were divided into these four categories. For a second group, the words were listed at <u>random</u>. Those who studied the material in organized categories consistently outperformed the others, recalling two to three times more words.

"Trying to digest new information in one lump is difficult," says Thomas R. Trabasso, professor of education and behavioral science at the University of Chicago. "By analyzing new material and dividing it into meaningful chunks, you make learning easier."

For example, to remember the names of all former U.S. Presidents in proper order, cluster the leaders into groups—those before the War of 1812, those from 1812 until the Civil War, those from the Civil War to World War I, and those after World War I. By thus organizing complex material into logical categories you create a permanent storage technique.

5. *Focus your attention.* The next time you are faced with new material you need to master, ask yourself, What do I want to learn from reading this, and how will I benefit from the knowledge gained? "By telling ourselves what the learning will do for us, we reduce our <u>resistance</u> to studying and become better learners," says Russell W. Scalpone, a psychologist and manager at A. T. Kearney, Inc., an international management-consulting firm.

Scalpone recommends four other techniques for improving concentration and focus:

- Establish a time and a place for learning. Take the phone off the hook; close the door. By regulating your environment, you create the expectation that learning will occur.

- Guard against <u>distractions</u>. Don't be shy about hanging a "Do Not Disturb" sign on your door. You have a right to your time.
- Try a variety of learning methods. Diagramming, note taking, outlining, even talking into a tape recorder are study techniques that can increase concentration. Use whatever study skills you are most comfortable with. Be creative.
- Monitor your progress. Being busy is not always the same as being productive. Stop occasionally and ask yourself, Am I contributing right now to my learning goal? If the answer is yes, keep working. If no, ask yourself why. If you're not making progress because of tension or <u>fatigue</u>, take a break—without feeling guilty. Regular breaks can improve the learning process.

6. *Discover your own learning style.* Educators Rita and Ken Dunn tell the story of three children who each received a bicycle for Christmas. The bikes, purchased unassembled, had to be put together by parents. Tim's father read the directions carefully before he set to work. Mary's father laid out the pieces on the floor and handed the directions to Mary's mother. "Read this to me," he said, as he surveyed the <u>components</u>. George's mother <u>instinctively</u> began fitting pieces together, glancing at the directions only when stymied. By day's end, all three bikes were assembled, each from a different approach.

"Although they didn't realize it," says Rita Dunn, professor of education at St. John's University in New York City, "the parents had worked according to their own learning styles".

"Our approaches to unfamiliar material are as unique and specialized as we are, and a key to learning is recognizing—and accommodating—the style that suits us best," says Ken Dunn, professor of education at Queens College in New York City.

Learning styles can vary dramatically. The Dunns have developed a Productivity Environment Preference Survey, which identifies 21 elements that affect the way we learn. These factors include noise level, lighting, amount of supervision required, even the time of day.

What's *your* style? Try some self-analysis. What, for example, is your approach to putting together an un-assembled item? Do you concentrate better in the morning or in the evening? In a noisy environment or a quiet one? Make a list of all the pluses and minuses you can identify. Then use this list to create the learning environment best for you.

Whichever style works for you, the good news is that you *can* expand your learning capacity. And this can make your life fuller and more productive.

Check Your Understanding

Review

Write each of the keys here. Skim the text for the keys if you need to.

1. _____
2. _____
3 _____
4. _____

5. _____

6. _____

Fill in the Blanks

Write in the word or words from the article to complete the statement.

1. STM stands for _____.

2. LTM stands for _____.

3. The Spanish word for "duck" is _____.

4. _____ are important for finding information in your memory.

5. Human intelligence is _____.

Multiple Choice

Write the letter or letters of the best choices to complete each statement.

1. The article is mainly about
   a. how your learning skills can be improved.
   b. how some people have good memories and others do not.
   c. how everyone learns the same way.
   d. how organizing is an aid to learning.
2. According to the article, good readers
   a. vocalize, either silently or aloud.
   b. become actively involved.
   c. think about what they read.
   d. all of the above.
3. Research into cognitive or intellectual development
   a. is no longer of interest.
   b. continues.
   c. has changed ideas about learning ability.
   d. is a waste of time.
4. The writer suggests that you can enhance your learning by
   a. using mnemonics.
   b. talking to yourself.
   c. organizing facts to be learned.
   d. all of the above.
5. The article suggests that
   a. some people are smarter than others.
   b. reading slowly is harmful to learning.
   c. everybody has the potential to become a successful learner.
   d. speed-reading of college texts is a timesaver.

True/False

Write the word *true* if the statement is correct or *false* if it is not correct.

1. The example of three parents who assemble bicycles shows that mechanical skills are easy to learn.
2. A good memory is very important to improving your intelligence.
3. Mental pictures or images are an aid in helping you remember things.

4. Your physical surroundings are not important in influencing your ability to learn.
5. You can improve your memory by transferring information from short-term memory to long-term memory.
6. Many people don't use the techniques mentioned in the article because they don't believe they'll work.
7. Some experts believe that good learners vocalize or read material aloud.
8. Mnemonics were once thought to be a gimmick or a game.
9. You can learn more easily if you divide new material into meaningful chunks.
10. We all learn in exactly the same way.

Vocabulary

Match the words in Column A with the words or phrases in Column B by writing the letter from Column B in the space before Column A for both exercises. Consult a dictionary for help with unfamiliar words.

I.

Column A	Column B
1. tentative	a. say aloud
2. absorbent	b. able to increase
3. retention	c. intellectual
4. enhancing	d interference
5. gimmick	e. ability
6. cognitive	f. ability to hold on to
7. distraction	g. uncertain
8. capacity	h. capable of taking in, soaking up
9. expandable	i. improving
10. vocalize	j. trick

II.

Column A	Column B
1. plunge	a. blocked
2. isolated	b. ways to improve memory
3. stymied	c. opposition to
4. mnemonics	d. part of a larger whole
5. retrieve	e. without order
6. random	f. dive
7. fatigue	g. kept apart
8. component	h. by nature
9. instinctively	i. bring back
10. resistance	j. weariness

Writing

Write a detailed description of a key to quicker learning that you intend to use immediately. Explain why you think this key will be helpful and mention at least one occasion when you will use it.

Group Discussion: Thinking beyond the Text

An important way to assure that you have understood your reading is to participate in group discussions or collaborative learning experiences. Research shows that students who study in groups do better than students who work alone. This text offers opportunities in each chapter for small group discussions to discuss readings, compare answers, clarify material, and extend your learning beyond the text by doing critical thinking about your activities and your reading.

Group work requires your active participation as a listener, a leader, a recorder, or a responder. Work with other members of your group to discuss the following questions. Your instructor may ask for a report from your group following the discussion:

1. The writer has used quotes from books and interviews with friends and experts to support her ideas. Do you find the ideas convincing? Is there anything she could have done to make her points more convincing?
2. Who do you think is the intended audience for this article?
3. Which key do you think would be most helpful to you? Explain your reasons.
4. Do you think that some of the suggestions are just the opinion of the writer? Why or why not?

Learning to Learn

Lester A. Lefton

> The following is an excerpt from *Psychology* (5th ed., Allyn & Bacon, 1995). Professor Lefton has taught undergraduate and graduate courses in psychology for more than twenty years at the University of South Carolina.
>
> Most college seniors believe they are much better students now than they were as first-year students. What makes the difference? How do students learn to learn better? Today, educators and cognitive researchers are focusing on how information is learned, as opposed to what is learned. To learn new information, students generate hypotheses, make interpretations, make predictions, and revise earlier ideas. They are active learners (Wittrock, 1987).

Human beings learn how to learn; they learn special strategies for special topics, and they devise general rules that depend on their goals (McKeachie, 1988). The techniques for learning foreign languages differ from those needed to learn mathematics. Are there general cognitive techniques that students can use to learn better? McKeachie, Pintrich, and Lin (1985) have argued that lack of effective learning strategies is a major cause of low achievement by university students. They conducted a study to see whether grades would improve overall when rote learning, repetition, and memorization were replaced by more efficient cognitive strategies.

To help students become better learners, McKeachie, Pintrich, and Lin developed a course on learning to learn; it provided practical suggestions for studying and a theoretical basis for understanding learning. It made students aware of the processes used in learning and remembering. This awareness (thinking about thinking, learning about learning) is called *metacognition*. Learning-skills practice, development of motivation, and development of a positive attitude were also included. Among specific topics were learning from lectures, learning from textbooks, test taking, self-monitoring, reduction of test anxiety, discovering personal learning styles, and learning through such traditional strategies as SQ3R plus (Survey, Question, Read, Recite, Review, plus write and reflect). The course focused on learning in general, not on specific courses such as history or chemistry. The goal was to develop generalized strategies to facilitate learning.

The voluntary learning-to-learn course attracted 180 students. They were tested at the beginning and end of the semester, and their test scores were compared with those of control groups enrolled in other psychology classes. Various measures were used to assess whether the course had any impact on SAT scores, reading test scores, anxiety test scores, and especially academic grades.

The results showed that the learning-to-learn students made gains in a number of areas, including grades and motivation. In later semesters, the students continued to improve. This straightforward study tells an important story about psychology in general and about learning psychology in particular. First, it shows that psychologists are engaged in activities that help people, not just in esoteric laboratory studies. Second, it shows a shift in emphasis from studies of learning specific facts or of specific stimuli and responses to studies of learning strategies. Third, it shows that research into thought processes can lead to more effective thought and, subsequently, to high levels of motivation. Last, this simple study shows that people can be taught to be more efficient learners.

McKeachie, Pintrich, and Lin argued: "The cognitive approach has generated a richer, deeper analysis of what goes on in learning and memory, increasing our understanding and improving our ability to facilitate retrieval and use of learning.... We need to be aware of several kinds of outcomes—not just *how much knowledge* was learned, but *what kinds of learning* took place" (p. 602). Students can better grasp history, chemistry, or economics if they understand *how* to go about studying these topics. Law, psychology, and medicine require different learning strategies. After we learn how to learn, the differences become obvious; indeed, some researchers think of creativity as a metacognitive process involving thinking about our own thoughts (Pesut, 1990). Individuals can learn to learn, reason, and make better choices across a variety of domains (Larrick, Morgan, & Nisbett, 1990).

Comprehension Check

Finish each of the following sentences by adding a word or phrase that best completes the idea.

1. College students become better students because _____

_____.

2. Thinking about the processes of thinking and learning is known as _____

_____.

3. The learning-to-learn course stressed the importance of a _____

_____.

4. Creativity can be defined as a process of _____

_____.

5. Different subjects require different _____

_____

_____.

Expanding Vocabulary

Match each word in the left column with its definition in the right column by placing the correct letter in the space next to each word.

hypotheses   a. make easier

theoretical   b. judge or evaluate

facilitate   c. the process of obtaining knowledge from memory

assess   d. conjectures or assumptions given to explain a situation, event, or behavior

retrieval   e. areas of study

domains   f. based on principles or ideas

For Discussion and Reflection

1. Has this analysis of "learning-to-learn" convinced you that "people can be taught to be more efficient learners"? If so, why? If not, why not?
2. The learning-to-learn students improved in several areas of learning. In what, if any, skill areas do you need improvement? What strategies could you use in your current reading course to work on those skills?
3. In the last paragraph one definition of creativity is offered. How would you define the term? Try to include specific examples of creativity.
4. The selection says that different strategies are needed to learn different subjects. In a group with classmates or on your own, make a list of the strategies that would be best for learning a subject that you are taking or plan to take.

7

Applying Learning Theory to a Course of Study in Technology

KEY STRATEGIES FOR MAXIMIZING PERFORMANCE IN TECHNOLOGY COURSES

When successful technology students are asked to describe their study or work habits and any *special techniques* they may have used to achieve their particular level of success, year after year, the same answers keep coming back. These answers indicate clearly that the most successful technology students practice, in common, a set of *key study strategies specific to technology courses.* Perhaps even more significant is the fact that almost every one of these strategies is absent from the study habits of the less successful students. This is no surprise: These same skills used to be taught as part of any basic high school curriculum. Recently, however, weaknesses in the secondary education system have meant that most first-year technology students arrive without these skills, and very few of them take the time to acquire them for themselves. As a result, many new technology students find it difficult to make the transition between high school and college. This almost always leads to poor performance in the first year.

In this chapter, we address the issue of performance and present that very collection of study strategies used by the most successful technology students. The strategies themselves are sufficiently general to be applicable to *all* technology courses at *any* level. In particular, we discuss:

- Time management strategies
- Preparing for a technology course and making sure that your prerequisite works
- Effective note taking
- Making effective use of the course textbook
- How to be effective on assignments
- Using posted solutions to assignments
- Using tutors and study guides

TIME MANAGEMENT STRATEGIES

Time is perhaps our most precious commodity: We cannot create more of it, and we cannot save it up and use it later. All we can do is learn to use the time we have as effectively as possible. Unfortunately, most of us have never been taught how to manage our time. Instead, we tend to learn these skills naturally, later in life, when faced with the usual commitments and responsibilities that come with having a full-time job, a new home, and raising a family.

The need for time management skills in technology is well understood. Only recently, however, is time management being recognized as one of the most important skills required for success in engineering study—despite the fact that the very best technology students have been practicing it for years! Fortunately, a simple, easy-to-follow time management system is not difficult to establish, and it's one of the most effective ways to give yourself even more time!

Prioritize

Think of your time as you would money. Since you have only a finite amount of money, you have to plan, monitor, and review how you spend it. Most of us do this by formulating a budget: We look at how much money we have and then prioritize our expenditures. First we account for necessities (rent, food, clothing, etc.). Then we distribute the remainder of our money according to our particular needs and circumstances. The same strategy can be applied to managing our time.

Make a Schedule

Schedules are personal reminders. The exact format should reflect the most advantageous way for you to be reminded of information. Individuals with strong visual intelligence create schedules that are often accented by color and/or icons. Individuals with strong verbal linguistic intelligence often include more explanation or the schedule may be more of a list format. The important thing is that the schedule communicates to the individual.

Effective time management begins with detailed scheduling. Get yourself a good diary, planner, or calendar, one that will allow you to record your commitments (both long and short term) and schedule your time on a daily basis. There are many advantages to doing this, including the following:

- You have a *visual representation* of your year, month, week, or day, so that you know what's ahead and can prepare accordingly.
- You can *see* if you are using your time as effectively as possible.
- A *picture* of how you are using your time makes it easier to reschedule events or change priorities.
- You are less likely to forget appointments or important events.
- You can note things and forget about them until the appointed time nears.
- You can set up *flags* to remind you of forthcoming important events (e.g., "Exam in one week!").
- You feel more organized and your confidence increases.
- You will receive excellent training for the work world.

Plan from the long term to the short term, as follows:

Long Term: In your diary or planner, mark any important dates for the current academic year. These will be special one-time dates occurring perhaps once or twice a year. For example, you might note midterm and final exam dates, the first and last day of classes, birthdays, and dental appointments, and you might set flags to remind you that certain events are coming up (e.g., two weeks before a final exam is scheduled, you might write "Get sample final exams for review!"). Having these recorded in your planner means that you can forget about them until a later time and be safe in the knowledge that your diary will serve as your *reminder*. I have used this method throughout my professional life as a student and as a professor, and I have found that it is an excellent way to reduce stress and avoid anxiety.

Short Term: It's always useful to be able to take a look at your week or day. That way you can easily reschedule events—for example, to go out with a surprise guest or to attend an upcoming sporting event. Scheduling your entire week also ensures that you don't forget to do anything you are required or intend to do that week. The best way to do this is to use a weekly planner. I have included an example (from a typical first-year technology student) in Figure 7.1.

Weekly Planner

Like schedules, weekly planners are individual tools to communicate information. The step-by-step presentation is consistent with the linear learner style and the daily task will lead to the final task. This type of learner will have to take care to keep the big picture in mind. The holistic learner will want to include more detail so that the task is broken down into workable steps.

The student whose weekly planner is shown in Figure 7.1 is taking three courses labeled (1), (2), and (3). Courses 1 and 2 meet on Monday, Wednesday, and Friday, and Course 3 meets on Tuesday and Wednesday. There are also various laboratories associated with different courses. You should schedule your week in the same way, as follows:

- First schedule all your commitments (shown in bold in the figure)
  1. Classes
  2. Laboratories (referred to as labs in the figure)
  3. Jobs (referred to as work in the figure)
  4. Meals
- Next, schedule blocks of time for study. Make sure you use *all available time*. For example, if one class ends at 1:50 P.M. and the next doesn't begin until 3:00 P.M., schedule approximately an hour for study. (Remember, you need to take into account the time it takes to move between classes and the place you choose to study.) You'll be amazed at how productive you can be even in short periods of time, time that might otherwise be wasted in deciding whether or not to study. To do this efficiently, you need to do two things *beforehand:*
  1. Write down *where* you will study. Decide beforehand where the best place to study will be, given the particular circumstances at that time. This will avoid wasting valuable time. For example, if your class finishes at 10:00 A.M., and your next class is at 11:00 A.M., choose a location near either the classroom you just vacated or the one you are about to enter.
  2. Write down *what* to study. Again, so many students waste valuable time procrastinating about what to do during study time. Choose small jobs for short periods of time and longer assignments for extended periods of time. Deciding this beforehand allows you to spend the maximum amount of time actually studying—just get there and get to it!
     Making these decisions in advance will improve your effectiveness tremendously. You'll be amazed at how much you can get done during time that would otherwise have been wasted.
- Finally, in the time that's left, try to fit in entertainment, leisure, and recreational activities. You may find yourself working out at different times on different days. That may not make for effective bodybuilding, but that's

Figure 7.1 Weekly planner for a 3-course schedule/3 days per week

	Monday	Tuesday	Wednesday	Thursday	Friday	Saturday	Sunday
0700	B/fast	Workout	B/fast	Workout	B/fast		
0800	Class (1)	B/fast	Class (1)	B/fast	Class (1)		
0900	Class (2)	Class (3)	Class (2)	Class (3)	Class (2)		
1000	Research-Libr. See Prof	Class (3) See Prof.	Study-Library	Class (3) Study-Library	Research-Libr./ See Prof.		
1100	Class (1) Theory in Lab	Class (2) Theory in Lab	Study-Library	Study-Library	Study-library	Workout	
1200	Lunch	Lunch	Lunch	Lunch	Lunch		
1300	Class (1) Lab	Class (2) Lab	Study Grp. Class (1) Lab	See Professor	Study-Library	See Professor	
1400	Class (1) Prepare Study Grp.	Class (2) Prepare Study Grp.	Class (1) Prepare Study Grp.	Class (2) Prepare Study Grp.	Study-Library	Study Paper #1– Library	Study Grp. (1)
1500	Study Grp. (Assn. #1)	Study Grp. (Assn. #4)	See Professor	Study Grp. Class (2) Lab	Seminar	Coffee (Mike) Cafe	Study Grp. (2)
1600	Study Grp. (Assn. #1)	Study Grp. (Assn. #4)	Workout	Study Grp. Class (1) Lab	Study Grp. Class (2) Lab	Study Paper#1– Library	Study Grp. (1)
1700	Review Lecture Notes	Review Lecture Notes	Review Lecture Notes	Dinner	Study Grp. Class (2) Lab	Dinner	Study Grp. (2)
1800	Dinner	Dinner	Dinner	Work	Dinner	Work	Dinner
1900	Relax	Relax	Relax	Work	Relax	Work	Review Week's Notes-Home
2000	Study Class (1)–Home	Study Class (2)–Home	Study Class (3)–Home	Work	Fun!	Work	Review Week's Notes-Home
2100				Work	Fun!	Work	
2200				Work	Fun!	Work	Sleep

Class (1) = Tech 1 Theory, Class (2) = General Education, Class (3) = Tech 2 Theory okay, since your priorities lie in technology study. Remember to schedule enough relaxation and leisure time. Your performance in technology also will depend on your stress and anxiety levels, as well as how happy you are in your everyday life.

Scheduling your entire week might seem awkward and difficult at first, but persevere. You'll find it becomes easier the more you do it, and the benefits are enormous. Soon, your study time will become scheduled study time and reach *commitment status.* This is exactly what the very best technology students do. They are quick to realize that study time is every bit as important as scheduled time, if not more important. Remember, study time is when you *process* the information *gathered* during scheduled time (e.g., in class, labs, etc.). Being a technology student is very much like working for yourself: the benefits are directly proportional to the amount of effort expended in the appropriate directions.

Figure 7.2 contains a blank weekly planner similar to that shown in Figure 7.1. Why not take this opportunity to look at your weekly schedule. I'll bet there is significant room for improvement.

Make a List!

Linear learners often make very detailed lists and check off each step. Holistic learners may make lists and not look at them or make lists with broad categories. Linear learners might benefit from including the overall goal on the list while holistic learners might want to include more detail and create a column to check off when tasks are completed.

Making lists is a great way of ensuring that you accomplish what you need to accomplish. Whenever you have several things to do in any period of time, write them down in order of priority, and work your way through the list, ticking off each item as it is completed. For example, suppose you allocate two hours' exam review time to calculus. Your list for that period of time might look like this:

1. Pick up sample exams.
2. Look at textbook for an explanation of a fundamental concept.

Figure 7.2 Weekly Planner

	Monday	Tuesday	Wednesday	Thursday	Friday	Saturday	Sunday
0700							
0800							
0900							
1000							
1100							
1200							
1300							
1400							
1500							
1600							
1700							
1800							
1900							
2000							
2100							
2200							

3. Review class notes on exam preparation.
4. Work through first sample exam.

Again, doing this beforehand means that the time allocated to study will be used entirely for study. Lists are easy to make and can be made anywhere, anytime. I make them in restaurants, on buses, in bed, or whenever anything occurs to me and anything resembling a piece of paper is at hand.

Save Yourself Time—It's Easy!

Almost everything you do as an technology student has been done before. The assignments, the lecture material, the experiments, and even the examinations have all been mastered and completed to perfection by other people ahead of you, either former technology students or professors. This gives you an excellent opportunity to save time by *learning from what other people have done.* Consequently, recognize that years of experience and wisdom and the successes that result from it are contained in the very many resources available to you, for example, your textbooks, this book, your professors, your fellow students, professional technologists in industry, and many more. Modeling those who have achieved what you hope to achieve can save you time, pain, and effort. Consequently, whenever possible, instead of embarking on an analysis by trial and error, seek out information that will give you answers and the most effective way of doing things. It never ceases to amaze me how many students will try to solve technical engineering technology problems off the top of their heads, without consulting class notes, reading textbooks, or asking for help. This is wasteful and stressful. There is no need to reinvent the wheel, and no one expects you to! Just find out how it was done, and do the same!

EFFECTIVE NOTE TAKING

Note taking is personal communication. The goal is to maximize your ability to recall information from lectures, text, or applicable media. Review your primary area of intelligence and your learning style and determine how your notes can be more effective. One of the challenges is we usually take notes in our natural style. Peter Drucker said, " Great strengths equals great weaknesses." By taking notes in our natural style we may miss important aspects. For example a holistic learner may take notes on the main points. In review they find they are missing needed detail. They need to develop a system that requires them to include more detail. The factual learner may miss the forest for the trees. They need to include headers that help them see the big picture. Determining your study techniques should reflect your types of intelligence and learning style.

We have already discussed the role of the lecture as a primary source of information in technology school. In this section, we concentrate on how best to *record* that information so that you take as much as possible of the lecture away with you.

First of all, let's establish that there is absolutely no point in attending a lecture in a technology school, *unless you take notes.* Some students like to explain their inactivity during a lecture by saying that they learn better by listening rather than spending the whole hour or so writing things down. Here's what happens: In class, they probably understand most of what has been presented. One hour later, it's all been forgotten or replaced by the next lecture. Remember, lectures are your main source of information, information that is almost always used (at least) several weeks later. Your efficiency in a lecture is measured by how much relevant information you take away with you, not by how much information you understand at the time.

Effective note taking depends on several factors. Perhaps the most important of these is the ability to adapt to the many different ways in which information is presented in a lecture. Most professors have their own style of lecturing and communicating information. It is up to you to learn to adapt your note taking to suit the particular style of the professor in front of you.

In general, lecturers fall into three basic categories:

1. The lecturer who writes everything down. These lecturers are most common in technical courses, such as mathematics or science, where the *language of communication* is mainly mathematics and most examples, methods, and theories are presented with the intention that you copy them *word for word*. Your main responsibility in this type of lecture is to write down everything the professor writes (and the odd thing that he or she says, but doesn't write down). You are primarily gathering information; most of the thinking and understanding will come later, on your own time, when you review your notes.

2. The lecturer who writes down very little and instead prefers to *talk* his or her way through the lecture with the aid of, for example, an overhead and (many) different slides. This type of lecturer is more common in less technical courses (e.g., history, economics, sociology, English, etc.), where the information is more easily communicated using spoken English together with pictures, diagrams, and perhaps demonstrations. In these courses, it is usually very difficult to write down everything that the lecturer says: Most people cannot write as fast as the lecturer speaks. Consequently, it becomes necessary to learn how to isolate the most important information and record it most effectively for later review.

3. The lecturer who employs a combination of the previous two methods.

The following are suggestions that will help you improve your note-taking system. They are classified into the following three groups:

- *General remarks*. These suggestions are applicable to all three categories of lecturers.
- *Group* 1. These suggestions apply mainly to the first category of lecturers.
- *Group* 2. These suggestions apply mainly to the second category of lecturers.

Those of you with a Category 3 lecturer can combine the hints and suggestions given for Category 1 and 2 lecturers.

General Remarks

- Go to any lecture with the right attitude and objectives. The lecturer is there to help you—to give you the information you require to be successful.
- Don't talk while the lecturer is talking. Apart from the fact that it's rude, distracting (to the lecturer and to other students), and unfair to your fellow students, your conversation is likely being heard all over the room. Lecture rooms are specifically designed to carry sound.
- Take and keep notes in a loose-leaf binder. This has the following advantages:
  —It gives you the ability to insert and remove pages, in the appropriate places, as necessary. This is particularly important when the lecturer uses a combination of handouts and board or overhead materials, or when you wish to supplement or correct notes later upon reviewing them.

—You don't need to carry around the whole semester's lecture notes with you all the time. Simply take the day's (new) lecture notes and insert them in the binder, at home, at the end of the day.

—You can select the notes from any specific lecture(s) simply by removing them from the binder.

- Number, title, and date each page in the upper right-hand corner. This makes for easy reference and good organization.
- Leave a header at the top of each page, and use it to note any important information (e.g., midterm exam dates, assignments, etc.)
- Use standard paper and write on one side only! This will make it easier to supplement or edit notes later.
- Don't try to save paper. It may be good for the environment, but it will reduce the effectiveness of your note taking dramatically!
- Leave blanks for information you missed or for things that require further clarification. See the instructor after class or talk with fellow students, and then fill in the blanks.
- Organize your page appropriately: Separate topics, leave margins (for additional notes), and emphasize points using asterisks, uppercase letters, and underlining.
- Sit as close as possible to the front of the class, where there are fewer distractions and it's easier to see, hear, read the board, and identify important material.
- Focus: *Get into* the lecture. Tune into the lecturer while tuning everyone and everything else out. Leave your emotions outside the lecture room.
- Maintain eye contact with the lecturer whenever possible. Try not to doodle or play with your pen. Doing so will serve only to distract you.
- Get instructions on assignments and examinations *precisely*. Leave no room for doubt—ask if you're unsure. (Most assignments are usually given in lectures.)
- Never write your final notes in a lecture. As often as possible, use abbreviations and rough sketches and diagrams. This will minimize the effort you put into the actual writing, leaving you more time to concentrate on the information itself.
- *As soon as possible after the lecture,* review and complete your notes. Write them out as if you were teaching the subject to yourself. (Remember, this is exactly what you will be doing at exam time.) Leaving your lecture notes to one side until days or weeks after is just a waste of time and paper.
- If you are part of a study group, consider appointing a (rotating) note taker, who writes everything down while the remaining group members concentrate on the material being presented. After the lecture, get the group together and perfect a set of lecture notes for the group based on what three or more people (depending on the number in the group) have heard.
- When you miss a class, *always* get the notes from either a conscientious and successful student who shares your objectives in technology study or, if possible, from the instructor. Use these notes as you would your own lecture notes (i.e., review, rewrite, supplement, and edit as necessary).
- If you want time to pass slowly, keep checking your watch. Otherwise don't check the time at all!

Category 1

- Try to prepare for the lecture by reading material assigned to the lecture beforehand, rereading the notes from the previous lecture, or *scanning* the material to be covered in the coming lecture from the textbook. You'll be amazed at how much more familiar lecture material appears if you've already thought about it or even just quickly read about it.
- Sit as close to the front of the class as possible, where you can easily see the board.
- Copy down *everything* on the board, regardless of whether or not it looks useful. Don't try to decide there and then what may not be relevant. Assume that if it's on the board, it's relevant. You will review your notes later anyway.
- Write down also anything the instructor might *say* (but not write down) by way of additional explanation.
- Note any references made to the textbook in the appropriate places, so you can look up an alternative explanation or more examples illustrating a challenging or difficult concept.
- After each lecture, if you haven't already, cross-reference your notes to the textbook. This will save you valuable time when you use your notes to complete an assignment or when you review for examinations.
- After each lecture, work through examples (presented in the lecture) *yourself*; and make a note of where (e.g., the textbook) other similar examples or the appropriate theory can be found.

Category 2

- Try to prepare for the lecture by reading material assigned to the lecture *beforehand,* rereading the notes from the previous lecture, or *scanning* the material to be covered in the coming lecture from the textbook or other sources of information. You'll be amazed at how much more familiar lecture material appears if you've already thought about it or even just quickly read about it.
- Do not try to take down everything the lecturer says. Most people just cannot write as fast as the lecturer speaks. Instead, spend more time listening and summarizing the main points in your own words: Not everything the lecturer says will be of equal importance.
- Listen *actively* by pausing to think before you write—but not for too long: You don't want to get too far behind.
- Write down the main ideas and any supporting details if possible.
- Don't let your own personal prejudices and biases affect your note taking. Be open minded and avoid arguing inside your head.
- Listen for any important clues as to what's important. For example, the professor might stress specific pieces of information, repeat certain points, change the tone of his or her voice, etc.
- Listen for words that signify an important idea or conclusion, such as "finally," "therefore," "consequently," "in conclusion," "to summarize," and so on.
- After the lecture, coordinate your reading and lecture notes, and expand on ideas and explanations as appropriate. Talk to the instructor and fellow students, if necessary, to reinforce ideas and understanding.

MAKING EFFECTIVE USE OF THE COURSE TEXTBOOK

Most technology courses require that you buy a particular textbook. This textbook is chosen by your instructor to satisfy several requirements, including the following:

- To provide a backup source of course material. In this respect, the textbook will include the vast majority of the material covered in the corresponding technology course.
- To provide a source of illustrative examples.
- To provide a good supply of practice problems.

It is important to understand that the textbook is intended to complement on your technology course and is in no way a substitute for lectures or labs. To illustrate this point, consider the following situation. You are enrolled in Physics. On the first day of classes, the professor gives you the following instructions: "There will be no lectures in this course. Everything you need to know is contained in the first five chapters of the prescribed textbook. I suggest you buy the textbook, study the first five chapters, and return to class on October 21 for the midterm examination and December 12 for the final examination." What kind of problems do you think you would encounter? Perhaps (at least) the following:

- The first five chapters of the textbook contain a wealth of information, but you can't hope to learn it all. What's important and what isn't? Which results can you omit without worrying about whether or not they will appear on the examinations? What are the main results of each section? Each chapter? There's just too much information.
- There are numerous practice exercises at the end of each section. You just do not have the time to work through every problem. Which of the problems are most important (e.g., for examination purposes)? Which of the problems are not relevant for this particular course (i.e., different professors emphasize and include different topics)? Which of the problems are of examination quality? Which of the problems are similar to the type likely to be asked on a test?

Without the professor's guidance, it is extremely difficult to target relevant material from the textbook. One of the main reasons for attending lectures is that the professor has spent considerable time and effort targeting relevant material, examples, and practice problems. In lectures, the professor will tell you what is important and what isn't, what material may appear on an examination and what material is not likely to, which examples best illustrate the theory and which don't, and which practice problems will give you the most effective preparation for assignments, class tests, and examinations.

This is not to say that the textbook is not important. It is an integral part of any technology course. However, there are ways to make sure that the textbook works *for you* in conjunction with the usual series of lectures, labs, and seminars.

- Use the lecture material as your *guide* to what's relevant. If you need a second opinion (or alternative explanation) or more detail on a particular result, consult the textbook. The alternative (or more detailed) explanation may be clearer to you.
- Again, with the class material as your guide, use the textbook as a source of more illustrative examples of the material covered in class. The more examples you see, the more likely it is that you will understand the basic concepts and that you will be able to apply the procedure to a new problem.

- Use the textbook as a supply of additional practice problems, but target problems *similar* to the ones solved in class or appearing on assignments or tests. This gives you smart practice, that is, relevant practice in the areas deemed to be important by your professor. In this respect, it is always a good idea to ask your professor to point out which problems in the textbook are most relevant. Many textbooks illustrate important theories and concepts using real-world examples and applications. These illustrations might help to make both theory and applications a little clearer to you. Hence, in addition to using the textbook as a source of problems and worked-out examples to help you solve homework problems and prepare for examinations, read through the accompanying text, it will enhance your understanding of the subject matter.
- Often, when a particular theory or concept is confusing, look ahead in the textbook to an application of the theory or concept in question. This might make things clearer for you.

HOW TO BE EFFECTIVE ON ASSIGNMENTS

Why are assignments (or homework problems) important? Certainly, one reason is that they can be worth anything from 5 percent to 20 percent of the final course grade. Another, perhaps more important, reason is illustrated in Figure 7.3.

The data in the figure represent average (final) examination scores for groups of students missing up to a maximum of 5 assignments in one of my courses. It is interesting to note that the average score among those students submitting all ten assignments was close to 70 percent, while the average score for those missing even four assignments was less than 50 percent.

It is clear that missing assignments also affect one's performance on an examination! To see why, we need only recall the basic principle that *we learn best by seeing examples and practicing for ourselves*. Assignments are vehicles for relevant and targeted practice. In other words:

- Assignments tell you *where* you should concentrate your practice. They identify relevant practice problems in relevant areas, as suggested by your professor! Assignments identify problems that best illustrate key concepts to enhance understanding.

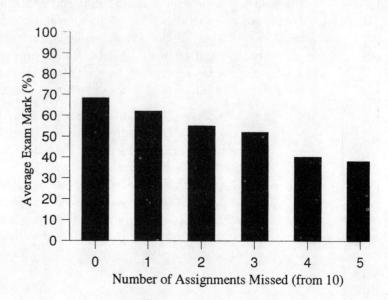

Figure 7.3 Missed assignments and their effect on final course grade

- Assignments identify problems similar to those that may be asked on tests. (Your professor is giving you clues!)
- Assignments identify required standards and expectations. The problems chosen indicate the standard expected in particular technology courses.
- In technology courses, working through relevant practice problems allows you to see patterns and note repetitions in solution techniques, making subsequent problems easier to solve. Assignments provide an excellent source of such problems.

Now that we have established the importance of assignments, the next step is to examine how you can be most effective when *writing* assignments. As previously mentioned, the three main purposes of an assignment are:

- To get *practice* in relevant techniques.
- To get that 10 to 20 percent of the course grade allocated to assignments.
- To help you review for examinations.

All three of these objectives depend on how you *present* solutions to assignment problems—in other words, *what* you write and how it is *recorded.* Before proceeding further, go to your *Strategies for Problem Solving Workbook* and reread the introductory material on problem solving and Polya's four-step process (approximately eight pages). The workbook presents a clear, logical procedure for arriving at the correct answer. Using the procedure consistently and methodically will help you in your mathematics course.

As far as the first purpose of an assignment is concerned (to get *practice* in relevant techniques), the procedure by which you arrive at the correct answer is just as important as the answer itself. It is exactly the development and repeated application of a set procedure that will allow you to begin to see patterns and repetitions in solutions, which is the main reason for practice in any technology course. For example, if you were now asked to solve a related problem, you could mimic the solution to the preceding example. The reasoning is clear and easy to follow, because of the effort invested the first time around. In this respect, solutions to assignments should resemble *maps or recipes,* recording *where* and *how* to proceed when you want to repeat a similar calculation.

The following are additional reasons to record as much as possible of your solution procedure (bear in mind the other two purposes of an assignment: to get that 10 to 20 percent of the course grade allocated to assignments and to help you review for examinations):

- A good step-by-step solution procedure enhances understanding; it's like teaching or explaining the material to yourself.
- It may take some *hard thinking* to solve certain problems. Recording the steps will save time next time you encounter a similar exercise, leaving you more time to practice with new problems. (Recall the *map* concept, i.e., that maps basically allow us to draw from our own or someone else's experience of having already worked out how to get to a desired location.)
- The person grading the assignment will be impressed by your clear and logical thinking (indicating understanding) and will find it much easier to allocate partial credit when, for example, an arithmetic slip or a careless omission has led to an incorrect final answer.
- When it comes to tests (remember, assignment questions are excellent as practice test problems), a detailed approach to assignment solutions allows for *reviewing* as opposed to *relearning.* There's nothing worse than trying to remember how you did something and then having to spend the same time (again) *relearning* how to do it. Just keep a record, and then consult your *map* or *recipe.*

- Detailed solution procedures will help you organize your thoughts and develop effective problem-solving techniques.

There is no doubt that more detailed solutions will, at first, take more time. This extra time should be thought of as an investment in the future. Soon, the *step-by-step* approach will become automatic, and you will have developed an effective procedure for solving many different kinds of problems.

Doing Assignments Yourself Versus Doing Them in a Group

The benefits of collaborative learning are particularly attractive when it comes to working on assignments in groups. We review some of them here for your convenience. Working on your assignment as part of a group will give you the following advantages:

- You will see and learn alternative problem-solving strategies,
- You will learn from your fellow students. This will add to and improve your overall learning experience.
- If you get stuck on a particular problem, the group tends to keep things going by *brainstorming* new and alternative suggestions instead of just giving up. The group atmosphere provides for active, cooperative learning: People in groups tend to verbalize their thinking, which adds to the problem-solving process.
- Working as part of a group will also lead to an improvement in self-esteem and a decrease in anxiety levels. (Talking about things relieves anxiety.)

However, when all is said and done (unless you are required to submit a group assignment), the final assignment you submit must reflect your *own* understanding—you will not have the benefit of a group in examinations. For this reason, it is perhaps best to adopt a middle-of-the-road approach. By all means, formulate and discuss ideas and opinions in collaboration with your colleagues. Think of this as part of the information-gathering process. Then use the information to put together your own assignments. Do not submit anything you do not understand, even if it is correct. First, make sure you understand how to solve all of the problems yourself, and then (with the three objectives of an assignment in mind) write and submit your own assignment.

Using Posted Solutions to Assignments

In many technology courses, professors will provide detailed solutions to assignment problems. It is always a good idea to consult these solutions, irrespective of your grade on a particular assignment. There are two main reasons for doing so:

1. By consulting the professor's solutions, you see exactly what constitutes a proper, correct solution (procedure) in the eyes of the professor (usually the person who grades examinations). This way, you know exactly what's *expected* of you.
2. Remember, an assignment is not just a way of accumulating points (recall the three purposes of assignments); it is also a way of developing efficient solution procedures and an important component of preparation for tests. For these reasons, whenever possible, you should always check your assignment against the professor's solutions, just to make sure that you are doing what you should be doing.

Determining your study techniques should reflect your types of intelligence and learning style. The goal is to maximize your strengths and minimize your weaknesses.

Using Tutors and Study Guides

There are a variety of school resources available to technology students. In some schools, such resources include free tutoring services in, for example, writing skills, mathematics, and learning strategies. You are strongly encouraged to make use of all free tutoring available to you, throughout your time in school, whether it is offered as part of your technology program or as an additional school resource.

In many cases, however, particularly when free tutoring is not available, technology students choose to seek help by hiring a personal (or group) tutor or by purchasing self-study manuals or study guides. Whereas there are many advantages to using any of the latter, the biggest drawback, by far, is the additional cost. For this reason, *before* spending any additional money on help, it is always best to utilize, as much as possible, the sources of help available as part of your technology program and those offered by school organizations.

Finding a Tutor

The main reason for hiring a tutor should be to obtain *specific, targeted, intensive, one-on-one help,* at convenient, selected times during a course. The additional cost involved means that most people hire tutors only when it is absolutely necessary to do so, such as at critical times during the course, when an extra injection of intensive help is required (e.g., in preparing for examinations).

Choosing a tutor, however, can be fraught with difficulties. Let's begin by noting a few important facts concerning tutors.

A tutor is *not:*

- Someone who "sort of" remembers something about the material or was "once able" to do something similar.
- A student who has recently passed the same technology course, even if he or she was at the top of the class! Passing a course (even with a perfect score) does not qualify someone to teach the material!

A tutor is:

- Someone with considerable expertise in the course in which help is required. A general rule of thumb is that the tutor should have completed at least two levels above that with which he or she is required to assist.
- Someone who can communicate ideas easily, effectively, and with a great deal of patience!
- Someone who can answer specific questions quickly, efficiently, and without any uncertainty.

The best way to find a tutor is through *word-of-mouth referral,* usually from your professor, a fellow student, or an informed advisor. Some institutions claim to have lists of *approved tutors.* Be careful here! Make sure you ascertain what qualifies a tutor for inclusion on the list. Sometimes it's nothing more than the fact that someone made a phone call to the person.

Once you have found a suitable tutor, it is necessary to take steps to ensure the most effective use of *(paid)* time spent in consultation. In this regard, the following suggestions may help you:

- *Prepare.* Before you meet with the tutor, make a list of all the questions you need to have answered. Keep the questions brief and specific. Make sure you are familiar with the material behind each question and the reason that you have asked a particular question. This will ensure that you make the time spent in consultation as effective as possible.

- *Control the session.* The tutor is there *for you.* Consequently, run the session according to *your* requirements. In this respect, make sure you tell the tutor exactly what you want. Stick closely to your list of questions. Don't let the tutor *stray* from the topic, and don't waste time.
- *Stay focused.* Every minute of time spent with a tutor costs money. Hence, stay alert and focused on your requirements. Don't leave a particular point or question until you are entirely satisfied with the explanation.
- *Get targeted help.* Use the tutor as a *source of help,* not to replace your efforts on assignments and practice problems. The tutor should *add to,* not replace, the overall learning experience. The tutor cannot, and should not, do the work for you. Rather, he or she should *show you how* to do the work yourself.
- *Learn as part of a group if you can.* If you require less in the way of one-on-one attention, but would like to have access to a tutor for the purpose of discussing a certain number of specific points and questions (e.g., while reviewing or working through old examinations), consider getting together with your study group or a few classmates and hiring a tutor *for the group.* This will save you money and afford you the advantages of group discussion.

Using Self-Study Manuals

Self-study manuals are similar to tutors in that they can be used to provide *specific, targeted help* in relevant areas. Your tools book is such a reference and self-study manual. It contains targeted information and is intended to help you quickly review, find and research information that you need.

Problems

1. Using a form similar to that in Figure 7.2, schedule your time for the next school day. Try to stick to this schedule, but feel free to make any minor adjustments as they arise. Explain any difficulties that arose. Did you find any advantages to scheduling your time?
2. Repeat Problem 1, but schedule your time for a whole week.
3. Make up five-question tests to test *prerequisite skills* required for each of your technology courses. Use your own experience so far (which prerequisite skills did or do you think are most important for each of your technology courses?) and any information offered by your professors or second-year technology students.
4. For each of your technology courses, list five skills that are prerequisites for entering the course.
5. List what you regard as the five main purposes of attending a lecture.
6. What do you think are the five main skills required to be effective in a lecture?
7. Explain the importance of taking notes in a one-page paper entitled "Why Bother Taking Notes in a Lecture?"
8. Suppose you were given a choice of using lectures or a textbook. List five advantages associated with not having to attend lectures and having to rely on the textbook instead. List five disadvantages associated with not having to attend lectures and having to rely on the textbook instead.

9. Write a one-page paper on the importance of assignments and homework. List the reasons that professors assign homework and what you think homework adds to your overall performance in technology courses.

10. Look over a problem from one of your previous assignments, preferably from two or more weeks ago. Pick one of the more difficult questions. Read over your solution to this problem. Does the solution still explain how to solve the problem today? If not, improve the solution, so that in two weeks' time you can read it through and understand immediately how to solve the problem.

11. Does reading through the solution to a problem provide the same level of understanding as solving the problem yourself? Explain. List five differences between the two procedures.

12. Suppose you get stumped on a particularly difficult question. One of your study buddies has solved the problem and gives you a copy of his solution. What do you do?

13. Of the study strategies presented in this section, list those in which you actively engage. List those that you have never tried before. List those that you think would help your effectiveness as an technology student. Resolve to implement as many of these strategies as possible throughout your time in technology school.

14. So far we have discussed the following study skills and strategies:
    - Interacting with, and making effective use of, your professors
    - Collaborative learning and group study
    - Time management
    - Making the most of class time: lectures, and laboratories
    - Effective note taking
    - Goal setting
    - Getting yourself motivated
    - Making use of school and other resources
    - Preparing for your technology courses; making sure your prerequisites work
    - Making effective use of the course textbook
    - How to be effective on assignments

    Which of these above strategies do you think are most important for success in technology study? Rank your choices from 1 (most important) to 5 (least important). Which skills or strategies do you need to improve in? Devise a plan for improving these skills.

How to Be Successful on Examinations

Examinations invariably make up the single largest contribution to your final grade in any technology course. This simple fact explains why many technology students are focused on examinations (quizzes, midterms, and finals), rather than on an appreciation of the course material. Like it or not, your performance on examinations will more or less determine how well you do in your technology courses. For this reason, it is essential to understand *why* the very best technology students are so successful in examinations and to learn how to use this information to your advantage.

So why do certain students perform so much better then others on examinations? Some students put it down to a simple matter of intelligence: "Oh, that girl is really smart. Her father is a physics teacher and her mother has a Ph.D. No wonder she scores over 90 percent on all her tests." Others put it down to the lack of a social life: "That guy never goes out. He does nothing but study. No wonder he performs so well on tests!" I suggest that neither is entirely correct and that the truth lies somewhere in between. Once you've reached college level, *intelligence* alone is no longer sufficient to place someone in the top 5 percent of the class. There is far too much material to absorb and not enough time in which to absorb it—even if you devote all your time to studying. Usually, the very best students have an extremely active social life. Indeed their level of success often increases with their level of activity. Achieving success has more to do with *how* you prepare for an examination and *what* you do to prepare.

Knowing the course material does not necessarily ensure success in course examinations.

I recall my midterm examination from one of my first technology courses. I had worked consistently throughout the year, understanding the course material, doing every assignment, and working through extra practice problems (in much the same way as I did when I was in high school). I understood the main ideas and concepts, and I was able to apply them in different situations. So I was quite confident that I would do well on the examination. Imagine my surprise when I discovered that I had scored only 58 percent! Worse than that, many of those students scoring above me had performed poorly throughout the course, having missed assignments and often asking *me* for help. I couldn't understand why this happened, I had worked hard and I knew the material, so why wasn't I performing to the best of my ability? I began to discover the answer to my question when I asked one of my classmates (who had the highest score on the test) how she had prepared for the examination. It became clear to me that there were some *missing ingredients* in my test preparation routine. Basically, it came down to two things:

- Smart practice
- Examination technique

My friend and I had both prepared well during the course. What made the difference in our midterm scores was what we did in preparing for the test itself. She had obviously regarded the test as a separate entity, targeting and tailoring all her efforts not solely toward reviewing the course material (as I did), but toward doing well *on the test itself (smart practice)*. She had obtained many former and practice midterm examinations and rehearsed her performance, so that she had a much better idea of what was expected and how to demonstrate the required knowledge under a time constraint *(examination technique)*. She was entirely focused on doing well on the examination. I, on the other hand, was focused on the course material, believing that to be sufficient to perform to the best of my ability on the midterm.

To understand why my friend's strategy was so much more effective than mine, let's return to the car-driving analogy. None of us believe that we can pass a standard driving test simply by driving the way we do in everyday life. We recognize that a driving test requires us to demonstrate a distinct collection of maneuvers and exercises, based on basic driving skills, under examination conditions. Conversely, no one continues to drive the way they did during their driving test. The latter is a rehearsed performance, requiring specific targeted practice based on a knowledge of exact requirements *(smart practice)* and a focused effort to perform well under specific test conditions *(examination technique)*. Consequently, in preparing for a driving test, we find out as much as we can about *what* is required and *target* our preparation (as effectively as possible) toward those particular goals. Exactly the same principles apply to preparing for any test, academic or otherwise.

In fact, since that first midterm, an acknowledgment of these basic principles has allowed me to perform to the best of my abilities on all subsequent examinations, such as academic examinations (in many different disciplines), driving tests, athletics competitions, or whatever requires me to demonstrate performance under a given set of constraints.

In this section, we discuss, in detail, the many different aspects of maximizing performance on examinations, including, in particular, the two main ingredients: *smart practice* and *examination technique*.

PREPARING FOR EXAMINATIONS: SMART PRACTICE AND EXAMINATION TECHNIQUE

To prepare effectively for course examinations, it is important to think about *both* long- and short-term preparation. Each is an essential component of an effective overall exam-preparation strategy. Long-term preparation builds a solid base or foundation in the course material, allowing time for learning, understanding, and asking questions. The material is slowly digested and assimilated into long-term memory, where it can be recalled relatively simply (with, for example, a few practice problems) and as required.

Short-term preparation is more concerned with the details of the examination itself and involves fine-tuning, targeted (or smart) practice, and practice in one's examination technique.

There are many examples in real life where this type of long- and short-term strategy is employed. For example, when training for competition, athletes build a solid base throughout the year using weight training and a combination of speed and endurance exercises (long-term preparation). Only as competition time approaches, do they tend to devote most of their training to *specific* events (short-term preparation).

Long-Term Preparation

Clearly, what you do during the semester will affect your performance on course examinations. As previously noted, long-term preparation is not, in itself, sufficient to guarantee maximum performance on examinations, but it is certainly necessary. Those who omit the long-term component of exam preparation engage in what is more commonly known as *cramming*.

Cramming describes an effort to fit a significant amount of work (for example, a month's or an entire quarter's worth of work) into a single night or weekend. *Cramming never works in technology*, basically because most disciplines contributing to the subject are not fact-based. Rather, they are method-based, cumulative (the understanding of one part depends heavily on the understanding of previous parts), and example-driven. There is just no way to read, understand, and practice every technique in such a short period of time. It simply doesn't work. Technology students who try cramming for examinations *never* perform to the best of their abilities.

Fortunately, long-term preparation takes place automatically for those who work consistently and conscientiously throughout the semester. The main components are summarized as follows for your convenience:

- *Lectures and classroom time*
  —Collect information in a clear, concise, and organized fashion. This will make the information easier to understand when it comes to reviewing for examinations.
  —Pay particular attention to specific topics and sections of the course material and examples emphasized in class. They often unexpectedly show up on examinations.
  —Make notes of any hints or extra information that a professor might give during the course.

—Use class and lecture materials to identify relevant sets of practice problems from the textbook or any other source. These will be useful when it comes to practicing, or *fine-tuning*, for examinations.

- *Assignments and homework*
  —Write clear, concise, and logical solutions. This will help tremendously when it comes to reviewing for examinations, since it is always easier to *review* than to *relearn*.
  —If you answered any assignment problems incorrectly during the quarter, make sure you understand your mistakes and make a note of the correct solution(s). It is always best to do this as soon after realizing the error as possible, when the topic is current and fresh in your mind. When you return to these solutions (for example, in reviewing assignments), not only do you have the correct solution, but you also have a note of what *not to* do—that is, your original error.
  —Use assigned problems as an indication of what material the professor deems most important in the course and of the standard expected by the professor. I often tell my students to think of assignments as a collection of *study guides* for each particular topic covered in the course.
- *Developing efficient problem-solving techniques.* Using clear and logical procedures to solve a wide range of problems over the entire semester cannot help but develop efficient problem-solving techniques. These techniques improve only with experience and practice, neither of which cannot be achieved in the short term. By examination time, many of these techniques will become *automatic*, requiring only fine-tuning when you review for examinations.
- *Asking for help.* Fix problems as they arise (not all at once near exam time, which leads to panic and *exam anxiety*). Use all of the resources at your disposal, including your instructor. Make a note of the help you receive, because you may need it later if you encounter similar difficulties upon reviewing course material.

The most successful students continue to demonstrate the importance of consistent long-term effort as a necessary foundation on which effective exam-preparation strategies are based. There is no doubt that this has always been, and will continue to be, an extremely significant factor in distinguishing optimum from mediocre performance on course examinations.

Short-Term Preparation

Short-term preparation is mostly concerned with preparing for the examination itself and involves fine-tuning, *targeted* (smart) practice, and practice in examination technique. The following are the main components of an effective short-term strategy:

- *Find out what will be covered on the examination.* It is always extremely useful to know which material is likely to be on an examination and which isn't. This allows you to target your efforts toward the relevant areas. There are basically two ways to get such information:
  1. *From (recent) past examinations in the same course.* In many introductory technology courses, examinations tend to cover the same standard material, year after year. Use this information to your advantage. Note any patterns, relative emphasis of one topic as opposed to another, and, perhaps how and where to obtain old or practice examinations.

2. *From your professor:* Ask your professor what material will be covered on the examination. This is a perfectly valid question, and you have nothing to lose by asking it. (But remember to be polite, courteous, and professional.) In most cases, the professor makes up the examinations, so there is no better person to ask. Similarly, when you peruse old examinations, show them to your professor. Ask whether the old practice examination is a good example of what will be on the [professor's] exam. Ask the professor if he or she recommends that you work through any *specific* past examinations or set of practice problems.

- *Apply smart practice.* Once you have a good idea of the topics most likely to appear on the examination, concentrate and target your efforts toward these particular areas by using the following steps:
  1. Review the relevant theory from course notes and the course textbook.
  2. Review relevant worked-out examples from the course notes and the course textbook.
  3. Review your solved assignments.
  4. Work through relevant problems:
     a. *Practice problems.* Work out sets of relevant practice problems from the textbook or any other source (preferably suggested by your professor). Choose these practice problems carefully. The main purpose here is to develop fluency and a working knowledge of selected techniques. Consequently, the practice problems should be mainly repetitive. Once you feel comfortable with any particular method, try a different style of problem using the same technique, but perhaps in a different setting. (These types of problems usually appear towards the end of a particular problem set in the textbook.) If you are unsure whether a particular set of problems is relevant, *ask* your professor. A good rule of thumb is to perform at least five (standard) practice problems per technique (to develop fluency), followed by one or two *different* or unusual problems in the same technique (for fine-tuning).
     b. *Assigned problems.* Redoing assigned problems is excellent practice, since you have the correct solution in front of you against which to check your work. Also, assigned problems are good indicators of the required standard and are chosen specifically to reinforce relevant lecture material that is likely to appear on examination.
     c. *Suggested problems.* Your professor may have worked through or suggested specific problems in class while a particular topic was under discussion. Do these problems (again if necessary), for they have been chosen specifically to reinforce or demonstrate a particular method or technique. Finally, *ask* your instructor to recommend some practice problems. You can be sure that this information will be relevant
     d. *Old or past examinations.* This is discussed in detail next.
- *Work through old or practice examinations.* Without a doubt, this is the most crucial stage of *smart practice.* An old or practice examination affords you the opportunity to actually rehearse the event. The questions are as relevant as they can be (they are actual examination questions for the very same technology course), and the examination conditions are probably identical, or at least extremely similar, to those that you will encounter. There are two equally important components of an old or practice examination package:

1. *The examinations themselves.* It is always a good idea to ask your professor which old or practice examinations are most relevant and which he or she would recommend.

2. *Detailed solutions to the examinations.* These are usually extremely difficult to obtain, but get them when you can. They are extremely valuable. Not only do they allow you to check your own solutions, but they let you see what is expected of you. Sometimes, professors will make solutions available, and sometimes the solutions are sold in packages in departmental offices or bookstores. It may take a little effort to find them, but it is always worthwhile: They make a particular examination much more effective as a tool for practice or rehearsal. Be careful, however, to use the solutions properly. Don't read them as a substitute for working through the problems. (*Reading the solution is not the same as doing the problem yourself.*) The solutions will always look easier than expected, and there is no substitute for performing the procedure yourself. You should pretend that you don't have the solutions, struggle with the problems as necessary (this is where the majority of the learning takes place), and consult the solutions only after you feel you have finished. Remember, there will be no solutions available when you take the examination. If you cannot get solutions to a particular practice examination, try the examination yourself, and then ask a member of the teaching staff to help you with any difficulties or to check your solution technique for obvious mistakes. Remember, the correct answer is only part of the solution; the technique by which you arrive at the answer is just as important.

There are two ways to use old or practice examinations:

1. *As an excellent source of relevant practice problems.* Ignore the examination conditions, and just do the problems. This will develop the required fluency and fine-tune your skills.

2. *As a way to develop your examination technique.* When you take into account the actual examination conditions, practice examinations allow you to rehearse, while actual old examinations are equivalent to a dress rehearsal; you can actually simulate the examination itself. Simulating the examination will allow you to develop the skills required to perform under the constraints (time, stress, or otherwise) of an actual examination.

   You should work through at least three practice examinations before writing your particular examination. At least one of the three examinations should be an actual past examination, and you should treat it as a *dress rehearsal.*

- *Examination technique.* Examination technique is concerned with two things: *acknowledging* that an examination requires you to perform under certain constraints and *practicing,* as much as possible, to overcome any difficulties associated with those constraints (for example, exam anxiety and time management). The following are the constraining elements inherent in most examinations:

1. Examinations always incorporate an unknown element: You are never 100% sure of what you may be asked.

2. Examinations require that you perform under a time constraint.

3. Examinations require that you demonstrate your knowledge precisely and logically. This means that, to be most effective, you must present your solution in a manner compatible with that expected by the person grading the examination.

   We shall discuss the different aspects of writing an examination, including the most efficient way to present solutions and what the person grading the examination looks for, in the upcoming section, "Taking the Examination."

   Taken together, these constraints are largely responsible for the two most common complaints associated with writing examinations: *exam anxiety* and *insufficient time*.

- *Exam anxiety.* It has been my experience that the most successful technology students overcome exam anxiety by making the examination an *anti-climax.* By the time they get to the examination, they have worked through so many practice problems and practice examinations, that they are on "autopilot." They know what to expect, many of their reactions during the examination are instinctive, and they are focused on their particular goal. There will always be the usual adrenaline rush associated with writing an examination, but when it comes to overcoming exam anxiety, *preparation* is the key—particularly short-term preparation, in the form of *rehearsal* and *dress rehearsal.* I have found that the process of working through practice examinations is one of the most significant components of overcoming exam anxiety in technology.

- *Insufficient time.* This is again symptomatic of inadequate practice and rehearsal with actual examinations. Working through an adequate number of practice problems allows you to develop fluency in the necessary skills, making your approach and problem-solving procedure almost automatic. This means that, in the examination, you solve problems quickly and effectively. Practice or old examinations, on the other hand, tell you what to expect in the allotted time. Working through a sufficient number of practice examinations cannot help but inform you of how much material you are likely to encounter in the examination itself. You will know (approximately) what to expect, and you can practice performing the required number of problems in the allotted time. We will return to this particular topic later, when we discuss writing the examination.

It is clear that old or practice examinations play an important role in developing one's *examination technique.* Other important factors that determine your effectiveness when you take an examination also will be discussed.

PREPARING FOR EXAMINATIONS: GETTING ORGANIZED

We have discussed the specifics of how to study for a test: *smart practice* and *examination technique.* In this section, we take one step back and examine the more general issues related to exam preparation.

How you prepare for an examination depends very much on the particular type of examination you are required to take. For this reason, it is important to obtain as much general information as possible about the examination itself, as soon as it becomes available. The following are things to find out about the examination:

- *Details of the examination*
    1. Is it a quiz, midterm, or a final examination?
    2. What are the place, time, and duration of the examination?

3. Is it an open-book or a closed book examination?
4. Is it a multiple choice, a written examination, or both?
5. Are *"cheat sheets"* (formula sheets) allowed?
6. Are calculators allowed?
7. How much is this examination worth as a percentage of the final grade?
8. What happens if you miss the examination for any reason?

- *What might appear on the examination?* Once you have discovered the type of test facing you, you should then enter your *short-term* preparation routine, as previously discussed. The first step in this routine is to find out what is likely to be asked on the test and what isn't. This will begin the process of *smart practice,* as discussed before.

We have already considered, in detail, some of the things you should do as part of an effective long-term preparation strategy. The following are additional suggestions that may help you during your short-term preparation:

- *Prepare a review schedule.* Prepare a structured review schedule. This schedule will vary in length and depth, depending on the volume of material you have chosen to study. This, in turn, will depend on the type of test you are required to write. For a final examination, prepare your schedule at least two weeks in advance. For a midterm examination, prepare one to two weeks in advance. For a quiz, preparing a few days in advance often will suffice. When preparing your schedule:
  1. Scan the relevant course material, and divide it into separate sections; usually based on different theories, techniques, or applications.
  2. Identify the material that you think is likely to appear on the examination.
  3. Allocate study time to each section according to the volume of material, its relevance to the examination, and its importance (i.e., the likelihood that it will appear on the examination).
  4. For each section, identify a set of relevant practice problems from the textbook, course notes, past assignments, or otherwise. Make note of these.
  5. Decide which practice or old examinations you will work through and when you will do it. (Remember to keep one such examination for the final stages of your review as a *dress rehearsal*)
  6. Remember to allocate more time for particularly difficult concepts or examples that require more thought—such as word problems.
- *Review section by section.*
  1. Begin with an overview of the technique illustrated in a particular section.
  2. Read through worked-out examples that use that technique (e.g., from course notes or your textbook) until you feel confident enough to be able to apply the technique for yourself (i.e., until you understand the main ideas behind the method.)
  3. Begin practicing the technique for yourself using the sets of (targeted) practice exercises identified earlier. Be sure to write clear, logical, and *methodical* solutions to the problems, as if you were teaching the material to yourself. This will help you pick up extra points when you actually take the examination.

4. Once you feel comfortable with the technique in a particular section, move on to the corresponding practice problems from course notes and old assignments. You should have access to the solutions to these problems, so make sure you check your *method* as well as your answer. (The former is more important.)

5. By this stage, you should have a good working knowledge of the section of material you are reviewing. To *fine-tune* your skills, pick a problem or two (dealing with this material) from some recent or practice examinations, and see if you can confidently and competently write a full solution to each problem. Do not skip any steps. Get into the habit now of writing full comprehensive solutions. Remember, when you take the examination, you must demonstrate your knowledge. Don't assume that any particular step is trivial; it may not be to the person grading the examination.

6. Finally, to complete the review of a section, write a summary of the section as follows:
   —List the important concepts, techniques, and formulas in the section.
   —Link each concept, technique, and formula with practice problems, assignment problems, examples in course notes or the textbook, and practice examination problems that you have worked through as part of your review and have found to be particularly good for understanding and developing fluency in the technique. You may want to return to these problems and examples for a quick review of the section as the examination draws closer.
   —Make any notes that you think may help you when you return to this material later.
   —Follow the foregoing procedure for each section of examinable material.

- *Study groups: discussion.* Group review is particularly effective for the following reasons:
   1. Group review represents active, cooperative learning. It is always a good idea to *talk* about the material under review.
   2. You see and learn problem-solving strategies.
   3. You learn from other students.
   4. When you get stuck, the group will tend to keep the momentum going.
   5. Group review improves self-esteem and decreases anxiety levels.

Consequently, *in addition to* (not instead of) following these review procedures, make an effort to discuss the material, examples, and problems with other people. Be careful to use this activity properly (as a *supplement* to your review). I have witnessed many situations in which students working in groups believed that they were reviewing effectively, but were, in fact, merely taking notes from the efforts of the well-organized students who always led the discussions. When all is said and done, you will face the examination alone. It pays to keep this at the back of your mind at all times!

- *Final review and fine-tuning.* Following the suggestions discussed here will allow you to learn the material, develop fluency and method in the particular techniques, and commit all of this to a part of your brain from which it can be easily retrieved. Then, one or two days before the examination you can review the collection of summaries you made when you reviewed each individual section. Build confidence and reinforce what you already know by selecting random practice problems from your collection and solving them *"blindly"* (i.e., without any supplementary information, such as that obtained from notes or a textbook, as you will do in the examination). Finally, fine-tune your skills by *rehearsing* with one or two complete examinations. After this, you will be well prepared for anything!

In closing this section, we make a few common sense suggestions relating to the logistics of studying.

- *Where to study.* To study effectively, it is necessary to free yourself of distractions and competing associations. The thinking part of the brain really *warms up* only after a period of deep thought or effort, usually after struggling or trying very hard to solve a particular problem. For this reason, you should never mix business with pleasure when it comes to studying for examinations. Instead, you should try to make your study time as efficient and as effective as possible. One hour of concentrated, focused study is worth three hours of watered-down, distracted study any day. Try to keep the following simple rules in mind:

  1. *Pick a quiet room that is free of distractions.* For example, the bedroom or library, and *not* your bed, the living room of your home, the kitchen table, a local fast-food restaurant, or a cafeteria or coffee shop.

  2. *Get comfortable.* Make sure that when you are studying, you wear comfortable clothes and use a comfortable chair. Any discomfort will distract you from your main purpose.

  3. *Take frequent breaks.* Be sure to get out of your study environment for a break whenever you feel the need, perhaps every hour or so. This will keep you sharp and maximize your effectiveness. Beware, however: Breaks shouldn't occur too frequently. It usually takes at least 30 minutes of effort to warm up your thinking. You shouldn't interrupt your concentration just when you get into things. Breaking too frequently will mean that you are constantly warming up and never working at the most effective level. Keep the breaks short (e.g., five minutes) and simple. Get up for a stretch, a snack, or something else, but be careful to minimize distractions during your break. Keep things rolling over in your mind, and don't get into some deep (unrelated) conversation with a friend!

  4. *Eat well and get plenty of rest.* To perform well mentally, you need to stay healthy. If you organize your study time effectively, you will have sufficient time to eat well and get lots of sleep.

  5. *Engage in physical activity.* For some reason, after spending a significant period of time thinking about a problem, things often come to people in the most unusual places or when they are doing something completely unrelated, such as jogging or working out at the local gym. The complete change in activity (from studying) seems to make things clearer. Have you ever had that experience? Even if you haven't, some good physical activity does tend to refresh and reenergize our minds and our bodies. And it doesn't have to be anything sophisticated: Even taking a brisk walk seems to have the desired effect.

TAKING THE EXAMINATION

The day has arrived! You're well prepared, confident, and ready to go. Nevertheless, to maximize your performance during the examination, there are certain essential components of taking an exam of which you must be aware:

- *Eat something.* Make sure you have a good meal on the day of the examination. You will expend lots of energy when you take the examination, so make sure you fuel your body sufficiently.
- *Dress comfortably.* Wear comfortable clothes. Remember, you may be sitting in the same position for up to three hours.
- *Do you have everything?* Before you leave for the examination room, go through a checklist of all the things you will need when you take the examination. For example, you may need any or all of the following things:
  —Writing instruments
    Pens
    Pencils
    Rulers
    Erasers
  —A calculator. If you do need one *remember* to check the batteries. Also bring spares if possible.
  —A textbook or other supplementary materials allowed by the examiner (if you will be taking an open-book examination)
  —A watch

Bring as many replacements of these items as you think you will need.

Get There Early

Arrive at the examination site at least 15 minutes before the examination begins. This will give you time to compose yourself, note the seating plan, and make yourself aware of any new instructions.

Get a Good Seat

When you enter the examination room, make sure you choose a good seat, one that is relatively free of distraction. In some cases, large rooms are used for a variety of different examinations, of varying styles and duration. If your examination is two hours long, and the row next to yours is being used for a one-hour examination, you will be distracted by students packing up midway through *your* examination. In such cases, it always pays to take a few minutes before the examination to study the seating plan. Similarly, try not to sit near students with heavy colds, they tend to sniff and cough a lot. Also students (even friends) with a different examination philosophy (i.e., those that tend not to take examinations seriously) should be avoided when it comes to seating. You have invested too much time and energy to risk being distracted by someone who is not focused. Find a nice quiet area not too far from the people proctoring the examination, because you may need to ask questions.

The large majority of examinations in technology are of the written type, multiple-choice, or an element of each. We begin with a discussion of the written examination and return to the subject of multiple-choice tests later in the chapter.

Maximizing Performance in Written Examinations: The First Few Minutes

When the examination begins, spend the first few minutes scanning the questions (including the distribution of points). When you do, note (in writing, near each question) which technique you will use and how much time you think you will need to answer each question. These little notes help you allocate your time effectively and act like doors, opening compartments to the (now) more-than-familiar corresponding review sections. Scanning the entire test at the start also gives you an opportunity to make sure that your examination paper is complete. Imagine finding out with five minutes to go that you are missing a question worth 20 percent of the grade! Once you have looked at all the questions, rank them according to level of difficulty. The easier problems usually require you to demonstrate methods and set procedures. The more difficult problems require more thought and less routine application of course material.

At this point, you can proceed in one of two ways, depending on your particular preference:

1. Start with the easier problems and work towards the more difficult problems. There are three main advantages to this strategy:
   a. In solving the easier problems, you slowly *warm up* your thinking in preparation for the more difficult ones.
   b. Solving a series of problems successfully means that you gain immediate confidence that you can tackle the more challenging problems.
   c. Getting the easier problems out of the way first will maximize the amount of time remaining to consider the more challenging problems,
2. Start with the most difficult problem and work towards the easiest problem. The main advantage in using this approach is that you can tackle the questions requiring the most thought at the beginning of the examination, when you are less tired and more alert.

The majority of the top students have consistently favored the first approach, but it depends on your particular preference. Once things are underway, bear in mind the following points, which will add to your overall effectiveness when you take the examination:

- *Note the point distribution.* Use the point distribution to allocate time for each question. Clearly, a question worth five points should not require as much time as one worth 20. Use the point distribution also as an indication of what is expected. The 20-point question requires 20 points worth of effort, and so on.
- *Show details in open-book examinations.* Open-book examinations rely less on memory and more on method and technique. Consequently, you are expected to demonstrate more detail in open-book examinations than in closed-book examinations. For example, in a closed-book examination, you may get a point or two for writing down a correct formula. In an open-book examination, by contrast, the formula is considered as being *supplied* (in the text), so it carries no weight. Instead, open-book examinations emphasize more method and problem-solving techniques.
- *Use formula sheets.* If a formula sheet is supplied with your examination, use it as a guide to the techniques that are to be employed on the examination. For example, if a complicated formula does not appear in the formula sheet, it is unlikely that you will need to use that formula on the examination.
- *Attempt every question.* Don't be afraid to try to answer every question, even if you're not sure how to proceed. Write down your thoughts, and try to develop a solution using logical steps. Partial credit may be awarded for some of the things you write down.

- *Watch your time.* Pace yourself, and try to stick as closely as possible to the time you have allocated to each question (on your initial appraisal of the examination). If you get stuck and can't seem to make any progress on a particular problem within the allocated time, leave the problem, and return to it at the end of the examination if there is time. It is better to lose points on one problem and gain points on the remaining problems than to sit for the rest of the examination wasting valuable time. Remember, even if you have been engaged in active thought in answering a particular question, if there is nothing on paper, the instructor will assume that you have done nothing in time. There is no way for the instructor to believe otherwise.
- *Ask for clarification.* If you are unsure about anything to do with how the examination is written, including the wording of a particular problem or the way it is stated, *ask* about the problem. There is nothing to lose, and you gain the added advantage that a verbal clarification might jog your memory.
- *Write with the purpose of getting the maximum number of points.* This is perhaps the most important aspect of writing examinations. An examination is just that—an *examination* or *investigation* of your performance, in a particular subject, on a particular day. Accordingly, you are required to *perform*, that is, to demonstrate your knowledge of the subject. When you bear in mind that in a written examination the only way to demonstrate ability or knowledge is by writing it down, the person grading the examination will use the written response as the *sole* criterion for judging your ability to answer a particular question. This is the crucial consideration that must be taken into account when writing solutions to a problem or an exam. Solutions must be written with the person grading the examination in mind.

After examination, some students always return to their professor to discuss their performance. Some wish to see their paper in an effort to pick up more points. What follows are some of the explanations heard whenever students have tried to explain blank or partial solutions to examination problems:

- "I knew what I was doing; I just didn't write it down!"
- "You [meaning the professor] know that I know how to do this stuff! I've done it many times in the assignments, and you gave me 100% each time. Surely you didn't expect me to produce all the details. There is a time limit, you know!"
- "I worked out the problem on a piece of scrap paper. I didn't write the details down because I didn't think they were important. I did get the correct answer, however; look!" (The student then points to the one equation $x = 3$ on the otherwise blank page.) "Don't I deserve full credit for this problem?"
- "I didn't have time to write the complete solution, so I did the calculation quickly in my head and obtained the correct answer. Why did you give me only 1 point out of 10?"

I answer these comments by informing the students (yet again; I do this in class at least three or four times *before* the examination) of exactly what I (and instructors, in general) look for when grading examinations:

- A set procedure or method illustrating clear, logical thinking and understanding, leading to the correct answer

- An ability to use the most appropriate technique in the most efficient way possible
- An ability to communicate ideas effectively
- An ability to develop a scientific argument, stage-by-stage, step-by-step, and with any necessary mathematics, leading to the desired result
- An ability to use problem-solving strategies and explain the significance of any results obtained

Clearly, the final answer (e.g., $x = 3$) is only one part of the *solution;* accordingly, it carries only a proportion of the points allocated to a *complete* solution.

We discussed the importance of writing clear, logical, step-by-step solutions to assignment problems. Exactly the same is true of writing solutions to examination problems, except that in this case it is even more crucial. Your professor will equate what you have on paper to what you know about solving a particular problem. There is nothing else to look at.

Below are three different solutions to the same problem taken from a final examination. The first two solutions were submitted by Students #1 and #2 as part of the written examination for this course. Both solutions have been graded (using the solution key provided in Solution #3—the professor's solution) and show the number of points awarded for each correct step in the solution.

Example 1

A bulletproof vest consists of a series of identical thin-coated metal sheets fixed together. A bullet, moving at 900ft/s, is directed in a straight line towards the vest. The bullet loses 20% of its speed as it passes through the first sheet in the vest. How many such sheets should the vest contain to ensure that the bullet stops before passing completely through the vest? (Neglect air resistance and assume that the bullet's mass is conserved).

Solution:
(Student #1)

$$T_1 + \text{work} = T_2$$
$$p \text{ sheets} \qquad ②$$

$$\frac{1}{2}\frac{W}{g}(900)^2$$

$$? \quad \frac{1}{2}\frac{W}{g}(720)^2 \quad ①$$

$$\int F \, da$$

$$p = \frac{145800\,\frac{W}{g}}{\frac{1}{2}\frac{W}{g}(900)^2} = 2.78 \checkmark$$

$$\frac{5}{10}$$

$$\sim \underline{3 \text{ sheets required}} \checkmark \quad ②$$

Example 2

A bulletproof vest consists of a series of identical thin-coated metal sheets fixed together. A bullet, moving at 900ft/s, is directed in a straight line towards the vest. The bullet loses 20% of its speed as it passes through the first sheet in the vest. How many such sheets should the vest contain to ensure that the bullet stops before passing completely through the vest? (Neglect air resistance and assume that the bullet's mass is conserved.)

Solution #2
(Student #2)

$$\frac{1}{2}mv_1^2 + \text{W.D.} = \frac{1}{2}mv_2^2$$

Particle dynamics

Work + E ②

$$\frac{1}{2}m(900)^2 \qquad\qquad \frac{1}{2}m\left(900 - \frac{900}{5}\right)^2$$

$$\frac{1}{2}m(900)^2 + N\left[\frac{1}{2}m(900)^2 - \frac{1}{2}m(720)^2\right]$$

$\frac{5}{10}$

$$= 0 \qquad ②$$

$$\underline{N = 3} \checkmark ①$$

Example 3

A bulletproof vest consists of a series of identical thin-coated metal sheets fixed together. A bullet, moving at 900ft/s, is directed in a straight line towards the vest. The bullet loses 20% of its speed as it passes through the first sheet in the vest. How many such sheets should the vest contain to ensure that the bullet stops before passing completely through the vest? (Neglect air resistance and assume that the bullet's mass is conserved).

Solution #3
(Professor)

- **Strategy:** Regard the bullet as a particle. The bullet is moving with an initial speed that changes after it comes into contact with the first metal sheet. In other words, the bullet's kinetic energy is altered as a result of the sheet. Try principle of work and energy.
- **Principle of work and energy.** Consider the situation arising when the bullet passes through the first sheet.

$$T_1 + Work\ (1 \rightarrow 2) = T_2 \qquad (1)$$

Here, T_1. T_2 represent the kinetic energies of the bullet just before and just after it passes through the sheet, respectively. (2)
- **Calculate kinetic energies and work**

$$T_1 = \frac{1}{2}mv_1^2 = \frac{1}{2}m(900)^2$$

$$T_2 = \frac{1}{2}mv_2^2 = \frac{1}{2}m(720)^2$$

where m is the mass of the bullet and v_1 v_2 ($= \frac{4}{5} v_1$) are the speeds of the bullet before and after impact, respectively. Before impact, the sheet does no work on the bullet. As the bullet passes through the sheet, however, the sheet does work equal to $-I$ on the bullet (since the force exerted by the sheet on the bullet is in the direction opposite to the bullet's motion). Hence the total work done by the sheet on the bullet from time 1 → time 2 is

$$0 - I = -I \qquad 2 \tag{3}$$

- **Apply principle of work and energy for a single sheet.** From (1) – (3),

$$\frac{1}{2}m(900)^2 + (0 - I) = \frac{1}{2}m(720)^2$$

- **Apply principle of work and energy for the required number of sheets.** Suppose we require n sheets to stop the bullet. Noting that, in this case, since the bullet is stopped in the final state,

$$T_2 = 0$$

From (1), we obtain

$$\frac{1}{2}m(900)^2 + (0 - nI) = 0$$

From (4), we have:

$$\frac{1}{2}m(900)^2 + [0 - n(145800m)] = 0 \qquad \textcircled{2}$$

- **Solve for n to obtain**

$$n = 25/9$$
$$\cong 2.78$$

In other words, at least three sheets are required to stop the bullet.

Notice that, although both Student #1 and Student #2 arrive at the correct answers, neither demonstrates the complete, correct logical procedures required to arrive at these answers (illustrated in the professor's solution). Consequently, both score only 5 points out of a possible 10, even though they each obtained the correct answers. They may have *known* the correct procedures, and they may even have *thought* through the problem using these procedures, but the point is that they did not write down the details. The grader cannot be expected to read between the lines or work out what you are trying to say. Only what you write down will be used toward assessing your grade. Solutions are almost always graded on a partial-credit basis, meaning that points are allocated to different parts of the procedure, of which the correct answer is but one part. To get a perfect score, you must demonstrate *all* of the components of the procedure. This grading methodology also works *for* you, when, for example, you demonstrate the correct procedure, but arrive at the wrong answer through an incorrectly performed calculation or some other misstep. In this case, you will receive all the points except those allocated to the correct answer itself. Try to apply the following guidelines when you write solutions in examinations:

- Recognize what the instructor will look for when grading your solution.
- Develop a clear, logical procedure leading to the correct answer.
- Don't be messy! The person grading your exam will not take the time to decipher what you are trying to say.
- Don't assume that the person grading the exam knows what you are talking about. Tell the grader exactly what you want to say.
- Label diagrams and place them where they belong, near the part of the solution to which they are most relevant.

Finally,

- *Don't leave early*
  Devote the entire examination period to maximizing your performance. If you finish the examination early, use the extra time to check your solutions. Add details, tidy up explanations, or think about alternative strategies for dealing with problems you couldn't solve. Even if you think you have aced the test, stay and check anyway.
- *Ignore everyone else*
  Sometimes when fellow students leave the examination early, there is a tendency to think that the examination should be easy and that you are missing something. This is nonsense. Take all the time you need. For all you know, those people leaving early may have failed. Many times, examinations submitted ahead of time almost never account for the top scores in the class. Quite the contrary, the very best students use every available minute to their advantage.

MAXIMIZING PERFORMANCE IN MULTIPLE-CHOICE TESTS

Most of what has just been said of written tests is true also of multiple-choice tests. After all, both types of tests have the same objective: to test your knowledge of the course material. From your point of view, the main difference and the biggest drawback to a multiple-choice test is that, since each question requires only a simple answer, for example, A, B, C, or D, there is little opportunity to *demonstrate* understanding of the course material through the presentation of well-written, clear, and logical solutions. Consequently, unlike written tests, in which method and procedure contribute significantly to the number of points awarded for each solution, multiple-choice tests exclude the opportunity to accumulate points from a detailed and methodical solution.

Nevertheless, in technology, the approach to solving problems on a multiple-choice test should, essentially, be the same as that used in solving problems on a written test. The main difference is that, at the end of the procedure, only the final answer is returned, not the solution (the *method* leading to the final answer). In other words, in a multiple-choice test, you will be answering the same types of questions you would on a written test, only shorter ones (a consequence of asking many equally weighted questions in a relatively short period of time). Hence, you should be prepared to work through each problem *anyway,* on a separate sheet of paper, and *arrive* at the correct answer through the same logical reasoning used to solve problems on a written test. Accordingly, make sure you bring a supply of *scrap paper!*

Of course, in a multiple-choice test, since the correct answer appears alongside each question (although hidden among decoys), there is always the opportunity to *guess.* This method, however, should be used only as a last resort. By far the most efficient and effective way of tackling a multiple-choice test in a technology subject is to treat it, essentially, as a written test and return only the final answers (at the end of your solution) on the answer sheet.

The following procedure may help you in answering multiple-choice questions:

Step 1 Identify any key words to help get you through the *padding* (extraneous information) and to the real meaning of the question. Identify the appropriate technique or theory to be used in the solution.

Step 2 Ignore the (given) answers and solve the problem for yourself on a separate sheet of paper. Do so clearly and methodically, as if you were supplying the solution to the same problem on a written test. If necessary, draw a diagram, it may help you to *see* things more clearly.

Step 3 Compare your answers with the given alternatives. If your answer is among them, enter the appropriate choice on the answer sheet. If your answer is not among the alternatives but *close* to one, go back and check how you worked out your solution. (This will be easy to do if you have solved the problem methodically.) Locate and correct any errors you find, and repeat each step until you believed you have identified the correct alternative. If, despite your best efforts, you cannot arrive at any of the given alternatives, choose the one that is *closest* to your answer.

Step 4 Move on to the next question.

The following tips may prove helpful in answering multiple-choice questions:

- If you are completely *stumped* and unable to begin to solve a particular problem, eliminate any alternatives that you *know* are incorrect, and make an *informed guess* from the remaining alternatives.

- The solution to a multiple-choice question is usually short and should take no more than 5 to 10 minutes (a consequence of asking many equally weighted questions in a relatively short period of time). If you find yourself spending more than this amount of time on a particular question, you are probably using the wrong method, so either guess or move on to the next question. Remember, each problem is worth the same number of points.

- If you complete the test with time remaining, return to those questions that you answered with any degree of uncertainty. Reexamine the *logical alternatives* (i.e., exclude the alternatives previously identified as incorrect), and check your answers.

- Often, *working backwards* is a good way to check your answer. Take your answer and make sure it fits the problem.

AFTER THE EXAMINATION

After the examination, you should take any opportunity to view your graded paper. For class quizzes and midterms, this is usually done in class, on the day the professor returns the grades. For final examinations, it may be necessary to make a separate appointment with the professor. No matter how well you did, reviewing your examination is a learning experience and a vitally important exercise in preparing you for the next examination, in the same course or otherwise. The following are some of the more important advantages associated with reviewing your examination:

- *Identification of errors in grading.* The professor may have made an arithmetic error in adding the different points awarded to each problem. Check the addition yourself. Similarly, the professor may have missed a question or forgotten to grade part of a problem. Point this out if he or she did. Ask the professor to outline his or her grading scheme. This way, you can ascertain the various points allocated to each solution and ensure that your paper was graded accordingly. Remember to be professional and courteous at all times.

- *Learning from your mistakes.* Use what you have learned from reviewing your examination to improve your performance in any future examinations. While the material is fresh in your mind, check any posted solutions, try to understand any errors in your solutions, and rework problems as necessary. This is particularly important in reviewing quizzes and midterms where you have the opportunity to correct any errors in method, understanding, and presentation (writing) *before the all-important* final examination. Consult with your professor as necessary.
- *Self-critique.* An examination affords you the opportunity to *try out* your studying, preparation, and examination-writing strategies. Use the review to analyze, improve, develop, and fine-tune your approach. Look for weaknesses, and decide how you will not make the same mistakes again.
- *Learning from the examination.* In the case of a quiz or midterm, you now have an actual examination made up by the very professor who will be responsible (entirely or in part) for your final examination. Note the style, the emphasis, and, above all, what the professor requires in a perfect solution. Be sure to use this information to your advantage in the final examination. Quizzes and midterms also afford you the opportunity to have your instructor critique and comment on all aspects of *your performance, before* the final examination. What better way to improve your studying, preparation, and examination-writing strategies than to have the *examiner* comment on the results of your efforts!

What to Do if You Failed Miserably

If you really made a mess of the examination and you're not sure why, apart from doing the things previously mentioned, you should make an appointment with your professor and try to explain or discuss what went wrong. The professor may see errors in your studying, preparation, or examination-writing strategies that may be easy to correct. Following are some of the same recurring reasons that students have performed so badly on examinations:

- Most admit to never having worked through a past or practice examination *by themselves.*
- Most have never engaged in smart practice.
- Most have never thought about *rehearsing* and practicing their examination technique.

In most cases, it is the *short-term preparation* that is inadequate or, in some cases, missing entirely. This is easily corrected using the procedures outlined in the first part of this chapter.

It is important that you maintain adequate communication with your professor in this and in all course-related matters. At the end of the course, the professor is charged with the responsibility of assessing your performance using the usual sources of information (assignments, examination scores, etc.) and any other information that you care to make available. Thus, you can make a good impression on your professor by frequently asking sensible questions in a courteous and professional manner. In this way, you appear conscientious and committed. Consulting with your professor after an examination adds to that impression and works to your advantage. For example, in some cases, professors will discard a disastrous midterm grade and move the appropriate weight to the final examination. This usually happens only when the professor is convinced that you have the potential to demonstrate the required knowledge by the end of the course, but, for example, you have "gotten off to a bad start." Such a decision is almost always *ad hoc,* based on the professor's *impression* of your individual *demonstrated* abilities, a significant part of which depends on good communication between you and your professor.

Problems

1. Write a one-page paper entitled, "Why Examinations Are an Essential Part of Technology" and discuss reasons this is so.
2. Write a 500-word essay entitled, "What I Do to Prepare for Examinations" in which you discuss your examination preparation procedures.
3. Think about your examination preparation routine. Write down its main components, in chronological order. What are its main strengths and weaknesses? Suggest ways to improve the weaker aspects.
4. Using the information in this chapter, devise a new examination preparation strategy. Implement this strategy when you prepare for your next test.
5. Write down five advantages of using past or practice examinations as part of your exam preparation.
6. List three places at school where you can obtain past or practice examinations for each of your technology courses. Find out if solutions are available.
7. How would you find out which topics are likely to appear on an upcoming test?
8. Produce a detailed *study schedule* for any one of your technology courses. You should allocate sufficient time for studying and demonstrate how and when you will cover the necessary material, as well as perform the necessary practice examples.
9. Which of the three solutions presented in the chapter example most resembles your solution to an examination problem? How could you improve on the way in which you present solutions in examinations?
10. Ask each of your professors how they go about grading examinations. Use this information to help you maximize your effectiveness when you take an examination.
11. Have you ever had a really bad examination? Explain why it was so bad and what you did or will do to ensure that you don't make the same mistakes again.
12. Make up an examination question from any one of your technology courses. Try to be as original as possible. Produce the detailed solution and allocate partial credit accordingly. Make sure you test all the necessary skills the examinee should possess.
13. Make up a one-hour examination for any one of your technology courses, You should produce a full solution key and grading scheme. You should also ensure that the best students are adequately challenged and that the time allotted is neither too little nor too great.
14. From your experiences answering Problems 12 and 13, write a one-page paper on "What a Professor Looks for When Grading Examinations."
15. Having read the material in this chapter, describe how your approach to preparing for and taking examinations will change. If you feel that there is no need for you to change anything, say why.
16. Describe a (nonacademic) real-life example in which you have prepared, taken, and successfully passed a test of some kind. Identify the most important factors leading to your success, Draw parallels with technology examinations.

17. Write a one-page paper detailing what you would do if you discovered that you had failed an examination that you expected to *ace.* Include a discussion relating to how you would use the experience to improve your subsequent performance on tests.

18. Have you ever failed an examination? What went wrong? What did you change about your examination preparation and writing routines to prevent the same thing from happening again?

READINGS

[From Paul Nolting: *Different Skills to Be Used for Math Courses.*]

Purpose

Your purpose for reading the following selection is to learn some key techniques for a good start in math courses. You will also practice looking for main ideas and marking your text with helpful notes.

Preview

Paul Nolting, a mathematics professor, offers advice for math study in his book, *Winning at Math.* This first chapter talks about things to consider before enrolling in a math course.

1. Scan the subheadings carefully.
2. Check the questions and the vocabulary at the end.

Anticipate/Associate

1. Have you ever had difficulty with previous math courses? If you did, do you know why? _____

   _____

2. What ideas do the subheads suggest that might be clues to making math easier? _____

   _____

Different Skills to Be Used for Math Courses

Paul Nolting

Mathematics courses are considered to be totally different from other college courses and require different study procedures. Passing most of your other college courses requires only that you read and understand the subject material. However, to pass mathematics, an extra step is required: applying the material by doing the problems.

Example: Political science courses require reading the textbook and understanding the material. But your instructor isn't going to make you run for political office to apply knowledge you obtained.

In mathematics you must understand the material, comprehend the material, and apply the material. Applying mathematics is the hardest task.

Linear Learning Pattern

Another characteristic of mathematics is its linear learning pattern. *Linear learning pattern means that the material learned on one day is used the next day and the next day, and so forth.*

If you fail to understand the classroom material the first week, you may never catch up. Linear learning affects studying for tests in mathematics as well. If you study Chapter One and understand it, study Chapter Two and understand it and study Chapter Three and *do not understand it,* then when you have a test on Chapter Four, you're not going to understand it, either.

In a history class, if you study for Chapter One and Chapter Two, and do not understand Chapter Three, and end up studying and having a test on Chapter Four, you could pass. Understanding Chapter Four in history is not totally based on comprehending Chapter Three.

To succeed in mathematics each previous chapter has to be understood before continuing to the next chapter.

When students get behind in mathematics it is difficult to catch up. Mathematics learning is a building process. All building blocks must be included to win at math. Mathematics learning builds up geometrically and compounds itself. Math is not a subject in which you can forget the material after a test. REMEMBER: To learn the new math material for the test on Chapter Five, first, you must go back and learn the material in Chapter Four. This means you will have to go back and learn Chapter Four while learning Chapter Five. The best of us can fall behind under these circumstances. However, if you do not understand the material in Chapter Four, you will not understand the material in Chapter Five either and will fail the test on Chapter Five.

Math as a Foreign Language

Another way to understand studying for mathematics is to consider it a foreign language. Looking at mathematics as a foreign language can improve your study procedures. In the case of a foreign language, if you do not practice it, what happens? You forget it. If you do not practice mathematics, what happens? You are likely to forget it, too. Students who excel in a foreign language study and practice it at least every other day. The same study habits apply to mathematics, because it is considered a foreign language.

Like a foreign language, mathematics has unfamiliar vocabulary words or terms to be put in sentences called expressions or equations. Understanding and solving a mathematics equation is the same as speaking and understanding a foreign language. Mathematics sentences have words in them, such as equal (=), less (<), and unknown (a).

Learning how to speak mathematics as a language is the key to success. Currently most universities consider computer and statistics (a form of mathematics) courses as foreign languages. Universities have now gone as far as to make mathematics a foreign language.

Mathematics is not a popular topic. You do not hear Dan Rather on TV talking in mathematics formulas. He talks about major events in countries like Korea to which we can relate politically, geographically, and historically. Through TV—the greatest of learning tools—we can learn English, humanities, speech, social studies, and natural sciences, but not mathematics. Mathematics concepts are not constantly reinforced like English or other subject areas in our everyday lives. Mathematics has to be learned independently. Therefore, it requires more study time.

High School Versus College Math

Mathematics as a college level course is almost two to three times as difficult as high school mathematics. In college, the fall and spring math class time has been cut to three hours a week. High school math gives you five hours a week. Furthermore, college courses are taught twice as fast as high school courses; what is learned in one year in high school is learned in one semester (four months) in college. This enhances mathematics study problems for the college student, you are receiving less instructional time and proceeding twice as fast. The responsibility for learning mathematics has now shifted from the school to the student, and most of your learning will have to occur outside the college classroom.

Course Grading System

The course grading system for mathematics is different in college than in high school. While in high school, if you make a D or borderline D/F the teacher more than likely will give you a D and you may go on to the next course. However, in some college mathematics courses, students cannot make a D, or if a D is made, the course will not count toward graduation. Also, college instructors are more likely to give an N (no grade), W (withdraw from class), or F for barely knowing the material, because you will be unable to pass the next course.

Most colleges require students to pass two college level algebra courses to graduate. In high school you may graduate by passing one to three arithmetic courses. In college you might have to take four mathematics courses and make Cs in all of them to graduate. *The first two high school mathematics courses will be preparation for the two college level algebra courses. Therefore you must <u>dramatically</u> increase the quality and quantity of your mathematics study skills to pass more mathematics courses with higher grades.*

Your First Math Test

Making a high grade on the first major math test is more important than making a high grade on the first major test in other college subjects. The first major math test taken is the easiest and most often least prepared for. Students feel that the first major math text is mainly review and they can make a B or C without much study. These students are overlooking an excellent opportunity to make an A on the easiest major math test of the semester which counts the same as the more difficult remaining major math tests. These students, at the end of the semester, sometimes do not pass the math course or do not make an A because their first major test grade was not high enough to pull up a low test score on one of the remaining major tests.

Studying hard for the first major math test and obtaining an A has several advantages:

- A high score on this math test *can <u>compensate</u> for a low score on a more difficult fourth or fifth math test*—and major tests count the same.
- Knowing you have learned the basic math skills required to pass the course. *This means you will not have to spend time relearning the misunderstood material covered on the first major test while learning new material for the next test.*
- *Improving <u>motivation</u> for higher test scores.* Improved motivation can cause you to increase your math study time, allowing you to master the material.
- *Improving confidence for higher test scores.* With more confidence you are more likely to work harder on the difficult math homework assignments, which will increase your chances of doing well in the course.

College math instructors treat students differently than high school mathematics instructors. High school mathematics teachers warn you about your grades. Some college instructors may ask you, "How are you doing in the course?"

Do not expect them to say, "You have been making Ds and Fs on your tests and you need to come to see me." That would be a rare response. *You must take responsibility and make an appointment to seek help from your instructor.*

Sometimes, due to the increase in the number of college math courses, there are more adjunct math faculty than full-time math faculty. This problem can restrict student and instructor interaction. Fulltime faculty have regular office hours and are required to help students a certain number of hours per week in their office or math lab. However, adjunct faculty are only required to teach their mathematics courses; they don't have to meet students after class even though some adjunct faculty will provide this service. Since mathematics students usually need more instructor assistance after class than other students, having an adjunct math faculty member could require you to find another source of course help. *Try to select a full-time math faculty member as your instructor.*

Finding a Study Buddy

Getting a study buddy is suggested. You can't always depend on having the instructor available for help. A study buddy is someone in your class to call when you have difficulty working mathematics problems. *A study buddy can improve your study time.*

Check Your Understanding

Before beginning to check your understanding, reread the selection and make marginal notes.

Review

Using the subheads and your marginal notes, write a main-idea sentence for each of the subheads.

Linear Learning Pattern: _____

_____

Math as a Foreign Language: _____

_____

High School versus College Math: _____

_____

Course Grading System: _____

_____

Your First Math Test: _____

_____

Finding a Study Buddy: _____

_____

Fill in the Blanks

Complete the statements by writing the best word in the blank.

1. Math has a _____ learning pattern.
2. To learn math, you need to _____ it; consequently, you will have many problems to solve for homework.
3. Your first math test is the _____.
4. Summer is not the _____ time to take a math course.
5. When you get behind in math, it is _____ to catch up.

Multiple Choice

Select the letter of the answer that best completes the statement.

_____ 1. The main idea of the whole selection is:
   a. Math is difficult.
   b. You have to have special intelligence for math.
   c. Learning math is different from learning other subjects for several reasons.
   d. Math teachers try to make the courses difficult.

_____ 2. Passing college math can prove difficult
   a. if you take the course in fall or winter.
   b. if you don't learn it in a linear pattern.
   c. if you don't make an A on the first test.
   d. because you can guess at the answers.

_____ 3. You can be successful on a chapter math test if you
   a. take your best estimated guess at the answers.
   b. understand the chapters preceding the test chapter.
   c. understand equations.
   d. do most of the assigned homework.

_____ 4. Math is like a foreign language because
   a. you must practice it frequently.
   b. it is a popular subject.
   c. math concepts are reinforced in daily living.
   d. everyone needs to understand more than one language.

_____ 5. Which of the following reasons is _not_ an important reason for getting an A on the first math test?
   a. A high score on the first test will make up for a lower test score later.
   b. A good score on one test improves your motivation.
   c. A good score gives you confidence.
   d. Your instructor will be impressed.

True/False

Label the statements true or false.

_____ 1. Applying math is the hardest task.
_____ 2. If you don't understand Chapter 3 in math, go ahead to Chapter 4. It may get easier.
_____ 3. Learning how to speak math as a language is a key to success.
_____ 4. College math is usually easier than high school math.
_____ 5. The best time to take math is during the summer because you can complete it faster.
_____ 6. It is easy to get behind in math.
_____ 7. Even if you get a D in math, you can go to the next course because it will be different.
_____ 8. When you're having difficulty in math, it's a good idea to make an appointment to see your instructor.
_____ 9. Getting a good grade on the first math test can help motivate you for the next test.
_____10. The linear learning pattern of math is like building with blocks. Each one must be solidly in place before you add another one.

Vocabulary

Use the words from the list to complete the statements that follow.

kamikaze	equation	reinforce	circumstance
enhance	linear	motivation	procedure
dramatically	compensate		

1. If one thing follows another in a line, it has a(n) _____ pattern.
2. A(n) _____ is an expression that asserts the equality of two quantities.
3. Having good _____ leads to better grades.
4. If you follow a set _____ in a math problem, you should reach the correct conclusion.
5. If a person experiences difficulty with math, seeking appropriate help will _____ for the weakness.
6. Spaced review will _____ ideas to be learned.
7. Attempting a math course without sufficient time for homework and review is called _____, because you won't survive.
8. Learning each chapter of a math text completely will _____ increase your chances for success.
9. The _____ or the surroundings of your study area can…
10. _____ your learning.

Writing

1. Write a paragraph about your previous experiences with math courses. How were you successful or not so successful?
2. Write a paragraph or letter to someone taking math for the first time in college. What advice would you give this person?

Group Discussion

1. How can the skills learned in math be helpful to you in daily living? (You might want to brainstorm this question.)
2. Why do colleges require math courses for graduation?

PART V
Societal Demands on the Individual in an Information Society

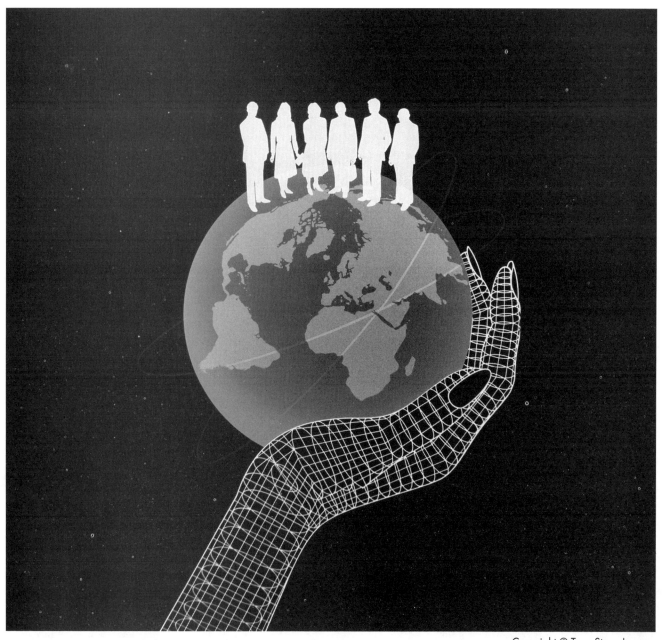

8

Solving Problems

PROBLEM SOLVING AND CRITICAL THINKING

Why Study Problem Solving Here?

As a first quarter student you may question why you have two courses that study problem solving. There is an entire course on problem solving. In that course you will learn how to be a technical problem solver. Not all problems are technical in nature. We know of many students who have become excellent technical problem solvers only to drop out of college or loose their job because they could not systematically solve other types of problems.

What makes it so difficult? The complex problems in our everyday life are often wrapped with emotional issues, values, and collaboration with other people. In this chapter we will focus on a systematic way to approach these problems. You will see a similarity with the process used in technical problems. Becoming an effective problem solver is an essential element of your professional training.

HOW TO BE SUCCESSFUL IN PROBLEM SOLVING

To be successful in college, the technical student must be a good problem solver. The dictionary defines a *problem* as "a *perplexing* question *demanding settlement,* especially when it is difficult or *uncertain* of solution." The key words are italicized. All problems demand settlement—require good problem solvers.

How often have you observed individuals refusing to make a decision or take action when decisive action is obviously needed? Is fate the only operative in this universe, or could better problem solving on the part of world leaders have changed history and improved the lives of all of us? How often have *you* failed to make a decision and act on that decision, causing yourself and those who depend on you to suffer?

There are many valid reasons that effective problem solving is so rare. Some of the most important reasons are:

- A lack of information
- Fear of making a wrong decision (or fear of failure)
- The time and energy needed to generate appropriate solutions and test the outcomes
- The absence of an effective problem-solving model

The first reason for not solving important problems, *lack of information,* can be overcome simply by realizing that we never have enough information. Problems become *perplexing,* or puzzling, because there is no neat solution that flows out of perfect knowledge. Good problem solvers enjoy the challenge of making decisions that others cannot or will not attempt. Being able to make these real-world decisions, made without full knowledge of the outcomes, is essential to your future happiness.

Fear of making a wrong decision, the second reason, may be easily put aside. The world's most successful people have failed. Winston Churchill, the great British statesman, was voted out of office after his decision to revaluate the British pound led to a general strike in 1929. He did not hold a cabinet position for ten years after that, at times living with extreme depression. He went on to become the heroic prime minister of Great Britain during World War II. The most successful technologist will often make wrong decisions. If you feel you have never failed you have not attempted much and *actually have failed* to reach your potential. And remember that *failure can result in success if we learn from our failures.*

Your choice to work in technology means *you must find time and energy to solve problems.* You will be confronted with problems on a daily basis: with equipment that doesn't always work the way it should, supervisors pushing seemingly impossible deadlines, or irate customers who cannot understand why their business is suffering because of a faulty computer. Good problem solving does not require great intelligence or creativity as much as hard work. The most successful people in business and industry will tell you that problem solving is "99 percent perspiration and 1 percent inspiration."

A top executive officer in the telecommunications industry discussed the necessity for hard work to overcome shortcomings:

To be honest, I like some days more than others, and some days I truthfully believe that the company cannot possibly survive my rash of bad judgments, but you will never find me quitting. Why? Because that is *my strength.* That is what I bring to the table. I have failings. I make mistakes. But no one, not ever, will outwork me. No one, not ever, will stick to a task longer than myself. No one, not ever, will out-plan me, will out-detail me, or outperform me. Again why? Because those are my strengths! Am I an intellectual giant? Not hardly. Am I an outstanding design engineer? Not in your or my lifetime. Is my English always correct? Don't I wish. But am I street smart, practical, and *hard working?* You bet!

Jack A. Shaw
Capitol College News
Graduation 1994

HOW TO DEFINE A PROBLEM

You constantly encounter problems to be solved, ranging from typical daily problems (how to manage study time or learn not to misplace your keys) to life-altering situations (how to adjust to a severe injury to design a custody plan during a divorce). Problems pop up in every aspect of your life. You will encounter school problems (how to get into courses required for your major), work problems (how to get along with a difficult supervisor), and personal problems (how to increase your income). Being a skilled and thoughtful problem solver can help you succeed at whatever you do.

> A little knowledge that acts is worth infinitely more than much knowledge that is idle.
> —Kahlil Gibran

THE EFFECTS OF NOT THINKING CRITICALLY

Making a decision or solving a problem without thinking critically can have negative effects. Think about a decision you have made in the past that you now consider unwise. What do you wish you had done? Perhaps you have said things to yourself such as, "I should have taken more time" or, "I should have asked someone for help" or, "I should have considered other options."

EMOTIONAL INTELLIGENCE

Many people find problem solving easy when they approach it from critical and creative thinking skills. It can be more difficult to solve problems, though, when you are too personally involved to see the situation clearly. Consider the story from the book *Emotional Intelligence:*

> A friend was telling me about her divorce, a painful separation. Her husband had fallen in love with a younger woman at work, and suddenly announced he was leaving to live with the other woman. Months of bitter wrangling over house, money, and the custody of the children followed. Some months later she was saying that her independence was appealing to her, that she was happy to be on her own. "I just don't think about him anymore—I really don't care," she said. But as she said it, her eyes momentarily filled up with tears. The moment of teary eyes could easily pass unnoted. But the empathic understanding that someone's watering eyes means she is sad despite her words to the contrary is an act of comprehending just as surely as distilling meaning from words on a printed page. One is an act of the emotional mind and the other an act of the rational mind. In a very real sense, we have two minds, one that thinks and one that feels.

> It is with the heart that one sees clearly, what is essential is invisible to the eye.
> —Antoine De Saint-Exupery

Only recently, researchers have realized that there are many ways of gathering information. As you learned previously, multiple intelligences affect how you learn, process, store, and retain information. In addition to the research done on multiple intelligences, Daniel Goleman, author of *Emotional Intelligence,* says that there are "two fundamentally different ways of knowing." One, the rational mind, is how we comprehend information. The other, the emotional mind, responds to information through feeling.

The rational mind:	The emotional mind:
reflects	feels
analyzes	controls impulse
thinks	regulates moods
ponders	motivates

Often, problems or elements of problems carry emotional weighting. In some problems, choosing the appropriate weighting is an important part of the solution process.

Although it is extremely important to develop your creative and critical thinking skills, having healthy responses to life can be equally important to both your well-being and success. Look at the list of benefits below and imagine how they might help you perform your job more effectively:

- Responding to others with skill
- Recognizing other's emotions
- Knowing how to delay gratification
- Understanding your own feelings and responses to others
- Effectively managing your responses

Following are three categories of ways people emotionally respond, adapted from *Emotional Intelligence*.

Usually individuals will fall into one of these three categories. Either make a mental note to yourself or place a checkmark next to the areas where you rate yourself.

Self-aware people:

____ are aware of their moods
____ have sophistication over their emotional life
____ are generally autonomous
____ are in good psychological health
____ understand and honor their personal needs
____ manage bad days with relative ease
____ do not obsess

Engulfed people:

____ feel overwhelmed by their emotions
____ allow their moods to take charge
____ have wide mood swings
____ often feel out of control
____ are unaware of their emotional life

Accepting people:

____ have no compelling urge to analyze their feelings
____ may not address their feelings and therefore be prone to depression
____ may be generally happy and therefore not feel the need to change

Having emotional self-awareness is an important part of decision making in school, in the workplace, and in life. The following exercise can help you see your emotional strengths and areas of your emotional life that need improvement. Read through the following chart and check the responses that apply to you.

Emotional Skills

Skills	Never	Usually	Always
I can identify what I am feeling.			
I can assess the intensity of what I'm feeling.			
I can delay gratification.			
I can control impulses.			
I can reduce the stress I'm feeling.			
I know the difference between feeling and action.			

Cognitive Skills

Skills	Never	Usually	Always
I conduct inner dialogues as a way of managing behavior.			
I read social cues from others.			
I utilize problem-solving skills.			
I understand the perspective of others.			
I understand what is acceptable behavior.			
I understand realistic expectations for my life.			
I have a positive attitude toward life.			

Behavioral Skills

Skills	Never	Usually	Always
I understand nonverbal communication.			
I respond effectively to criticism.			
I help others.			
I like participating in peer groups.			

Once you have checked your responses to the above exercise, analyze whether or not your emotional life needs more attention. If you checked the boxes marked Usually or Always, you probably have a fairly solid emotional life. On the other hand, if you checked the box marked Never, you probably need to spend some time getting to know your emotions. A good place to start is to become aware of what you are feeling. Try observing your feelings for the next several days. Keep a journal and note how often you are frustrated, happy, angry, etc. For many, journals offer the opportunity to process emotions that may have been suppressed during the day.

Can you see how emotional intelligence can help you to either avoid or deal more effectively with certain forms of problems? Being emotionally self-aware adds an important perspective that brings balance to the decision-making process.

NON-CRITICAL THINKING TENDENCIES

It's human to act impulsively, and people often short-circuit their problem-solving and decision-making success by doing so. Non-critical thinking tendencies include the following:

Acting on a problem or decision before thinking it through. Sometimes people don't believe they have time to think about the problem or decision, or just plain don't. For example, you may have said something that you regretted later, or you may have dated someone whom you later wished you hadn't. You may not even have an answer to the question, "Why did I do that?"

Doing what someone else says to do without thinking it over. At times it seems easier just to follow someone else's advice, especially if the advice comes from someone you like and trust. Even so, it isn't always the smartest choice for you and your particular circumstances. Another person may not understand your needs and may not ask the questions you need to ask. For example, a friend who liked a certain class recommends that class to you, and it turns out that you like it least of all your classes. You took the advice without thinking about it and did not ask questions stemming from your own needs.

Doing nothing and waiting for the problem or decision to sort itself out. Some problems and decisions are difficult or frightening. Sometimes it seems easier just to ignore them, hoping they will resolve on their own. Unfortunately, this often results in worsened conditions. If you have a mole that seems irregularly shaped or enlarged, for example, letting it go could lead to more serious medical problems, perhaps even skin cancer.

You won't always have the ideal amount of time, energy, and available resources to solve a problem or make a decision in the way that would benefit you most. Making your best effort to think critically before acting, however, will almost always make for a better solution or decision than you would have found had you not thought at all. Give yourself the best chance to succeed by thinking critically, using whatever time and energy you have.

For more information on Critical Thinking, consult your *Tools Reference* book and review Part III.

PROBLEM-SOLVING PROCESS

The six-step problem-solving process is introduced in your *Tools* book and each of the steps is defined briefly. The steps are as follows:

1. State the problem clearly.
2. Analyze the problem.
3. Brainstorm possible solutions.
4. Determine the criteria for your solution.
5. Explore each solution.
6. Choose and execute the solution you decide is best.

We are going to go into each of the steps in considerable detail, but you may wish to review the brief descriptions in your *Tools* reference book before you proceed.

1. State the Problem Clearly

The first step is to state and define the problem clearly and accurately. Although this step may seem obvious and easy, it can be difficult and often demands a great deal of energy. If you define the problem incorrectly at the start, the most flawless problem-solving technique won't help you fix what's really wrong.

The key to defining a problem correctly is to focus on the causes of the problem rather than the effects. Take, for example, the student described in your *Tools* book in the section on Inductive Logic who developed shoulder soreness from using a computer mouse. If he states the problem as, "My shoulder is sore" and stops there, he may design solutions such as "use a salve that helps muscle aches" or "get regular massages." He then may be surprised to find that the soreness keeps coming back. If, however, he defines the problem cause as, "The way I use the mouse is not comfortable for my body," he may come up with a solution such as raising his chair seat so his arm is lower when using the mouse. This solution, based on the true cause, is the one that will solve the problem.

As another example, you may have heard the Chinese saying, "Give a man a fish, and he will eat for a day. Teach a man to fish, and he will eat for a lifetime." If you state the initial problem as "The man is hungry," giving him a fish seems like a perfectly good solution. Unfortunately, the problem returns the next day, and the day after that. You could assume that this is a recurring problem or you could think in more depth about causes and redefine the problem, focusing on this cause: "The man does not know how to find food." Given that his lack of knowledge is the true cause, teaching him to fish will truly solve the problem.

This scenario can apply to how governments deal with homeless people. Although it's important to provide food and shelter for them, simply giving them something to eat day after day is not necessarily going to improve their situation. The real problem is that most homeless people do not have jobs, or the skills necessary for jobs, that could help them provide for themselves. Therefore, a better solution would involve therapy and training programs that could help people get off the streets and into the workplace. How to do that effectively, and find the funding for it, would be the next problem to solve.

There are four steps to defining a problem. Figure 8.1 is a visual representation of these steps.

1. *Collect information about the problem.* The more you know about the problem, the more likely you will be to identify its causes accurately and solve it effectively. This step has steps within it:
   - *Look at different perspectives.* The more views you can gather about the problem, the more you will be able to clearly define it. Talk with anyone involved with the problem (or anyone who has observed the problem) to get their direct input and observations.
   - *Break the problem into parts, if it has them.* Sometimes one problem is actually a combination of smaller problems. Analyze the problem to make sure you have gotten as specific as possible about its parts. If it consists of smaller problems, for example, you may want to solve each separately.
   - *Be specific and clear.* As with any critical thinking process, the better information (facts and evidence) you work with, the better your final product will be.

2. *If possible, observe the problem first-hand.* If this is your own problem, you are already "in the know." If, however, you are helping to solve a problem with which you are not directly involved, a first-hand view of it will help you better understand what's at stake. For example, if you are a supervisor at work and an employee comes to you with a problem, observing it rather than coming up with a solution on the spot probably will lead you to a more effective solution.

3. *Confirm your findings about the problem.* Once you have gathered all the information you can about the problem, check it for accuracy. Did you observe well and completely? Did people with whom you spoke give you the whole story?

Once you have gathered information about the problem, you have one more decision to make before you begin to solve it.

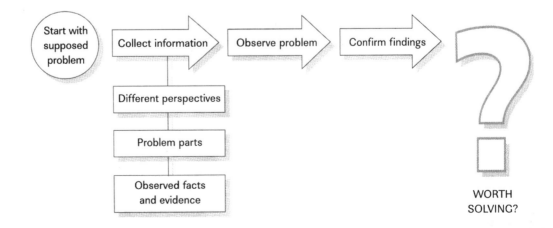

Figure 8.1 Defining a problem.

Ask If It's Worth Solving

In today's world, people are often overwhelmed with work, responsibilities, and relationships that seem to take up far more time than they should have. There are only 24 hours in a day, and it is impossible to sit down and give every problem in your life a complete, thoughtful, time-taking, problem-solving treatment. You will have to perform "problem triage"—make a quick evaluation of any problem or decision to see if it is worth your time.

For example, on a given day you begin to realize that you might not have time to grab some lunch. Is it worth troubling yourself over? Well, that's your call. Evaluate the situation by weighing the effects. If you know that you will have a chance to get a bite to eat in mid-afternoon, for example, you might want to let this problem pass by. Conversely, if you are diabetic and need to eat regularly to keep your body functioning normally, you may evaluate that this problem is worth solving.

You can use the question "So what?" to help you look at any potential problem and decide if it is worth your energy. When a problem comes up, ask yourself, "So what?" If you don't have an answer, you may be better off just letting it be. If you do have an answer, explore what makes the problem important for you to solve. Then move on and apply the problem-solving process.

2. Analyze the Problem

Once you have defined a problem and established that you want to solve it, walking yourself through a critical-thinking-based problem-solving plan will give you the best chance of coming up with a favorable solution. One way of getting a big-picture overview of where you want to go with a problem is to consider "present state" and "desired state."

Present state. This refers to where the situation currently stands. For example, you are having a conflict with your instructor. More specifically, you need to speak with her one on one. You have another class during her office hours, and you don't think she is trying to accommodate your needs.

Desired state. This refers to where you or anyone else involved in the problem would like the situation to be. Continuing the example, your desired state may be to have access to your instructor for a private meeting.

Getting from the present state to the desired state is where the problem-solving process comes in. The process, however, might not always bring you to exactly where you thought you wanted to be. It may lead you to the conclusion that the desired state is not possible (or not *yet* possible). It may introduce new possibilities of desired states to you. It may raise ideas about how you can put a twist on the present state and improve the situation that way. You won't find out, however, until you try. That's what the process is for.

You may wish to use graphical methods to analyze a problem. For example, you may find that cause and effect diagrams, also known as fishbone or Ishikawa diagrams, or free field diagrams will help you clarify potential causes that contribute to a problem.

A simple fishbone diagram might look like the following:

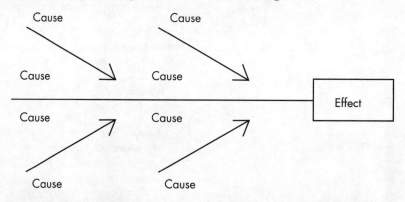

Figure 8.2 A simple fishbone diagram.

Complexity may be added by modifying the diagram somewhat:

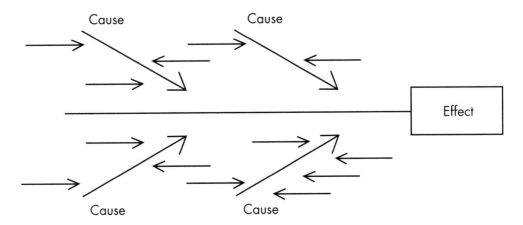

Figure 8.3 A complex fishbone diagram.

A force field diagram is constructed as follows:

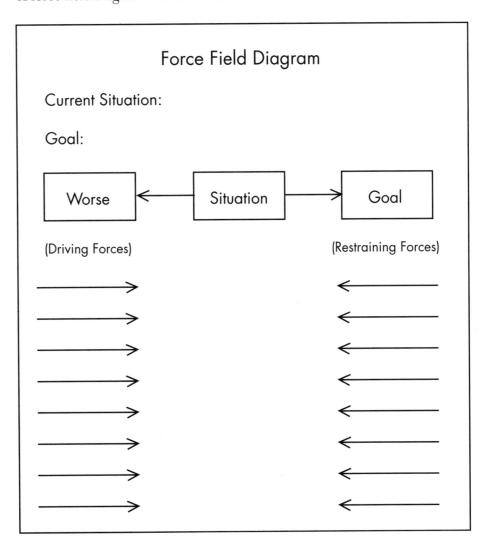

Figure 8.4 A force field diagram.

These methods are tools that you can use to help visualize and reduce a problem to its core component.

3. Brainstorm Possible Solutions

You are brainstorming when you approach a problem by letting your mind free-associate and come up with as many possible ideas, examples, or solutions as you can, without immediately evaluating them as good or bad. Brainstorming is also referred to as *divergent thinking;* you start with the issue or problem and then let your mind diverge, or go in as many different directions as it wants, in search of ideas or solutions. Here are some guidelines for successful brainstorming:

Don't evaluate or criticize an idea right away. Write down your ideas so you remember them. Evaluate later, after you have had a chance to think about them. Try to avoid criticizing other people's ideas as well. Students often become stifled when their ideas are evaluated during brainstorming.

Focus on quantity; don't worry about quality until later. Generate as many ideas or examples as you can. The more thoughts you generate, the better is the chance that one of them may be useful. Brainstorming works well in groups. Group members can become inspired by, and make creative use of, one another's ideas.

Consider wild and wacky ideas. Trust yourself to go off the beaten track. Sometimes the craziest ideas end up being the most productive, positive, workable solutions.

Creativity can be developed if you have the desire and patience. Nurture your creativity by being accepting of your own ideas. Your creative expression will become more free with practice.

4. Determine the Criteria for Your Solution

Criterion is a standard, guideline, or yardstick by which a solution is measured. The following areas should be considered:

Values: Many forget to consider the values that impact the decision. They often find themselves implementing a solution that is destined to fail because it conflicts with a key personal value. A student who valued coaching little league for his son's age group started a two-year intensive evening college in the fall. Things went well until spring. Suddenly the student started missing class and his grades began to suffer. He had not considered the impact little league would have on his college classes. He clearly wanted to be supportive of his son but he also knew completing the degree would result in significantly higher income that would help pay for his son's college.

Priorities: In the case above the student had to weigh his priorities. Once the criteria is set one should rate each priority according to its importance. While some priorities carry the same weight, others may be important but not necessary while others may be non-negotiable.

Feasibility: A solution must be feasible. Often problems have solutions but the solution is not possible given the set of circumstances. Feasible solutions often deal with resources of time, money, and ability. A student may know that hiring a tutor is a partial solution to his problem, but he clearly does not have the financial resources for this. Sometimes the feasible solution depends on whether we have control over certain aspects of the problem. The father did not have control over the little league schedule or his college schedule.

Results of solution: Criteria are included that are based on the effect of the solution. A frequent criterion is that the solution must not cause a bigger problem. The father could pay someone to go to class for him. Even if the person took excellent notes, the student's risk of being expelled if caught would be a greater problem.

Setting parameters: There are often elements that need to be included in any solution. In the case of the father and his little leaguer, the father may include that the son must feel supported and he must pass his courses.

Once the criteria has been set . . . .

5. Explore Each Solution

Why might your solution work or not work? Might a solution work partially, or in a certain situation? *Evaluate* ahead of time the pros and cons (positive and negative effects) of each plan. Create a chain of *causes* and *effects* in your head, as far into the future as you can, to see where this solution might lead.

Ask these important questions as you evaluate:

- What resources are available to help solve the problem? Do the solutions take advantage of these resources? Does any solution require resources we cannot access?
- When does the problem have to be solved? Does each solution fit the timeline? Can the timeline be changed?
- Whom does each solution benefit? Is there a solution that is truly best for everyone involved? If not, which solution benefits the most people? Is there a workable compromise?
- Does each solution adequately address the cause(s)?
- Does each solution help reach the desired state—or improve/change the present state?

Evaluate this step: Ask: Have I thought through each solution completely? Considered solutions for the sample problem? What are the other possible solutions for the problem?

6. Choose and Execute the Solution You Decide Is Best

The final step in the problem-solving process includes the following substeps:

Step 1. Choose and Execute the Solution You Decide Is Best
This is the action step. First, decide how you will put your solution to work, Then execute your solution.

Evaluate this step: Ask: Did I execute the solution completely and effectively?

Step 2. Evaluate the Solution
Look at the effects of the solution that you acted upon. What are the positive and negative *effects* of what you did? In terms of your needs, was it a useful solution or not? Could the solution benefit from any adjustments? Would you do the same again or not? In evaluating, you are collecting data. You are doing a form of research.

Evaluate this step: Ask: Did I acknowledge all of the effects, on every aspect of the situation, and weigh them all thoughtfully?

Step 3. Continue to Evaluate and Refine the Solution
Problem solving is a continual process. You may have opportunities to apply the same solution, or similar solutions, again and again. Evaluate repeatedly, making changes that you decide make the solution better (that is, more reflective of the causes of the problem).

Evaluate this step: Ask: Am I continuing to learn from what happened with this problem? Have I retained important knowledge that will help me with similar problems in the future? Is there an important idea (principle) of which this problem is an example?

Figure 8.5 Problem-solving plan.

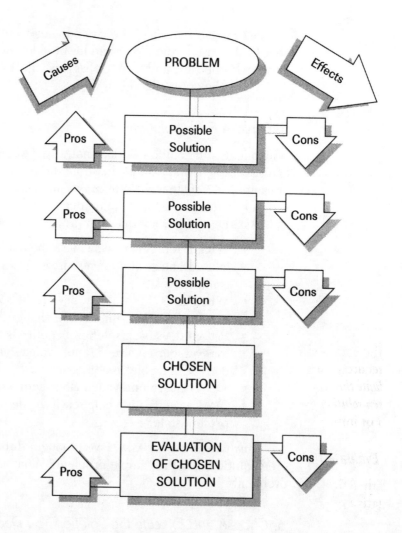

Using this process will enable you to solve school, work, and personal problems in a thoughtful, comprehensive way. The think link in Figure 8.5 demonstrates a way to visualize the flow of problem solving.

OBSTACLES TO PROBLEM SOLVING

Problem solving is often complicated, requiring a lot of effort. Along the way, problem solvers may make mistakes that prevent them from successfully solving their problems. You already have examined one common mistake—addressing effects or false causes in the first problem statement. Some other common obstacles follow:

The perfect solution. Believing that every problem has one perfect solution can intimidate you. If you come up with fifty ideas but none seems exactly right, you may think you just aren't good enough to find the right one, and you might give up. Even if you continue to try, looking for the perfect solution may drag out the process indefinitely, leading to your never getting around to solving the problem. Don't imagine there is one perfect solution. Instead, look for the *best* solution, using whatever time frame you have.

The smart-people complex. If you run into a snag while trying to solve a problem, you might get yourself off the hook by deciding that only a really smart person could solve this problem—and, of course, you refuse to define yourself as "a really smart person." This leads to both an unsolved problem and a negative assessment of your abilities. Think positive. Believe that any person, thinking critically and carefully, can solve this problem.

The first choice is the best. If you come up with a good idea right away, it's tempting to go with it. Even if you think you accomplished something, will the problem be solved effectively? If the first choice turns out not to be the best choice, you risk having to go back and start the whole process again. Be sure to give your ideas equal time, even if the first one is good. Evaluate each idea so you can be sure you have covered every angle. The more solutions you generate, the better chance you have at finding the absolute best one.

Focusing on the "easier" cause. If you aren't doing very well in a course, you may want to believe it is because your instructor is incompetent. Is that really the cause? You might feel relieved to blame someone other than yourself. If the true cause is that you aren't putting effort into your work, however, you do yourself a disservice. Blaming the instructor won't solve your difficulties in the course if the true cause lies elsewhere. Actually, it may add to the problems you already are experiencing.

Watch for these pitfalls as you work to solve the problems that come your way from day to day. Keep an eye out for them when making decisions, too.

USE THE STEPS FOR EFFECTIVE PROBLEM SOLVING

By following the steps for effective decision making, you will make better decisions. Consider the following example of a simple problem that will walk you through the problem-solving process. There are seven steps in the process:

1. **State the problem**
   What exactly is the problem? Be as specific as possible. For instance, you have just been hired at a company several miles away and have determined that you may need transportation. After analyzing your situation, and determining that other modes of transportation are not feasible, you can narrow your statement of the problem down even further. For the purpose of this case, the identified problem is that you need an automobile.

2. **Determine the criteria**
   What are the important factors to you in the decision you're about to make? In this case, you may determine that the criteria you think are important in looking for a car are:
   - Price
   - Gas mileage
   - Style
   - Comfort

3. **Rate the importance of the criteria**
   This is not a scientific formula, and you can rate factors in several ways. What you want to do is try to quantify your subjective feelings about the factors. One of the easiest ways to rate the importance of each factor is to use a scale of 1 to 10, with 10 being the most important factor to you. For example, in this case, the rating may look something like this:

Price	This is the most important factor, by far, in your decision so you give this a 10.
Gas mileage	This is important to you, but compared to price, you would rate this as a 5
Style	This is very important—and, compared to price and gas mileage, you would rate this as a 7.

Comfort   This is the least important factor to you, and you give it a rating of 2.

4. **Brainstorm solutions**

Write down as many possible solutions as you can. At this point, don't assess whether the ideas are practical—just let the ideas flow freely without deciding if they're good or bad. For the purpose of illustrating this process, we will only use three possible solutions, though there would, of course, be several more. The possible solutions we will use are:

a. Volkswagen Beetle
b. Jeep Wrangler
c. Honda Accord

5. **Analyze each possible solution**

To analyze the possible solutions, we will rate the possible solutions according to the criteria. For example, we can look at the cars' qualities in terms of price, gas mileage, style, and comfort by developing a chart:

Criteria	Volkswagen Beetle	Jeep Wrangler	Honda Accord
Price			
Gas mileage			
Style			
Comfort			

Now rate the cars in terms of the criteria. For example, how does a Beetle rank in terms of gas mileage? Again, you can use a scale of 1–10, with 10 being the best. After getting information on each car, you might rate the Beetle and the Accord as 8 and 10, respectively, on gas mileage. The Jeep you may rate as 4 because its gas mileage is very low, compared to the other cars. After completing the chart, it may look something like this:

Criteria	Volkswagen Beetle	Jeep Wrangler	Honda Accord
Price	5	6	7
Gas mileage	8	4	10
Style	9	10	5
Comfort	6	5	8

6. **Choose the best solution**

At this point, consider whether you have included all of the important criteria. If there are others you would like to include, go back and add them to your chart. One you have rated all of the possible solutions by criteria, enter the importance of each criteria, which you determined in step 3, on the next chart.

Criteria	Volkswagen Beetle	Jeep Wrangler	Honda Accord
Price	5	6	7
10			
Gas mileage	8	4	10
7			
Style	9	10	5
5			
Comfort	6	5	8
2			

Now, multiply the value of the criteria rating by the value you assigned to each possible solution. For example, the Volkswagen Beetle, which you rated as 5 for price will be multiplied by the price criteria rating of 10, the total value of which will be 50. Complete the multiplication for each solution and criteria value.

Criteria	Volkswagen Beetle	Jeep Wrangler	Honda Accord
Price	5	6	7
10	50	60	70
Gas mileage	8	4	10
7	56	28	70
Style	9	10	5
5	45	50	25
Comfort	6	5	8
2	12	15	16
Total Value	163	153	181

Sum the values for each solution. In this case, the value for the Honda Accord of 181 (70 + 70 + 25 + 16) is a higher value than that of the other options. If you selected the criteria and their weights appropriately, then this should be the solution you choose. By going through this process, even if you choose to implement another solution than the one chosen, you will be more aware of your thinking processes and the value of alternative solutions.

7. **Implement the solution and evaluate the outcome**

   Once you purchase your car, in this case, or implement any decision, you'll want to evaluate it. There may be other criteria that you might find are important, or more important, than what you had originally thought. If this is the case, start again at the beginning of the process and state your new problem. For every decision you make, you will want to analyze its outcome.

   Using your mind to come up with effective solutions is a skill. Just like any skill, the more you practice, the better you will become. Brainstorming is one method for increasing your creative problem-solving juices.

Creativity is the ability to create something, whether it is a solution, tangible product, work of art, idea, system, program, or format. Everyone is creative in some form or fashion. Some people assume that the word *creative* refers primarily to visual and performing artists—writers, designers, musicians, actors, and others who work in creative fields. *Creativity, though, is inside everyone and exists in every field.*

Imagine if part of your day was spent envisioning new products. What would you create? In the aerospace industry, people are envisioning and building the International Space Station and the new shuttle that will efficiently carry people back and forth from earth to the station. In the automobile industry, they are developing solar-powered engines and rubber cars for safety. People are thinking of ways to preserve the rain forest for medical research. You can apply creative thinking to any job and come up with innovative ways to increase your company's effectiveness in the market place. You can develop your creative thinking skills when you:

- **Open Yourself to Different Types of People**
  By meeting people from different cultures and people with different skills and likes, you expand your own frame of reference giving you a wider array of ideas from which to work.

- **Solicit Input from Others**
  Creative thinking is even more effective when you do it with others. The ideas another person has can spark ideas within your own mind. When your creative juices are tapped, solicit help from others.

HOW WELL CAN YOU EXPLAIN IT ALL?

Our ability to understand and explain the reasons for why things happen are a central part of our thinking skills. The three questions below are part of a series of such questions used to analyze critical thinking skills.

See how well you can reason out the correct response to each.

Goal: To illustrate examples of logical thinking.

Directions: Read Fact 1 and Fact 2 below, then answer the question underneath the facts.

1. Fact 1—A camper started a fire to cook food on a windy day in a forest.
   Fact 2—A fire started in dry grass near a campfire in the forest.

   Both of these facts took place in the same forest. Could one have at least partly caused the other?

   a. Yes; Fact 1 could have at least partly caused Fact 2.
   b. Yes; Fact 2 could have at least partly caused Fact 1.
   c. No; neither is likely to have caused the other.

2. Fact 1—A camper started a fire to cook food on a windy day in a forest.
   Fact 2—A fire started in dry grass near a campfire in the forest.

   Could any of the following statements be used to explain any of the possible cause-and-effect connections between Facts 1 and 2? If so, which *one* would be best?

   a. The heat from burning trees can set other trees on fire.

b. Burning coals from a campfire are hot enough to start a fire in dry grass.

c. Food requires heat for cooking.

d. None of these.

3. Fact 1—A camper started a fire to cook food on a windy day in a forest.
Fact 2—A fire started in dry grass near a campfire in the forest.
Here is another fact that happened later that day in the same forest:

Fact Y—A house in the forest burned down.
Imagine that you have been asked to explain what might have caused the house to burn down in Fact Y. Could Facts 1 and 2 be useful as part of the explanation?

a. Yes; both 1 and 2 and the cause-and-effects between them would be useful.

b. Yes; both 1 and 2 would be useful even though neither was likely a cause of the other.

c. No; because *only one* of Facts 1 and 2 was a likely cause of Y.

d. No; because *neither* 1 or 2 was a likely cause.

Did You Know That . . .

Psychologist Jean Piaget first put forth the concept of developmental stages for thinking skills. To solve the problems in this exercise, an individual must have had to reach, at a minimum, the Stage of Formal Operations. Individuals of normal intelligence generally reach this stage in early adolescence. During the Stage of Formal Operations, the individual is able to conceptualize hypothetical situations and to engage in scientific thinking.

The correct answers are as follows:

1. a
2. b
3. a

Source: Wallen, N. E., Durkin, M. C., Fraenkel, J. R., McNaughton, A. H., and Sawin, E. I. *The Taba Curriculum Development Project in Social Studies.* Final report, Project No.5-1314, Grant No. OE-6-10-182, U.S. Department of Health, Education and Welfare. San Francisco State College, California, 1969. ERIC document no. ED 040106.

PART VI
Small Groups and the Information Society

9

Speaking in Small Groups

Never doubt that a small group of thoughtful, committed citizens can change the world. Indeed, it's the only thing that ever has.

—Margaret Mead

In recent years, it has become increasingly important that technologists and students know how to work in groups. Students regularly use small groups to problem solve, study, and master materials. For its part, industry, in response to actual job demands, has requested technical schools to produce students who understand how to work in and manage groups. The following chapter provides an introduction to groups and how to make them work for you.

The Importance of Small Groups

Take out a sheet of paper and start listing all the small groups to which you belong. Think of committees, subcommittees, boards, and councils on which you serve. Include your network of close friends. Add your family to the list. What about athletic teams, honor societies, fraternities or sororities, the chess club, the debating society, the arts council, study groups, and other groups? After a few minutes of this brainstorming, you will probably be surprised at the length of your list. In light of that discovery, you probably won't be surprised that one survey estimated that "35 to 60 percent of the average manager's day is taken up by meetings." In fact, groups are so prevalent in our society that it is estimated that there are more groups in America than there are people.

Not only are groups plentiful, they are also influential. They shape our society and our behavior. Government, businesses, educational institutions, and other organizations depend on groups to gather information, assess data, and propose courses of action. Our families and our close friends give us counsel and support in times of need. We do so much planning, problem solving, and recreating in small groups that we can all relate to the humorist's remark that "there are no great people, only great committees."

Because groups significantly influence our lives, it is essential that groups communicate effectively. Unfortunately, small group communication seems not to be a skill most of us master easily. For example, a communication professor and a consultant note that "poor meeting preparation, ad hoc scheduling, and lack of participant training in meeting management are causing many companies to lose the *equivalent of thirty man-days and 240 man-hours a year for every person who participates in business conferences.*" Clearly, poor group communication can be costly. You will work more effectively in groups if you understand the subjects covered in this chapter: the relationship between small group communication and public speaking, the characteristics of a group, the types of groups, the principles of group decision making, the responsibilities of group leaders and members, and the most frequently used formats for group presentations.

SMALL GROUP COMMUNICATION AND PUBLIC SPEAKING

Why study group work as an adjunct to public speaking? The answer is twofold: (1) Groups of people often make presentations, either internally or to the public, and (2) the quality of those presentations depends on how well group members have functioned together.

For most of your work in your public speaking class, you have operated alone. You selected your speech topics. You researched as much as you wanted and at your own convenience. You organized your speeches as you thought best and practiced them as much as you thought necessary. Your individual work continues in a group. You must still present, support, and defend your ideas. As you'll see in this chapter, group communication involves a variety of speeches, from the chairperson's orientation speech, to internal reports to other group members, to public presentations about the group's work. Each time you share your ideas and opinions with other group members, you will, in effect, be giving an impromptu speech. The more you know about effective speech content, organization, and delivery, the better your individual speeches within the group will be.

As part of a group solving a problem and preparing a presentation, your work is more complex, however. On-the-spot interaction in a group elevates the importance of listening and critiquing. You will need to utilize all of the critical thinking skills we discussed in Chapter 1. You'll also be challenged to provide feedback to other group members. Using the guidelines for critiquing that we discussed will help you do your part to create and maintain a constructive, supportive communication environment. Group processes will truly test your ability to work productively and congenially with other people.

SMALL GROUPS DEFINED

A **small group** is a collection of three or more individuals who interact with and influence each other in pursuit of a common goal. This definition includes four important concepts: individuals, interaction, influence, and goal.

The number of *individuals* in a group may vary. At a minimum, there must be three. Two people are not a group but rather an interpersonal unit, sometimes called a dyad. The addition of a third person adds a new dynamic, a new perspective. Paul Nelson describes the new relationship in the following way:

> Something happens to communication when it involves more than two people: It becomes much more complex. For example, imagine two people, A and B, having a conversation. There is only *one* possible conversation, A–B. Add one more person, C, however: Now there are four possible interactions, A-B, A-C, B-C, and A-B-C. Add another person, D, and there are *eleven* possible interactions. And so on.

Although we can all agree that three is the minimum number for a small group, we do not always agree on the maximum number. Even communication experts disagree, with some using seven as a workable maximum and others stretching the range to twenty. What characterizes a small group is not a specific number of participants but the *type* of communication they undertake. A group that is too large cannot maintain meaningful interaction among members and may have to be divided into smaller working groups.

A group's size, then, affects a second characteristic of a small group: *interaction*. A small group offers each participant an opportunity to interact with all other members of the group. A group cannot function if its participants fail to interact, and it functions ineffectively when a few members dominate. Generally, the larger the group, the fewer opportunities for any one member to participate and the greater the likelihood that a few members will dominate the flow of communication, making certain that meaningful interaction does not take place.

A third characteristic of small groups is *influence*. Members of a group interact in order to influence others. As journalist Walter Lippman observed, "When all think alike, no one thinks very much." Groups function best when members express differences of opinions openly and try to persuade others with data and arguments.

Finally, a group has a purpose. As we noted in Chapter 1, a group is more than simply a collection of individuals who interact; it exists for a reason. Members interact and influence each other over a period of time in order to achieve a *goal*. The group process fails when members are unsure of their goal or when they fail to resolve conflicting perceptions of that goal.

TYPES OF GROUPS

People form groups for two reasons: because they enjoy interacting with each other or because they need to accomplish a task. Therefore, we can classify groups into two general types: social-oriented and task-oriented. A **social-oriented group** is one whose main goal is social. Group members may not have a major task in mind but rather be concerned mainly with relationships, enjoying time spent with other members of the group. A **task-oriented group** is more formal. Members interact having a specific goal in mind. For example, you and a few classmates may form a study group to review for examinations and to be an audience for each other as you practice your speeches.

The objectives of social- and task-oriented groups often intermingle. Say you and your friends decide to go to a movie. Clearly, this is a social occasion, but you still must accomplish certain tasks: What movie does the group want to see? When is the best time for everyone to see it? Will you carpool or will everyone meet at the theatre? Do you want to get a bite to eat before or after the movie? You have probably, at times, been frustrated when your social group was unable to make some of these "easy" task decisions.

While social-oriented groups may have task objectives, the converse is also true. You form a study group to accomplish certain tasks, but as you get to know the others in the group you discover that you enjoy their company. As social objectives emerge, the group meets more frequently and functions more effectively. If social purposes predominate,

Although a task-oriented group functions more effectively if members enjoy one another's company, social interactions should not take precedence over the group's basic objective: to accomplish the task.

however, you may find that your group sacrifices studying for socializing. Even though most groups have both social and task objectives, one purpose usually takes precedence according to the situation. That purpose determines the structure of your group and the nature of the communication among its members.

In this chapter, we will focus on task-oriented groups, sometimes called working groups. These include study groups, problem-solving groups, and action groups. The objective of a study group is to learn about a topic. It gathers, processes, and evaluates information. When you and your classmates work together to prepare for an exam, you are a study group. A problem-solving group decides on courses of action. This type of group explores a problem, suggesting solutions to remedy it. The objective of an action group is, as its name implies, to act. It has the power to implement proposals. These categories may overlap. In fact, you may be a member of a group that studies a situation, devises a solution, and implements it.

As you go through this chapter, you will find that participating in task groups and delivering public speeches are similar in several ways. Both usually involve research, analysis of information and ideas, and the presentation of that information to others. In small groups your presentation may be to other group members, although sometimes a group will present its findings to an external body. Yet despite these similarities, there are notable differences between public speaking and group communication. The effective communicator will seek to master both sets of skills.

GROUP DISCUSSION AND DECISION MAKING

One of the most important reasons we form groups is to make decisions. We may seek a friend's guidance because we believe that two heads are better than one. The philosophy behind this decision is the foundation of group decision making. You may have heard the expression that in communication "the whole is greater than the sum of its parts." This is particularly true in group communication. What this means is that, if a group of five functions effectively, its product will be qualitatively or quantitatively superior to the total product of five people working individually. But a group is able to work most effectively when members follow certain principles of group decision making. We discuss these five principles next.

Key Points: Principles of Group Decision Making

1. Group decision making is a shared responsibility.
2. Group decision making requires a clear understanding of goals.
3. Group decision making benefits from a clear but flexible agenda.
4. Group decision making is enhanced by open communication.
5. Group decision making requires adequate information.

Principles of Group Decision Making

Group Decision Making Is a Shared Responsibility

It is true that the group leader plays a special role in the group. As a matter of fact, we include separate sections in this chapter about the responsibilities of the group leader as well as of members. The presence of a group leader does not necessarily establish a leader-follower, or even an active-passive, association. In fact, this relationship is usually better represented as a partnership. Group decision making requires the active participation of all members performing mutually reinforcing responsibilities.

Group Decision Making Requires a Clear Understanding of Goals

As we have stated earlier, every group has a goal. Sometimes that goal is predetermined. Your instructor may, for example, divide your class into small groups, assigning each group to generate a list of twenty-five topics suitable for a speech to inform. In your career, you may be part of a small group having the task of studying specific job-related problems and proposing workable solutions. In both of these instances, the group has a clear statement of its objective. In other situations, the goal of your group may be less clear. If that is the case, you will have to clarify, specify, or even determine your goals.

Group Decision Making Benefits from a Clear but Flexible Agenda

Every group needs a plan of action. Because a group's process affects its product, it is vital that members spend sufficient time generating an action plan. The leader can facilitate this process by suggesting procedures that the group may adopt, modify, or reject. The best plan, or agenda, however, is one not dictated by the leader but rather developed by both the leader and the members of the group. Remember, the leader and the group members form a partnership.

A group's agenda should be both specific and flexible. Group participants must know what is expected of them and how they will go about accomplishing the task at hand. Raising $1,000 for charity could be accomplished by dividing the membership into five teams, each having the responsibility for generating $200. These teams would need to communicate and coordinate to avoid unnecessary overlap as they decided on their fund-raising projects. Groups also need to be flexible as they pursue their goals. Unexpected obstacles may require revising the agenda. The group needs a backup plan, for example, if its car wash is canceled because of rain.

Group Decision Making is Enhanced by Open Communication

If all members of a group think alike, there is no need for the group. One person can simply make the decision. Diversity is what gives a group breadth of perspective. Both the group leader and individual members should protect and encourage the expression of minority views.

What a group wants to avoid is the problem of groupthink, a term coined by Irving Janis. **Groupthink** occurs when group members come to care more about conforming and not making waves than they do about exercising the critical evaluation necessary to weed out bad ideas. Groupthink reduces open communication and adversely affects the quality of decision making. In order to be effective, a group must encourage each member to exercise his or her independent judgment.

Group Decision Making Requires Adequate Information

Access to information that is sufficient and relevant is extremely important. A group suffers if its information is based on the research of only one or two of its members. To avoid this problem, a group should follow a few simple steps. First, the leader should provide essential information to the group as a starting point. Second, each member of the group should contribute critical knowledge to the group. Third, the group should divide the gathering of information in a way that is efficient and yet provides some overlap. Later in this chapter, we provide some suggestions for gathering information. Now that we understand the principles of group decision making, let's take a look at how the group makes decisions.

The Process of Group Decision Making

In his celebrated book *How We Think,* published in 1910, John Dewey argued that decision making should be a logical, orderly process. His "Steps to Reflective Thinking" have provided one of the most useful, and we think one of the best, approaches to problem solving. Authors and theorists differ in their adaptations of the reflective thinking model, organizing it around five, six, or seven steps. We prefer a seven-step approach.

If you are a member of a problem-solving discussion group or a task-oriented group and you have not been assigned a topic, the group will need to select a topic and word it. A good discussion topic is current, is controversial, and has a body of data and opinion from which to construct and refute positions. Once you select a topic meeting these criteria, you must word the topic according to the following guidelines.

First, it should be worded as a question the group will seek to answer. "The campus parking problem" fails to meet this criterion and, consequently, does not direct participants in the discussion toward a goal. A better wording is evident in the examples presented in the second criterion.

Second, the question should be open rather than closed. Open wording might include "What can be done to alleviate the parking problem on campus?" or "How should this college solve the campus parking problem?" These questions are open because they do not direct the group to one particular solution. They invite a variety of solutions and can generate lively and productive discussion. The question "Should the campus build a multistory parking facility to solve the campus parking problem?" is an example of a closed question, because it focuses attention on only one solution. This yes-or-no question limits discussion of alternative proposals. Because it forces individuals to choose sides, a closed question is probably more appropriate for a debate than for a discussion format.

After members have agreed upon a topic question, the group should begin answering it in a logical, methodical manner. The following seven-step process, based on Dewey's model, will aid your group. It is important that you go through these steps chronologically and not jump ahead in your discussion. Solutions are best discussed and evaluated only after a problem is thoroughly defined and analyzed.

Key Points: The Steps to Problem Solving

1. Define the problem.
2. Analyze the problem.
3. Determine the criteria for the optimal solution.
4. Propose solutions.
5. Evaluate proposed solutions.
6. Select a solution.
7. Suggest strategies for implementing the solution.

Define the Problem

Before you can solve a problem, you must first define it. By defining the key terms of the question, group members decide how they will focus the topic, thus enabling them to keep on track and to avoid extraneous discussion. Suppose your college asks you to be part of a student advisory committee to address the issue, "What can be done to alleviate the parking problem on campus?" In order to answer the question, members must agree on what constitutes "the parking problem." Are there too few parking spaces? If there are sufficient spaces, are they not geographically located to serve the campus best? Is there congestion only during certain times of the day or week? Is the problem how the spaces are designated—or example, is there adequate parking for faculty but not for students? Is the problem not the number of spaces but the condition of the parking lots? How your group defines the problem determines, to a large extent, how you will solve it. If there is not a problem with the condition of the lots or the number of spaces for faculty, you can safely delete these considerations from your discussion agenda.

Analyze the Problem

In analyzing any problem, a group looks at both its symptoms and causes. We gauge the severity of a problem by examining its *symptoms*. For example, the group needs to know not only the approximate number of students unable to find parking spaces, but also why that is detrimental. Students may be late for class or may avoid going to the library because of parking congestion; accidents may occur as cars crowd into small spaces; the college may spark resentment from students who pay to attend but have no place to park; students may transfer to another school having more convenient access; students walking to dimly lit and distant parking spaces after an evening class may worry about physical attacks. These symptoms point to the magnitude of the problem. Certainly, some symptoms are more serious than others, and group members must identify those needing immediate action.

However, the group is still not ready to propose remedies. The group must now consider the *causes* of the problem. By examining how a difficulty developed, a group may find its solution. The parking problem may stem from a variety of causes, including increased enrollment, parking spaces converted to other uses, lack of funds to build new parking lots, too many classes scheduled at certain times, inadequate use of distant parking lots, and some student parking spaces earmarked for faculty and administrators.

Determine the Criteria for the Optimal Solution

Decision-making criteria are the standards we use to judge the merits of proposed solutions. It is wise to state these criteria before discussing solutions. Why select an action plan only to discover later that sufficient funding is unavailable? The group studying campus parking worked to avoid this pitfall. Some of the criteria they considered were as follows:

Criteria	Explanation
Economics	The proposal should be cost-effective.
Aesthetics	The proposal should not spoil the beauty of the campus.
Legality	The proposal cannot force residents and businesses adjacent to campus to sell their land to the college.
Growth	The proposal should account for future increases in enrollment.
Security	Students should be safe as they go to and from parking lots.

The group could also have considered ranking parking privileges according to student seniority or giving students parking status equal to faculty.

Propose Solutions

Only after completing the first three steps is the group ready to propose solutions. This is essentially a brainstorming step with emphasis on the quantity, not quality, of suggestions. At this stage, the group should not worry about evaluating any suggested solutions, no matter how farfetched they may seem. This group's brainstorming list included the following:

- Building a multistory parking lot in the center of campus.
- Constructing parking lots near the edge of campus.
- Reclaiming some faculty spaces for student use.
- Lighting and patrolling lots in the evening.
- Initiating bus service between apartment complexes and the campus.
- Encouraging students to carpool or to ride bicycles to campus.

Evaluate Proposed Solutions

Now the group is ready to evaluate each of the proposed solutions. Each possibility is judged using the criteria listed in the third step. Next, the group considers the advantages of the proposed solution. Finally, they assess its disadvantages. The centrally located, high-rise parking garage may not be cost-efficient, and may intrude on the beauty of the campus, but may use valuable land efficiently and limit the extent of late-night walking.

Select a Solution

After evaluating each proposed solution, you and your fellow group members should have a pretty good idea of those solutions to exclude from consideration and those to retain. You will then weigh the merits and deficiencies of each. Your final solution may be a combination of several of the proposed remedies. For example, the group working on the campus parking problem could issue a final report advocating a three-phase solution: short-range, middle-range, and long-range goals. A short-term approach may involve converting a little-used athletic practice field to a parking facility, creating more bicycle parking areas, and encouraging carpooling. A middle-range solution could involve creating a bus system between student apartment houses and the campus, or trying to get the city transit system to incorporate new routes. The proposal for the long-term could involve building a well-lit multistory parking facility, not in the middle of campus, but near the athletic complex, to be used during the week for general student parking and on weekends for athletic and entertainment events.

Suggest Strategies for Implementing the Solution

Once the small group has worked out a solution, members would normally submit their recommendations to another body for approval, action, and implementation. Sometimes, however, decision makers should not only select feasible and effective solutions but also show how they can be implemented. How would the small group incorporate suggestions for implementing its solution? Members would probably recommend coordinating their plan with the long-range master plan for the college. Other administrators would have to be included. The group would probably also suggest a timetable detailing short-term and long-term projects, and might also identify possible funding sources.

In summary, the reflective thinking model enables a group to define a problem, analyze it, determine the criteria for a good solution, propose solutions, evaluate solutions, select a solution, and suggest ways to implement it. Decisions made by following this process are generally better, and group members are more satisfied with their work. Not only can this model benefit groups in business, government, education, and other organizations, it can also improve your individual decision making.

The Responsibilities of Group Members

As we argued earlier, the leader-member relationship is not an active-passive partnership. In order to enhance the quality of the group's product, all members must participate actively. At this stage, you may be asking yourself, "What do group participants do?" If you reflect on our example of the group tackling the campus parking problem, you can see how those group members handled their responsibilities. Productive group members undertake five key responsibilities.

Key Points: Responsibilities of Group Members

1. Inform the group.
2. Advocate personal beliefs.
3. Question other participants.
4. Evaluate ideas and proposals.
5. Support other group members.

Inform the Group

"Just the facts, ma'am."—Sgt. Joe Friday, *Dragnet*

Group members should enlarge the information base upon which decisions are made and action taken. As we have said elsewhere, a decision is only as good as the information upon which it is based. If the group does not know all the causes of a problem, for example, its proposed solution may not solve it. The greater the number of possible solutions a group considers, the greater its chance of selecting the best one.

You enlarge the group's information base in two ways. First, you contribute what you already know about the issue being discussed. Hearsay information is worth mentioning at this stage, as long as you acknowledge that it is something you have heard but cannot prove. Another member may be able to confirm or refute it, or it can be put on the agenda for further research. Dispelling popular misconceptions so that they do not contaminate the decision-making process is important.

Second, group members contribute to a group's understanding of a topic by gathering additional relevant information. Ideas surfacing during a group meeting may help shape the agenda for the next meeting. You may hear ideas that you want to explore further. You may need to check out facts before the group can clarify the dimensions of a problem or adopt a particular plan of action. The research and thought you give to a topic before a meeting will make the meeting itself more efficient and productive.

Advocate Personal Beliefs

Group members should not only provide information to help make decisions, but they also should use that data to develop positions on the issues being discussed. Participants should be willing to state and defend their opinions. A good participant is open-minded, though willing to offer ideas and then revise or retract them as additional facts and expert opinion surface. Your opinions may change as they are challenged throughout the discussion.

Question Other Participants

Effective participants not only give but also seek information and opinions. Knowing how and when to ask an appropriate question is an important skill for group members. As one advertisement claims, "When you ask better questions, you tend to come up with better answers." The ability to ask effective questions requires active listening, sensitivity to the feelings of others, and a desire to learn. Group members should seek clarification of ideas they do not understand and encourage others to explain, defend, and extend their ideas.

Evaluate Ideas and Proposals

Too often we either accept what we hear at face value or remain silent even though we disagree with what is said. Yet challenging facts, opinions, and proposals benefits the quality of discussion. As Adlai Stevenson proclaimed, "Freedom rings where opinions clash." It is the obligation of the group to evoke a range of positions on the issue being discussed and then separate the good ideas from the bad. Each idea should be discussed thoroughly and analyzed critically. A decision based on incorrect information or faulty reasoning may be ineffective or even counterproductive. Thus, all group members are obligated to evaluate the contributions of others and to submit their own positions to rigorous testing. This is sometimes difficult to do. Yet participants should not be defensive about their ideas, but instead be open to constructive criticism.

Support Other Group Members

A group is a collection of individuals having different personalities. Some may be less assertive than others and may have fragile egos. Reluctant to express their ideas because they fear criticism, they may cause the group to lose important information and to rush into a decision. They may even foster the groupthink we discussed earlier. The climate of the group should encourage openness and acceptance. It is the job of both the leader and the group members to create and reinforce a climate of openness and acceptance.

The Responsibilities of Group Leaders

When individuals complain about the lack of cohesiveness and productivity of their group, much of their criticism is often directed toward the group's leader. Just as effective leadership depends on effective membership, so does effective membership depend on effective leadership. Leaders have certain responsibilities that, if fulfilled, will help the group meet its goal.

Key Points: Responsibilities of Group Leaders

1. Plan the agenda.
2. Orient the group.
3. Establish an information base.
4. Involve all members in the discussion.
5. Encourage openness and critical evaluation.
6. Secure clarification of ideas and positions.
7. Keep the group on target.
8. Introduce new ideas and topics.
9. Summarize the discussion.
10. Manage conflict.

Plan the Agenda

A group leader has the primary responsibility for planning an agenda. This does not mean dictating the agenda; rather, the leader offers suggestions and solicits group input into the process.

Orient the Group

How a meeting begins is extremely important in setting expectations that affect group climate and productivity. A leader may want to begin a meeting with some brief opening remarks to orient the group to its mission and the process it will follow. In analyzing business meetings, Roger Mosvick and Robert Nelson conclude, "The chairperson's orientation speech is the single most important act of the business meeting." They describe this speech as follows:

> It is a systematically prepared, fully rehearsed, sit-down speech of not less than three minutes nor more than five minutes (most problems require at least three minutes of orientation; anything over five minutes sets up a pattern of dominance and control by the chairperson).

For some groups that you lead, it will not always be appropriate or even desirable to begin a meeting with a structured speech. Still, leaders should try to accomplish several objectives early in the group's important first meeting. They should (1) stress the importance of the task, (2) secure agreement on the process the group will follow, (3) encourage interaction among members, and (4) set an expectation of high productivity.

Establish an Information Base

Leaders may wish to introduce background information to the group in an opening statement, or forward some relevant articles with background information to members before the first meeting. This sometimes makes the initial meeting more productive by establishing a starting point for discussion. Leaders should encourage input from all members, however, as the primary means of ensuring sufficient information for making decisions.

Involve All Members in the Discussion

A leader must make certain that participation among group members is balanced. A person who speaks too much is as much a problem as one who speaks too little. In either case, the potential base of information and opinion is narrowed. Remember our position that all members share the responsibility of group leadership. If someone is not contributing to the discussion, any member of the group can ask the silent person for his or her opinion.

Encourage Openness and Critical Evaluation

After the group has shared information and ideas, the leader must guide the group in evaluating them. The leader may do this by directing probing questions to specific individuals or to the group as a whole. To achieve and maintain a climate of free and honest communication, the group leader must be sensitive to the nonverbal communication of participants, encouraging them to verbalize both their reluctance and their excitement about the ideas other members are expressing. At the same time, the sensitive leader will keep criticism focused on ideas rather than on personalities.

Secure Clarification of Ideas and Positions

Effective leaders are good at getting members of the discussion to make their positions and ideas clearer and more specific. They do this in two ways. First, the leader may encourage a member to continue talking by asking a series of probing follow-up questions ("So what would happen if . . . ?"). Even the use of prods ("Uh-huh." "Okay?") can force discussants to think through and verbalize their ideas and positions. Second, the leader may close a particular line of discussion by paraphrasing the ideas of a speaker ("So what you're saying is that . . ."). This strategy confirms the leader's understanding, repeats the idea for the benefit of other group members, and invites their reaction.

Keep the Group on Target

Effective leaders keep their sights on the group's task while realizing the importance of group social roles. There is nothing wrong with group members becoming friendly and socializing. This added dimension can strengthen your group. However, when social functions begin to impede work on the task, the group leader must "round up the strays" and redirect the entire group to its next goal.

ETHICAL DECISIONS

An anonymous benefactor has contributed funds to sponsor a Career Day on Emily's campus. The president of the Student Government Association appoints Emily, a first-year student, to chair a committee charged with drafting a detailed proposal for Career Day activities. Despite Emily's efforts to encourage open discussion and to distribute the workload, two of the five committee members have contributed little. Kate, a junior, opposes most of the ideas offered by others, seldom volunteers any concrete suggestions of her own, and often wants to discuss issues unrelated to the committee's task. Gary, a senior, seldom attends meetings, and when Emily asks for his input, he usually shrugs and says, "Whatever you decide is fine with me." After three unproductive meetings with all five members present, Emily is concerned that the committee may not meet its deadline for the report. She decides to call a private meeting with the two productive members and draft the report. They finish it in a few hours, then present it to the full committee at the next meeting, allowing all of the members to discuss and vote on it.

Is Emily's strategy an ethical one for a committee chair? When a group is not functioning effectively, should the leader do everything possible to ensure that all members participate in the decision-making process, or is it more important to ensure that the group takes action, even if it means giving more power to selected members? What responsibility do the members have to ensure equal participation?

Introduce New Ideas and Topics

We've already mentioned that it is important for leaders to prepare for the first group meeting, either by researching and preparing an orientation speech or by circulating background materials to group members. In addition, the leader should be the most willing researcher among the group. If discussion stalls because the group lacks focus or motivation, the leader must be willing and able to initiate new topics for research and talk. If a lapse in the group's progress signals that research and discussion have been exhausted,

A democracy cannot function without effective group communication. Committees must reach agreement before they can enact policies and legislation.

the leader must recognize this situation and be willing to move on to the next phase of group work.

Summarize the Discussion

A leader should provide the group periodic reviews of what has been decided and what remains to be decided. These summaries keep members focused on the group's task. Leaders may begin a group meeting with an initial summary, a brief synopsis of what the group decided previously. They may offer internal summaries during the discussion to keep the group on target. At the conclusion of the group task, leaders should provide a *final summary*, reviewing what the group accomplished.

Manage Conflict

Conflict is not only inevitable in group discussion, it is essential. When ideas collide, participants must rethink and defend their positions. This process engenders further exploration of facts and opinions and enhances the likelihood of a quality outcome. It is important, then, that a group not discourage conflict but manage it.

While conflict of ideas contributes to group effectiveness, interpersonal antagonism may undermine it. When conflict becomes personal, it ceases to be productive. Such conflict disrupts the group. Some members may stop expressing their opinions for fear of attack. If the climate becomes too uncomfortable, members may withdraw from the group. Thus, it is essential that when conflict surfaces, the group responds appropriately. At some point, it may become evident that conflict cannot be solved by the group or in the presence of group members. In this event, the leader may have to meet with the disruptive member one-on-one and discuss the problem.

When a group, following the seven steps of problem solving, is composed of members and a leader fulfilling the various roles we have just outlined, it should produce results quickly. At times, the problem solving will benefit the group alone and no external report is needed. Often, however, the group will be requested or will want to present its findings to a larger group: company workers, company stockholders, or just an interested public audience, for example. In such cases, the group must continue to work together to plan its presentation.

THE GROUP PRESENTATION

In the following sections of this chapter, we discuss two popular formats for group presentations and provide a systematic checklist to help you develop a first-rate presentation.

Formats for the Presentation

There are several different formats for a group presentation, two of which are the public discussion and the symposium.

The Public Discussion

In a **public discussion,** a group sits, usually in a semicircle, in front of the audience. Members are aware of an audience but usually address others in the group. The audience, in effect, eavesdrops on the group's conversation. If your public speaking class includes group presentations, your small group may be asked to use this format to present your report to the class.

The problem-solving classroom discussion usually requires extensive preparation. The group has researched the topic, planned the discussion, and possibly practiced the presentation. Members have a general idea of the content and organization of their own and other participants' remarks, although the presentation is not memorized or scripted. The presentation is intended to inform and persuade the audience on the issue being discussed. Sometimes a question-answer period follows.

The Symposium

A **symposium** is a series of speeches on a single topic presented to an audience. It differs from a public discussion in at least two ways. First, there is no interaction among the speakers during the presentation, unless a discussion period follows. Each speaker has a designated amount of time to present his or her remarks. Second, speakers address members of the audience directly. Sometimes speakers are seated at a table; often they use a lectern. In most public symposiums, the speakers have not met beforehand to discuss what they will say. If you are assigned to a group for a presentation in this class, you will likely want to meet several times, following some of the guidelines we discuss in the following section.

Preparing a Group Presentation

A **group presentation** offers you a variety of learning experiences. You can enhance your research, organization, oral communication, and group interaction skills. This assignment, therefore, is a significant learning opportunity. In addition, your group presentation can be a positive learning experience for your classmates.

Although there is no one correct way to prepare for a group presentation, the following suggestions will help you work more efficiently and produce a more effective product. This symbol (•) denotes those steps requiring group interaction; the other steps can be done individually.

Key Points: Steps in Preparing a Group Presentation

- •1. Brainstorm about the topic.
- 2. Do some exploratory research.
- •3. Discuss and divide the topic into areas of responsibility.
- 4. Research your specific topic area.
- 5. Draft an outline of your content area.
- •6. Discuss how all the information interrelates.
- •7. Finalize the group presentation format.
- •8. Plan the introduction and conclusion of the presentation.
- 9. Prepare and practice your speech.
- •10. Rehearse and revise the presentation.

• Brainstorm about the Topic

If you've read the previous chapters, our first suggestion for preparing a group presentation shouldn't surprise you. Through brainstorming, you will discover knowledge that group members already possess, and you will uncover numerous ideas for further research. In addition to providing content, brainstorming also serves a relationship function. By giving all members an opportunity to participate, brainstorming affords you a glimpse of your peers' personalities and their approaches to group interaction. You get to know them, and they get to know you. Maintaining an atmosphere of openness and respect during this first meeting gets the group off to a good start. Once you have generated a list of areas concerning your group's topic, you are ready for the second step.

Do Some Exploratory Research

Through brainstorming, you discover areas that need further investigation. The second phase of your group process is individual research. While there may be some merit in each person's selecting a different topic to research, research roles should not be too rigid. Rather than limit yourself by topic, you may wish to divide your research by resource. One member may look at popular news magazines, another at government documents, while a third may interview a professor who is knowledgeable on the topic, and so forth. It is important that you not restrict your discovery to the list of topics you have generated. Exploratory research is also a form of brainstorming. As you look in indexes and read articles you find, you will uncover more topics. Each member of the group should try to find a few good sources that are diverse in scope.

• Discuss and Divide the Topic into Areas of Responsibility

After exploratory research, your group should reconvene to discuss what each member found. Which expectations were confirmed by your research? Which were not? What topics did you find that you had not anticipated? Your objective at this stage of the group process is to decide on the key areas you wish to investigate. Each person should probably be given primary responsibility for researching a particular area. That person becomes the content expert in that area. While this approach makes research more efficient, it has a drawback. If one person serves as a specialist, the group gambles that he or she will research thoroughly and be objective in reporting findings. If either assumption is not valid, the quantity of information can be insufficient and its quality contaminated. An alternative approach is to assign more than one person to a specific area.

Research Your Specific Topic Area

Using strategies we have discussed, research your topic area. Your focus should be on the quality of the sources you discover, not on quantity. While your primary goal should be to gather information on your topic, you should also note information related to your colleagues' topics. As you consult indexes, jot down on a card sources that may be helpful to another member in the group. Group members who support each other in this way make the process more efficient and, hence, more enjoyable. This usually results in a better product.

Draft an Outline of Your Content Area

After you have concluded your initial research but before you meet again with your group, construct an outline of the ideas and information you've found. This step is important for two reasons. It forces you to make sense of all the information you have collected, and it will expedite the next step when you will share your information with the rest of the members of your group.

• Discuss How All the Information Interrelates

You are now ready to meet again with the other members of your group. Members should briefly summarize what they have discovered through their research. After all have shared their ideas, the group should decide which ideas are most important and how these ideas relate to each other. There should be a natural development of the topic that can be divided among the members of the group.

• Finalize the Group Presentation Format

The speaking order should already be determined. There are, nevertheless, certain procedural details that the group must decide. Will the first speaker introduce all presenters, or will each person introduce the next speaker? Where will the participants sit when they are not speaking, facing the audience, or in the front row? The more details you decide beforehand, the fewer distractions you will have on the day you speak.

• Plan the Introduction and Conclusion of the Presentation

A presentation should appear to be that of a group and not that of four or five individuals. Consequently, you must work on introducing and concluding the group's comments, and you must incorporate smooth transitions from one speaker's topic to the next. An introduction should state the topic, define important terms, and establish the importance of the subject. A conclusion should summarize what has been presented and end with a strong final statement.

Prepare and Practice Your Speech

By this time in the course, you know the requirements of an excellent speech and have had the opportunity to deliver a few. Most of our earlier suggestions also apply to your speech in your group's presentation. Some differences are worth noting, however. For example, as part of a group presentation, you will need to refer to members' speeches and perhaps even use some of their supporting materials. The group presentation may also impose physical requirements you haven't encountered as a classroom speaker, such as using a microphone, speaking to those seated around you in addition to making direct contact with the audience, or speaking from a seated position.

• Rehearse and Revise the Presentation

Independent practice of your individual speech is important, but that is only one part of rehearsal. The group should practice its entire presentation. Group rehearsal will not only make participants more confident about their individual presentations, but will also give the group a feeling of cohesion.

SUMMARY

Whether they are part of our business, social, or personal lives, numerous formal and informal groups are important to us because they solve problems, get things done, and provide us with emotional support. A small group is a collection of three or more people influencing and interacting with one another in pursuit of a common goal.

Groups usually fulfill both *social-oriented* and *task-oriented* needs for their participants, though one of these types of needs will predominate depending upon the situation. Three types of task-oriented groups include the *study group*, which learns about a topic; the *problem-solving group*, which decides on courses of action; and the *action group*, which implements proposals. This chapter focused on the ways groups function and the tasks they accomplish: gathering, analyzing, and spreading information; and formulating, advocating, and implementing courses of action.

Group decisions are usually superior to decisions individuals make by themselves. To ensure valid decisions, groups must abide by five principles. First, group decision making is a shared responsibility and requires active participation of all members. Second, group members must share a goal that is specific and realistic. Third, groups make decisions best under a clear but flexible schedule or agenda. Fourth, groups can avoid *group-*

think and make the best decisions when members are free to express opinions openly. Fifth, group decision making requires and benefits from the research and information shared by all participants.

Problem-solving groups can speed their progress and simplify their task by following a seven-step modification of John Dewey's steps to reflective thinking. First, define the problem. Second, analyze the symptoms and the causes of the problem. Third, determine the criteria that an optimal solution to the problem must satisfy. Fourth, propose various solutions to the problem. Fifth, evaluate each possible solution against the established criteria. Sixth, decide on the best solution, and seventh, suggest ways of putting the solution into action. Following these steps in this order will streamline group problem-solving work.

Group participation involves five functions: sharing information, advocating personal beliefs, questioning other participants, evaluating data and opinions, and supporting other participants in the group. Responsibilities of group leaders include planning the group's agenda; orienting the group to the task at hand; providing background information on the problem to be discussed; involving all members in the group's discussion; encouraging a climate of open, honest critical evaluation; seeking clarification of members' ideas and positions; keeping the group focused on its task; introducing new ideas and topics for discussion; summarizing the discussion at various points; and managing interpersonal conflict. If group members and leaders perform these functions during the seven-step problem-solving process, they should reach a satisfactory conclusion, and may then be asked to present their findings in a public presentation.

The presentation may take the form of a *public discussion* before an audience. In this situation, participants speak to one another about aspects of the problem after researching, organizing, and practicing the presentation. Another popular form of group presentation is the *symposium*, a series of formal individual speeches on different aspects of a problem.

When given the opportunity to meet and plan a group presentation before delivering it, members should always do so. Both those experienced and inexperienced in preparing group presentations can benefit from a logical ten-step approach to developing them. First, brainstorm the topic with colleagues in the group. Second, do some individual exploratory research to gauge the scope of the topic. Third, discuss the topic with group members and divide areas of research responsibility by topic or source. Fourth, individually research your assigned area, noting sources in other group members' areas. Fifth, organize the data your research has yielded. Sixth, discuss with other group members how all the generated information interrelates. Seventh, determine the presentation format. Eighth, plan the introduction of group members and the material under discussion. Ninth, prepare and practice speeches individually. And tenth, rehearse and revise the entire group presentation.

PRACTICE CRITIQUE: ANALYZING A GROUP'S INTERACTIONS

Arrange to attend a meeting of a student, faculty, city, or some other decision-making group. Select a group with a limited number of members so that you can observe interactions among them. Take notes during the meeting and then, using the lists of responsibilities for group members and group leaders on pages 283 and 284 as a guide, write a brief analysis of the group's interactions. Which responsibilities did the group perform well? Which responsibilities seemed to receive little attention? What could the group do to foster more effective interactions? If the group had a leader, what strengths and weaknesses did you observe in his or her communication behaviors?

PROBLEMS

1. Select someone in a leadership position to interview. The person may be a business executive, an officer in an organization, a school principal, a college president, or any other leader. Construct and ask a series of questions designed to discover his or her views on characteristics of effective and ineffective leaders. Record the answers and be prepared to discuss them in class.

2. Using the topic areas listed below, select a specific problem area and word it in the form of a problem-solving discussion question.
   a. crime
   b. education
   c. international relations
   d. political campaigning
   e. public health

3. Choose four campus problems you think need to be addressed—for example, class registration. Word the topics as problem-solving questions. Analyze each topic, asking the following questions:
   a. How important is the problem?
   b. What information do you need to analyze and solve the problem?
   c. Where would you find this information?
   d. What barriers keep the problem from being solved now?
   e. Which steps in the problem-solving process do you think will generate the most conflict? Why?

   Based on your answers to these questions, select the best topic for a problem-solving discussion. Justify your choice.

4. Think of a problem you are experiencing that you need to solve. Work through the seven steps of the reflective thinking model to arrive at a solution to the problem. Did the model help you arrive at a decision? If so, which steps were most helpful? If not, what are some limitations of the model?

5. Observe a meeting of a student, faculty, city, or some other decision-making group. What examples did you observe of good and bad group communication skills? Could the meeting have been conducted better? If so, how?

6. Discuss when it would be better for a group presentation to take the form of a public discussion. When would the symposium format be preferable?

APPENDIX A
Readings for Further Study

Computers, Networks, and Work

Lee Sproull and Sara Kiesler

> This contribution explores how electronic interactions that take place on a computer network differ significantly from those face to face exchanges that occur within work environments. The authors of this article—Dr. Lee Sproull, a social scientist, and Dr. Sara Kiesler, a social psychologist—are communication scholars who focus their reassert on electronic conversations. As Sproull and Kiesler note, our conceptions of both time and space are altered when electronic conversations become a main means of communication.
>
> This article originally appeared in a special issue of *Scientific American* that focused on "communications, computers, and networks." This special issue, aimed at an informed and educated readership interested in issues broadly associated with science and more specifically aquatinted with computers, was published in September 1991, just as electronic global communication systems were beginning a stage of exponential growth and expansion.

Although the world may be evolving into a global village, most people still lead local lives at work. They spend the majority of their time in one physical location and talk predominantly to their immediate coworkers, clients and customers. They participate in only a few workplace groups: their primary work group, perhaps a committee or task force and possibly an informal social group.

Some people, however, already experience a far more cosmopolitan future because they work in organizations that have extensive computer networks. Both individuals can communicate with people around the world as easily as they talk with someone in the next office. They can hold involved group discussions about company policy, new product design, hiring plans or last night's ball game without ever meeting other group members.

The network organization differs from the conventional workplace with respect to both time and space. Computer-based communication is extremely fast in comparison with telephone or postal services, denigrated as "snail mail" by electronic mail converts. People can send a message to the other side of the globe in minutes; each message can be directed to one person or to many people. Networks can also essentially make time stand still. Electronic messages can be held indefinitely in computer memory. People can read or reread their messages at any time, copy them, change them or forward them.

Managers are often attracted to networks by the promise of faster communication and greater efficiency. In our view the real potential of network communication has less to do with such matters than with influencing the overall work environment and the capabilities of employees. Managers can use networks to foster new kinds of task structures and reporting relationships. They can use networks to change the conventional patterns of who talks and who knows what.

The capabilities that accompany networks raise significant questions for mangers and for social scientists studying work organizations. Can people really work closely with one another when their only contact is through a computer? If employees interact through telecommuting, teleconferencing and electronic group discussions, what holds the organization together? Networking permits almost unlimited access to data and other people. Where will management draw the line on freedom of access? What will the organization of the future look like?

We and various colleagues are working to understand how computer networks can affect the nature of work and relationships between managers and employees. What we are learning may help people to exploit better the opportunities that networks offer and to avoid or mitigate the potential pitfalls of networked organizations.

Our research relies on two approaches. Some questions can be studied through laboratory experiments. For instance, how do small groups respond emotionally to different forms of communication? Other questions, particularly those concerning organizational change, require field studies in actual organizations that have been routinely using computer networks. Data describing how hundreds of thousands of people currently use network communications can help predict how other people will work in the future as computer-based communications become more prevalent. Drawing on field studies and experiments, researchers gradually construct a body of evidence on how work and organizations are changing as network technology becomes more widely used. The process may sound straight forward, but in reality it is often full of exciting twists. People use technology in surprising ways, and effects often show up that contradict both theoretical predictions and managerial expectations.

One major surprise emerged as soon as the first large-scale computer network, known as the ARPANET, was begun in the late 1960s. The ARPANET was developed for the Advanced Research Projects Agency (ARPA), a part of the U.S. Department of Defense. The ARPANET was intended to link computer scientist at universities and other research institutions to distant computers, thereby permitting efficient access to machines unavailable at the home institutions. A facility called electronic mail, which enabled researchers to communicate with one another, was considered a minor additional feature of the network.

Yet electronic mail rapidly became one of the most popular features of the ARPANET. Computer scientists around the country used ARPANET to exchange ideas spontaneously and casually. Graduate students discussed problems and shared skills with professors and other students without regard to their physical location. Heads of research projects used electronic mail to coordinate activities with project members and to stay in touch with other research teams and funding agencies. A network community quickly formed, filled with friends and collaborators who rarely if ever, met in person. Although some administrators objected to electronic mail because they did not consider it a legitimate use of computer time, demand grew sharply for more and better network connections.

Since then, many organizations have adopted internal networks that link anywhere from a few to a few thousand employees. Some of those organizational networks have also been connected to the Internet, the successor to ARPANET. Electronic mail has continued to be one of the most popular features of these computer networks.

Anyone who has a computer account on a network system can use electronic mail software to communicate with other users on the network. Electronic mail transmits messages to a recipient's electronic "mailbox." The sender can send a message simultaneously to several mailboxes by sending the message to a group name or to a distribution list. Electronic bulletin boards and electronic conferences are common variants of group electronic mail; they too have names to identify their topic or audience. Bulletin boards post messages by topic and display grouped messages together.

The computer's communications technology in most networked organizations today is fairly similar, but there exist large differences in people's actual communication behavior that stem from policy choices made by management. In some networked organizations, electronic mail access is easy and open. Most employees have networked terminals or computers at their desks, and anyone can send mail to anyone else. Electronic mail costs are considered part of the general overhead expenses and are not charged to the employees or to their departments. In the open-network organizations that we have studied, people typically send and receive between 25 and 100 messages a day and belong to between 10 and 50 electronic groups. These figures hold across job categories, hierarchical position, age and even amount of computer experience.

In other network organizations, managers have chosen to limit access or charge costs directly to users, leading to much lower usage rates. Paul Schreiber, a *Newsday* columnist, describes how his own organization changed from an open-access network to a limited-access one. Management apparently believed that reporters were spending too much time sending electronic mail; management therefore had the newspaper's electronic mail software modified so that reporters could still receive mail but no longer could send it. Editors, on the other hand, could still send electronic mail to everyone. Clearly technology by itself does not impel change. Management choices and policies are equally influential.

But even in organizations that have open access, anticipating the effect of networks on communication has proved no easy task. Some of the first researchers to study computer network communications thought the technology would improve group decision making over face-to-face discussion because computer messages were plain text. They reasoned that electronic discussions would be more purely intellectual, and so decision making would be less affected by people's social skills and personal idiosyncrasies.

Research has revealed a more complicated picture. In an electronic exchange, the social cues that usually regulate and influence group dynamics are missing or attenuated. Electronic messages lack information regarding job titles, social importance, hierarchical position, race, age and appearance. The context also is poorly defined because formal and casual exchanges look essentially the same. People may have outside information about senders, receivers and situations, but few cues exist in the computer interaction itself to remind people of that knowledge.

In a series of experiments at Carnegie Mellon University, we compared how small groups make decisions using computer conferences, electronic mail and face-to-face discussion. Using a network induced the participants to talk more frankly and more equally. Instead of one or two people doing most of the talking, as happens in many face-to-face groups, everyone had a more equal say. Furthermore, networked groups generated more proposals for action than did traditional ones.

Open, free ranging discourse has a dark side. The increased democracy associated with electronic interactions interfered with decision making. We observed that three-person groups took approximately four times as long to reach a decision electronically as they did face-to-face. In one case, a group never succeeded in reaching consensus, and we were ultimately forced to terminate the experiment. Making it impossible for people to interrupt one another slowed decision making and increased conflict as a few members tried to dominate control of the network. We also found that people tended to express extreme opinions and vented anger more openly in an electronic face-off than when they sat together and talked. Computer scientists using the ARPANET have called this phenomenon "flaming."

We discovered that electronic communication can influence the effect of people's status. Social or job position normally is a powerful regulator of group interaction. Group members typically defer to those who have higher status and tend to follow their direction. Members' speech and demeanor become more formal in the presence of people who have high status. Higher-status people, in turn, talk more and influence group discussion more than do lower-status people.

Given that electronic conversations attenuate contextual cues, we expected that the effect of status differences within a group should also be rescued. In an experiment conducted with Vitaly Dubrovsky of Clarkson University and Beheruz Sethna of Lamar University, we asked groups constituting high- and low-status members to make decisions both by electronic mail and face-to-face. The results confirmed that the proportion of talk and influence of higher-status people decreased when group members communicated by electronic mail.

Is this a good state of affairs? When higher-status members have less expertise, more democracy could improve decision making. If higher-status members truly are better qualified to make decisions, however, the results of the consensus decision may be less good.

Shoshanash Zubof of Harvard Business School documented reduced effects of status on a computer conference system in one firm. People who regarded themselves as physically unattractive reported feeling more lively and confident when they expressed themselves over the network. Others who had soft voices or small stature reported that they no longer had to struggle to be taken seriously in a meeting.

Researchers have advanced alternative explanations for the openness and democracy of electronic talk. One hypothesis is that people who like to use computers are childish or unruly, but this hypothesis does not explain experimental results showing that the same people talk more openly on a computer than when they are face-to-face. Another hypothesis holds that text messages require strong language to get a point across; this hypothesis explains flaming but not the reduction of social and status differences. The most promising explanation of the behavior of networked individuals is that when cues about social context are absent or weak, people ignore their social situation and cease to worry about how others evaluate them. Hence, they devote less time and effort to posturing and social niceties, and they may be more honest.

Researchers have demonstrated decreased social posturing in studies that ask people to describe their own behavior. In one of our experiments, people were asked to complete a self-evaluation questionnaire either by pencil and paper or via electronic mail. Those randomly assigned to reply electronically reported significantly more undesirable social behaviors, such as illegal drug use or petty crimes. John Greist and his colleagues at the University of Wisconsin found similar decreases in posturing when taking medical histories from clinical patients. People who responded to a computerized patient history interview revealed more socially and physically undesirable behavior than did those who answered the same questions asked by a physician.

These studies show that people are willing to reveal more about undesirable symptoms and behavior to a computer, but are these reports more truthful? An investigation of alcohol consumption conducted by Jennifer J. Waterton and John C. Duffy of the University of Edinburgh suggests an affirmative answer. In traditional surveys, people report drinking only about one half as much alcohol as alcohol sales figures would suggest. Waterton and Duffy compared computer interviews with personal interviews in a survey of alcohol consumption. People who were randomly assigned to answer the computer survey reported higher alcohol consumption than those who talked to the human interviewer. The computer-derived reports of consumption extrapolated more accurately to actual alcohol sales than did the face-to-face reports.

These and other controlled studies of electronic talk suggest that such communication is relatively impersonal, yet paradoxically, it can make people feel more comfortable about talking. People are less shy and more playful in electronic discussions; they also express more opinions and ideas and vent more emotion.

Because of these behavioral effects, organizations are discovering applications for electronic group activities that nobody had anticipated. Computers can be valuable for counseling and conducting surveys about sensitive topics, situations in which many people are anxious and cover their true feelings and opinions. Networks are now being used for applications ranging from electronic Alcoholics Anonymous support groups to electronic quality circles.

Just as the dynamics of electronic communications differ from those conducted orally, so electronic groups are not just traditional groups whose members use computers. People in a networked organization are likely to belong to a number of electronic groups that span time zones and job categories. Some of these groups serve as extensions of existing work groups, providing a convenient way for members to communicate between face-to-face meetings. Other electronic groups gather together people who do not know one another personally and who may in fact have never had the opportunity to meet in person.

For example, Hewlett-Packard employs human-factors engineers who work in widely scattered locations around the world. These engineers may meet one another in person only once a year. An electronic conference creates ongoing meetings in which they can frequently and routinely discuss professional and company issues.

In some ways, electronic groups resemble nonelectronic social groups. They support sustained interactions, develop their own norms of behavior and generate peer pressure. Electronic groups often have more than 100 members, however, and involve relationship among people who do not know one another personally.

Employees whose organization is connected to the Internet or to a commercial network can belong to electronic groups whose members come from many different organizations. For example, Brian K. Reid of Digital Equipment Corporation reports that some 37,000 organizations are connect to USENET, a loosely organized network that exchanges more than 1,500 electronic discussion groups, called newsgroups. Reid estimates that 1.4 million people worldwide read at least one newsgroup.

Networked communication is only beginning to affect the structure of the workplace. The form of most current organizations has been dictated by the constraints of the nonelectronic world. Interdependent jobs must be situated in physical proximity. Formal command structures specify who reports to whom, who assigns tasks to whom and who has access to what information. These constraints reinforce the centralization of authority and shape the degree of information sharing, the number of organizational levels, the amount of interconnectivity and the structure of social relationships.

Organizations that incorporate computer networks could become more flexible and less hierarchical in structure. A field experiment conducted by Tora K. Bikson of Rand Corporation and John E. Eveland of Claremont Colleges supports the point. They formed two task forces in a large utility firm, each assigned to analyze employee retirement issues. Both groups contained 40 members, half of whom had recently retired from the company and half of whom were still employed but eligible for retirement. The only difference between the two groups was that one worked on networked computer facilities, whereas the other did not.

Both task forces created subcommittees, but the networked group created more of them and assigned people to more than one subcommittee. The networked group also organized its subcommittees in a complex, overlapping matrix structure. It added new subcommittees during the course of its work, and it decided to continue meeting even after its official one-year life span had ended. The networked task force also permitted greater input from the retirees, who were no longer located at the company. Although not every electronic group will be so flexible, eliminating the constraints of face-to-face meetings evidently facilitates trying out different forms of group organization.

Another effect of networking may be changed patterns of information sharing in organizations. Conventional organizations have formal systems of record keeping and responsibilities for distributing information. Much of the information within an organization consists of personal experience that never appears in the formally authorized distribution system: the war stories told of service representatives (which do not appear in service manuals), the folklore about how the experimental apparatus really works (which does not appear in the journal articles) or the gossip about how workers should behave (which is not described in any personal policy).

In the past, the spread of such personal information has been strongly determined by physical proximity and social acquaintance. As a result, distant or poorly connected employees have lacked access to local expertise; this untapped knowledge could represent an important informational resource in large organizations. Electronic groups provide a forum for sharing such expertise independent of spatial and social constraints.

One significant kind of information flow begins with the "Does anybody know. . .?" message that appears frequently on computer networks. A sender might broadcast an electronic request for information to an entire organization, to a particular distribution list or to a bulletin board. Anyone who sees the message can reply. We studied information inquiries on the network at Tandem Computers, Inc., in Cupertino, Calif., a computer company that employs 10,500 workers around the world. In a study we conducted with David Constant, we found an average of about six does-anybody-know messages broadcast every day to one company-wide distribution list.

Information requests typically come from field engineers or sales representatives who are soliciting personal experience or technical knowledge that they cannot find in formal documents or in their own workplace. At Tandem, about eight employees send electronic mail replies to the average question. Fewer than 15 percent of the people who answered the question are personally acquainted with the questioner or are even located in the same city.

Question askers can electronically redistribute the answers they receive by putting them in a public computer file on the network. About half of the Tandem questioners make their reply files publicly available over the company network to other employees. Tandem takes this sharing process one step further by maintaining an electronic archive of question-and-reply files that is also accessible over the company network. The firm has thereby created a repository of information and working expertise that is endlessly accessible through space and time (for example, the expertise remains available when an employee is out of the office or he or she leaves the organization). A study by Thomas Finholt in our research program found that this archive is accessed more than 1,000 times a month by employees, especially those located in field offices away from the geographic center of the company.

The discretionary information sharing we discovered at Tandem and at other networked organizations seems to run contrary to nonelectronic behavior in organizations. The askers openly admit their ignorance to perhaps hundreds or even thousands of people. The repliers respond to requests for help from people they do not know with no expectation of any direct benefit to themselves.

One might wonder why people respond so readily to information requests made by strangers. Part of the explanation is that networks make the cost of responding extremely low in time and effort expended. Also, open-access networks favor the free flow of information. Respondents seem to believe that sharing information enhances the overall electronic altruism quite different from the fears that networks would weaken the social fabric of organizations.

The changes in communication made possible by networks may substantially alter the relationship between an employee and his or her organization, the structure of organizations and the nature of management. Senior managers and key professionals usually have strong social and informational connections within their organizations and within their broader professional communities. Conversely, employees who reside on the organizational periphery by virtue of geographic location, job requirements or personal attributes have relatively few opportunities to make contact with other employees and colleagues.

Reducing the impediments to communication across both physical and social distance is likely to affect peripheral employees more than central ones. We, along with Charles Huff of St. Olaf College, studied this possibility for city employees in Fort Collins, Colo. Employees who used electronic mail extensively reported more commitment to their jobs and to their co-workers than did those who rarely used the network. This correlation was particularly strong for shift workers, who, because of the nature of their work, had fewer opportunities to see their colleagues than did regular day workers. As one policewoman told us, "Working the night shift, it used to be that I would hear about promotions after they happened, though I had a right to be included in the the discussion. Now I have a say in the decision making."

Organizations are traditionally built around two key concepts: hierarchical decomposition of goals and tasks and the stability of employee relationships over time. In the fully networked organization that may become increasingly common in the future, task structure may be much more flexible and dynamic. Hierarchy will not vanish, but it will be augmented by distributed interconnections.

In today's organizations, executives generally know whom they manager and manage whom they know. In the future, however, managers of some electronic project groups will face the challenge of working with people they have never met. Allocating resources to projects and assigning credit and blame for performance will become more complex. People will often belong to many different groups and will be able to reach out across the network to acquire resources without management intervention or perhaps even without management knowledge.

A recent case in mathematics research hints at the nature of what may lie ahead. Mathematicians at Bell Communications Research (Bellcore) and at Digital Equipment sought to factor a large, theoretically interesting number known as the 9th Fermat number. They broadcast a message on the Internet to recruit researchers from universities, government laboratories and corporations to assist them in their project. The several hundred researchers who volunteered to help received—via electronic mail—software and a piece of the problem to solve; they also returned their solutions through electronic mail.

After results from all the volunteer were combined, the message announcing the final results of the project contained a charming admission:

We'd like to thank everyone who contributed computing cycles to this project, but I can't; we only have records of the person at each site who installed and managed the code. If you helped us, we'd be delighted to hear from you; please send us your name as you would like it to appear in the final version of the paper. (Broadcast message from Mark S. Manasse, June 15, 1990.)

Networking in most organizations today is limited to data communications, often for economic or financial applications such as electronic data interchange, electronic funds transfer or remote transaction processing. Most organizations have not yet begun to continue the opportunities and challenges afforded by connecting their employees through networks.

Among those that have, managers have responded in a variety of ways to changes that affect their authority and control. Some managers have installed networks for efficiency reasons but ignored their potential for more profound changes. Some have restricted who can send mail or have shut down electronic discussion groups. Others have encouraged using the network for broadening participation and involving more people in the decision-making process. The last actions push responsibility down and through the organization and also produce their own managerial issues.

A democratic organization require competent, committed, responsible employees. It requires new ways of allocating credit. It increases unpredictability, both for creative ideas and for inappropriate behavior. Managers still have to come up with new kinds of worker incentives and organizational structures to handle these changes.

The technology of networks is changing rapidly. Electronic mail that includes graphics, pictures, sound and video will eventually become widely available. The advances will make it possible to reintroduce some of the social context cues absent in current electronic communications. Even so, electronic interactions will never duplicate those conducted face-to-face.

As more people have ready access to network communications, the number and size of electronic groups will expand dramatically. It is up to management to make and shape connections. The organization of the future will depend significantly not just on how the technology of networking evolves but also on how managers seize the opportunity it presents in transforming the structure of work.

THINKING AND LEARNING

As you reread this piece, focus on some of the questions that Sproull and Kiesler have identified as guiding their research: Can people really work closely and effectively with one another when their only contact is through a computer? If employees interact through telecommuting, teleconferencing, and electronic group discussions, what holds the organization together? Where will management draw the line in freedom access to electronic mail? What will the organization of the future look like? How do small groups respond emotionally to different forms of communications?

Sproull and Kiesler claim that in groups containing both high- and low-status people, the relative influence of high-status people decreased when group members communicated by e-mail. As you read this piece, consider what Sproull and Kiesler mean by high status. How is such a characteristic determined in a group that communicates via face-to-face exchanges? Why? How might status be determined in a group that converses online? Why? How might these different ways of determining status affect Sproull and Kiesler's findings?

WRITING AND LEARNING

1. Conduct your own research project on E-mail communication. First, compose a list of ten or more questions that you'd like answered—some of these questions might be suggested from your reading of the Sproull and Kiesler article. Avoid yes-no questions and questions that yield only single-word answers. Try to focus on questions that get at technology practices as they happen in real social settings and the nature of computer-mediated communication as a form of social exchange. Among them, you might want to ask the following: Do you use E-mail to communicate with others? If so, with whom do you communicate most often via E-mail? Least often? Why? How many E-mail messages do you send a day? How many E-mail messages do you receive? From whom do you receive E-mail on a regular basis? An irregular basis? What features do you like most about E-mail? Least? How do the messages you write on E-mail differ from those you write with a paper and pen/pencil? How do the features of these two sets of technologies (i.e., paper/pen/pencil and computer/E-mail) differ? For what purposes do you think E-mail is best suited? Least suited? When you have identified a set of at least ten questions that interest you, identify a group of ten people at random in the student union. Ask each of these people to answer the questions you have identified. Either obtain their written permission for you to tape-record their answers, have them write their answers, or take notes of their answers. Finally, in a report

written to inform your classmates, summarize your findings about the E-mail practices of these ten people.

2. In a letter to Lee Sproull and/or Sara Kiesler, respond to the following claim: "In an electronic exchange, the social and contextual cues that usually regulate and influence group dynamics are missing or attenuated. Electronic messages lack information regarding job titles, social importance, hierarchical position, race, age, and appearance." Examine at least ten E-mail messages that you have written or responded to in the last few weeks. Or find a friend who will give you written permission to look at his or her messages and who will answer a few questions about the origins and authors of these messages. In your letter, discuss whether Sproull and Kiesler's claims hold up when you examine these messages and interview the author. Can you see evidence that contradicts their conclusion? If so, explain. If their claims do seem to be true, explain the corroborating evidence that you found. For support, you will want to quote from specific messages; however, make sure you have the written permission of the author before you do so.

3. Sproull and Kiesler note that organizations have both formal system of record keeping and communications (i.e., communication systems set up by and maintained by the organization for its own official purposes) and informal systems (i.e., systems of communication established primarily by employees for their own purposes). In an observational report written to your teacher, describe one of the more important formal as well as one of the more important informal communication systems within a typical college classroom. Describe the various systems of communication, identify their purposes, and analyze how and why they work as they do. Who generally initiates information within such systems and how? For what purposes? To whom is information communicated? Why? How are responses generated? Why? In what form is the information put? Why? How is information received? What are the social contexts that influence such communications? Why? Your purpose in this report is to provide your teacher with an informative report that includes a student's eye view of classroom communication systems that the teacher might not have noticed or might not have fully analyzed.

Mythinformation

Landon Winner

Langdon Winner is the author of *The Whale and the Reactor*, a book that looks at the challenges posed by the contemporary age of new technology and tries to identify some social limits that we might productively consider adopting in our headlong rush for "progress." The following contribution by Winner represents one chapter, entitled "Mythinformation," of that book. This chapter, which we can consider an example of technology criticism, explores the implications of the "computer revolution," calling into question the goals of such a revolution, the participants, their motives, and the resulting social developments.

As you read this chapter—which is written for a serious and educated audience—try to recall all the times when you have heard the term *computer revolution* and considered that movement an inevitable mark of technological progress. When you read Winner's analysis, consider which goals of the computer revolution you would prefer to be associated with, and why.

> Computer power to the people is essential to the realization of a future in which most citizens are informed about, and interested and involved in, the processes of government.
>
> —J. C. R. Licklider

In nineteenth-century Europe a recurring ceremonial gesture signaled the progress of popular uprisings. At the point of which it seemed that forces of disruption in the streets were sufficiently powerful to overthrow monarchical authority, a prominent rebel leader would go to the parliament or city hall to "proclaim the republic." This was an indication to friend and foe alike that a revolution was prepared to take its work seriously, to seize power and begin governing in a way that guaranteed political representation to all the people. Subsequent events, of course, did not always match these grand hopes; on occasion the revolutionaries were thwarted in their ambitions and reactionary governments regained control. Nevertheless, what a glorious moment when the republic was declared! Here, if only briefly, was the promise of a new order—an age of equality, justice, and emancipation of humankind.

A somewhat similar gesture has become a standard feature in contemporary writings on computers and society. In countless books, magazine articles, and media specials some intrepid soul steps forth to proclaim "the revolution." Often it is called simply "the computer revolution;" my brief inspection of a library catalogue revealed three books with exactly that title published since 1962.[1]

Other popular variants include the "information revolution," "microelectronics revolution," and "network revolution." But whatever its label, the message is usually the same. The use of computers and advanced communications technologies is producing a sweeping set of transformations in every corner of social life. An informal consensus among computer scientists, social scientists, and journalists affirms the term "revolution" as the concept best suited to describe these event. "We are all very privileged," a noted computer scientist declares, "to be in this great information Revolution in which the computer is going to affect us very profoundly, probably more so than the Industrial Revolution."[2] A well-known sociologist writes, "This revolution in the organization and processing of information and knowledge, in which the computer plays a central role, has as its context the development of what I have called the post-industrial society."[3] At frequent intervals during the past dozen years, garish cover stories in *Time* and *Newsweek* have repeated this story, climaxed by *Time's* selection of the computer as its "Man of the Year" for 1982.

Of course, the same society now said to be undergoing a computer revolution has long since gotten used to "revolutions" in laundry detergents, underarm deodorants, floor waxes, and other consumer products. Exhausted in Madison Avenue advertising slogans, the image has lost much of its punch. Those who employ it to talk about computers and society, however, appear to be taking much more serious claims. They offer a powerful metaphor, one that invites us to compare the kind of disruptions seen in political revolutions to the changes we see happening around computer information systems. Let us take that invitation seriously and see where it leads.

A Metaphor Explored

Suppose that we were looking at a revolution in a Third World country, the revolution of the Sandinistas in Nicaragua, for example. We would want to begin by studying the fundamental goals of the revolution. Is this a movement truly committed to social justice? Does it seek to uphold a valid ideal of human freedom? Does it aspire to a system of democratic rule? Answers to those questions would help us decide whether or not this is a revolution worthy of our endorsement. By the same token, we would want to ask about the means the revolutionaries had chosen to pursue their goals. Having succeeded in armed struggle, how will they manage violence and military force once they gain control? A reasonable person would also want to learn something of the structure—the situational authority that the revolution will try to create. Will there be frequent, open elections? What systems of decision making, administration, and law enforcement will be put to work? Coming to terms with its proposed ends and means, a sympathetic observer could then watch the revolution unfold, noticing whether or not it remained true to its professed purposes and how well it succeeded in its reforms.

Most dedicated revolutionaries of the modern age have been willing to supply coherent public answers to questions of this sort. It is not unreasonable to expect, therefore, that something like these issues must have engaged those who so eagerly used the metaphor "revolution" to describe and celebrate the advent of computerization. Unfortunately, this is not the case. Books, articles, and media specials aimed at a popular audience are usually content to depict the dazzling magnitude of technical innovations and social effects. Written as if by some universally accepted format, such accounts describe scores of new computer products and processes, announce the enormous dollar value of the growing computer and communications industry, survey the expanding uses of computers in offices, factories, schools, and homes, and offer good news from research and development laboratories about the great promise of the next generation of computing devices. Along with this one reads of the many "impacts" that computerization is going to have on every sphere of life. Professionals in widely separate fields—doctors, lawyers, corporate managers, and scientists—comment on the changes computers have brought to the work. Home consumers give testimonials explaining how personal computers are helping educate their children, prepare their income tax forms, and file their recipes. On occasion, this generally happy story will include reports on people left unemployed in occupations undermined by automation. Almost always, following this formula, there will be an obligatory sentence or two of criticism of the computer culture solicited from a technically qualified spokesman, an attempt to add balance to an otherwise totally sanguine outlook.

Unfortunately, the prevalence of such superficial unreflective descriptions and forecasts about computerization cannot be attributed solely to hasty journalism. Some of the most prestigious journals of the scientific community echo the claim that "a revolution is in the works."[4] A well-known computer scientist has announced unabashedly that "revolution, transformation and salvation are all to be carried out."[5] It is true that more serious approaches to the study of computers and society can be found in scholarly publications. A number of social scientists, computer scientists, and philosophers have begun to explore important issues about how computerization works and what developments, positive and negative, it is likely to bring society.[6] But such careful, critical studies are by no means the ones most influential in shaping public attitudes about the world of microelectronics. An editor at a New York publishing house stated the norm, "People want to know what's new with computer technology. They don't want to know what could go wrong."[7]

It seems all but impossible for computer enthusiasts to examine critically the *ends* that might guide the world-shaking developments they anticipate. They employ the metaphor of revolution for one purpose only—to suggest a drastic upheaval, one that people ought to welcome as good news. It never occurs to them to investigate the idea or its meaning any further.

One might suppose, for example, that a revolution of this type would involve a significant shift in the locus of powers; after all, that is exactly what one expects in revolutions of a political kind. Is something similar going to happen in this instance?

One might also ask whether or not this revolution will be strongly committed, as revolutions often are, to a particular set of social ideals. If so, what are the ideals that matter? Where can we see them argued?

To mention revolution also brings to mind the relationships of different social classes. Will the computer revolution bring about the victory of the one class over another? Will it be the occasion for a realignment of the class loyalties?

In the busy world of computer science, computer engineering, and computer marketing such questions seldom come up. Those actively engaged in promoting the transformation—hardware and software engineers, managers of microelectronics firms, computer salesmen, and the like—are busy pursuing their own ends: profits, market share, handsome salaries, the intrinsic joy of invention, the intellectual rewards of programming, and the pleasures of owning and using powerful machines. But the sheer dynamism of technical and economic activity in the computer industry evidently leaves its members little time to ponder the historical significance of their own activity. They must struggle to keep current, to be on the crest of the next wave as it breaks. As one member of Data General's Eagle computer project describes it, the prevailing spirit resembles a game of pinball. "You win one game, you get to play another. You win with this machine, you get to build the next."[8] The process has its own inertia.

Hence, once looks in vain to the movers and shakers in computer fields for the qualities of social and political insight that characterized revolutionaries of the past. Cromwell, Jefferson, Robespierre, Lenin, and Mao were able to reflect upon the world historical events in which they played a role. Public pronouncements by the likes of Robert Noyce, Marvin Minsky, Edward Feigerbaum, and Steven Jobs show no similar wisdom about the transformations they so actively help to create. By and large the computer revolution is conspicuously silent about its own ends.

GOOD CONSOLE, GOOD NETWORK, GOOD COMPUTER

My concern for the political meaning of revolution in this setting may seem somewhat misleading, even perverse. A much better point of reference might be the technical "revolutions" and associated social upheavals of the past, the industrial revolution in particular. If the enthusiasts of computerization had readily taken up this comparison, studying earlier historical periods for similarities and differences in patterns of technological innovation, capital formation, employment social change, and the like, then it would be clear that I had chosen the wrong application of this metaphor. But, in fact, no well-developed comparisons of that kind are to be found in the writings on the computer revolution. A consistently ahistorical viewpoint prevails. What one often find emphasized, however, is a vision of drastically altered social and political conditions, a future upheld as both desirable and, in all likelihood, inevitable. Politics, in other words, is not a secondary concern for many computer enthusiasts; it is a crucial, albeit thoughtless, part of their message.

We are, according to a fairly standard account, moving into an age characterized by the overwhelming dominance of electronic information systems in all areas of human practice. Industrial society, which depended upon material production for its livelihood, is rapidly being supplanted by a society of information services that will enable people to satisfy their economic and social needs. What water- and steam—powered machines were to the industrial age, the computer will be to the era now dawning. Ever-expanding technical capacities in computation and communications will make possible universal, instantaneous access to enormous quantities of valuable information. As these technologies become less and less expensive and more and more convenient, all the people of the world, not just the wealthy, will be able to use the wonderful services that information machines make available. Gradually, existing differences between rich and poor, advantaged and disadvantaged, will begin to evaporate. Widespread access to computers will produce a society more democratic, egalitarian, and richly diverse than any previously known. Because "knowledge is power," because electronic information will spread knowledge into every corner of world society, political influence will be much more wide. With the personal computer serving as the great equalizer, rule by centralized authority and social class dominance will gradually fade away. The marvelous promise of a "global village" will be fulfilled in a worldwide burst of human creativity.

A sample from recent writings on the information society illustrates these grand expectations:

> The world is entering a new period. The wealth of nations, which depended upon land, labor, and capital during its agricultural and industrial phase—depended upon natural resources, the accumulation of money, and even upon weaponry—will come in the future to depend upon information, knowledge and intelligence.[9]
>
> The electronic revolution will not do away with work, but it does hold out some promises: Most boring jobs can be done by machines; lengthy commuting can be avoided; we can have enough leisure to follow interesting pursuits outside our work; environmental destruction can be avoided; the opportunities for personal creativity will be unlimited.[10]

Long lists of specific services spell out the utopian promise of this new age: interactive television, electronic funds transfer, computer-aided instruction, customized news service, electronic magazines, electronic mail, computer teleconferencing, on-line stock market and weather reports, computerized Yellow Pages, shopping via home computer, and so forth. All of it is supposed to add up to a cultural renaissance:

> Whatever the limits to growth in other fields, there are no limits near in telecommunications and electronic technology. There are no limits near in the consumption of information, the growth of culture, or the development of the human mind.[11]
>
> Computer-based communications can be used to make human lives richer and freer, by enabling persons to have access to vast stores of information, other "human resources," and opportunities for work and socializing on a more flexible, cheaper and convenient basis than ever before.[12]
>
> When such systems become widespread, potentially intense communications networks among geographically dispersed persons will become actualized. We will become Network Nation, exchanging vast amounts of information and social and emotional communications with colleagues, friends and "strangers" who share similar interests, who are spread all over the nation.[13]
>
> A rich diversity of subcultures will be fostered by computer-based communications systems. Social, political, technical changes will produce conditions likely to lead to the formation of groups with their own distinctive sets of values, activities, language and dress.[14]

According to this view, the computer revolution will, by its sheer momentum, eliminate many of the ills that have vexed political society since the beginning of time. Inequalities of wealth and privilege will gradually fade away. One writer predicts that computer networks will "offer many opportunities to disadvantaged groups to acquire the skills and social ties they need to become full members of society."[15] Another looks forward to "a revolutionary network where each node is equal in power to all others."[16] Information will become the dominant form of wealth. Because it can flow so quickly, so freely through computer networks, it will not, in this interpretation, cause the kinds of stratification associated with traditional forms of property. Obnoxious forms of social organization will also be replaced. "The computer will smash the pyramid," one best-selling book proclaims. "We created the hierarchical, pyramidal, managerial system because we needed it to keep track of people and things people did; with the computer to keep track, we can restructure our institutions horizontally,"[17] Thus, the proliferation of electronic information will generate a leveling effect to surpass the dreams of history's great social reformers.

The same viewpoint holds that the prospects for participatory democracy have never been brighter. According to one group of social scientists, "The form of democracy found in the ancient Greek city-state, the Israeli kibbutz, and the New England town meeting, which gave every citizen the opportunity to directly participate in the political process, has become impractical in America's mass society. But this need not be the case. The technological means exist through which millions of people can enter into dialogue with one another and with their representatives, and can form the authentic consensus essential for democracy."[18]

Computer scientist J. D. R. Licklider of the Massachusetts Institute of Technology is one advocate especially hopeful about a revitalization of the democratic process. He looks forward to "an information environment that would give politics greater depth and dimension than it now has." Home computer consoles and television sets would be linked together in a massive network. "The political process would essentially be a giant tele-conference, and a campaign would be a months-long series of communications among candidates, propagandists, commentators, political action groups and voters." An arrangement of this kind would, in his view, encourage a more open, comprehensive examination of both issues and candidates. "The information revolution," he exclaims, "is bringing with it a key that may open the door to a new era of involvement and participation. The key is the self-motivating exhilaration that accompanies truly effective interaction with information through a good console through a good network to a good computer."[19] It is, in short, a democracy of machines.

Taken as a whole, beliefs of this kind constitute what I would call mythinformation: the almost religious conviction that a widespread adoption of computers and communications systems along with easy access to electronic information will automatically produce a better world for human living. It is a peculiar form of enthusiasm that characterizes social fashions of the latter decades of the twentieth century. Many people who have grown cynical or discouraged about other aspects of social life are completely enthralled by the supposed redemptive qualities of computers and telecommunications. Writing of the "fifth generation" supercomputers, Japanese author Yoneji Masuda rhapsodically predicts "freedom for each of us to set individual goals of self-realization and then perhaps a worldwide religious renaissance, characterized not by a belief in a supernatural god, but rather by awe and humility in the presence of the collective human spirit and its wisdom, humanity living in a symbolic tranquility with the planet we have found ourselves upon, regulated by a new set of global ethics."[20]

It is not uncommon for the advent of a new technology to provide an occasion for flights of utopian fancy. During the last two centuries the factory system, railroads, telephone, electricity, automobile, airplane, radio, television and nuclear power have all figured prominently in the belief that a new glorious age was about to begin. But even within the great tradition of optimistic technophilia, current dreams of a "computer age" stand out as exaggerated and unrealistic. Because they have such a broad appeal, because they overshadow other ways of looking at the matter, these notions deserve closer inspection.

THE GREAT EQUALIZER

As is generally true of a myth, the story contains elements of truth. What were one industrial societies are being transformed into service economics, a trend that emerges as more material production shifts to developing countries where labor costs are low and business tax breaks lucrative. At the same time that industrialization takes hold in less-developed nations of the world, deindustrialization is gradually altering the economics of North America and Europe. Some of the service industries central to this pattern are ones that depend upon highly sophisticated computer and communications systems. But this does not mean that future employment possibilities will flow largely from the microelectronics industry and information services. A number of studies, including those of the U.S.

Bureau of Labor Statistics, suggest that the vast majority of new jobs will come in menial service occupations paying relatively low wages.[21] As robots and computer software absorb an increasing share of factory and office tasks, the "information society" will offer plenty of opportunities for janitors, hospital orderlies, and fast food waiters.

The computer romantics are also correct in noting that computerization alters relationships of social power and control, although they misrepresent the direction this development is likely to take. Those who stand to benefit most obviously are large transnational business corporations. While their "global reach" does not arise solely from the application of information technologies, such organizations are uniquely situated to exploit the efficiency, productivity, command, and control the new electronics make available. Other notable beneficiaries of the systematic use of vast amounts of digitized information are public bureaucracies, intelligence agencies, and an ever-expanding military, organizations that would operate less effectively at their present scale were it not for the use of computer power. Ordinary people are, of course, strongly affected by the workings of these organizations and by the rapid spread of new electronic systems in banking, insurance, taxation, factory and office work, home entertainment, and the like. They also counted upon to be eager buyers of hardware, software, and communications services as computer products reach the consumer market.

But where in all of this motion do we see increased democratization? Social equality? The dawn of a cultural renaissance? Current developments in the information age suggest an increase in power by those who already had a great deal of power, an enhanced centralization of control by those already prepared for control, an augmentation of wealth by the already wealthy. Far from demonstrating a resolution in patterns of social and political influence, empirical studies of computers and social change usually show powerful groups adapting computerized methods to retain control.[22] That is not surprising. Those best situated to take advantage of the power of a new technology are often those previously well situated by dint of wealth, social standing, and institutional position. Thus, if there is to be a computer revolution, the best guess is that it will have a distinctly conservative character.

Granted, such prominent trends could be alternated. It is possible that a society strongly rooted in computer and telecommunications systems could be one in which participatory democracy, decentralized political control, and social equality are fully realized. Progress of that kind would have to occur as the result of that society's concerted efforts to overcome many difficult obstacles to achieve those ends. Computer enthusiasts, however, seldom propose deliberate action of that kind. Instead, they strongly suggest that the good society will be realized as a side effect, a spin-off from the vast proliferation of computing devices. There is evidently no need to try to shape the institutions of the information age in ways that maximize human freedom while placing limits upon concentrations of power.

For those willing to wait passively while the computer revolution takes its hold, technological determinism ceases to be mere theory and becomes an ideal: a desire to embrace conditions brought on by technological change without judging them in advance. There is nothing new in this disposition. Computer romanticism is merely the latest version of the nineteenth- and twentieth-century faith we noted earlier, one that has always expected to generate freedom, democracy, and justice through sheer material abundance. Thus there is no need for serious inquiry into the appropriate design of new institutions or the distribution of rewards and burdens. As long as the economy is growing and the machinery in good working order, the rest will take care of itself. In previous versions of this homespun conviction, the abundant (and therefore democratic) society was manifest by a limitless supply of houses, appliances, and consumer goods.[23] Now "access to information" and "access to computers" have moved to the top of the list.

The political arguments of computer romantics draw upon a number of key assumptions: (1) people are bereft of information; (2) information is knowledge; (3) knowledge is power; and (4) increasing access to information enhances democracy and equalizes social power. Taken as separate assertions and in combination, these beliefs provide a woefully distorted picture of the role of electronic systems in social life.

It is true that people face serious shortages of information. To read the literature on the computer revolution one would suppose this to be a problem on par with the energy crisis of the 1970s. The persuasiveness of this notion borrows from our sense that literacy, education, knowledge, well-informed minds, and the widespread availability of tools inquiry are unquestionable social goods, and that, in contrast, illiteracy, inadequate education, ignorance, and forced restrictions upon knowledge are among history's worst evils. Thus, it appears superficially plausible that a world rewired to connect human beings to vast data banks and communications systems would be a progressive step. Information shortage would be remedied in much the same way that developing a new fuel supply might solve an energy crisis. Alas, the idea is entirely faulty. It mistakes sheer supply of information with an educated ability to gain knowledge and act effectively based on that knowledge. In many parts of the world that ability is sadly lacking. Even some highly developed societies still contain chronic inequalities in the distribution of good education and basic intellectual skills. The U.S. Army, for instance, must now reject or dismiss a fairly high percentage of the young men and women it recruits because they simply cannot read military manuals. It is no doubt true of these recruits that they have a great deal of information about the world—information from their life experiences, schooling, the mass media, and so forth. What makes them "functionally illiterate" is that they have not learned to translate this information into a mastery of practical skills.

If the solution to problems of illiteracy and poor education were a question of information supply alone, then the best policy might be to increase the number of well-stocked libraries, making sure they were built in places where libraries do not presently exist. Of course, that would do little good in itself unless people are sufficiently well educated to use those libraries to expand their knowledge and understanding. Computer enthusiasts, however, are not noted for their calls to increase support of public libraries and schools. It is *electronic information* carried by *networks* they uphold as crucial. Here is a case in which an obsession with a particular kind of technology causes one to disregard what are obvious problems and clear remedies. While it is true that systems of computation and communications, intelligently structured and wisely applied, might help a society raise its standards of literacy, education, and general knowledgeability, to attend to those instruments first while ignoring how to enlighten and invigorate a human mind is pure foolishness.

"As everybody knows, knowledge is power,"[24] This is an attractive idea, but highly misleading. Of course, knowledge employed in particular circumstances can help one act effectively and in that sense enhance one's power. A citrus farmer's knowledge of frost conditions enables him/her to take steps to prevent damage to the crop. A candidate's knowledge of public opinion can be a powerful aid in an election campaign. But surely there is no automatic, positive link between knowledge and power, especially if that means power in a social or political sense. At times knowledge brings merely an enlightened impotence or paralysis. One may know exactly what to do but lack the wherewithal to act. Of the many conditions that affect the phenomenon of power, knowledge is but one and by no means the most important. Thus, in the history of ideas, arguments that expert knowledge ought to play a special role in politics have always been offered as something contrary to prevailing wisdom. To Plato and Verlen it was obvious that knowledge was *not* power, a situation they hoped to remedy.

An equally serious misconception among computer enthusiasts is the belief that democracy is first and foremost a matter of distributing information. As one particularly flamboyant manifesto exclaims: "There is an explosion of information dispersal in the technology and we think this information has to be shared. All great thinkers about democracy said that the key to democracy is access to information. And now we have a chance to get information into people's hands like never before."[25] Once again such assertions play on our belief that a democratic public ought to be open-minded and well informed. One of the great evils of totalitarian societies is that they dictate what people can know and impose secrecy to restrict freedom. But democracy is not founded solely (or even primarily) upon conditions that affect the availability of information. What distinguishes it from other political forms is a recognition that the people as a whole are capable of self-government and that they have a rightful claim to rule. As a consequence, political society ought to build institutions that allow or even encourage a great latitude of democratic participation. How far a society must go in making political authority and public information available to ordinary people is a matter of dispute among political theorists. But no serious student of the question would give must credence to the idea that creating a universal gridwork to spread electronic information is, by itself, a democratizing step.

What, then, of the idea that "interaction with information through a good console, through a good network to a good computer, will promote a renewed sense of political involvement and participation? Readers who believe that assertion should contact me about some parcels of land my uncle has for sale in Florida. Relatively low levels of citizen participation and prevail in some modern democracies, the United States, for example. There are many reasons for this, many ways a society might try to improve things. Perhaps opportunities to serve in public office or influence public policy are too limited; in that case, broaden the opportunities. Or perhaps choices placed before citizens are so pallid that boredom is a valid response; in that instance, improve the quality of those choices. But it is simply not reasonable to assume that enthusiasm for political activity will be stimulated solely by the introduction of sophisticated information machines. The role that television plays in modern politics should suggest why this is so. Participation in voting has steadily declined as television replaced the face-to-face politics of precincts and neighborhoods. Passive monitoring of electronic news and information allows citizens to feel involved while dampening the desire to take an active part. If people begin to rely upon computerized data bases and telecommunications as a primary means of exercising power, it is conceivable that genuine political knowledge based in first-hand experience would disappear altogether. The vitality of democratic politics depends upon people's willingness to act together in pursuit of their common ends. It requires that on occasion members of a community appear before each other in person, speak their minds, deliberate on paths of action, and decide what they will do.[26] This is considerably different from the model now upheld as a breakthrough for democracy: logging onto one's computer, receiving the latest information, and sending back as (tantaneous) digitized response.

A chapter from recent political history illustrates the strength of direct participation in contrast to the politics of electronic information. In 1981 and 1982 two groups of activists set about to do what they could to stop the international nuclear arms race. One of the groups, Ground Zero, chose to rely almost solely upon mass communications to convey its message to the public. Its leaders appeared on morning talk shows and evening news programs on all three television networks. They followed up with mass mail solicitation using addresses from a computerized data base. At the same time another group, the Nuclear Weapons Freeze Campaign, began by taking its proposal for a bilateral nuclear freeze to New England town meetings, places where active citizen participation is a long-standing tradition. Winning the endorsement of the idea from a great many town meetings, the Nuclear Freeze group expanded its drive by launching a series of state initiatives. Once again the key was a direct approach to people, this time through thousands of meetings, dinners, and parties held in homes across the country.

The effects of the two movements were strikingly different. After its initial publicity, Ground Zero was largely ignored. It had been an ephemeral exercise in media posturing. The Nuclear Freeze campaign, however, continued to gain influence in the form of increasing public support, successful ballot measures, and an ability to apply pressure upon political officials. Eventually, the latter group did begin to use computerized mailings, television appearances, and the like to advance its cause. But it never forgot the original source of its leverage: people work together toward common ends.

Of all the computer enthusiasts' political ideas, there is none more poignant than the faith that the computer is destined to become a potent equalizer in modern society. Support for this belief is found in the fact that small "personal" computers are becoming more and more powerful, less and less expensive, and ever more simple to us. Obnoxious tendencies associated with the enormous, costly, technically inaccessible computers of the recent past are soon to be overcome. As one writer explains, "The great forces of centralization that characterized mainframe and minicomputer design of that period have now been reversed." This means that "the puny device that sits innocuously on the desktop will, in fact, within a few years, contain enough computing power to become an effective equalizer."[27] Presumably, ordinary citizens equipped with microcomputers will be able to counter the influence of large, computer-based organizations.

Notions of this kind echo beliefs of eighteenth- and nineteenth-century revolutionaries that placing the fire arms in the hands of the people was crucial to overthrowing entrenched authority. In the American Revolution, French Revolution, Paris Commune, and Russian Revolution the role of "the people armed" was central to the revolutionary program. As the military defeat of the Paris Commune made clear, however, the fact that the popular forces have guns may not be decisive. In a contest of force against force, the larger, more sophisticated, more ruthless, better equipped competitor often has the upper hand. Hence, the availability of low-cost computing power may move the baseline that defines electronic dimensions of social influence, but it does not necessarily alter the relative balance of power. Using a personal computer makes one no more powerful vis-à-vis, say, the National Security Agency, than flying a hang glider establishes a person as a match for the U.S. Air Force.

In sum, the political expectations of computer enthusiasts are seldom more than idle fantasy. Beliefs that widespread use of computers will cause hierarchies to crumble, inequality to tumble, participation to flourish, and centralized power to dissolve simply do not withstand close scrutiny. The formula information that knowledge = power = democracy lacks any real substance. At each point the mistake comes in the conviction that computerization will inevitably move society toward the good life. And no one will have to raise a finger.

INFORMATION AND IDEOLOGY

Despite its shortcomings as political theory, mythinformation is noteworthy as a expressive contemporary ideology. I use the term "ideology" here in a sense common in social science: a set of beliefs that expresses the needs and aspirations of a group, class, culture, or subculture. In this instance the needs and aspirations that matter most are those that stem from operational requirements of highly complex systems in an advanced technological society; the groups most directly involved are those who build, maintain, operate, improve, and market these systems. At a time in which almost all major components of our technological society have to depend upon the application of large and small computers, it is not surprising that computerization has risen to ideological prominence, an expression of grand hopes and ideals.

What is the "information" so crucial in this odd belief system, the icon now so greatly cherished? We have seen enough to appreciate that the kind of information upheld is not knowledge in the ordinary sense of the term; not is it understanding, enlightenment, critical thought, timeless wisdom, or the content of a well-educated mind. If one looks carefully at the writings of computer enthusiasts, one finds that information in a particular form and content offered as a paradigm to inspire emulation. Enormous quantities of data, manipulated within various kinds of electronic media and used to facilitate the transactions of today's large, complex organizations is the model we are urged to embrace. In this context the sheer quantity of information presents a formidable challenge. Modern organizations are continually faced with overload, a flood of data that threatens to become unintelligible to them. Computers provide one way to confront that problem; speed conquers quantity. An equally serious challenge is created by the fact that the varieties of information most crucial to modern organizations are highly time specific. Data on stock market prices, airline traffic, weather conditions, international economic indicators, military intelligence, public opinion pool results, and the like are useful for very short periods of time. Systems that gather, organize, analyze, and utilize electronic data in these areas must be closely tuned to the very latest developments. If one is trading on fast-paced international markets, information about prices an hour old or even a few second old may have no value. Information is itself a perishable commodity.

Thus, what looked so puzzling in another context—the urgent "need" for information as a social world filled with many pressing human needs—now becomes transparent. It is, in the first instance, the need of complex human/machine systems threatened with debilitating uncertainties or even breakdown unless continually replenished with up-to-the-minute electronic information about their internal states and operating environments. Rapid information-processing capabilities of modern computers and communications devices are a perfect match for such a marriage made in technological heaven.

But is it sensible to transfer this model, as many evidently wish, to all parts of human life? Must activities, experiences, ideas, and ways of knowing that take a longer time to bear fruit adapt to the speedy processes of digitized information processing? Must education, the arts, politics, sports, home life, and all other forms of social practice be transformed to accommodate it? As one article on the coming of the home computer concludes, "running a household is actually like running a small business. You have to worry about inventory control—of household supplies—and budgeting for school tuition, housekeepers' salaries, and all the rest."[28] The writer argues that these complex, rapidly changing operations require a powerful information—processing capacity to keep them functioning smoothly. One begins to wonder how everyday activities such as running a household were even possible before the advent of microelectronics. This is a case in which the computer is a solution frantically in search of a problem.

In the last analysis, the almost total silence about the ends of the "computer revolution" is replaced by a conviction that information processing is something valuable in its own right. Faced with an information explosion that strains the capacities of traditional institutions, society will renovate its structure to accommodate computerized, automated systems in every area of concern. The efficient management of information is revealed as the *telos* of modern society, its greatest mission. It is that fact to which mythinformation adds glory and glitter. People must be convinced that the human burdens of an information age—unemployment, de-skilling, the disruption of many social patterns—are worth bearing. Once again, those who push the plow are told they ride a golden chariot.

EVERYWHERE AND NOWHERE

Having criticized a point of view, it remains for me to suggest what topics a serious study of computers and politics should pursue. The question is, of course, a very large one. If the long-term consequences of computerization are anything like the ones commonly predicted, they will require a rethinking of many fundamental conditions in social and political life. I will mention three areas of concern.

As people handle an increasing range of their daily activities through electronic instruments—mail, banking, shopping, entertainment, travel plans, and so forth—it becomes technically feasible to monitor these activities to a degree heretofore inconceivable. The availability of digitized footprints of social transactions affords opportunities that contain a menacing aspect. While there has been a great deal written about this problem, most of it deals with the "threat to privacy," the possibility that someone might gain access to information that violates the sanctity of one's personal life. As important as that issue certainly is, it by no means exhausts the potential evils created by electronic data banks and computer matching. The danger extended beyond the private sphere to affect the most basic of public freedoms. Unless steps are taken to prevent it, we may develop systems capable of a perpetual, pervasive, apparently benign surveillance. Confronted with omnipresent, all-seeing data banks, the populace may find passivity and compliance the safest route, avoiding activities that once represented political liberty. As a badge of civic pride a citizen may announce, "I'm not involved in anything a computer would find the least bit interesting."

The evolution of this unhappy state of affairs does not necessarily depend upon the "misuse" of computer systems. The prospect we face is really much more insidious. An age rich in electronic information may achieve wonderful social conveniences at a cost of placing freedom, perhaps inadvertently, in a deep chill.

A thoroughly computerized world is also one bound to alter conditions of human sociability. The point of many applications of microelectronics, after all, is to eliminate social layers that were previously needed to get things done. Computerized bank tellers, for example, have largely done away with small local branch banks, which were not only ways of doing business, but places where people met, talked, and socialized. The so-called electronic cottage industry, similarly, operates very well without the kinds of human interactions that once characterized office work. Despite greater efficiency, productivity, and convenience, innovations of this kinds do away with the reasons people formerly had for being together, working together, acting together. Many practical activities once crucial to even a minimal sense of community life are rendered obsolete. One consequence of these developments is to pare away the kinds of face-to-face contact that once provided important buffers between individuals and organized power. To an increasing extent, people will become even more susceptible to the influence of employers, news media, advertisers, and national political leaders. Where will we find new institutions to balance and mediate such power?

Perhaps the most significant challenge posed by the linking of computers and telecommunications is the prospect that the basic structures of political order will be recast. Worldwide computer, satellite, and communication networks fulfill, in large part, the modern dream of conquering space and time. These systems make possible instantaneous action at any point on the globe without limits imposed by the specific location of the initiating actor. Human beings and human societies, however, have traditionally found their identities within spatial and temporal limits. They have lived, acted, and found meaning in a particular place at a particular time. Developments in microelectronics tend to dissolve these limits, thereby threatening the integrity of social and political forms that depend on them. Aristotle's observation that "man is a political animal" meant in its most literal sense that man is a *polis* animal, a creature naturally suited to live in a particular kind of community within a specific geographical setting, the city-state. Historical experience shows that it is possible for human beings to flourish in separate units—kingdoms, empires, nation-states—larger than those the Greeks thought natural. But until recently the crucial conditions created by spatial boundaries of political societies were never in question.

That has changed. Methods pioneered by transnational corporations now make it possible for organizations of enormous size to manage their activities effectively across the surface of the planet. Business units that used to depend upon spatial proximity can now be integrated through complex electronic signals. If it seems convenient to shift operations from one area of the world to another far distant, it can be accomplished with a flick of a switch. Close an office in Sunnyvale; open an office in Singapore. In the recent past corporations have had to demonstrate at least some semblance of commitment to geographically based communities; their public relations often stressed the fact that they were "good neighbors." But in an age in which organizations are located everywhere and nowhere, this commitment easily evaporates. A transnational corporation can play fast and loose with everyone, including the country that is ostensibly its "home." Towns, cities, regions, and whole nations are forced to swallow their pride and negotiate for favor in that process, political authority is gradually redefined.

Computerization resembles other vast, but largely unconscious experiments in modern social and technological history, experiments of the kind noted in earlier chapters. Following a step-by-step process of instrumental improvements, societies create new institutions, new patterns of behavior, new sensibilities, new contexts for the exercise of power. Calling such changes "revolutionary," we tacitly acknowledge that these are matters that require reflection, probably even strong public action to ensure that the outcomes are desirable. But the occasions for reflection, debate, and public choice are extremely rare indeed. The important decisions are left in private hands inspired by narrowly focused economic motives. While many recognize that these decisions have profound consequences for our common life, few seem prepared to own up to that fact. Some observers forecast that "the computer revolution" will eventually be guided by new wonders in artificial intelligence. Its present course is influenced by something much more familiar: the absent mind.

Notes

1. See, for example, Edward Berkeley, *The Computer Revolution* (New York: Doubleday, 1962); Edward Tomeski, *The Computer Revolution: The Executive and the New Information Technology* (New York: Macmillan, 197); and Nigel Hawkes, *The Computer Revolution* (New York: E.P. Dutton, 1972). See also Aaron Sloman, *The Computer Revolution in Philosophy* (Hassocks, England: Harvester Press, 1978); Zenon Pylyshyn, *Perspectives on the Computer Revolution* (Englewood Cliffs, N.J.: Prentice Hall, 1970); Paul Stoneman, *Technological Diffusion and the Computer Revolution* (Cambridge: Cambridge University Press, 1976); and Ernest Braun and Stuart MacDonald, *Revolution in Miniature: The History and Impact of Semiconductor Electronics* (Cambridge University Press, 1978).
2. Michael L. Dertouzos in an interview on "The Today Show," National Broadcasting Company, August 8, 1983.
3. Daniel Bell, "The Social Framework of the Information Society," in *The Computer Age: A Twenty Year View,* Michael L. Dertouzos and Joel Moses (eds.) (Cambridge: MIT Press, 1980), 163.
4. See, for example, Philip H. Abelson, "The Revolution in Computers and Electronics," Science 215:751-753, 1982.
5. Edward A. Feigenbaum and Pamela McCorduck, *The Fifth Generation: Artificial Intelligence and Japan's Computer Challenge to the World* (Reading, Mass.: Addison-Wesley, 1984), 8.

6. Among the important works of this kind are David Burnham, *The Rise of the Computer State* (New York: Random House, 1983); James N. Danziger et al., *Computers and Politics: High Technology in American Local Governments* (New York: Columbia University Press, 1982): Abbe Moshowitz, *The Conquest of Will: Information Processing in Human Affairs* (Reading, Mass.: Addition; Wesley, 1986); James Rule et al., *the Politics of Privacy* (New York: New American Library, 198); and Joseph Weizenbaum, *Computer Power and Human Reason: From Judgment to Calculation* (San Francisco: W. H. Freeman, 1976).

7. Quoted in Jacques Vallee, *The Network Revolution: Confessions of a Computer Scientist* (Berkeley: And/Or Press, 1982), 10.

8. Tracy Kidder, *Soul of a New Machine* (New York: Avon Books, 1982), 228.

9. *The Fifth Generation*, 14.

10. James Martin, *Telematic Society: A Challenge for Tomorrow* (Englewood Cliffs, N.J.: Prentice-Hall, 1981), 172.

11. Ibid, 4.

12. Starr Roxanne Hiltz and Murray Turoff, *The Network Nation: Human Communication via Computer* (Reading, Mass.: Addison-Wesley, 1978), 489.

13. Ibid., xxix.

14. Ibid., 484.

15. Ibid., xxix.

16. *The Network Revolution*, 198.

17. John Naisbitt, *Megatrends: Ten New Directions Transforming Our Lives* (New York: Warner Books, 1984). 282.

18. Amitai Etzioni, Kenneth Laudon, and Sara Lipson, "Participating Technology: The Minerva Communications Tree," *Journal of Communications*, 25:64, Spring 1975.

19. J. C. R. Licklider, "Computers and Government,: in Dertouzos and Moses (eds.), *The Computer Age*, 114, 126.

20. Quoted in *The Fifteen Generation*, 240.

21. *Occupational Outlook Handbook*, 1982-1983, U.S. bureau of Labor Statistics, Bulletin No. 2200, Superintendent of Documents, U.S. government, Printing Office, Washington, D.C. See also Gene I. Maeroll, "The Real Job booms Likely to Be Low-Tech," *New York Times*, September 4, 1983, 16E.

22. See, for example, James Danziger et al., *Computers and Politics*.

23. For a study of the utopia of consumer products in American democracy, see Jeffrey L. Meikle, *Twentieth Century Limited: Industrial Design in America*, 1925–1939 (Philadelphia: Temple University Press, 1985. For other utopian dreams see Joseph J. Corn, *The Winged Gospel: American's Romance with Aviation, 1900-1950* (Oxford: Oxford University Press, 1983); Joseph J. Corn and Brian Horrigan, *Yesterday's Tomorrows; Past Vision of America's Future* (New York: Summit Books 1984); and Erik Barnow, *the Tube of Plenty* (Oxford University Press, 1975).

24. *The Fifth Generation*, 8.

25. "The Philosophy of US," from the official program of The US Festival held in San Bernardino, California: September 4–7, 1982. The outdoor rock festival, sponsored by Steven Wozniak, co-inventory of the original Apple Computer, attracted an estimated half million people. Wozniak regaled the crowd with large-screen video presentations of his message, proclaiming a new age of community and democracy generated by the use of personal computers.

26. *"Power* corresponds to the human ability not just to act buy to act in concert. Power is never property of an individual; it belongs to a group and remains in existence only so long as the group keeps together." Hannah Arendt, *On Violence* (New York: Harcourt Brace & World, 1969), 44.

27. John Markoff, "A View of the Future: Micros Won't Matter," *Info-World*, October 31, 1983, 69.

28. Donald H. Dunn, "The Many Uses of the Personal Computer,: *Business Week,* June 23, 1980, 125–126.

THINKING AND REREADING

1. As you reread this piece, consider Winner's quote from an editor at a New York publishing firm, "People want to know what's new with computer technology. They don't want to know what could go wrong." Think about why such a statement might be true. Why would people avoid an analysis of the problems associated with technology?
2. Furthermore, identify for yourself the specific goals of the computer revolution as it has been manifested in our culture. What is the revolution against? What is it for? Who are the participants? Who are the victims? How do they stand to benefit? To lose?

WRITING AND LEARNING

1. In a letter written to the current president or vice president of the United States, identify the goals of the computer revolution as you think they have been manifested in our country. You are writing from the point of view of an informed citizen and a taxpayer, so you have both the right and the responsibility to express your opinion on this matter. In your letter, identify which of these specific goals you agree with and think we should be able to attain, which you consider less worthwhile and less attainable, and which you disagree with and believe we are unable to attain. Explain your opinions about each goal.

APPENDIX B

Using the Internet

What Does It Mean to "Be on the Internet"?

"Being on the Internet" means having full access to all Internet services. Any commercial service or institution that has full Internet access provides the following:

- Electronic mail (E-mail)
- Telnet
- File Transfer Protocol (FTP)
- World Wide Web

Electronic Mail

Electronic mail is the most basic, the easiest to use, and for many people, the most useful Internet service. E-mail services allow you to send, forward, and receive messages from people all over the world, usually at no charge. You can then easily reply to messages, save, file, and categorize received messages.

Electronic mail also makes it possible to participate in electronic conferences and discussions. You can use E-mail to request information from individuals, universities, and institutions.

Telnet

Telnet provides the capability to log in to a remote computer and to work interactively with it. When you run a Telnet session, your computer is remotely connected to a computer at another location, but will act as if it were directly connected to that computer.

File Transfer Protocol (FTP)

File Transfer Protocol is a method that allows you to move files and data from one computer to another. File Transfer Protocol, most commonly referred to as FTP, enables you to download magazines, books, documents, free software, music, graphics, and much more.

World Wide Web

The World Wide Web is a collection of standards and protocols used to access information available on the Internet. World Wide Web users can easily access text documents, images, video, and sound.

The Web and the Internet

The World Wide Web (WWW or Web) is a collection of documents linked together in what is called a *hypermedia system*. Links point to any location on the Internet that can contain information in the form of text, graphics, video, or sound files.

Using the World Wide Web requires "browsers" to view Web documents and navigate through the intricate link structure. Currently there are between 30–40 different Web browsers. In this chapter you will learn how to use two of the premiere Web browsers —Netscape Navigator and Microsoft's Explorer. Both of these browsers combine a point-and-click interface design with an "open" architecture that is capable of integrating other Internet tools such as electronic mail, FTP, Gopher, WAIS, and Usenet newsgroups. This architecture makes it relatively easy to incorporate images, video, and sound into text documents.

The World Wide Web was developed at the European Particle Physics Laboratory (CERN) in Geneva, Switzerland. Originally it was developed as a means for physicists to share papers and data easily. Today it has evolved into a sophisticated technology that links hypertext and hypermedia documents.

The Web and the Internet are not synonymous. The World Wide Web is a collection of standards and protocols used to access information available on the Internet. The Internet is the network used to transport information.

The Web uses three standards:

- URLs (Uniform Resource Locators)
- HTTP (Hypertext Transfer Protocol)
- HTML (Hypertext Markup Language)

These standards provide a mechanism for WWW servers and clients to locate and display information available through other protocols such as Gopher, FTP, and Telnet.

URLs (Uniform Resource Locators)

URLs are a standard format for identifying locations on the Internet. They also allow an addressing system for other Internet protocols such as access to Gopher menus, FTP file retrieval, and Usenet newsgroups. URLs specify three types of information needed to retrieve a document:

- the protocol to be used;
- the server address to which to connect; and
- the path to the information.

The format for an URL is: protocol//server-name/path

Figure B.1

Sample URLs
World Wide Web URL: http://home.netscape.com/home/Welcome.html
Document from a secure server: https://netscape.com
Gopher URL: gopher://umslvma.umsl.edu/Library
FTP URL: ftp://nic.umass.edu
Telnet URL: telnet://geophys.washington.edu
Usenet URL: news:rec.humor.funny

Note: The URL for newsgroups omits the two slashes. The two slashes designate the beginning of a server name. Since you are using your Internet provider's local news server, you do not need to designate a news server by adding the slashes.

URL Tips

- Do not capitalize the protocol string. For example, the HTTP protocol should be http:// not HTTP://. Some browsers such as Netscape correct these errors. Others do not.
- If you have trouble connecting to a Web site, check your URL and be sure you have typed in the address correctly.
- You do not need to add a slash (/) at the end of an URL, such as http://home.netscape.com because a slash indicates that there is another path to follow.

HTTP (Hypertext Transfer Protocol)

HTTP is a protocol used to transfer information within the World Wide Web. Web site URLs begin with the http protocol: http://
  This Web URL connects you to Netscape's Home Page: http://home.netscape.com

HTML (Hypertext Markup Language)

HTML is the programming language used to create a Web page. It formats the text of the document, describes its structure, and specifies links to other documents. HTML also includes programming to access and display different media such as images, video, and sound.

The Adventure Begins . . .

Now that you have a basic understanding of the Internet you are ready to begin your adventure. Before you can travel and explore the information superhighway you will first need the following:

- An Internet account
- A username and password (required to log onto your Internet account)
- Instructions from your institution on how to log on and log off

Getting Started

1. Turn on your computer.
2. Log onto your network using your institution's login procedures.
3. Open Netscape Navigator, Explorer, or the Internet browser that you will be using.

GUIDED TOUR—INTERNET BROWSERS

This section provides you with a guided tour of the two most widely used Internet browsers—Netscape Navigator and Microsoft's Internet Explorer. You will learn how to navigate the Internet by using toolbar buttons and pulldown menus, and how to save your favorite Internet sites (URLs) as bookmarks.

Netscape Navigator

Netscape Navigator is a user-friendly graphical browser for the Internet. Netscape makes it possible to view and interact with multimedia resources (text, images, video, and sound) by pointing and clicking your mouse on pull-down menus and toolbar buttons.

Netscape Navigator (Version 1.0) was developed in 1994 by Marc Andreeseen and others who developed the first graphical Internet browser, Mosaic, at the National Center for Supercomputing Applications (NCSA) at the University of Illinois at Urbana-Champaign. It quickly became the standard and was the premiere Internet information browser in 1995. Netscape 2.0 was introduced in February 1996 and remains at the head of its field.

Features and Capabilities

Netscape Navigator features include the ability to:

- use Netscape as your electronic mail program.
- connect to Gopher, FTP, and Telnet sites without using any additional software.
- read Usenet newsgroups.
- save your favorite Internet addresses (URLs) as bookmarks.
- download images, video, and sound files to your computer desktop.
- view, save, or print the HTML programming code for Web pages as either text or HTML source code.
- use forms for collecting information.
- use plug-in programs, such as JAVA, that extend the capabilities of Netscape.

THE NETSCAPE WINDOW (PAGE)

The World Wide Web is unique in that its architecture allows for multimedia resources to be incorporated into a hypertext file or document called a page. A Web page or window may contain text, images, movies, and sound. Each multimedia resource on a page has associated locational information to link you to the resource. This locational information is called the URL.

The Netscape Navigator 2.0 window includes the following features to assist you with your Internet travels:

- The Window Title Bar shows the name of the current document.
- Page display shows the content of the Netscape window. A page includes text and links to images, video, and sound files. Links include highlighted words (colored and/or underlined) or icons. Click on a highlighted word or icon to bring another page of related information into view.
- Frames is a segmented portion of a Netscape page that contains its own page.
- Progress Bar shows the completed percentage of your document layout as your page downloads.
- Mail Icon (the small envelope in the bottom-right corner of the Netscape page, or the Mail and News pages) provides you with information on the status of your mail. A question mark next to the mail envelope indicates that Netscape cannot automatically check the mail server for new E-mail messages.
- Address location field shows the URL address of the current document.
- Toolbar buttons activate Netscape features and navigational aids.
- Directory buttons display resources for helping you to browse the Internet.

- Security indicators (doorkey icon in the lower-left corner of the window) indicate whether a document is secure (doorkey icon is blue) or insecure (doorkey icon is grey).

The Home Page

The Home Page as shown in Figure B.2 is the starting point for your journey using a Web browser such as Netscape Navigator. Home pages are created by Internet providers, colleges and universities, schools, businesses, individuals, or anyone who has information they want to make available on the Internet. For example, a college or university may have links to information on the college and courses taught.

Figure B.2 A Home page for Intel: http://www.Intel.com.

Navigating with Netscape

This guided tour introduces you to Netscape's graphical interface navigational tools:

- hyperlinks
- toolbar buttons
- pull-down menus

Hyperlinks

When you begin Netscape you will start with a Home Page. Click on highlighted words (colored and/or underlined) to bring another page of related information to your screen.

Images will automatically load onto this page unless you have turned off the **Auto Load Images** found under the **Options** menu. If you have turned off this option you will see this icon that represents an image that can be downloaded.

If you want to view this image, click on this highlighted icon or on the **Images** button.

As you travel the World Wide Web, you will find other icons to represent movies, video, and sound. Click on these icons to download (link) you to these resources.

Toolbar Buttons

Netscape toolbar buttons.

Back: Point and click on the **Back** button to go to your previous page.

Forward: This button takes you to the next page of your history list. The history list keeps track of the pages you link to.

Home: This button takes you back to the first opening page that you started with.

Reload: Click on this button to reload the same page that you are viewing. Changes made in the source page will be shown in this new page.

Images: Clicking on this button downloads images onto your current page. Netscape provides you with an option to not download images when you access a page. This makes page downloading faster. If you have selected this option (found in **Options** menu—**Auto Load Images**) and decide that you would like to view an image, just clink on the Images button.

Open: Use this button to access a dialog box for typing in URLs for Web sites, newsgroups, Gopher, FTP, and Telnet.

Print: Select this button to print the current page you are viewing.

Find: If you are searching for a word in the current page you are viewing, click on the **Find** button for a dialog box to enter the word or phrase.

Stop: This button stops the downloading of the Web pages: text, images, video, or sound.

Netscape navigational buttons for exploring the Net.

What's New: Visit *What's New* to link to the best new sites.

What's Cool: Netscape's selection of cool Web sites to visit.

Handbook: Links you to on-line Netscape tutorials, references, and index.

Net Search: Clicking on this button links you to available search engines that help find a particular site or document. Search engines use key words and concepts to help find information in titles or headers of documents, directories, or documents themselves.

Net Directory: Click on this button to explore Internet resources categorized by topic. Some directories cover the entire Internet; some present only what they feel is relevant; others focus on a particular field.

Software: This button connects you to information about Netscape Navigator software: subscription programs, upgrade information, and registration.

Pull-down Menus

Nine pull-down menus offer navigational tools for your Netscape journeys: File, Edit, View, Go, Bookmarks, Options, Directory, Window, and Help (Windows only).

File Menu

Many of the File menu options work the same as they do in other applications. You also have options to open a new Netscape window, Home Page, or Internet site.

Figure B.3 Netscape **File** pull-down menu.

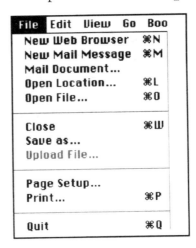

New Web Browser: Creates a new Netscape window. This window displays the first page you viewed when you connected to Netscape.

New Mail Message: Opens an E-mail composition box that allows you to create and send a message or attach a document to your mail message.

Mail Document (or **Mail Frame**): Lets you send an e-mal message with the Web page you are viewing attached. The page's URL will be included.

Open Location: Works the same as the **Open** toolbar button. Enter an URL address in the dialog box.

Open File: Provides a dialog box for you to use to open a file on your computer's hard drive without being connected to the Internet.

Close: Closes the current Netscape page. On Windows, this option exits the Netscape application when you close the last page.

Save as . . . (or **Save Frame as**): Creates a file to save the contents of the current Internet page you are viewing in the Netscape window. The page can be saved as plain text or in source (HTML) format.

Upload File: Click on this option to upload a file to the FTP server indicated by the current URL. You can also upload images by dragging and dropping files from the desktop to the Netscape window. Note: This command is active only when you are connected to an FTP server.

Page Setup: Click on this to specify your printing options.

Print: Click on this button to print the current page or frame. To print a single frame, click in the desired frame.

Print Preview (Windows only): Previews the printed page on the screen.

Exit (on Macintosh—**Quit**): Exits the Netscape application.

Edit Menu

The **Edit** menu makes it possible to cut and paste text from a Web page to your computer's clipboard. This option can be used to copy and paste text from a page or frame to a word processing document or another application of your choice. The options under this menu are similar to what you have available to you in many of your computer software applications under their **File** menu (i.e., word processing, desktop publishing, and graphics applications).

Figure B.4 Netscape **Edit** menu.

Edit	View	Go	
Can't Undo		⌘Z	
Cut		⌘X	
Copy		⌘C	
Paste		⌘V	
Clear			
Select All		⌘A	
Find...		⌘F	
Find Again		⌘G	

Undo: (or Can't Undo): May reverse the last action you performed.

Cut: Removes what you have selected and places it on the clipboard.

Copy: Copies the current selection to the computer's clipboard.

Paste: Puts the current clipboard's contents in the document you are working on.

Clear (for the Macintosh only): Removes the current selection.

Select All: Selects all you have indicated by using the application's selection markers. May be used to select items before you cut, copy, or paste.

Find: Lets you search for a word or phrase within the current Web page.

Find Again: Searches for another occurrence of the word or phrase specified when you used the **Find** command.

View Menu

The **View** menu offers options for viewing images, the Netscape page, HTML, source code, and information on the current Web's document structure.

Figure B.5 **View** menu options from Netscape.

View	Go	Bookmar
Reload		⌘R
Reload Frame		
Load Images		⌘I
Document Source		
Document Info		

Reload: Downloads a new copy of the current Netscape page you are viewing to replace the one originally loaded. Netscape checks the network server to see if any changes have occurred to the page.

Reload Frame: Downloads a new copy of the currently selected page within a single frame on the Netscape page.

Load Images: If you have set **Auto Load Images** in your Netscape **Options** menu, images from a Web page will be automatically loaded. If this option has not been selected, choose **Load Images** to display the current Netscape page.

Refresh (Windows only): Downloads a new copy of the current Netscape page from local memory to replace the one originally loaded.

Document Source: Selecting this option provides you with the format of HTML (hypertext Markup Language). The HTML source text contains programming commands used to create the page.

Document Info: Produces a page in a separate Netscape window with information on the current Web document's structure and composition, including title, location (URL), date of the last modification, character set encoding, and security status.

Go Menu

The **Go** menu has Netscape navigational aids.

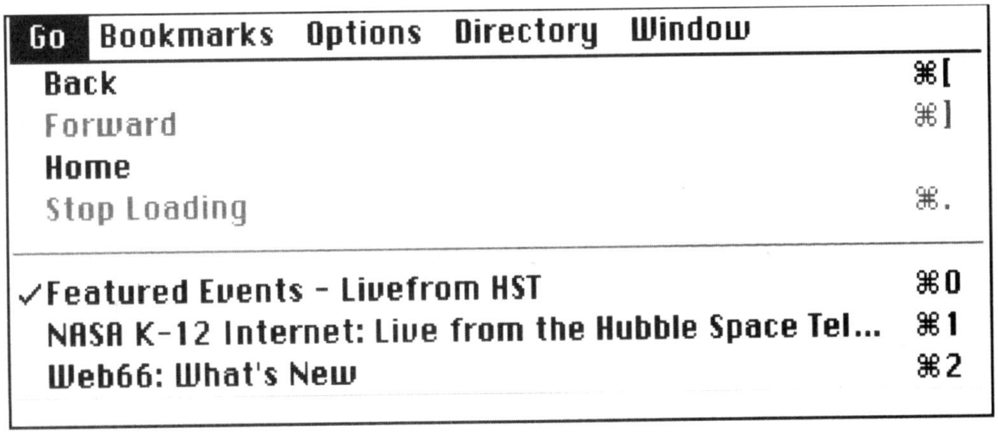

Figure B.6 Netscape **Go** menu.

Go	Bookmarks	Options	Directory	Window	
Back					⌘[
Forward					⌘]
Home					
Stop Loading					⌘.
✓Featured Events – Livefrom HST					⌘0
NASA K-12 Internet: Live from the Hubble Space Tel...					⌘1
Web66: What's New					⌘2

Back: Takes you back to the previous page in your history list. Same as the **Back** button on the toolbar. The history list keeps track of all the pages you link to.

Forward: Takes you to the next page of your history list. Same as the **Forward** button on the toolbar.

Home: Takes you to the Home Page. Same as the **Home** button on the toolbar.

Stop Loading: Stops downloading the current page. Same as the **Stop** button.

History Items: A list of the titles of the places you have visited. Select menu items to display their page. To view the History list, select the **Window** menu and then choose **History**.

Bookmarks Menu

Bookmarks make it possible to save and organize your favorite Internet visits. Opening this pull-down menu allows you to view and download your favorite page quickly.

Figure B.7 Netscape **Bookmark** menu.

Add Bookmark: Click on **Add Bookmark** to save this page n your bookmark list. Behind the scenes, Netscape saves the URL address so you can access this page by pointing-and-clicking on the item in your list.

Bookmark Items: Below **Add Bookmark**, you will see a list of your saved pages. Point and click on any item to bring this page to your screen.

To view your bookmarks, add new bookmark folders, arrange the order of your bookmarks, or to do any editing, select the Window menu and choose **Bookmarks**.

Options Menu

The Options menu offers customization tools to personalize your use of Netscape Navigator. Several uses for these customization tools include:

- showing the toolbar buttons.
- showing the URL location of a page.
- showing the Directory buttons.
- automatic loading of images.
- selecting styles for pages to appear.
- selecting which Home Page you want to appear when you log onto Netscape.
- selecting link styles (colors).
- selecting your news server to interact with Usenet newsgroups.
- up E-mail on Netscape.

There are additional customization tools available that are more advanced. Refer to the Netscape on-line handbook for more information on **Options** and **Preferences**.

Note: Before you can use the E-mail and Usenet newsgroup tools available in Netscape, you will need to customize the **Mail and New Preferences**.

Figure B.8 Netscape **Options** menu.

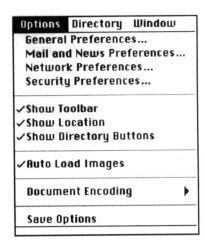

General Preferences: Presents tab buttons for selecting preferences. Each tab presents a panel for customizing Netscape's operations for your personal needs, preferences, and interests.

Mail and News Preferences: Panel for entering information on your mail and news server, so you can use Netscape to send and receive E-mail and to participate in Usenet newsgroups.

Network Preferences: Options for cache, network connections, and proxy configurations.

Security Preferences: Panel for setting security features.

Show Toolbar: If selected, the Toolbar buttons are visible on the Netscape page.

Show Location: If selected, the URL location for the page is displayed.

Show Directory Buttons: If selected, the Directory buttons are visible.

Show Java Console (Windows only): If selected, displays the Java Console window.

Auto Load Images: If selected, images embedded onto a page will be loaded automatically. If not checked, images can be loaded by clicking on the **Load Images** button. Deselecting this option increases the speed of downloading a page.

Document Encoding: Lets you select which character set encoding a document uses when document encoding is either not specified or unavailable. The proportional and fixed fonts are selected using the **General Preferences/Fonts** panel.

Save Options: Click on this option to save the changes you made to any of the above options.

Directory Menu

The **Directory** pull-down menu directs you to a few navigational aids to help you begin your Web exploration.

Figure B.9 Netscape **Directory** menu.

Netscape's Home: Takes you to the Netscape Home Page.

What's New: Click on this item to see what's new on the Internet.

What's Cool: Netscape's selection of interesting places to visit.

Netscape Galleria: A showcase of Netscape customers who have built Net sites using Netscape Server software. Visit the Galleria to learn more about how to build and maintain innovative Web sites.

Internet Directory: Same as the Internet Directory button. Links you to Internet directories for finding information and resources.

Internet Search: Connects you to many of the best on-line search engines.

Internet White Pages: Links you to tools to help you find people connected to the Internet.

About the Internet: Links to resources to help you learn more about the Internet.

Window Menu

The **Window** menu makes it possible for you to navigate easily between your E-mail, Usenet news, and Bookmarks windows, and to see and visit places you have already traveled.

Figure B.10 Netscape **Window** menu.

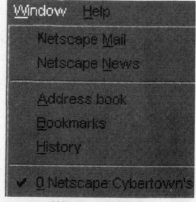

Macintosh **Window**

Windows **Window**

Netscape Mail: Click on this option to access the Netscape E-mail program.

Netscape News: Click on this option to access the Usenet newsgroups.

Address Book: Displays an Address Book window for use with the E-mail program.

Bookmarks: Displays bookmarks and pull-down menus for working with or editing your bookmarks.

History: Displays a history list of the pages (their titles and URLs) that you have recently viewed. Select an item and press the **Go To** button (or double-click) to revisit the page.

INTERNET EXPLORER

Now that you're familiar with Internet navigation using Netscape, you will be able to transfer that knowledge to the use of other Internet browsers. Most browsers have similar or the same navigational tools in the form of toolbar buttons and pull-down menus. Microsoft's Internet Explorer is another widely used and highly sophisticated browser that is integrated with the Windows 95 operating environment. Explorer is the primary Internet browser for America On-line (AOL) and CompuServe. Notice in Figure B.10 how similar the navigational tools are to those of Netscape's Navigator.

Figure B.11 Microsoft's Internet Explorer window.

Navigating with Internet Explorer

Toolbar buttons and pull-down menus are your Internet navigational tools when using Internet Explorer.

Toolbar Buttons

 Open: Accesses a dialog box for typing in URLs, documents, or folders for Windows to open.

 Print: Prints the page you are viewing.

 Send: Information services for using Microsoft's fax, E-mail, Netscape Internet transport, or Microsoft's Network On-line Services.

 Back/Forward: Takes you either back to your previous page or forward to the next page in your history list.

 Stop: Stops the downloading of a Web page: text, images, video, or sound.

 Refresh: Brings a new copy of the current Explorer page from local memory to replace the one originally loaded.

 Open Start Page: Takes you back to the first opening page.

 Search the Internet: Click this button for a list of search services to help you find information on the Internet.

 Read Newsgroups: This option brings up a list of Usenet newsgroups available from your Internet provider or college/university.

 Open Favorites: Click this button to see a list of your favorite URLs.

 Add to Favorites: Click on this button to add a favorite URL to your list.

 Use Larger/Smaller Font: Increase or decrease the size of the font on the page you are viewing.

 Cut: Removes what you have selected and places it on the clipboard.

 Copy: Copies the current selection to the computer's clipboard.

 Paste: Puts the current clipboard's contents in the document you are working on.

Pull-down Menus

Pull-down menus offer navigational tools for your Internet exploration. Some of the options are similar to the toolbar buttons: File, Edit, View, Go, Favorites, Help.

> **Note:** The pull-down menus will not be discussed or shown *unless* their functions differ significantly from the discussion of pull-down menus under Netscape Navigator.

File Menu

Explorer's **File** menu provides options for connecting to new Internet sites, printing Web pages, creating desktop shortcuts to your favorite Web pages, and finding information about the page you are viewing.

Figure B.12 Explorer's **File** pull-down menu.

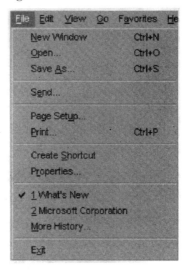

Create Shortcut: Select this option to create a shortcut to the current page that will be placed on your desktop.

Properties: Provides you with general information about the page you are viewing, including security information.

Edit Menu

The **Edit** menu offers cut, copy, and paste options as well as a find command for keyword searches.

Figure B.13 Explorer's **Edit** menu.

View Menu

The **View** menu provides options for how your Explorer page appears. **Toolbar, Address Bar,** and **Status Bar** provide options for viewing or not viewing these Explorer tools.

Figure B.14 Explorer's
View menu with active tools
checked.

Go Menu

The **Go** menu provides options for moving forward to the next page in your history list or backward to a previous page.

Start Page: Takes you back to the first opening page you started with.

Search the Internet: Takes you to search tools for finding information on the Internet.

Read Newsgroups: This option takes you to Explorer's newsreader for Usenet newsgroups.

Figure B.15 Explorer's **Go**
menu.

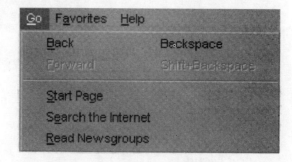

Favorites Menu

Explorer's **Favorites** list is the same as Netscape's Bookmarks, or what other browser's refer to as a hotlist.

Add To Favorites: Select this option to add the URL of a Web site to Explorer's Favorites list.

Open Favorites: Use this option to select an URL for Explorer to open.

Figure B.16 Explorer's
Favorites menu.

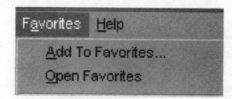

Help Menu

The **Help** menu provides help with using Internet Explorer.

Note: Internet browsers such as Netscape Navigator and Internet Explorer support many additional capacities such as electronic mail, Usenet newsgroups, Gopher, FTP, Telnet, and downloading and viewing image, video, and sound files. For a more in-depth discussion and practice using these features, refer to *Netscape Adventure—Step-By-Step Guide to Netscape Navigator and The World Wide Web* by Cynthia Leshin and published by Prentice Hall, 1997.

Figure B.17 Explorer's **Help** menu.

Figure B.18 Explorer's **Help** Contents panel.

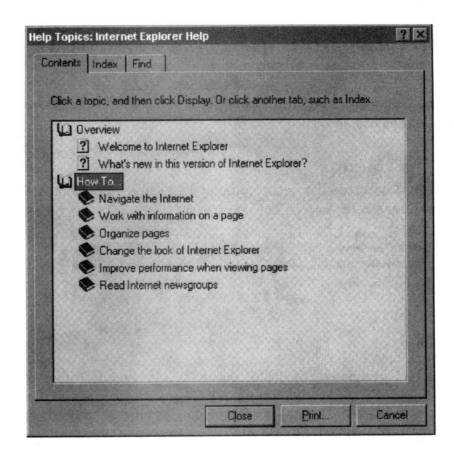

HANDS-ON PRACTICE

In this section, you will practice using Netscape and/or Explorer for navigating the Internet, organizing and using bookmarks, and exploring the Internet.

Practice 1: Browsing the Internet

In this guided practice you will use Netscape Navigator or Explorer to:

- connect to World Wide Web sites and Home Pages;
- use pull-down menus and navigational toolbar buttons to navigate World Wide Web sites; and
- save bookmarks of your favorite pages.

1. *Log onto your Internet account.* When you have connected, open the Explorer browser by double-clicking on the application icon.

Microsoft Explorer Icon

You will be taken to a Home Page. Notice the Location/Address URLs in Figure B.19 and Figure B.20. This Home Page may belong to Microsoft (http://www.microsoft.com) or it may have been designed by your college or university. Look at the top of the Home Page in the Title Bar to see whose Home Page you are visiting.

URLs are a standard for locating Internet documents. Highlighted text on Netscape pages contains built-in URL information for linking to that information. You can also type in new URL text to link a page.

Figure B.19 Netscape Navigator toolbar button.

Figure B.20 Microsoft's Internet Explorer toolbar buttons.

2. *Begin exploring* the World Wide Web by using Netscape's toolbar buttons and pull-down menus. Click on the **What's New** button. You will see a list of highlighted underlined links to Web sites. Click on a link and EXPLORE. HAVE FUN! If you are using Explorer, investigate the Home Page that you are viewing.
3. *Save your favorite pages* by making a bookmark or an addition to your Favorites List.

When you find a page that you may want to visit at a later time, click on the pull-down menu, **Bookmarks**. Next, click on the menu item **Add Bookmark**. (Explorer—select the **Favorites** menu.)

Click on the **Bookmarks (Favorites)** pull-down menu again. Notice the name of the page you marked listed below the **View Bookmarks** menu item. To view this page again, select the **Bookmarks** pull-down menu and click on the name of the page you saved.

4. Continue your exploration by clicking on the **What's Cool** button.
5. After you have linked to several pages, click on the **Go** pull-down menu. Notice the listing of the places you have most recently visited. If you want to revisit any of the pages you have already viewed, click on the name of the Web site.

Practice 2: Organizing and Using Bookmarks

In this practice you will learn how to organize, modify, save, and move bookmark files. If you are using Explorer, save your favorite URLs by using either the **Favorites** button or the **Favorites** menu.

Before you can organize and work with bookmark files, you must access Netscape's **Bookmark** window. There are two ways to access the **Bookmark** window:

*   Go to the **Bookmarks** pull-down menu and select **Go To Bookmarks**; or
*   Go to the Window pull-down menu and select **Bookmarks**.

1. *Organizing your bookmarks.* Before you begin saving bookmarks it is helpful to consider **how** to organize saved bookmarks. Begin by thinking of categories that your bookmarks might be filed under such as Software, Business, Education, Entertainment, Research, etc. For each category make a folder. These are the steps for making your bookmark folders.
    a. Go the **Bookmarks** menu and select **Go To Bookmarks,** or go to the **Window** menu and select **Bookmarks**.

Figure B.21 The Netscape **Bookmarks** window.

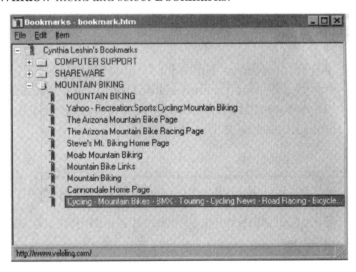

Notice the Web sites saved in the bookmark folders in Figure B.21. This Bookmarks window provides you with three new menus for working with your bookmarks: **File, Edit,** and **Item**.

b. Create a new folder for a bookmark category by selecting the **Item** menu (Fig. B.22)

Figure B.22 Opened **Item** menu from within.

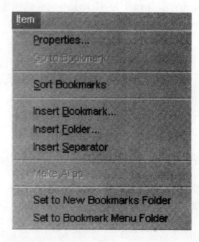

c. Select **Insert Folder** (see Fig. B.23).

Figure B.23 **Insert Folder** window

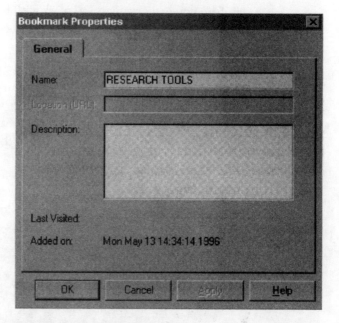

d. Type in the name of your folder in the Name dialog box.
e. Enter in any description of the bookmark folder.
f. Click OK.

2. *Adding bookmarks to a folder.* Netscape provides an option for identifying which folder you would like to select to drop your bookmarks in.

a. Select the folder you would like to add your new bookmarks to by clicking on the name of the folder once. The folder should now be highlighted.
b. Go to the **Item** menu and select **Set to New Bookmarks Folder** shown near the bottom of Figure B.22.
c. Go back to your Bookmark window and notice how this newly identified folder has been marked with a colored Bookmark identifier. All bookmarks that you add will be placed in this folder until you identify a new folder.

3. *Modifying the name of your bookmark.* Bookmark properties contain the name of the Web site and the URL. You may want to change the name of the bookmark to indicate more clearly the information available at this site. For example, the bookmark name *STCil/HST Public Information* has very little meaning. Changing its name to *Hubble Space Telescope Public Information* is more helpful later when selecting from many bookmarks.

   a. To change the name of a bookmark, select the bookmark by clicking on it once.

   b. Go to the **Item** menu from within the Bookmark window.

   c. Select **Properties**.

Figure B.24 Properties window from Bookmark **Item** Options.

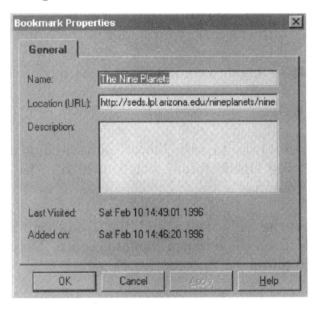

d. Enter in the new name for your bookmark by either deleting the text shown in Figure B.24 or begin typing the new name when the highlighted text is visible.

   e. Notice the URL for the bookmark; you can also enter in a new description for the URL.

4. *Making copies of your bookmarks for adding to other folders.* Occasionally you will want to save a bookmark in several folders. There are two ways to do this:

   a. Select the bookmark that you would like to copy. Go to the **Edit** menu from within the Bookmark window and select **Copy**. Select the folder where you would like to place the copy of the bookmark. Go to the **Edit** menu and select **Paste**.

   b. Make as alias of your bookmark by selecting **Make Alias** from the **Item** menu. When the alias of your bookmark has been created, move the alias bookmark to the new folder (see "Note").

Note: Bookmarks can be moved from one location to another by dragging an existing Bookmark to a new folder.

5. *Deleting a bookmark.* To remove a bookmark:

   a. Select the bookmark to be deleted by clicking on it once.

   b. Go to the **Edit** menu from within the Bookmark window.

   c. Choose either **Cut** or Delete.

6. *Exporting and saving bookmarks.* Netscape provides options for making copies of your bookmarks to either save as a backup on your hard drive, to share with others, or to use on another computer.

Follow these steps for exporting or saving your bookmarks to a floppy disk:

a. Open the **Bookmark** window.
b. From within the Bookmark window, go to the **File** menu. Select **Save As**.
c. Designate where you would like to save the bookmark file – on your hard drive or to a floppy disk—in the **Save** in box.

Figure B.25 Netscape Bookmark Window for saving Bookmark files.

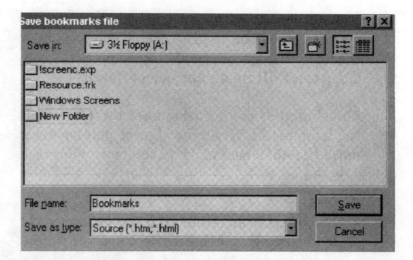

d. Enter in a name for your bookmark file in the **File name** dialog box.
e. Click **Save**.

7. *Importing Bookmarks.* Bookmarks can be imported into Netscape from a previous Netscape session saved on a floppy disk.

a. Insert the floppy disk with the bookmark into your computer.
b. Open the **Bookmark** window.
c. From within the Bookmark window, go to the **File** menu and select **Import** (see Fig. B.26)
d. Designate where the bookmark file is located: The **Look in** window displays a floppy disk or you can click on the scroll arrow to bring the hard drive into view.

Figure B.26 **Import** window
allows bookmark files from a
floppy disk to be imported into
your Netscape application.

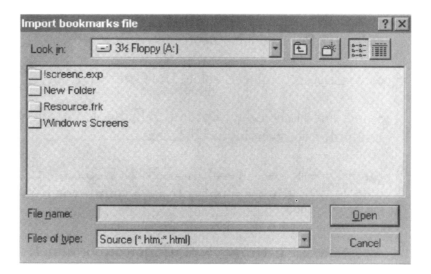

e. *Click on **Open***. The bookmarks will now be imported into your Netscape
bookmark list.

Practice 3: Exploring the Internet with Your Web Browser

In this practice you will enter in URL addresses to link to World Wide Web (WWW)
sites.

There are three options in Netscape for entering in an URL:

* the **Location** text field;
* the **File menu—Open Location;** or
* the **Open** toolbar button.

If you are using Explorer, select the **Open** button

1. Select one of the above options to bring you to the window where you
    can enter your choice of URL text.
2. Listed below are several interesting Web sites to visit. Type an URL and
    EXPLORE. Remember to save your favorite sites of Bookmarks/Favorites.
    * Awesome List: http://www.clark.net/publ/journalism/awesome.html
    * CityNet: http://www.city.net
    * ESPNetSportsZone: http://espnet.sportzone.com
    * NASA: http://www.nasa.gov
    * Time Warner Pathfinder:
      http://www.timeinc.com/pathfinder/Greet.html
    * The White House: http://www.whithouse.gov
    * Wired: http://www.hotwired.com

INDEX